# The Philosophical Challenge of Religious Diversity

# The Philosophical Challenge of Religious Diversity

*Edited by*

Philip L. Quinn
Kevin Meeker

New York Oxford
OXFORD UNIVERSITY PRESS
2000

**Oxford University Press**

Oxford New York
Athens Auckland Bangkok Bogotá Buenos Aires Calcutta
Cape Town Chennai Dar es Salaam Delhi Florence Hong Kong Istanbul
Karachi Kuala Lumpur Madrid Melbourne Mexico City Mumbai
Nairobi Paris São Paulo Singapore Taipei Tokyo Toronto Warsaw

*and associated companies in*

Berlin Ibadan



Published by Oxford University Press, Inc.,
198 Madison Avenue, New York, New York, 10016
http://www.oup-usa.org
1-800-334-4249



**Library of Congress Cataloging-in-Publication Data**

The philosophical challenge of religious diversity / edited by Philip L. Quinn, Kevin Meeker.
p. cm.
ISBN 0-19-512154-6 (paper). — ISBN 0-19-512155-4 (pbk. : paper)
1. Religion—Philosophy. 2. Religions. 3. Religious pluralism.
I. Quinn, Philip L. II. Meeker, Kevin, 1968– .
BL51.P5255 1999
291.1'72—dc21 98-33341
CIP

Printing (last digit): 10 9 8 7 6 5 4 3 2

Printed in the United States of America
on acid-free paper

# CONTENTS

Contents

# LIST OF CONTRIBUTORS

**William P. Alston** is Professor Emeritus of Philosophy at Syracuse University.

**David Basinger** is Professor of Philosophy at Roberts Wesleyan College.

**William Lane Craig** is Research Professor of Philosophy at the Talbot School of Theology, Biola University.

**Paul R. Eddy** is Assistant Professor of Theology at Bethel College, Minnesota.

**John Hick** is Danforth Professor Emeritus of the Philosophy of Religion at the Claremont Graduate School.

**George I. Mavrodes** is Professor Emeritus of Philosophy at the University of Michigan, Ann Arbor.

**Alvin Plantinga** is John A. O'Brien Professor of Philosophy at the University of Notre Dame.

**Philip L. Quinn** is John A. O'Brien Professor of Philosophy at the University of Notre Dame.

**J. L. Schellenberg** is Associate Professor of Philosophy at Mount Saint Vincent University.

**Ninian Smart** is J. F. Rowny Professor of Comparative Religions in the Department of Religious Studies at the University of California, Santa Barbara.

**Sumner B. Twiss** is Professor of Religious Studies at Brown University.

**William J. Wainwright** is Distinguished Professor of Philosophy at the University of Wisconsin, Milwaukee.

**Keith Ward** is Regius Professor of Divinity at Oxford University.

# The Philosophical Challenge of Religious Diversity

# Introduction

## *The Philosophical Challenge of Religious Diversity*

Kevin Meeker
Philip L. Quinn

Imagine that you were raised in a small, mostly evangelical Christian farming community in South Dakota. As far back as you can remember, you have believed in a personal God. While growing up, you were taught various Christian doctrines in Sunday School. Almost all the adults you knew accepted these doctrines, and so you took most of them for granted. You tried your best to live a good Christian life.

But now you are at the university. You elect to take a course in religious studies on Hinduism. In it you learn that advaita Hindus do not believe in a personal God; instead, for them, ultimate reality is the nonpersonal Brahman. As it happens, a classmate who also resides on your dormitory floor is a practicing advaita Hindu. The material from the class and discussions with this classmate inspire you to study the issue of what reasons there are for being a Christian.

You discover that arguments for the existence of a personal God come in many varieties: ontological, cosmological, teleological, and so on. But you also learn that scholars disagree on whether such arguments are any good. By the same token, you find out that there are arguments for the existence of Brahman and learn that they too are disputed. You read about Christians who report experiences of God. Indeed, when you reflect on the matter, you recall a couple of experiences of your own that could well be taken to be experiences of God guiding you. But you also read reports by advaita Hindus about their experiential contact with Brahman. You read reports about how the Christian system of belief and practice has helped many people become good and holy, but you also find out that there are reports of a lot of good and holy people among the advaita Hindus. You quickly realize that it is unlikely that you will discover undisputed arguments or reasons that will establish the superiority of your own evangelical Christianity to advaita Hinduism or vice versa. And, of course, you recognize that you probably would have reached similar conclusions if you had been investigating Buddhism or Islam or Judaism or Taoism instead of advaita Hinduism.

So what should you do? Should you stick with the Christian system of belief and practice in which you were raised? Should you try to switch to one of its competitors? Or should you become a skeptic about all the religious systems of belief and take a stand outside all the religious practices? Once you have become genuinely puzzled by questions like these, you have felt the challenge of religious diversity. Of course, you need not doubt your own religion to feel the force of this challenge; simply wondering what justifies you in remaining in a tradition as opposed to switching to some other perspective poses similar questions. Or you might wonder how rationally to convince someone from another tradition that yours is true. In all such situations, the challenge of religious diversity looms large.

Needless to say, the awareness of religious diversity is not new. But many scholars argue that this awareness has recently acquired new significance. Some of the essays collected in this volume discuss why many treat this problem with increased urgency. Among the factors involved in this change is the better acquaintance people have with religions other than their own. After all, modern technologies of travel and communication facilitate contacts between adherents of different religions. Along the same lines, modern scholarship has produced fine translations of texts from a variety of religious traditions, and cultural anthropologists have provided fascinating thick descriptions of the practices of such traditions. Moreover, those who live in religiously pluralistic democracies have ample opportunities to develop first-hand familiarity with religions other than their own without leaving home. Finally, twenty-four hour a day news broadcasts have confronted us with graphic illustrations of what can transpire when diverging religions clash in such places as Belfast, Beirut, and Bosnia. Brief reflection on these factors should make it easy to see why the issue of religious diversity has become increasingly significant.

The editors have collected in this volume what we regard as some of the best recent responses to the philosophical challenge of religious diversity. The published literature on this topic is enormous, and so we have had to be very selective. Our selections were guided by three considerations. First, we wanted to include in the volume only important work. We think that the essays selected for inclusion either develop and argue for or criticize and argue against positions that have played major roles in the recent discussion. Second, we wanted the volume to have an interdisciplinary focus. Religious diversity is of interest not only to philosophers but also to scholars in religious studies and theology, and some of them have made significant contributions to the philosophical discussion. The essays by John Hick, Ninian Smart, and Sumner B. Twiss represent the discipline of religious studies, and the essays by Paul R. Eddy and Keith Ward represent the discipline of theology. And third, we wanted to convey to readers our sense that the philosophical discussion is much like a conversation in which many people are taking part. This led us to favor essays by authors who take one another seriously enough to discuss one another's positions and to report in this introduction on further back and forth exchanges among some of the authors whose essays we have selected for inclusion in this volume.

Before we introduce the individual essays to readers and comment on some topics for further reflection they suggest to us, we need to say a few words about the terminology used in the conversation about religious diversity. In this introduction, we use the term *religious diversity* to refer to the undisputed fact that different religions espouse doctrines that are at least apparently in conflict and offer alternative paths of salvation or liberation. The authors of some of the essays use the term *religious pluralism* to refer to this fact, but we reserve that term to refer to the position John Hick adopts in response to the fact of religious diversity. The three main positions in the conversation are exclusivism, inclusivism, and pluralism. *Exclusivism* is the view that one religion has it mostly right and all the other religions go seriously wrong. Exclusivism has more than one dimension. Doctrinal exclusivism is the view that the doctrines of one religion are mostly true and the doctrines of all the others, when they conflict, are false. Soteriological exclusivism is the view that only the path proposed by one religion leads to salvation or liberation. And experiential exclusivism is the view that the religious experiences typical of one religion are mostly veridical while conflicting experiences typical of all the others are nonveridical. *Pluralism* is the view championed by John Hick and others according to which all the major religious traditions—the so-called world religions—are in contact with the same ultimate religious reality, and all of them offer paths to salvation or liberation that are, as far as anyone can tell, equally effective in producing transformations from self-centeredness to Reality-centeredness. *Inclusivism* is a family of views that occupy a middle ground between exclusivism and pluralism. Thus, for example, Christian soteriological inclusivism is the view that salvation through Christ is not restricted to Christians but is available to devout members of other religious traditions, who might be thought of as, to use Karl Rahner's memorable phrase, anonymous Christians.

The conversation about religious diversity occasionally makes contact with the realism and antirealism debate. A religious realist affirms that the ultimate religious reality (God, Brahman, the Tao, etc.) exists independent of human thought and experience. A religious antirealist denies that this is the case. There are several varieties of antirealism. Subjectivists hold that the ultimate religious reality is nothing but a product of human subjectivity. Freudians who think that God is nothing but an imaginary father-figure produced by wishful thinking are subjectivists. Constructivists hold that the ultimate religious reality is nothing but a cultural construction. Durkheimians who think religious thought and experience merely represent, in a disguised fashion, social facts and relations are constructivists. Some people think that the fact of religious diversity counts as evidence in favor of religious antirealism of one kind or another.

In our first selection, David Hume presents an argument for religious skepticism or, perhaps, for some form of religious antirealism. This argument appears in his famous discussion of miracles that occurs in the second part of Section 10 of his *An Enquiry Concerning Human Understanding.* Although Hume scholars disagree about the exact nature and force of his overall argument, they generally agree that Hume was at least trying to show that it was irrational to believe that a miracle had ever occurred. For our purposes, the most important part of his discussion is his fourth reason for discounting any report of a miracle. Hume here highlights the diversity of religions and points out that religious believers often appeal to miracles to try to show that their religion is more authentic than its competitors. Hume calls into question the testimony of anyone who reports a miracle because the conflicting testimonies in essence cancel each other out. Hume draws a legal analogy to support his point: Just as a judge must discount the conflicting testimonies of witnesses who seem equally truthful, so too should we assume a skeptical stance towards different religious traditions unless we have some independent reason to believe that one religion really is true. In other words, we should not accept any religious tradition given the contrary miracle reports that are presented to us. Hume's argument reveals that religious diversity is not a new issue for philosophers, but has played a role in philosophical reflections in the past. His reasoning also raises another important issue: If his legal analogy works, then it would only work for those not already committed to a particular religion. What of those already committed? Here is Hume's famous reply: "The *Christian Religion* not only was at first attended with miracles, but even at this day cannot be believed by any reasonable person without one. Mere reason is insufficient to convince us of its veracity: And whoever is moved by *Faith* to assent to it, is conscious of a continued miracle in his own person, which subverts all the principles of his understanding, and gives him a determination to believe what is contrary to custom and experience."

William Lane Craig's "'No Other Name': A Middle Knowledge Perspective on the Exclusivity of Salvation through Christ" presents and defends traditional Christian soteriological exclusivism. Tracing this exclusivism back to the New Testament writers, Craig argues that its most difficult problem is answering such questions as the following: *Why did God not create a world in which all people freely believe in Jesus Christ and are thus saved from eternal damnation?* To state this difficulty with more precision, he draws parallels with the traditional logical problem of evil. That is, Craig claims that we can plausibly read many who object to exclusivism as claiming that the proposition

1. God is omniscient, omnipotent, and omnibenevolent

is incompatible with

2. Some persons do not receive Christ and are damned.

To prove that these two propositions are compatible, Craig produces a possibly true proposition that is not only consistent with (1), but also entails (2) when conjoined with (1). The proposition Craig proposes is the following:

9. God has actualized a world containing an optimal balance between saved and unsaved, and those who are unsaved suffer from transworld damnation.

According to Craig, a person suffers from transworld damnation if, roughly speaking, that person would freely reject God and thus be lost in every world God could have actualized in which the person existed. Assuming that Craig has successfully proven that soteriological exclusivism is logically compatible with belief in God, we are still left with the following question: How should those (such as David Hume) not already committed to the exclusivist claims of a particular tradition view religious diversity? But, of course, Craig is not really addressing that particular issue; instead he is defending exclusivism against what he takes to be a major objection and suggesting that those within his tradition should adopt his view.

Interestingly, Craig goes on to claim that (9) itself is not implausible. He suggests that he has provided a plausible soteriological theodicy, that is, an explanation of why God has *in fact* actualized a world in which some are not saved because they do not believe in Christ. But how plausible is it to suppose that those who are not saved because they do not believe in Christ would have freely rejected God in every world God could actualize in which they exist? For many people religion seems to be an accident of birth; they wind up endorsing the religion of the culture in which they are brought up. Hence it seems that many people who do not believe in Christ because they are brought up outside Christian cultures would have accepted Christ if they had been brought up in a Christian culture. Perhaps this dependence of religious affiliation on cultural context provides us with reason to be skeptical of Craig's claim that his view is "quite plausible not only as a defense, but also as a soteriological theodicy."

In "Religious Pluralism and Salvation," John Hick provides an argument aimed at moving even those within particular traditions away from the exclusivistic outlook that Craig represents. Hick maintains that we should all recognize that the great religions of the world agree on the core ethical component of salvific transformation: unselfish regard for others. Given this core agreement, he argues for a pluralistic outlook that views all the great religions as equally efficacious in helping humans to turn from lives of self-centeredness to an appropriate relationship with the Real. Although these religions have different views of the Real, Hick claims that a reasonable interpretation of the various religious experiences and practices in different cultures is that there is a transcendent ultimate reality that is perceived through different religious "lenses," which are in turn shaped by history, culture, spiritual practices, and so forth. So while followers of the various religious traditions experience the Real in different ways, the unknowable divine reality for the most part exceeds human conceptualization. The obvious upshot of this hypothesis of religious pluralism is that the exclusivist claim that only a particular religion can save someone is misguided: One is not lost in virtue of not being a member of a particular tradition because salvation is occurring in many religions. (More explicit Hickian critiques of exclusivism are mentioned in the essays by Sumner B. Twiss and David Basinger included in this volume.)

Although this tack cannot reconcile contrary metaphysical doctrines about which religions disagree (e.g., reincarnation versus resurrection) or settle disputed historical questions (e.g., was Ishmael or Isaac almost sacrificed by Abraham?), Hick claims that such beliefs are irrelevant to whether or not one lives a life of Reality-centeredness. Finally, Hick claims that inclusivism is an invention of twentieth century Christians who have realized that other religions have salvific efficacy but still insist on the superiority of their own religious tradition. In a move reminiscent of William Lane Craig's appeal to the New Testament writers, Hick argues that inclusivism was "not taught by Jesus or his apostles." Hick discusses his pluralistic hypothesis in much greater detail in his book, *An Interpretation of Religion.*

It is worth noting that John Hick is the person who has dealt most fully with the topic of religious diversity, and his work has affected fields other than philosophy. Some evidence of this impact surfaces in Sumner B. Twiss's essay, "The Philosophy of Religious Pluralism: A Critical Appraisal of Hick and His Critics." Twiss, who works in religious studies, explains, clarifies, and sympathetically defends Hick's position. Twiss admits that Hick's view exhibits many tensions; most notably, Twiss highlights Hick's *antirealist* (Twiss labels it "noncognitive, neo-Wittgensteinian") tendency to emphasize the cultural and linguistic aspects of religions while maintaining that these practices presuppose the *realist* doctrine that the Real exists independent of these practices.

Nevertheless, Twiss defends the overall coherence of Hick's vision. In particular, Twiss concentrates on revealing the plausibility of four aspects of Hick's theory. First, he argues that we should not dismiss Hick's views about the transcendent unity of religions because this view discounts what the adherents of particular religions say (and in particular their exclusivistic doctrines). For Hick is not attempting to *describe* the beliefs of the religious adherents but rather to *explain* the amazing diversity of their beliefs in terms of a higher-order theory, that is, his theory of religious pluralism. Second, Twiss defends Hick's conviction that religious thought and experience put religious believers in contact with ultimate reality. Here a bit of background is needed. In other writings, Hick has argued that just as it is rational to accept one's sensory experiences (e.g., visual, auditory) as trustworthy, so too it is rational to accept religious experiences as veridical. In other words, he contends that a principle of credulity applies to religious experience. But then the difficulty is to account for all these rational beliefs in different ultimate realities. What shall we say about the experiences had by religious participants in other traditions? As we have seen, Hick argues that his pluralism is the most reasonable explanation of these experiences. He regards both exclusivism and inclusivism about the veridicality of religious experience as unreasonably arbitrary. At this point, Twiss notes that it might seem strange that Hick then proceeds to show that the religious experiences of all traditions are veridical by considering their practical fruits. Twiss suggests that this is not so odd if we keep in mind that for Hick veridical religious experiences and thoughts simply amount to "belief on the part of participants in religious forms of life (practices) that they are somehow in touch with, praying to, worshipping, and so forth, something that is real and not illusory." On behalf of Hick, Twiss points out that it is difficult to separate experience from belief. Moreover, Twiss claims that we should regard Hick's pluralist hypothesis as a serious candidate for explaining the facts of religious diversity.

Third, Twiss defends Hick's postulate of the divine noumenon against criticisms set forth by George Netland. Specifically, Twiss defends Hick against the following charges: (1) Given the incompatible properties assigned to their purported ultimate realities by different traditions, it is incredible that there could be *one* reality to which they all refer; and (2) if the Real is as inaccessible as Hick claims, then it seems illegitimate for it to perform such a unifying function in Hick's theory. Twiss begins his defense of Hick by saying that Netland has overlooked an analogy that Hick draws between his postulate and the complementarity principle in physics. Just as light exhibits contrary properties (i.e., wave and particle) when scientists experiment upon it in different ways, so too the divine noumenon exhibits contrary properties when religious believers from different traditions interact with it. Because we do not deny the reality of light, by parity of reasoning we should not deny the existence of the Real. Twiss also contends that Hick should be allowed to invoke this postulate because it is needed to explain the veridicality of religious experience in all traditions and is not implausible by virtue of the analogy with the complementarity principle.

Fourth, Twiss champions the adequacy of Hick's justification for his theory. While Hick claims that in this life we should adopt an attitude of tolerant agnosticism about many of the historical and metaphysical beliefs of the various religious traditions, he maintains that in the afterlife such beliefs could be verified, which means that religious accounts of history and the nature of the world make factual truth-claims. So why should we not be agnostic about Hick's position in this life? Twiss points out that Hick contends that, so far as we can tell, the major traditions are equally efficacious in producing salvific transformations and therefore equally veridical encounters with the divine. So Twiss interprets Hick as assuming a pragmatic view of justification: Beliefs that lead to transformation are more likely to correspond with reality, and this is the best that we can hope for in this life.

In "A Contemplation of Absolutes" Ninian Smart provides another sympathetic reading of John Hick's view. Smart's approach is informed by the comparative study of religions. Specifically, he focuses on Hick's Kantian description of the Real. In light of the difficulties in spelling out Hick's postulate of the Real as that toward which the major religions aim, Smart suggests that the Buddhist conception of an Empty may lead to Real insight when thinking about the Real. Employing the concept of Emptiness would have the advantage of avoiding the implication that the Real is singular (as opposed to a plurality) and a substance (as opposed to a process). Moreover, Smart contends that the Empty itself is not countable: Just as it makes no sense to say that love is singular or plural, so the same is true of the Empty. He notes that if we view the Real in this way, then we need not suppose that all religions point to the *same* Real; he suggests instead that these religions could have *overlapping* and *complementary* messages. On Hick's unity model, there is the hope that diverse religious traditions will honor one another and cooperate; on Smart's model there is also the possibility for friendly criticism and advice. Smart observes that diversity encourages creativity and progress and offers this as a reason for encouraging religious world-views to differ. Nevertheless, he admits that if Hick is correct in thinking that the conceptual framework that filters all our experiences is indeed contingent and culturally bound and not, as Kant thought, innate and immutable, then the interaction of traditions might very well alter our conceptual schemes so that we eventually converge on a single world religion.

Along these lines, Smart notes that the spread of individualism highlights the contingency of these traditions and precipitates their fragmentation. In such a situation in which people can "pick and choose" among various options, we should doubt that the religious traditions have as much sway over how we view the world as they once did. Because traditions have changed and continue to do so, there is no reason in principle to rule out the possibility of their convergence on a single religious world-view. Allowing that traditions can teach each other certain lessons helps to avoid the complacency and corruption that are concomitants of universal agreement and encourages a healthy stance of self-criticism. Smart also predicts that even though movements towards unity seem inevitably to produce backlash, "a world-view of world-views which looks to a future convergence will probably become more and more influential as the globe reflects upon its close texture, made dense by instantaneous communications and rapid travel."

Smart asks whether the ultimate should be thought of as a mere placeholder that just provides the space, so to speak, in which to lodge whatever each religious tradition takes to be ultimate. Conceiving of the ultimate as Emptiness would be a good way of representing it as a blank placeholder that is a space for alternatives rather than the point at which different paths meet. However, this thin conception of the ultimate can seem to be quite puzzling. It is difficult to see that there would be any real difference between an ultimate that is a mere placeholder and no ultimate at all. So perhaps we should be prepared to take seriously the idea that what each religious tradition takes to be ultimate is nothing but a human projection if we interpret the ultimate as an Empty that is a mere placeholder.

Keith Ward is a theologian who is less sympathetic to John Hick's views. While he does not advocate rejecting Hick's view completely, in his "Truth and the Diversity of Religions" he does argue that, as it stands, it is mostly unacceptable. Ward contends that insofar as Hick focuses on faiths that are concerned with a belief in the transcendent, he is *excluding* faiths that lack such a belief and thus is committed to a relatively abstract form of exclusivism. Moreover, Ward argues that Hick illicitly moves from the claim that many different religions speak of an ineffable transcendent reality to the conclusion that they all speak of the *same* ineffable transcendent reality. In a move reminiscent of Ninian Smart's discussion, Ward takes Hick to task for calling the Real "it," because Hick also admits that we cannot legitimately call the Real one or many. Ward notes that the view that the Real is one is opposed to the Tibetan Buddhist doctrine that there is no absolute at all. Unlike Smart, Ward takes such opposition to show that there is not much hope of uniting all the world religions. Even if we concentrate on those religions that do believe in one transcendent reality, Ward points out that their adherents affirm that something can be known about it, for example, that God is simple and infinite in the case of Aquinas, or that the ultimate reality is not the personal creator of the universe in the case of those who follow the Asvaghosa tradition of Japanese Buddhism. Ward argues that the only way that we could refer to the Real is by description, which requires attribution to the Real of many properties other than being able to be referred to in order to secure uniqueness of reference. He contends that Hick's own account of the Real is not merely formal because it attributes to the Real substantial properties such as goodness, as is implicit in Hick's endorsement of Anselm's conception of God as the greatest conceivable being. He then attacks Hick's claim that religious experience in all the major traditions is veridical and suggests that Hick does not recognize that while contradictory or contrary beliefs can be justified, they cannot all be true. Nevertheless, Ward admits that in a situation in which contradictory or contrary beliefs are justified we should refrain from judging others' beliefs as *obviously* mistaken. Moreover, Ward points out that we might regard our own religious beliefs as correct on important matters but not entirely correct and we might consistently think that others have a mixture of true and false religious beliefs.

An interesting feature of Ward's discussion is the way in which he distinguishes among different types of pluralism. Extreme pluralism is the view that all possible religious traditions are equally true, authentic, or valid. As Ward points out, extreme pluralism is necessarily false. Even if we did not have actual examples such as Satanism and Christianity, we could imagine possible religious traditions whose doctrines are logically incompatible and so cannot all be true. Hard pluralism is the view that many religious traditions do not contain mutually exclusive beliefs but are equally valid paths of salvation and authentic experience of the Real. Ward takes Hick to be a hard pluralist, and so hard pluralism is the target of his criticism. Soft pluralism is the view that the Real can manifest itself in many religious traditions and humans can respond appropriately to it in them. Ward considers soft pluralism to be defensible and important. It is consistent with the inclusivist view that a particular tradition is closer to having a complete understanding of the Real and the correct path to salvation or liberation. Revisionist pluralism is the view that all the major religious traditions need to revise their beliefs in order to make them mutually compatible. Ward suspects that "Hick wishes to commend revisionist pluralism, too." Ward himself thinks there is much to be said for revisionist pluralism. Must we agree with Ward in supposing that Hick is a hard pluralist? Surely Hick is aware that most of the practitioners of the world religions take at least some of their beliefs to be incompatible with beliefs held by practitioners of other religions. In other words, hard pluralism's claim that religious traditions do not contain mutually exclusive beliefs is inconsistent with the self-understandings of most members of the major religious traditions. So maybe if we are going to attribute one of Ward's varieties of pluralism to Hick, charity in interpretation requires us to think of him as a revisionist pluralist rather than a hard pluralist.

Paul R. Eddy is another theologian who is critical of John Hick's views. In "Religious Pluralism and the Divine: Another Look at John Hick's Neo-Kantian Proposal," Eddy argues that Hick's emphasis on religious experience and his commitment to a quasi-Kantian epistemology spell trouble: More precisely, they force him to an atheistic position. Of course, it is Hick's emphasis on the Real as the focus of the various religions that is supposed to separate his view from atheism. Following Keith Ward, Eddy points out that Hick has misunderstood what is entailed if one affirms an ineffable being: Such an affirmation entails that such a being cannot be known exhaustively, but does not entail that we can know nothing about such a being. If we can say nothing substantial about the Real, it is difficult to see what differentiates Hick's pluralism from atheism. Eddy summarizes the points at which Hick relies heavily on Kantian themes as well as the points at which he departs from Kant. He argues that when Hick draws on certain results from sociologists of knowledge to support his relativization of phenomenal manifestations of the Real to religious traditions, he arbitrarily neglects the constructivist and antirealist implications of these sociological theories. Because Kant was suspected of offering a subjectivist view, even though he took the categories to be universal and necessary, Hick is sure to be open to the charge of subjectivism when he makes them culture-relative and contingent. In addition, while for Kant the categories provide form for our sensory experiences, Eddy argues that for Hick our conceptual schemes also provide most of the content of our religious experiences. In other words, Kant needed to postulate a noumenal realm to provide the raw material of our sensory experiences that is then shaped by our concepts, but, for Hick, our conceptual schemes provide most of the content as well. So what need is there to postulate anything beyond our conceptual schemes to explain religious experience? Eddy thinks there is no need. He concludes that "it would appear that the noumenal Real in Hick's system is rendered a purely unnecessary and unjustifiable construct."

In a brief response to Eddy, Hick concedes that he should not have endorsed applying Anselm's description of God to the Real, but he denies that his distinction between the noumenal Real and the phenomenal manifestations of the Real implies that all the content of our religious experiences and traditions comes from us. Eddy, Hick charges, fails to consider the difference between Hick's justification for believing there is a transcendent reality, on the one hand, and his justification for believing that the Real is differently experienced within the different traditions, on the other. For Hick one's particular experience justifies one in the former belief, and in this respect Hick's view is similar to William P. Alston's, while the postulate of the Real in itself and its various manifestations is justified by its power to explain the differences among traditions. Hick denies that his view is a radical subjectivism and opts for a "critical realism" label that is "a middle way between the non-realism of Feuerbach (and his contemporary echoes) and the naive realism of evangelical theology. It is this moderate, rational, balanced, Anglican-style middle way that I have recommended."[1]

In light of Hick's response, should we accept Eddy's conclusion that the Real is, in Hick's system, an unnecessary and idle construct? As Eddy points out, Hick insists that the Real is a source of informational input into religious experience in all the major religious traditions. Hence it seems that, for Hick, the Real provides raw material for religious experience in a way similar to that in which Kant's noumenal realm provides raw material for sensory experience. To the extent that Hick insists upon this point, however, he is committed to the claim that the Real stands in causal relations to the human subjects of religious experience and exercises causal powers. This claim is not purely formal; it is a substantial claim about the Real. Hence it is in tension with Hick's view that only purely formal concepts apply to the Real. Perhaps the tension could be resolved if Hick were to allow that a limited number of substantial concepts do apply to the Real. After all, there seems to be no reason for Hick to deny that the Real has a genuine influence on believers in all the world religions. Maybe such an influence could provide part of the explanation of their salvific efficacy.

George I. Mavrodes begins his "Polytheism" with the astonishing claim that John Hick is "probably the most important philosophical defender of polytheism in the history of Western philosophy." But it is easy to see why this claim makes sense. For Hick holds that the absolutes of the major religious traditions, both personal (Allah, Jahweh, Holy Trinity) and impersonal (Brahman, the Dharmakaya, the Tao), are phenomenally real. And phenomenal reality is the kind of reality objects we experience have. So if we follow Mavrodes in thinking of a god as a very powerful nonembodied rational agent, it makes sense to say that Hick holds that several personal gods are phenomenally real. In other words, Hick is committed to the view that several personal deities are at least as real as, say, cantaloupes, and this makes him a polytheist. Of course, we should not identify any of these phenomenal realities with the noumenal reality that Hick postulates as their ground, what he calls the Real or the Real *an sich.* But then it seems appropriate to ask how this noumenal reality is related to the various phenomenal realities it stands behind.

Mavrodes finds an ambiguity in how Hick conceives of the relation of the Real *an sich* to the phenomenal gods and impersonal absolutes. He illustrates this ambiguity using a disguise model and a construct model. Mavrodes introduces the disguise model by telling a story of a prince who wants to go among his people incognito to attain an undistorted picture of their lives. At different times he disguises himself as a monk and as a stonemason. The Real *an sich* is like the prince. It appears to the practitioners of some of the religions as a personal deity; to others it appears as an impersonal absolute. On this model, the absolutes of various religious traditions are simply ways in which the Real *an sich* appears to the practitioners of the traditions. Those absolutes are not things in their own right; they are instead ways of appearing.

Mavrodes introduces the construct model with a story of several artists who paint while looking at a certain landscape. Because the artists work in different nonrepresentational styles, their paintings do not resemble one another or the landscape. Yet they say that their paintings were influenced by the landscape. The Real *an sich* is like the landscape, and the absolutes of various religions are like the paintings. On this model, those absolutes are things in their own right. They are, however, human constructs, though the Real *an sich* influences their construction.

Although Hick seems to endorse both models, they are incompatible. According to the disguise model, one and the same thing, the Real *an sich,* appears to the practitioners of various religions in various ways. According to the construct model, the Real *an sich* does not appear to the practitioners of any religion, but it does influence the things that do appear, which are things the practitioners construct. So we are entitled to ask whether Hick *actually* endorses either of these models and, if so, which one.

Hick's answer to this question appears in an article in which he responds to Mavrodes. He begins by admitting that he is "at one level a poly-something, though not precisely a poly-theist, and at another level a mono-something, though not precisely a mono-theist."[2] It is clear why Hick describes himself as being at one level a mono-something but not a mono-theist. He is a mono-something at the noumenal level at which he postulates the Real *an sich.* He is willing to speak of it in the singular, though strictly speaking it is supposed to be neither one nor many, but it is not a personal reality because it lacks all humanly conceivable intrinsic characteristics other than purely formal ones. It is less clear why he describes himself as being at one level a poly-something, but not a poly-theist. He is a poly-something at the phenomenal level, and so he is committed to the phenomenal reality of several gods. Perhaps he thinks he is not precisely a poly-theist because he is also committed to the phenomenal reality of the impersonal absolutes of non-theistic traditions.

When he discusses the two models that Mavrodes proposes, Hick says that he is using neither. He finds the disguise model misleading because the Real *an sich* is not at all like the prince in the story. The prince has definite describable characteristics, but the postulated Real *an sich* is ineffable. He also finds the construct model misleading. Unlike the landscape, the Real *an sich* cannot be experienced directly or as it is in itself. So Hick suggests a different analogy that he takes to be less misleading. Consider the way in which we experience, say, a wooden table top as solid, hard, and brown. Imagine that Martians and Alpha Centaurians experience the table top in ways vastly different from each other and from the way in which we experience it. And contrast all these experiences with the account physicists give of the table top according to which it is mostly empty space in which subatomic particles are rapidly moving. This is, Hick thinks, "a partial analogy for the way in which different spiritual practices (I-Thou prayer, non-I-Thou meditation) and different sets of religious concepts lead to a very different awareness of the Transcendent."[3]

It is worth noting that Hick's analogy is very much like the disguise model. In it one and the same physical object, the table top, appears in different ways to humans, Martians, and Alpha Centaurians. This is supposed to be comparable to different awarenesses of the Transcendent. Hence it seems reasonable to attribute to Hick the view that one and the same thing, the Transcendent, appears in different ways to the practitioners of different religions on the basis of his claim that the analogy, though only partial, is a good one. If this is correct, then Hick is operating, at least in this context, with something like the disguise model.

In his reply to Hick, Mavrodes wonders why Hick describes himself as a poly-something but not a poly-theist. He voices the suspicion that Hick really thinks that the gods and impersonal absolutes of religious traditions are much less real than cantaloupes. If that is what he thinks, then "what he is poly about is this whole group of shadowy *insubstantia*."[4] If Hick is operating with something like the disguise model in mind, then this suspicion is plausible. In the disguise model, the gods and the impersonal absolutes of religious traditions are ways of appearing of the Real *an sich*. They are not things in their own right, and so they are insubstantial. Moreover, Mavrodes makes the point in "Polytheism" that the construct model yields a genuine polytheism but the disguise model does not. So perhaps the lesson to be learned from the exchange between Mavrodes and Hick is that Hick is, after all, not a genuine polytheist because he presupposes something like the disguise model. In other words, Hick thinks the gods and impersonal absolutes of religious traditions are merely ways in which the Real *an sich* appears to the practitioners of different religions and have no substantial reality in their own right.

David Basinger's "Hick's Religious Pluralism and 'Reformed Epistemology': A Middle Ground" argues that both John Hick's pluralism and Alvin Plantinga's Reformed Epistemology contain valuable insights. Basinger takes the question of primary concern to Reformed Epistemology to be the following: Under what conditions is an individual rational or within her epistemic rights in affirming one of the mutually exclusive religious hypotheses? And he supposes that Hick is mainly interested in the following question: Given that an individual can be rational or within her epistemic rights in affirming either exclusivism or pluralism, upon what basis should her actual choice be made? These are obviously distinct but related questions.

How does Reformed Epistemology answer its primary question? According to Plantinga, belief in God is basic for most theists; that is, it is not based on other beliefs or arguments the theist has or can produce. Moreover, there are conditions in which theistic belief is properly basic, and in such conditions it is rational even in the absence of support from propositional evidence. To be sure, it is incumbent on the theist to consider objections to theistic belief such as various problems of evil. However, all the theist has to be able to do in order to remain rational is to undercut such potential defeaters of theistic belief. Basinger thinks Reformed Epistemology could extend this line of thought to the situation in which the theist is considering alternatives such as non-theistic religions or Hick's pluralism. To remain rational, the theist does not have to prove that theism is more plausible or more probable than the alternatives; it suffices to undercut arguments aimed at showing that theism is less probable or less plausible than a competitor. In other words, the theist "need ultimately only defend herself against the claim that a thoughtful assessment of the matter makes the affirmation of some incompatible perspective—i.e., pluralism or some incompatible exclusivistic perspective—the only rational option." So Reformed Epistemology's answer to its question is this: An individual is rational or within her epistemic rights in affirming an exclusive religious hypothesis if she can successfully defend it by undercutting the potential defeaters. It is this sort of defense that William Lane Craig tries to provide for Christian soteriological exclusivism. Basinger is confident that the exclusivist theist can accomplish at least this much, and no doubt he would allow that exclusivists of other stripes can do so too.

For Basinger we are confronted with a choice situation in which there is more than one rational option. There are, on the one hand, several rational exclusivist perspectives, and there is, on the other, Hick's pluralism. On what basis, if any, are we to choose among them, assuming choice is possible? It is at this point that he locates Hick's contribution. He sees Hick as offering a challenge to exclusivists who are aware of religious diversity. Most people find formed in themselves the dominant exclusive religious beliefs of the culture in which they grew up. Why should any group of exclusivists suppose that its belief-forming mechanisms are functioning properly while the analogous mechanisms in the other groups are not? Of course, exclusivists have answers to this question. Christian exclusivists, for example, can claim that human religious belief-forming mechanisms have been damaged as a result of sin and theirs alone are reliable because of a gift of the Holy Spirit. But such beliefs are outputs of the very mechanisms whose reliability is being questioned, and so they cannot be used without circularity to establish the reliability of those mechanisms. And if exclusivists of other sorts can only answer the question by appeal to claims internal to their own religious perspectives, they too cannot argue without circularity for the reliability of their religious belief-forming mechanisms.

Basinger thinks that in this situation the choice between exclusivism and pluralism should be based on inference to the best explanation. Exclusivists must, he suggests, "ultimately fall back on the contention that their belief-forming mechanisms can alone be trusted because that set of beliefs thus generated appears to them to form the most plausible religious explanatory hypothesis available." He envisages a comparative analysis of the explanatory virtues of Hick's pluralism and various forms of exclusivism and a conscious choice among competing religious explanatory hypotheses in favor of the hypothesis with the most explanatory virtues. He does not, however, assume that Hick's pluralism will win the competition, nor does he expect the analysis to produce consensus.

It seems proper to evaluate Hick's pluralism as an explanatory hypothesis because it was proposed to explain such things as the apparently equal efficacy of different religious traditions in transforming human existence from self-centeredness to Reality-centeredness. But it is not clear that it is appropriate to evaluate its exclusivist competitors as explanatory hypotheses, for it is not clear that they are meant to explain things. Perhaps they lack explanatory virtues but possess other virtues that make them choiceworthy. If the comparisons Basinger makes are focused exclusively on explanatory virtues, there is some risk that the deck will be stacked in favor of Hick's pluralism and the merits of its exclusivist rivals will be overlooked. And this risk may not be small. The view that traditional religious doctrines should not be understood as explanations enjoys considerable support among philosophers, and so it is a view that ought to be taken seriously.

Alvin Plantinga's "Pluralism: A Defense of Religious Exclusivism" defends the exclusivist, who holds that the doctrines of one religion are true and the propositions incompatible with them are false, against ethical/moral and intellectual/epistemic charges. The main ethical complaint is that the exclusivist exhibits vices such as arrogance or egotism. Plantinga observes that this complaint does not make sense unless the exclusivist believes she knows of no arguments for the beliefs with respect to which she is an exclusivist that would persuade all or most honest and intelligent inquirers. So he asks why we should think that an exclusivist who satisfies this condition is arrogant or egotistical, and he argues that there is no good reason for thinking so. Consider the doctrine of the Incarnation. John Hick is committed to the view that this doctrine is literally false and so must accept the denial of the doctrine in question. But he is aware that he knows of no argument for this denial that would persuade all or most honest and intelligent inquirers. Hence if the Christian exclusivist is guilty of arrogance or egotism, then the Hickian pluralist is likewise guilty. What is more, according to Plantinga, skeptical suspense of judgment about the doctrine of the Incarnation fares no better than affirmation or denial. Either the skeptic falls prey to the charge of arrogance or egotism, or the skeptic has no basis for launching the charge against others.

Plantinga likens religious disagreement to disagreement over moral questions, and the analogy seems to be fruitful. Consider an example Plantinga does not discuss. Imagine someone who believes that abortion is wrong except when necessary to save the life of the pregnant woman. He realizes that many disagree. He considers their objections to his position with as much care and sympathy as he can muster, but the objections seem to him to be flawed and unconvincing. However, he is also aware that he knows of no argument for his position that would persuade all or most honest and intelligent inquirers. If, after reflection, his position still seems to him to be correct, is he being arrogant or egotistical in sticking with it? It is difficult to see how to sustain such a charge. By parity of reasoning, it is difficult to see how to substantiate a parallel charge directed to the religious exclusivist.

The chief intellectual or epistemic complaint Plantinga considers is that the exclusivist is unjustified or irrational in holding her exclusivist beliefs.

With respect to justification, he examines two possibilities. One is that the exclusivist violates some epistemic duty; the other is that exclusivism is intellectually arbitrary because it violates some principle of epistemic parity. Plantinga quickly dismisses the charge that the exclusivist must violate some generally acknowledged duty. Someone who, after examining objections to her exclusivist beliefs and finding them wanting, continues to think they seem true and accordingly continues to hold them seems to be entirely within her intellectual rights. The charge of arbitrariness receives more extended consideration. Plantinga grants, for the sake of the argument, that conflicting religious beliefs can be on an epistemic par in some respects. They can have, for instance, relevantly similar internally available markers such as felt strength of conviction, experiential support, and propositional evidence for them. But he insists that the exclusivist must think they are not on a par in all epistemically relevant respects. As he puts it, "she must still think that there is an important epistemic difference: she thinks that somehow the other person has *made a mistake,* or *has a blind spot,* or hasn't been wholly attentive, or hasn't received some grace she has, or is in some way epistemically less fortunate." Of course the exclusivist may be mistaken, but she is not being arbitrary in retaining her exclusivist beliefs.

Plantinga goes on to argue that the exclusivist is not, in any of the five main senses of "irrational," necessarily irrational in holding her exclusivist beliefs. In the course of this argument he considers the charge that exclusivist beliefs are arbitrary because they are accidents of birth. Most people just find themselves with exclusivist religious beliefs of the cultures in which they grow up. But what are we to make of this sociological fact if it is, indeed, a fact? Plantinga concedes, for the sake of the argument, that his beliefs would have been quite different if he had been born in Madagascar. Of course the same goes for the Hickian pluralist. He probably would not have been a pluralist if he had been born in medieval France. Does it follow that it is irrational in any sense to be a Hickian pluralist? Plantinga doubts that it does. Similarly, the exclusivist's religious beliefs are not shown to be irrational merely by pointing out that she would not have had them if she had been raised elsewhere.

Plantinga does allow that an awareness of the facts of religious diversity can have an impact on the epistemic status of exclusivist beliefs. In his epistemology, warrant is the degreed property enough of which converts true belief into knowledge, and degree of warrant depends in part on degree of belief or level of confidence in a proposition. Knowledge of the facts of religious diversity can reduce the level of confidence in exclusivist beliefs and thereby diminish their degree of warrant. Indeed Plantinga thinks the impact could be sufficiently severe that exclusivist beliefs that would have been knowledge in the absence of awareness of the facts of religious diversity are not knowledge in the presence of that awareness.

In a response to Plantinga, John Hick distances himself from the ethical complaints against exclusivism and revisits one of the epistemic issues. He argues that we should look critically at or apply a hermeneutic of suspicion to exclusivist religious beliefs because they are instilled into believers by the surrounding religious culture in their youth. We do not, he thinks, have the same reason to be suspicious or critical of his pluralism. This is because "one is not usually a religious pluralist as a result of having been raised from childhood to be one, as (in most cases) one is raised from childhood to be a Christian or a Muslim or a Hindu, etc."[5] It is worth keeping in mind, however, that Hick's pluralism is the product of a certain kind of academic culture, one that is not universally shared. Perhaps that gives us some reason to be suspicious or critical of it.

Plantinga's reply to Hick returns to the question of arbitrariness. It distinguishes two claims. One is the claim that there is no relevant epistemic difference between, for example, exclusivist Christian beliefs and conflicting beliefs in other religions and hence the Christian exclusivist's stance is arbitrary. The other is the claim that the Christian exclusivist herself agrees that there is no relevant epistemic difference between her exclusivist beliefs and the conflicting beliefs in other religions and, retaining her own beliefs anyway, falls into arbitrariness. Plantinga thinks the second claim is unfair to the Christian exclusivist. She will not agree that there is no relevant epistemic difference; she will cite such things as their confirmation by the inner testimony of the Holy Spirit as epistemically relevant features her exclusivist beliefs have and their competitors lack. In doing so, she may, of course, be mistaken, but she is not being arbitrary. But if Hick wants to establish the first claim and show that there really is no relevant epistemic difference between exclusivist Christian beliefs and their rivals, then it is incumbent on him to argue that the Christian exclusivist's claims of epistemic privilege are false. What is more, according to Plantinga, "it is very probable that if Christian belief is true, then Christians *are* in a better position, epistemically speaking, than those who reject Christian belief; so what Hick really owes us is a good argument with respect to whose conclusion it is very unlikely that Christian belief is true."[6] Plantinga is willing to bet that Hick will not be able to bear this burden of proof. Of course Hick may not think that he needs to bear it. It is open to him to suggest that the Christian exclusivist's stance is arbitrary unless she can prove that her claims of epistemic privilege are true. Perhaps we should construe the disagreement between Plantinga and Hick on this issue as a dispute about where the burden of proof lies. If so, it will, like other burden of proof disputes in philosophy, be difficult to resolve.

In "Religious Diversity and Perceptual Knowledge of God," William P. Alston tackles the problem religious diversity raises for his thesis that experience of God provides *prima facie* justification for beliefs about how God is manifested to the experiencer. He defends this thesis within the context of his doxastic practice approach to epistemology. A doxastic practice is a practice of forming beliefs together with a series of possible overriders for the *prima facie* justification conferred on a belief by its emergence from the practice. Doxastic practices are to be epistemically assessed in terms of the likelihood that they produce true beliefs, that is, in terms of their reliability. Basic doxastic practices are socially established practices whose reliability cannot be established in a noncircular manner. Alston considers it rational to accord *prima facie* acceptance to all basic practices that are not demonstrably unreliable or otherwise disqualified from rational acceptance. He also argues that a practice's claim to rational acceptance is strengthened if it enjoys self-support.

Alston assumes that each of the major religions has a practice of forming beliefs about how Ultimate Reality is manifested on the basis of religious experience. Different religions have different practices because the possible overriders vary from one religious tradition to another. Among them is the Christian practice (CP). According to Alston, CP is a basic practice that is not demonstrably unreliable and derives self-support from the way in which its promises of spiritual development can be seen from within to be fulfilled. He supposes that, in addition to CP, there are other religious doxastic practices that are basic, are not demonstrably unreliable, and enjoy as much self-support as CP does. Does this disqualify CP from rational acceptance?

Alston thinks not. He admits that religious diversity diminishes the justification its practitioners have for engaging in CP, but he denies that it does so to the extent of its being irrational for them to engage in it. The denial is supported by two lines of argument.

The first contrasts intrapractice conflicts and interpractice conflicts. Consider various ways of predicting the weather, for example, scientific meteorology, going by the state of rheumatism in one's joints, observing groundhogs. As Alston sees it, if one employs one of these methods but has no non-question-begging reason for supposing it is more reliable than the others, then one lacks a sufficient rational basis for employing the method. But this is because the rival methods confront one another within a single doxastic practice, and we know how to get non-question-begging reasons for supposing one method is more reliable than the others. We can run a statistical test on the predictive success of the methods, and its outcome can give us a non-question-begging reason for supposing one of them is more reliable than the others. Alston thinks that the lack of such reasons clearly has strongly negative epistemic consequences because it is the lack of something we know how to get. But things are different in the religious case. Since in this case the conflict is between doxastic practices, there is no shared procedure for settling disputes. Hence the lack of non-question-begging reasons is not the lack of something we know how to get. Alston's conclusion is that this lack does not have the strongly negative epistemic consequences found in the intrapractice case or, at least, it is not clear that it has such consequences.

The second line of argument employs an analogy with a counterfactual assumption about some perceptual doxastic practices. Suppose that in certain cultures there were a socially established Cartesian practice of construing what is visually perceived as an indefinitely extended medium that is more or less concentrated at various points, rather than, as in our Aristotelian practice, as made up of more or less discrete objects scattered in space. Further suppose that in other cultures there were an established Whiteheadian practice in which the visual field is construed as made up of momentary events growing out of one another in a continuous process. Assume that each of these practices serves its practitioners equally well in their dealings with the environment and is associated with a well-developed physical science. Imagine us to be as firmly wedded to our Aristotelian practice as we in fact are but unable to find a non-question-begging reason for thinking it more accurate than either of the others. Alston thinks that, absent any non-question-begging reason for thinking that one of the other practices is more accurate than my own, "the only rational course for me to take is to sit tight with the practice of which I am a master and which serves me so well in guiding my activity in the world." But the imagined sense-perceptual situation is precisely parallel to our actual situation with regard to CP and its religious rivals. Hence, by parity of reasoning, the rational thing for a practitioner of CP to do is to sit tight with it and continue to form beliefs in accord with it.

In commenting on Alston's conclusion, John Hick makes two points. He notes that Alston is assuming that only one of the competing religious belief-systems can be completely true. From that assumption, Hick claims, it follows that religious experience generally produces false beliefs and so is a generally unreliable basis for belief-formation. What is more, he goes on to claim, "whilst it is possible that the doxastic practice of one's own community constitutes the sole exception to a general rule, the claim that this is so can only appear arbitrary and unjustified unless it is supported by good arguments."[7] Hick seems to think that Alston bears a special burden of proof if he claims that CP is the exception to a general rule. Perhaps this is indirect evidence that Hick's disagreement with Alvin Plantinga is also ultimately a matter of disagreement about where the burden of proof lies.

Alston's reply to Hick focuses on the first point. Alston challenges the claim that, on his assumption, religious experience is an unreliable source of religious belief. To get this conclusion from the assumption one would also have to suppose that most of the beliefs of each religious system contradict most of the beliefs of the others. Alston thinks it is by no means clear that this supposition is true and has the impression that it is false. Moreover, "even if the major religious belief-systems are mostly in contradiction," he argues, "there is still the question of the extent to which this is to be laid at the door of religious experience."[8] It could be that most of the beliefs that contradict one another derive from sources other than religious experience. Finally, even if most beliefs based on religious experience were false, that would not contradict Alston's epistemological thesis that religious experience provides *prima facie* justification for beliefs about the manifestations of Ultimate Reality. Since *prima facie* justification can be overridden, religious experience can render beliefs about manifestations of Ultimate Reality *prima facie* justified, even if most of this justification is overridden.

Hick's second point suggests one point that deserves further discussion. Alston is concerned with the situation in which the practitioner of CP has no non-question-begging reason for supposing that CP is more reliable than its religious rivals and also has no non-question-begging reason for supposing that any one of them is more reliable than it is. Even if Alston is correct in thinking that it is rational for the practitioner of CP to sit tight in this situation, Hick's suspicion that doing so will seem arbitrary might be on the right track. Why would it not be equally rational for the practitioner to switch to one of the other religious doxastic practices that is basic, is not demonstrably unreliable, and is self-supported? Perhaps Alston is mistaken in thinking that sitting tight is *the only* rational course for the practitioner of CP in this situation. Maybe the situation in which sitting tight is the only rational course, and so is not arbitrary, for the practitioner of CP is the situation in which the practitioner has a non-question-begging reason or, as Hick puts it, good arguments for the superior reliability of CP.

J. L. Schellenberg's "Religious Experience and Religious Diversity: A Reply to Alston" criticizes William P. Alston's solution to the problem of religious diversity. Schellenberg considers the presentation in Alston's book, *Perceiving God,* rather than the presentation in his article, "Religious Diversity and Perceptual Knowledge of God." But because essentially the same solution is presented in both places, successful criticism of the solution in the book would also be successful criticism of the solution in the article. There are, of course, terminological differences between the two presentations, but it is easy to translate from one terminology to the other.

Schellenberg takes Alston's first line of argument to be focused on the condition in which the lack of non-question-begging, that is, independent, reasons providing resolution of a dispute is the lack of something we know how to get. He supposes that the second premise in the argument is the claim that, in the situation of religious incompatibility, the lack of independent reasons is not the lack of something we know how to get. And he assumes that its conclusion is the claim that justification for belief is *not* removed in the situation of religious incompatibility. On these assumptions, if the argument is to be deductively valid, its first premise must be the claim that if justification for belief is removed in the situation of religious incompatibility, then, in that situation, the lack of independent reasons is the lack of something we know how to get. Schellenberg argues that this premise is false. He holds that justification for belief is removed in the situation of religious incompatibility, even though the lack of independent reasons is *not* the lack of something we know how to get. He will be right about this if justification for belief in the situation of religious incompatibility is removed by something other than the lack of independent reasons being the lack of something we know how to get.

Schellenberg thinks justification is removed in the situation of religious incompatibility by the unresolved incompatibility itself. He takes it to be a necessary truth that, for any person and proposition $p$, the person is justified in believing $p$ only if, for any proposition $q$ known by the person to be entailed by $p$, the person has justification for believing $q$. He also assumes that participants in the competing religious doxastic practices who are aware of the problem of religious diversity know that the denial of the reliability claims of other practices is entailed by their own reliability claim. He then argues as follows: (1) For each such participant, belief in the reliability of her own practice is justified only if she has justification for belief in the denial of the reliability claims of other practices; and (2) each participant does not have justification for belief in the denial of the reliability claims of the other practices; therefore, (3) for each participant, belief in the reliability of her own practice is not justified. The argument is deductively valid, and so if we accept its premises (1) and (2), we are committed to accepting its conclusion (3).

One important objection to the alleged necessary truth from which premise (1) is derived is that it opens the door to skepticism. Suppose someone bases the belief that there is a tree in front of her on her visual experience. Being a philosopher, she knows that this belief entails the denial of the claim that she is a brain in a vat. A skeptic argues that she does not have justification for the denial of that claim and then infers, using the allegedly necessary truth and *modus tollens,* that her belief that there is a tree in front of her is not justified. Of course, as Schellenberg points out, one can respond to the skeptic by insisting that her belief that there is a tree in front of her is justified and then inferring, using the allegedly necessary truth and *modus ponens,* that she has justification for the denial of the brain in a vat hypothesis. However, as he realizes, if he allows this response to the skeptic, he will be asked why Alston should not be allowed to make a similar move. Why not insist that, for each participant in a religious doxastic practice, belief in the reliability of her own practice is justified and then infer, using the alleged necessary truth and *modus ponens,* that each participant has justification for belief in the denial of the reliability claims of other practices? In other words, why is the antiskeptic granted the privilege of using a *modus ponens* argument while the Alstonian is not? Schellenberg's answer is that there is a significant difference between the two cases. As he puts it, "*competition* is obviously a factor in the case of an unresolved incompatibility." In the religious case, there is genuine competition; different communities of people actually believe the incompatible propositions that emerge from the rival doxastic practices. But there is no community that actually believes that we are brains in vats; typically this hypothesis figures in skeptical arguments merely as an uneliminated possibility.

There are, however, other cases of genuine competition we can examine when we are trying to assess Schellenberg's argument. Some philosophers believe that freedom and determinism are compatible; others believe they are incompatible. So compatibilism and incompatibilism are in genuine competition. Compatibilists know that their view entails the denial of incompatibilism, and incompatibilists likewise know that their view entails the denial of compatibilism. Moreover, there is no shared procedure for resolving the dispute. Whatever philosophers share, including the arguments for and against both positions, have not and probably will not resolve it. If we think that genuine competition is what authorizes the application of the *modus tollens* form of argument, we ought to be prepared to apply it to the compatibilists and incompatibilists. To the compatibilists we should say that, because you do not have justification for the belief in the denial of incompatibilism, your belief in compatibilism is not justified. And obviously the same judgment applies to the incompatibilists. But it is far from clear that we ought to make such judgments. After all, presumably at least some parties to the dispute on both sides have examined all the major arguments pro and con and done their level best to arrive at the truth. So perhaps we ought to be prepared to apply the *modus ponens* form of argument to them. To such compatibilists, maybe we should say that, since your belief in compatibilism is justified, you do have justification for belief in the denial of incompatibilism. And once again a similar judgment applies to such incompatibilists. However, if we ought to apply the *modus ponens* form of argument to some compatibilists and some incompatiblists, then perhaps we also ought to apply it to some participants in competing religious doxastic practices. If we do so, we are committed to rejecting premise (2) of Schellenberg's argument against Alston. Hence maybe that argument is less compelling than it might initially appear.

In a brief response to Schellenberg, Alston makes a similar point. Let *p* be one of the deliverances of CP, and let *q* be an inconsistent product of one of the rival forms of mystical practice. According to Schellenberg's principle, if a practitioner of CP is justified in believing *p* and realizes that *p* entails not-*q*, then the practitioner has justification for believing not-*q*. Alston admits that it would be question-begging for him to assume that the practitioner *is* justified in believing *p*. But he claims that, by the same token, it would be question-begging for Schellenberg to assume that the practitioner *does not have* justification for believing not-*q*. Alston says: "Either assumption would be begging the question."[9] So his view is that premise (2) of Schellenberg's argument is question-begging. If we agree with Alston on this point, we will think that in this case both the *modus ponens* argument and the *modus tollens* argument have a question-begging minor premise, in which case neither argument can be dialectically effective.

Schellenberg is also critical of Alston's second line of argument. He supposes that the counterfactual case of diverse sensory practices shows only that it would be imprudent or practically impossible to cease forming beliefs in accord with the Aristotelain practice to which we are firmly wedded. From this supposition he concludes that Alston's analogy is irrelevant to the question of whether it is *epistemically* rational to engage in religious doxastic practices such as CP.

William J. Wainwright's "Religious Experience and Religious Pluralism," which is excerpted from his "Religious Language, Religious Experience and Religious Pluralism," is a sympathetic but critical discussion of William P. Alston's solution to the problem of religious diversity. Like J. L. Schellenberg, Wainwright discusses the presentation of the solution in *Perceiving God*, but what he says applies, *mutatis mutandis*, to the presentation in "Religious Diversity and Perceptual Knowledge of God." Wainwright argues that Alston's defense of the rationality of engaging in an experiential religious doxastic practice such as Alston's Christian practice (CP), or in *Perceiving God*, Christian mystical practice (CMP), is only partly successful.

Wainwright begins by noting that Alston's discussion is primarily addressed to those who are already engaged in CMP or some other mystical practice. He wonders what Alston has to say to the religiously uncommitted. After pointing out that Alston thinks that those who do not engage in a mystical practice can have good reasons for accepting the testimony of those who do and hence for believing their claims, Wainwright raises the issue of conflicting testimony. What the practitioners of CMP tell the uncommitted is, to a large extent, incompatible with what the practitioners of Buddhist mystical practice (BMP) tell them. So whatever reasons the uncommitted have for assenting to the products of BMP are reasons against assenting to the products of CMP and vice versa. According to Wainwright, the uncommitted face an analogue of one of David Hume's arguments against miracles. Hume argued that since miracles are cited to support incompatible religious systems, cases for miracles destroy one another. Similarly, testimonial reasons for incompatible religious beliefs destroy one another. It seems to Wainwright that this provides the uncommitted with a rather decisive reason for a skeptical suspense of judgment.

Wainwright also doubts that Alston has shown that it is reasonable for Christians who engage in CMP or Buddhists who engage in BMP to retain their commitments. He does not think that there is the difference in kind between secular and religious disputes that Alston's first argument requires. On the one hand, we sometimes have compelling reasons for believing that a dispute between eyewitnesses to an event such as a car accident will never be resolved. We might know, for example, that there were no other witnesses and that the event was not videotaped. On the other hand, we know how the religious dispute could be resolved. It could be resolved by arguments from non-question-begging or neutral premises that show some mystical practices to be getting closer to the truth than others. So it seems to Wainwright that, if unresolved secular disputes have strongly negative epistemic consequences, unresolved religious disputes do too. What is more, Wainwright claims, many religious traditions contain certain doctrines that, if they are understood in certain ways, imply that competing mystical practices are at least partially reliable. He takes the Christian doctrine that God is love and the Buddhist doctrine of the universal accessibility of the Buddha nature to be examples. Because any reason for supposing an incompatible doxastic practice is reliable is also a *prima facie* reason for thinking one's own is not, mystical practices that involve such doctrines are to some extent self-undermining. These considerations lead Wainwright to give more weight to the diversity objection than Alston does.

When he discusses the counterfactual situation of competing sensory perceptual practices that is involved in Alston's second argument, Wainwright agrees with Alston's claim that it is pragmatically rational for the Aristotelian practitioner to sit tight. However, he also thinks the Aristotelian practitioner has a reason for doubting that beliefs that emerge from her practice are any more firmly grounded in reality than those that emerge from the rival Cartesian and Whiteheadian practices. Because engaging in a doxastic practice involves thinking that it is reliable and, hence, accepting its outputs as mostly true, that is, believing them, the Aristotelian practitioner will continue believing the outputs of her practice despite her reason for doubt. But, Wainwright suggests, she may conclude that it is not epistemically reasonable for her to do so. He is interested in the question of whether we should reach the same conclusion about those who engage in CMP or BMP.

According to Wainwright, it is epistemically rational to engage in a doxastic practice if there are good reasons for thinking it reliable and epistemically irrational to do so if there are good reasons for thinking it unreliable. Absent good reasons either way, engagement is epistemically nonrational. Wainwright agrees with Alston that the social establishment and self-support of CMP, together with the fact that it is not demonstrably unreliable, constitute a good reason for thinking it *prima facie* reliable, but he also believes that religious diversity is a good reason for thinking it *prima facie* unreliable. Absent a neutral or non-question-begging reason for thinking CMP is *ultima facie* reliable, it is not epistemically rational to engage in it. But if the reasons for thinking CMP is unreliable merely offset but do not outweigh or override the reasons for thinking it is reliable, then it is not epistemically irrational to engage in it. Hence, as Wainwright sees it, Alston has shown, at most, that sitting tight with CMP is pragmatically rational and not epistemically irrational. This makes his defense of the rationality of engaging in CMP partly successful. Wainwright thus thinks Alston has accomplished more than Schellenberg is willing to give him credit for. To establish the epistemic rationality of continuing to engage in CMP one would have to produce a non-question-begging argument or independent or neutral reason for thinking the reliability of CMP is superior to that of its rivals. If Alston's defense is to be fully successful, Wainwright concludes, "it must form part of a persuasive cumulative case argument for the Christian world-view."

There may be some interesting connections between Hick's and Wainwright's dissatisfactions with Alston's defense. Alston wants to show that, despite religious diversity, the only rational thing for a practitioner of CMP to do is to sit tight and continue engaging in CMP even in a "worst-case scenario" in which the practitioner has no non-question-begging or independent or neutral reason for thinking that the reliability of CMP is superior to that of its rivals. To Hick, sitting tight in the worst-case scenario seems arbitrary. Wainwright argues that sitting tight in the worst-case scenario is not epistemically rational, though it is not epistemically irrational and is pragmatically rational. Maybe both critics are right. If so, how are their complaints connected? Perhaps sitting tight in the worst-case scenario is arbitrary because it is not epistemically rational; perhaps it is not epistemically rational because it is arbitrary. Or maybe the lack of epistemic rationality and the arbitrariness are linked in some other way.

In "Towards Thinner Theologies: Hick and Alston on Religious Diversity," Philip L. Quinn criticizes the views about religious diversity set forth in the writings of both John Hick and William P. Alston. But he also tries to accomplish something more constructive and irenic. He argues that movement in the direction of a refined version of Hick's position, which amounts to movement towards thicker phenomenologies and thinner theologies, is a rational course of action within the framework of Alston's doxastic practice approach to religious epistemology.

Like George I. Mavrodes, Quinn discerns an ambiguity in the way Hick deploys the distinction between the phenomenal and the noumenal. On one interpretation, Hick's pluralistic hypothesis postulates a single noumenal Real or Real *an sich* and diverse ways in which *it* appears and is experienced in different religious traditions. Quinn finds the analogy in the disguise model proposed by Mavrodes helpful in understanding this interpretation. On the other interpretation, Hick's pluralistic hypothesis postulates not only a single noumenal Real but also many phenomenal Reals that are joint products of the interaction of the noumenal Real and various human religions. Quinn also finds the analogy in the construct model proposed by Mavrodes helpful in understanding this interpretation. His main complaint is that Hick falls into inconsistency because he switches back and forth between the two interpretations. He quotes a passage by Hick whose first sentence implies that the noumenal Real is experienced, albeit through our religious concepts (which would be the case if the pluralistic hypothesis on its first interpretation were true) and whose third sentence implies that the noumenal Real is not experienced, because it cannot be experienced (which would be the case if the pluralistic hypothesis on its second interpretation were true).

Quinn also sees difficulties for the pluralistic hypothesis arising from the way Hick tries to demarcate between claims that are literally true of the noumenal Real and those that are not. Hick distinguishes between statements and concepts that are purely formal and those that are not. He thinks that the noumenal Real falls under only purely formal concepts and only purely formal statements are true of it. However, he does not provide a definition of purely formal statements or concepts, and so the examples he gives provide the only clue to what he has in mind. Quinn finds some of them problematic. Hick claims that Anselm's definition of God as that than which no greater can be conceived is a formal statement. But, as Quinn points out, philosophers from Anselm to Alvin Plantinga have argued that maximal conceivable greatness entails such divine attributes as omniscience, omnipotence, and moral perfection, which in turn entail being personal. So if it is literally true that the noumenal Real satisfies Anselm's definition because it is a formal statement and if entailment transmits literalness, then it is literally true that the noumenal Real is personal, which contradicts Hick's claims that it is neither person nor thing. Quinn thus joins Keith Ward and Paul R. Eddy in criticizing Hick's appropriation of Anselm.

Quinn thinks the best way to respond to the problems Hick's pluralistic hypothesis faces is not to abandon it but to refine it. He suggests a recipe that he hopes will allow those who follow it to construct coherent pluralistic hypotheses if such constructions are possible. But anyone who proposes to follow this recipe should keep in mind Eddy's suggestion that the closer a pluralistic hypothesis comes to depriving the noumenal Real it postulates of all positive attributes the harder it will be to distinguish such a noumenal Real from nothing at all.

There is a disagreement between Quinn and J. L. Schellenberg about what to make of Alston's argument concerning the disanalogy between conflict within a single doxastic practice and conflict among diverse doxastic practices. Schellenberg thinks the argument is best understood as an unsound argument for the conclusion that justification for belief is not removed in the situation of religious incompatibility. Quinn agrees that the argument does not establish that conclusion. Lack of something we know how to get is the feature whose presence in the intrapractice case leads, at worst, to nullification or elimination of justification, and that feature is absent in the interpractice case. As Quinn notes, it does not follow from its absence that nullification or elimination of justification does not occur in the interpractice case. What follows is only that nullification or elimination does not occur on account of the presence of that feature, and so if it occurs, it occurs for some other reason. But Quinn disagrees with Schellenberg's view about the best way to understand Alston's argument. Quinn thinks the argument is best understood as aimed at undercutting a reason that might be offered for thinking that it is not rational to engage in CMP, and so he concludes that it succeeds in blocking "one path to the conclusion that it is not rational to engage in CMP."

Quinn disagrees with Alston about the conclusion that should be drawn from the imagined situation in which there are competing sensory practices. Alston thinks that the only rational course for the Aristotelian practitioner is to sit tight. Quinn agrees that sitting tight is rational but denies that it is the only rational course. He thinks another rational course is to revise the Aristotelian practice from within in a Kantian direction and work to get the revised sensory perceptual practice socially established. It might occur to the Aristotelian practitioner, Quinn supposes, that a plausible explanation of the success of the diverse sensory perceptual practices is the hypothesis that each of the established practices is reliable with respect to the appearances the physical environment presents to its practitioners, but none is reliable with respect to how the physical environment is in itself. This thought could motivate the decision to modify Aristotelian practice so that the new outputs are beliefs about the appearances the physical environment presents to the practitioner but not about how the physical environment really is independent of the practitioner.

By parity of reasoning, Quinn argues, though it is rational for practitioners of CMP to continue to engage in it, it is not *the only* rational course of action in light of the facts of religious diversity. Another rational course to take is to revise CMP from within in ways that would improve its reliability if some refined pluralistic hypothesis were true. Quinn thinks that each of these courses of action is a rationally permissible response to the competition of mystical practices. Neither of them is irrational, but neither is rationally required.

Of course, the plausibility of Quinn's conclusion depends on the assumption that we are operating within the constraints of Alston's worst-case scenario. If non-question-begging or independent or neutral reasons for supposing CMP is more reliable than the sort of Kantian religious doxastic practice Quinn envisages were forthcoming, then the plausibility of Alston's claim that the only rational course for a practitioner of CMP to take is to stick with it would be considerably enhanced. And maybe Alston's claim will be more plausible than Quinn's conclusion only if such independent reasons are forthcoming. So perhaps Alston can have his conclusion about the exclusive rationality of sitting tight with CMP only if he can get out of the worst-case scenario by coming up with independent reasons for regarding CMP as more reliable than its extant rivals in other religious traditions and the revisionary possibility Quinn suggests. If so, this gives us another reason for concurring with William J. Wainwright's conclusion that Alston's defense of CMP must be part of a larger cumulative case for the truth of the Christian world-view if it is to be fully successful.

So what have we learned? It goes without saying that there is absolutely no consensus in sight on the issue of religious diversity. Although at this point William P. Alston's defense of exclusivism and John Hick's defense of pluralism seem to be the most fully developed positions, both views encounter problems, as we have seen. Of course, these problems have not forced either Hick or Alston to abandon his view. Nevertheless, one might wonder if different approaches might avoid at least some of these problems. Hick constantly encounters criticism of his distinction between purely formal concepts that can apply to the noumenal Real and substantive concepts that do not. Perhaps, then, forsaking the Kantian aspects of his hypothesis would help him escape these difficulties, though it would no doubt exact other costs. But Alston's doxastic practice approach faces many difficulties of its own and might require modification or supplementation. Scholars will most likely continue to focus critical attention on these and similar issues in the near future.

Inclusivism faces a less certain future, however. Although many hold this view, no one has yet undertaken to provide the same *detailed* defense of inclusivism that is evident in Hick's defense of pluralism or Alston's defense of exclusivism. This is not to say, of course, that no one has thought to defend inclusivism at all. Keith Ward, in his essay in this volume, is an example of someone who sticks up for the plausibility of such a view. Nevertheless, it is difficult to deny that inclusivism has not yet garnered as much attention as its competitors. *Why* this is the case is unclear. Perhaps too many perceive it to exhibit many of the problems of exclusivism and pluralism but none of their advantages. Maybe it is because Christian inclusivism is an invention of twentieth century Christians, as Hick has argued. Because it has not been around as long as exclusivism has, it makes sense that it would not have received as much attention. But Hick's pluralism, which is also a recent invention, has received more attention than inclusivism from philosophers, and so the relative neglect of inclusivism cannot be entirely explained in terms of its novelty.

It is also worth noting that the issue of religious diversity in general has not been on the radar screen of *academic* philosophy in the twentieth century as much as one might expect. For philosophy of religion in the middle part of the century was almost exclusively preoccupied with abstract questions about the meaningfulness of religious language. Now that the range of topics discussed has widened considerably, the issue of religious diversity is again receiving critical attention. And this is a healthy sign. For religious diversity is a practical problem for many people. As we noted earlier, modern technology and demographics have made the problem more acute and pressing. Unlike many very abstract philosophical problems, then, this one has the potential to engage nonphilosophers in a down-to-earth issue, and the philosophical discussion of it promises to aid nonphilosophers in further reflecting about what is at stake. We hope that this volume works to that end.

## NOTES

1. John Hick, "Religious Pluralism and the Divine: A Response to Paul Eddy," *Religious Studies* **31** (1995), p. 420.
2. John Hick, "The Epistemological Challenge of Religious Pluralism," *Faith and Philosophy* **14** (1997), p. 283.
3. *Ibid.*, p. 283.
4. George I. Mavrodes, "A Response to John Hick," *Faith and Philosophy* **14** (1997), p. 290.
5. Hick, "Epistemological Challenge," p. 281.
6. Alvin Plantinga, "Ad Hick," *Faith and Philosophy* **14** (1997), p. 296.
7. Hick, "Epistemological Challenge," p. 278.
8. William P. Alston, "Response to Hick," *Faith and Philosophy* **14** (1997), p. 287.
9. William P. Alston, "Response to Critics," *Religious Studies* **30** (1994), p. 179.

CHAPTER 1

# Of Miracles

DAVID HUME

In the foregoing reasoning we have supposed, that the testimony, upon which a miracle is founded, may possibly amount to an entire proof, and that the falsehood of that testimony would be a real prodigy: But it is easy to shew, that we have been a great deal too liberal in our concession, and that there never was a miraculous event established on so full an evidence.

For *first,* there is not to be found, in all history, any miracle attested by a sufficient number of men, of such unquestioned good-sense, education, and learning, as to secure us against all delusion in themselves; of such undoubted integrity, as to place them beyond all suspicion of any design to deceive others; of such credit and reputation in the eyes of mankind, as to have a great deal to lose in case of their being detected in any falsehood; and at the same time, attesting facts performed in such a public manner and in so celebrated a part of the world, as to render the detection unavoidable: All which circumstances are requisite to give us a full assurance in the testimony of men.

*Secondly.* We may observe in human nature a principle which, if strictly examined, will be found to diminish extremely the assurance, which we might, from human testimony, have, in any kind of prodigy. The maxim, by which we commonly conduct ourselves in our reasonings, is, that the objects, of which we have no experience, resemble those, of which we have; that what we have found to be most usual is always most probable; and that where there is an opposition of arguments, we ought to give the preference to such as are founded on the greatest number of past observations. But though, in proceeding by this rule, we readily reject any fact which is unusual and incredible in an ordinary degree; yet in advancing farther, the mind observes not always the same rule; but when anything is affirmed utterly absurd and miraculous, it rather the more readily admits of such a fact, upon account of that very circumstance, which ought to destroy all its authority. The passion of *surprise* and *wonder,* arising from miracles, being an agreeable emotion, gives a sensible tendency towards the belief of those events, from which it is derived. And this goes so far, that even those who cannot enjoy this pleasure immediately, nor can believe those miraculous events, of which they are

From David Hume, *An Enquiry Concerning Human Understanding,* Section X, Part II, "Of Miracles."

informed, yet love to partake of the satisfaction at second-hand or by rebound, and place a pride and delight in exciting the admiration of others.

With what greediness are the miraculous accounts of travellers received, their descriptions of sea and land monsters, their relations of wonderful adventures, strange men, and uncouth manners? But if the spirit of religion join itself to the love of wonder, there is an end of common sense; and human testimony, in these circumstances, loses all pretensions to authority. A religionist may be an enthusiast, and imagine he sees what has no reality: he may know his narrative to be false, and yet persevere in it, with the best intentions in the world, for the sake of promoting so holy a cause: or even where this delusion has not place, vanity, excited by so strong a temptation, operates on him more powerfully than on the rest of mankind in any other circumstances; and self-interest with equal force. His auditors may not have, and commonly have not, sufficient judgement to canvass his evidence: what judgement they have, they renounce by principle, in these sublime and mysterious subjects: or if they were ever so willing to employ it, passion and a heated imagination disturb the regularity of its operations. Their credulity increases his impudence: and his impudence overpowers their credulity.

Eloquence, when at its highest pitch, leaves little room for reason or reflection; but addressing itself entirely to the fancy or the affections, captivates the willing hearers, and subdues their understanding. Happily, this pitch it seldom attains. But what a Tully or a Demosthenes could scarcely effect over a Roman or Athenian audience, every *Capuchin,* every itinerant or stationary teacher can perform over the generality of mankind, and in a higher degree, by touching such gross and vulgar passions.

The many instances of forged miracles, and prophecies, and supernatural events, which, in all ages, have either been detected by contrary evidence, or which detect themselves by their absurdity, prove sufficiently the strong propensity of mankind to the extraordinary and the marvellous, and ought reasonably to beget a suspicion against all relations of this kind. This is our natural way of thinking, even with regard to the most common and most credible events. For instance: There is no kind of report which rises so easily, and spreads so quickly, especially in country places and provincial towns, as those concerning marriages; insomuch that two young persons of equal condition never see each other twice, but the whole neighbourhood immediately join them together. The pleasure of telling a piece of news so interesting, of propagating it, and of being the first reporters of it, spreads the intelligence. And this is so well known, that no man of sense gives attention to these reports, till he find them confirmed by some greater evidence. Do not the same passions, and others still stronger, incline the generality of mankind to believe and report, with the greatest vehemence and assurance, all religious miracles?

*Thirdly.* It forms a strong presumption against all supernatural and miraculous relations, that they are observed chiefly to abound among ignorant and barbarous nations; or if a civilized people has ever given admission to any of them, that people will be found to have received them from ignorant and barbarous ancestors, who transmitted them with that inviolable sanction and authority, which always attend received opinions. When we peruse the first histories of all nations, we are apt to imagine ourselves transported into some new world; where the whole frame of nature is disjointed, and every element performs its operations in a different manner, from what it does at present. Battles, revolutions, pestilence, famine and death, are never the effect of those natural causes, which we experience. Prodigies, omens, oracles, judgements, quite obscure the few natural events, that are intermingled with them. But as the former grow thinner every page, in proportion as we advance nearer the enlightened ages, we soon learn, that there is nothing mysterious or supernatural in the case, but that all proceeds from the usual propensity of mankind towards the marvellous, and that, though this inclination may at intervals receive a check from sense and learning, it can never be thoroughly extirpated from human nature.

*It is strange,* a judicious reader is apt to say, upon the perusal of these wonderful historians, *that such prodigious events never happen in our days.* But it is nothing strange, I hope, that men should lie in all ages. You must surely have seen instances enough of that frailty. You have yourself heard many such marvellous relations started, which, being treated with scorn by all the wise and judicious, have at last been abandoned even by the vulgar. Be assured, that those renowned lies, which have spread and flourished to such a monstrous height, arose from like beginnings; but being sown in a more proper soil, shot up at last into prodigies almost equal to those which they relate.

It was a wise policy in that false prophet, Alexander, who though now forgotten, was once so famous, to lay the first scene of his impostures in Paphlagonia, where, as Lucian tells us, the people were extremely ignorant and stupid, and ready to swallow even the grossest delusion. People at a distance, who are weak enough to think the matter at all worth enquiry, have no opportunity of receiving better information. The stories come magnified to them by a hundred circumstances. Fools are industrious in propagating the imposture; while the wise and learned are contented, in general, to deride its absurdity, without informing themselves of the particular facts, by which it may be distinctly refuted. And thus the impostor above mentioned was enabled to proceed, from his ignorant Paphlagonians, to the enlisting of votaries, even among the Grecian philosophers, and men of the most eminent rank and distinction in Rome: nay, could engage the attention of that sage emperor Marcus Aurelius; so far as to make him trust the success of a military expedition to his delusive prophecies.

The advantages are so great, of starting an imposture among an ignorant people, that, even though the delusion should be too gross to impose on the generality of them (*which, though seldom, is sometimes the case*) it has a much better chance for succeeding in remote countries, than if the first scene had been laid in a city renowned for arts and knowledge. The most ignorant and barbarous of these barbarians carry the report abroad. None of their countrymen have a large correspondence, or sufficient credit and authority to contradict and beat down the delusion. Men's inclination to the marvellous has full opportunity to display itself. And thus a story, which is universally exploded in the place where it was first started, shall pass for certain at a thousand miles distance. But had Alexander fixed his residence at Athens, the philosophers of that renowned mart of learning had immediately spread, throughout the whole Roman empire, their sense of the matter; which, being supported by so great authority, and displayed by all the force of reason and eloquence, had entirely opened the eyes of mankind. It is true; Lucian, passing by chance through Paphlagonia, had an opportunity of performing this good office. But, though much to be wished, it does not always happen, that every Alexander meets with a Lucian, ready to expose and detect his impostures.

I may add as a *fourth* reason, which diminishes the authority of prodigies, that there is no testimony for any, even those which have not been expressly detected, that is not opposed by an infinite number of witnesses; so that not only the miracle destroys the credit of testimony, but the testimony destroys itself. To make this the better understood, let us consider, that, in matters of religion, whatever is different is contrary; and that it is impossible the religions of ancient Rome, of Turkey, of Siam, and of China should, all of them, be established on any solid foundation. Every miracle, therefore, pretended to have been wrought in any of these religions (and all of them abound in miracles), as its direct scope is to establish the particular system to which it is attributed; so has it the same force, though more indirectly, to overthrow every other system. In destroying a rival system, it likewise destroys the credit of those miracles, on which that system was established; so that all the prodigies of different religions are to be regarded as contrary facts, and the evidences of these prodigies, whether weak or strong, as opposite to each other. According to this method of reasoning, when we believe any miracle of Mahomet or his successors, we have for our warrant the testimony of a few barbarous Arabians: And on the other hand, we are to regard the authority of Titus Livius, Plutarch, Tacitus, and, in short, of all the authors and witnesses, Grecian, Chinese, and Roman Catholic, who have related any miracle in their particular religion; I say, we are to regard their testimony in the same light as if they had mentioned that Mahometan miracle, and had in express terms contradicted it, with the same certainty as they have for the miracle they relate. This argument may appear over subtile and refined; but is not in reality different from the reasoning of a judge, who supposes, that the credit of two witnesses, maintaining a crime against any one, is destroyed by the testimony of two others, who affirm him to have been two hundred leagues distant, at the same instant when the crime is said to have been committed.

One of the best attested miracles in all profane history, is that which Tacitus reports of Vespasian, who cured a blind man in Alexandria, by means of his spittle, and a lame man by the mere touch of his foot; in obedience to a vision of the god Serapis, who had enjoined them to have recourse to the Emperor, for these miraculous cures. The story may be seen in that fine historian[1]; where every circumstance seems to add weight to the testimony, and might be displayed at large with all the force of argument and eloquence, if any one were now concerned to enforce the evidence of that exploded and idolatrous superstition. The gravity, solidity, age, and probity of so great an emperor, who, through the whole course of his life, conversed in a familiar manner with his friends and courtiers, and never affected those extraordinary airs of divinity assumed by Alexander and Demetrius. The historian, a contemporary writer, noted for candour and veracity, and withal, the greatest and most penetrating genius, perhaps, of all antiquity; and so free from any tendency to credulity, that he even lies under the contrary imputation, of atheism and profaneness: The persons, from whose authority he related the miracle, of established character for judgement and veracity, as we may well presume; eye-witnesses of the fact, and confirming their testimony, after the Flavian family was despoiled of the empire, and could no longer give any reward, as the price of a lie. *Utrumque, qui interfuere, nunc quoque memorant, postquam nullum mendacio pretium.* To which if we add the public nature of the facts, as related, it will appear, that no evidence can well be supposed stronger for so gross and so palpable a falsehood.

There is also a memorable story related by Cardinal de Retz, which may well deserve our consideration. When that intriguing politician fled into Spain, to avoid the persecution of his enemies, he passed through Saragossa, the capital of Arragon, where he was shewn, in the cathedral, a man, who had served seven years as a doorkeeper, and was well known to every body in town, that had ever paid his devotions at that church. He had been seen, for so long a time, wanting a leg; but recovered that limb by the rubbing of holy oil upon the stump; and the cardinal assures us that he saw him with two legs. This miracle was vouched by all the canons of the church; and the whole company in town were appealed to for a confirmation of the fact; whom the cardinal found, by their zealous devotion, to be thorough believers of the miracle. Here the relater was also contemporary to the supposed prodigy, of an incredulous and libertine character, as well as of great genius; the miracle of so *singular* a nature as could scarcely admit of a counterfeit, and the witnesses very numerous, and all of them, in a manner, spectators of the fact, to which they gave their testimony. And what adds mightily to the force of the evidence, and may double our surprise on this occasion, is, that the cardinal himself, who relates the story, seems not to give any credit to it, and consequently cannot be suspected of any concurrence in the holy fraud. He considered justly, that it was not requisite, in order to reject a fact of this nature, to be able accurately to disprove the testimony, and to trace its falsehood, through all the circumstances of knavery and credulity which produced it. He knew, that, as this was commonly altogether impossible at any small distance of time and place; so was it extremely difficult, even where one was immediately present, by reason of the bigotry, ignorance, cunning, and roguery of a great part of mankind. He therefore concluded, like a just reasoner, that such an evidence carried falsehood upon the very face of it, and that a miracle, supported by any human testimony, was more properly a subject of derision than of argument.

There surely never was a greater number of miracles ascribed to one person, than those, which were lately said to have been wrought in France upon the tomb of Abbé Paris, the famous Jansenist, with whose sanctity the people were so long deluded. The curing of the sick, giving hearing to the deaf, and sight to the blind, were every where talked of as the usual effects of that holy sepulchre. But what is more extraordinary; many of the miracles were immediately proved upon the spot, before judges of unquestioned integrity, attested by witnesses of credit and distinction, in a learned age, and on the most eminent theatre that is now in the world. Nor is this all: a relation of them was published and dispersed every where; nor were the *Jesuits,* though a learned body, supported by the civil magistrate, and determined enemies to those opinions, in whose favour the miracles were said to have been wrought, ever able distinctly to refute or detect them.[2] Where shall we find such a number of circumstances, agreeing to the corroboration of one fact? And what have we to oppose to such a cloud of witnesses, but the absolute impossibility or miraculous nature of the events, which they relate? And this surely, in the eyes of all reasonable people, will alone be regarded as a sufficient refutation.

Is the consequence just, because some human testimony has the utmost force and authority in some cases, when it relates the battle of Philippi or Pharsalia for instance; that therefore all kinds of testimony must, in all cases, have equal force and authority? Suppose that the Cæsarean and Pompeian factions had, each of them, claimed the victory in these battles, and that the historians of each party had uniformly ascribed the advantage to their own side; how could mankind, at this distance, have been able to determine between them? The contrariety is equally strong between the miracles related by Herodotus or Plutarch, and those delivered by Mariana, Bede, or any monkish historian.

The wise lend a very academic faith to every report which favours the passion of the reporter; whether it magnifies his country, his family, or himself, or in any other way strikes in with his natural inclinations and propensities. But what greater temptation than to appear a missionary, a prophet, an ambassador from heaven? Who would not encounter many dangers and difficulties, in order to attain so sublime a character? Or if, by the help of vanity and a heated imagination, a man has first made a convert of himself, and entered seriously into the delusion; who ever scruples to make use of pious frauds, in support of so holy and meritorious a cause?

The smallest spark may here kindle into the greatest flame; because the materials are always prepared for it. The *avidum genus auricularum,*[3] the gazing populace, receive greedily, without examination, whatever sooths superstition, and promotes wonder.

How many stories of this nature have, in all ages, been detected and exploded in their infancy? How many more have been celebrated for a time, and have afterwards sunk into neglect and oblivion? Where such reports, therefore, fly about, the solution of the phenomenon is obvious; and we judge in conformity to regular experience and observation, when we account for it by the known and natural principles of credulity and delusion. And shall we, rather than have a recourse to so natural a solution, allow of a miraculous violation of the most established laws of nature?

I need not mention the difficulty of detecting a falsehood in any private or even public history, at the place, where it is said to happen; much more when the scene is removed to ever so small a distance. Even a court of judicature, with all the authority, accuracy, and judgement, which they can employ, find themselves often at a loss to distinguish between truth and falsehood in the most recent actions. But the matter never comes to any issue, if trusted to the common method of altercation and debate and flying rumours; especially when men's passions have taken part on either side.

In the infancy of new religions, the wise and learned commonly esteem the matter too inconsiderable to deserve their attention or regard. And when afterwards they would willingly detect the cheat, in order to undeceive the deluded multitude, the season is now past, and the records and witnesses, which might clear up the matter, have perished beyond recovery.

No means of detection remain, but those which must be drawn from the very testimony itself of the reporters: and these, though always sufficient with the judicious and knowing, are commonly too fine to fall under the comprehension of the vulgar.

Upon the whole, then, it appears, that no testimony for any kind of miracle has ever amounted to a probability, much less to a proof; and that, even supposing it amounted to a proof, it would be opposed by another proof; derived from the very nature of the fact, which it would endeavour to establish. It is experience only, which gives authority to human testimony; and it is the same experience, which assures us of the laws of nature. When, therefore, these two kinds of experience are contrary, we have nothing to do but substract the one from the other, and embrace an opinion, either on one side or the other, with that assurance which arises from the remainder. But according to the principle here explained, this substraction, with regard to all popular religions, amounts to an entire annihilation; and therefore we may establish it as a maxim, that no human testimony can have such force as to prove a miracle, and make it a just foundation for any such system of religion.

I beg the limitations here made may be remarked, when I say, that a miracle can never be proved, so as to be the foundation of a system of religion. For I own, that otherwise, there may possibly be miracles, or violations of the usual course of nature, of such a kind as to admit of proof from human testimony; though, perhaps, it will be impossible to find any such in all the records of history. Thus, suppose, all authors, in all languages, agree, that, from the first of January 1600, there was a total darkness over the whole earth for eight days: suppose that the tradition of this extraordinary event is still strong and lively among the people: that all travellers, who return from foreign countries, bring us accounts of the same tradition, without the least variation or contradiction: it is evident, that our present philosophers, instead of doubting the fact, ought to receive it as certain, and ought to search for the causes whence it might be derived. The decay, corruption, and dissolution of nature, is an event rendered probable by so many analogies, that any phenomenon, which seems to have a tendency towards that catastrophe, comes within the reach of human testimony, if that testimony be very extensive and uniform.

But suppose, that all the historians who treat of England, should agree, that, on the first of January 1600, Queen Elizabeth died; that both before and after her death she was seen by her physicians and the whole court, as is usual with persons of her rank; that her successor was acknowledged and proclaimed by the parliament; and that, after being interred a month, she again appeared, resumed the throne, and governed England for three years: I must confess that I should be surprised at the concurrence of so many odd circumstances, but should not have the least inclination to believe so miraculous an event. I should not doubt of her pretended death, and of those other public circumstances that followed it: I should only assert it to have been pretended, and that it neither was, nor possibly could be real. You would in vain object to me the difficulty, and almost impossibility of deceiving the world in an affair of such consequence; the wisdom and solid judgement of that renowned queen; with the little or no advantage which she could reap from so poor an artifice: All this might astonish me; but I would still reply, that the knavery and folly of men are such common phenomena, that I should rather believe the most extraordinary events to arise from their concurrence, than admit of so signal a violation of the laws of nature.

But should this miracle be ascribed to any new system of religion; men, in all ages, have been so much imposed on by ridiculous stories of that kind, that this very circumstance would be a full proof of a cheat, and sufficient, with all men of sense, not only to make them reject the fact, but even reject it without farther examination. Though the Being to whom the miracle is ascribed, be, in this case, Almighty, it does not, upon that account, become a whit more probable; since it is impossible for us to know the attributes or actions of such a Being, otherwise than from the experience which we have of his productions, in the usual course of nature. This still reduces us to past observation, and obliges us to compare the instances of the violation of truth in the testimony of men, with those of the violation of the laws of nature by miracles, in order to judge which of them is most likely and probable. As the violations of truth are more common in the testimony concerning religious miracles, than in that concerning any other matter of fact; this must diminish very much the authority of the former testimony, and make us form a general resolution, never to lend any attention to it, with whatever specious pretence it may be covered.

Lord Bacon seems to have embraced the same principles of reasoning. "We ought," says he, "to make a collection or particular history of all monsters and prodigious births or productions, and in a word of every thing new, rare, and extraordinary in nature. But this must be done with the most severe scrutiny, lest we depart from truth. Above all, every relation must be considered as suspicious, which depends in any degree upon religion, as the prodigies of Livy: And no less so, every thing that is to be found in the writers of natural magic or alchimy, or such authors, who seem, all of them, to have an unconquerable appetite for falsehood and fable."[4]

I am the better pleased with the method of reasoning here delivered, as I think it may serve to confound those dangerous friends or disguised enemies to the *Christian Religion,* who have undertaken to defend it by the principles of human reason. Our most holy religion is founded on *Faith,* not on reason; and it is a sure method of exposing it to put it to such a trial as it is, by no means, fitted to endure. To make this more evident, let us examine those miracles, related in scripture; and not to lose ourselves in too wide a field, let us confine ourselves to such as we find in the *Pentateuch,* which we shall examine, according to the principles of these pretended Christians, not as the word or testimony of God himself, but as the production of a mere human writer and historian. Here then we are first to consider a book, presented to us by a barbarous and ignorant people, written in an age when they were still more barbarous, and in all probability long after the facts which it relates, corroborated by no concurring testimony, and resembling those fabulous accounts, which every nation gives of its origin. Upon reading this book, we find it full of prodigies and miracles. It gives an account of a state of the world and of human nature entirely different from the present: Of our fall from that state: Of the age of man, extended to near a thousand years: Of the destruction of the world by a deluge: Of the arbitrary choice of one people, as the favourites of heaven; and that people the countrymen of the author: Of their deliverance from bondage by prodigies the most astonishing imaginable: I desire any one to lay his hand upon his heart, and after a serious consideration declare, whether he thinks that the falsehood of such a book, supported by such a testimony, would be more extraordinary and miraculous than all the miracles it relates; which is, however, necessary to make it be received, according to the measures of probability above established.

What we have said of miracles may be applied, without any variation, to prophecies; and indeed, all prophecies are real miracles, and as such only, can be admitted as proofs of any revelation. If it did not exceed the capacity of human nature to foretell future events, it would be absurd to employ any prophecy as an argument for a divine mission or authority from heaven. So that, upon the whole, we may conclude, that the *Christian Religion* not only was at first attended with miracles, but even at this day cannot be believed by any reasonable person without one. Mere reason is insufficient to convince us of its veracity: And whoever is moved by *Faith* to assent to it, is conscious of a continued miracle in his own person, which subverts all the principles of his understanding, and gives him a determination to believe what is most contrary to custom and experience.

## NOTES

1. Hist. lib. iv. cap. 81. Suetonius gives nearly the same account *in vita* Vesp.
2. By Mons. Montgeron, counsellor or judge of the Parliament of Paris.
3. Lucret.
4. Nov. Org. lib. ii. aph. 29.

CHAPTER 2

# "No Other Name": *A Middle Knowledge Perspective on the Exclusivity of Salvation through Christ*

WILLIAM LANE CRAIG

The conviction of the New Testament writers was that there is no salvation apart from Jesus. This orthodox doctrine is widely rejected today because God's condemnation of persons in other world religions seems incompatible with various attributes of God.

Analysis reveals the real problem to involve certain counterfactuals of freedom, e.g., why did not God create a world in which all people would freely believe in Christ and be saved? Such questions presuppose that God possesses middle knowledge. But it can be shown that no inconsistency exists between God's having middle knowledge and certain persons' being damned; on the contrary it can be positively shown that these two notions are compatible.

## INTRODUCTION

"There is salvation in no one else, for there is no other name under heaven given among men by which we must be saved" (Acts 4.12). So proclaimed the early preachers of the gospel of Christ. Indeed, this conviction permeates the New Testament and helped to spur the Gentile mission. Paul invites his Gentile converts to recall their pre-Christian days: "Remember that you were at that time separated from Christ, alienated from the commonwealth of Israel, and strangers to the covenants of promise, having no hope and without God in the world" (Ephesians 2.12). The burden of the opening chapters of Romans is to show that this desolate situation is the general condition of mankind. Though God's eternal power and deity are evident through creation (1.20) and the demands of His moral law implanted on the hearts of all persons (2.15) and although God offers eternal life to all who seek Him in well-doing (2.7), the tragic fact of the matter is that in general people suppress the truth in unrighteousness, ignoring the Creator (1.21) and flouting

From William Lane Craig, "'No Other Name': A Middle Knowledge Perspective on the Exclusivity of Salvation through Christ," *Faith and Philosophy* **6** (April 1989): 172–88. Reprinted by permission from the author and *Faith and Philosophy*.

the moral law (1.32). Therefore, "all men, both Jews and Greeks, are under the power of sin, as it is written: 'None is righteous, no, not one; no one understands, no one seeks for God'" (3.9–11). Sin is the great leveler, rendering all needy of God's forgiveness and salvation. Given the universality of sin, all persons stand morally guilty and condemned before God, utterly incapable of redeeming themselves through righteous acts (3.19–20). But God in His grace has provided a means of salvation from this state of condemnation: Jesus Christ, by his expiatory death, redeems us from sin and justifies us before God (3.21–26). It is through him and through him alone, then, that God's forgiveness is available (5.12–21). To reject Jesus Christ is therefore to reject God's grace and forgiveness, to refuse the one means of salvation which God has provided. It is to remain under His condemnation and wrath, to forfeit eternally salvation. For someday God will judge all men, "inflicting vengeance upon those who do not know God and upon those who do not obey the gospel of our Lord Jesus. They shall suffer the punishment of eternal destruction and exclusion from the presence of the Lord and from the glory of his might" (II Thessalonians 1.8–9).

It was not just Paul who held to this exclusivistic, Christocentric view of salvation. No less than Paul, the apostle John saw no salvation outside of Christ. In his gospel, Jesus declares, "I am the way, and the truth, and the life; no one comes to the Father, but by me" (John 14.6). John explains that men love the darkness of sin rather than light, but that God has sent His Son into the world to save the world and to give eternal life to everyone who believes in the Son. "He who believes is not condemned: he who does not believe is condemned already, because he has not believed in the name of the only Son of God" (John 3.18). People are already spiritually dead; but those who believe in Christ pass from death to life (John 5.24). In his epistles, John asserts that no one who denies the Son has the Father and identifies such a person as the antichrist (I John 2.22–23; 4.3; II John 9). In short, "He who has the Son has life; he who has not the Son of God has not life" (I John 5.12). In John's Apocalypse, it is the Lamb alone in heaven and on earth and under the earth who is worthy to open the scroll and its seven seals, for it was he that by his blood ransomed men for God from every tribe and tongue and people and nation on the earth (Revelation 5.1–14). In the consummation, everyone whose name is not found written in the Lamb's book of life is cast into the everlasting fire reserved for the devil and his cohorts (Revelation 20.15).

One could make the same point from the catholic epistles and the pastorals. It is the conviction of the writers of the New Testament that "there is one God, and there is one mediator between God and men, the man Christ Jesus, who gave himself as a ransom for all" (I Timothy 2.5–6).

Indeed, it is plausible that such was the attitude of Jesus himself. New Testament scholarship has reached something of a consensus that the historical Jesus came on the scene with an unparalleled sense of divine authority, the authority to stand and speak in the place of God Himself and to call men to repentance and faith.[1] Moreover, the object of that faith was he himself, the absolute revelation of God: "All things have been delivered to me by my

Father; and no one knows the Son except the Father, and no one knows the Father except the Son and anyone to whom the Son chooses to reveal him" (Matthew 11.27).[2] On the day of judgment, people's destiny will be determined by how they responded to him: "And I tell you, everyone who acknowledges me before men, the Son of Man also will acknowledge before the angels of God: but he who denies me before men will be denied before the angels of God" (Luke 12.8–9).[3] Frequent warnings concerning hell are found on Jesus's lips, and it may well be that he believed that most of mankind would be damned, while a minority of mankind would be saved: "Enter by the narrow gate, for the gate is wide and the way is easy, that leads to destruction, and those who enter by it are many. For the gate is narrow and the way is hard, that leads to life, and those who find it are few" (Matthew 7:13–14).[4]

A hard teaching, no doubt; but the logic of the New Testament is simple and compelling: the universality of sin and the uniqueness Christ's expiatory sacrifice entail that there is no salvation apart from Christ. Although this exclusivity was scandalous in the polytheistic world of the first century, with the triumph of Christianity throughout the Empire the scandal receded. Indeed, one of the classic marks of the church was its catholicity, and for men like Augustine and Aquinas the universality of the church was one of the signs that the Scriptures are divine revelation, since so great a structure could not have been generated by and founded upon a falsehood.[5] Of course, recalcitrant Jews remained in Christian Europe, and later the infidel armies of Islam had to be combatted, but these exceptions were hardly sufficient to overturn the catholicity of the church or to promote religious pluralism.

But with the so-called "Expansion of Europe" during the three centuries of exploration and discovery from 1450 to 1750, the situation changed radically.[6] It was now seen that far from being the universal religion, Christianity was confined to a small corner of the globe. This realization had a two-fold impact upon people's religious thinking: (i) It tended toward the relativization of religious beliefs. Since each religious system was historically and geographically limited, it seemed incredible that any of them should be regarded as universally true. It seemed that the only religion which could make a universal claim upon mankind would be a sort of general religion of nature. (ii) It tended to make Christianity's claim to exclusivity appear unjustly narrow and cruel. If salvation was only through faith in Christ, then the majority of the human race was condemned to eternal damnation, since they had not so much as even heard of Christ. Again, only a natural religion available to all men seemed consistent with a fair and loving God.

In our own day the influx into Western nations of immigrants from former colonies, coupled with the advances in telecommunications which have served to shrink the world toward a "global village," have heightened both of these impressions. As a result, the church has to a great extent lost its sense of missionary calling or been forced to reinterpret it in terms of social engagement, while those who continue to adhere to the traditional, orthodox view are denounced for religious intolerance. This shift is perhaps best illustrated by the attitude of the Second Vatican Council toward world mission. In its

Dogmatic Constitution on the Church, the Council declared that those who have not yet received the gospel are related in various ways to the people of God.[7] Jews, in particular, remain dear to God, but the plan of salvation also includes all who acknowledge the Creator, such as Muslims. People who through no fault of their own do not know the gospel, but who strive to do God's will by conscience can also be saved. The Council therefore declared that Catholics now pray for the Jews, not for the conversion of the Jews and also declares that the Church looks with esteem upon Muslims.[8] Missionary work seems to be directed only toward those who "serve the creature rather than the Creator" or are utterly hopeless.[9] Carefully couched in ambiguous language and often apparently internally inconsistent,[10] the documents of Vatican II could easily be taken as a radical reinterpretation of the nature of the Church and of Christian missions, according to which great numbers of non-Christians are salvifically related to the Church and therefore not appropriate subjects of evangelism.

The difficulty of the orthodox position has compelled some persons to embrace universalism and as a consequence to deny the incarnation of Christ. Thus, John Hick explains,

> For understood literally the Son of God, God the Son, God-incarnate language implies that God can be adequately known and responded to only through Jesus; and the whole religious life of mankind, beyond the stream of Judaic-Christian faith is thus by implication excluded as lying outside the sphere of salvation. This implication did little positive harm so long as Christendom was a largely autonomous civilization with only relatively marginal interaction with the rest of mankind. But with the clash between the Christian and Muslim worlds, and then on an ever broadening front with European colonization through the earth, the literal understanding of the mythological language of Christian discipleship has had a divisive effect upon the relations between that minority of human beings who live within the borders of the Christian tradition and that majority who live outside it and within other streams of religious life.
>
> Transposed into theological terms, the problem which has come to the surface in the encounter of Christianity with the other world religions is this: If Jesus was literally God incarnate, and if it is by his death alone that men can be saved, and by their response to him alone that they can appropriate that salvation, then the only doorway to eternal life is Christian faith. It would follow from this that the large majority of the human race so far have not been saved. But is it credible that the loving God and Father of all men has decreed that only those born within one particular thread of human history shall be saved?[11]

But what exactly is the problem with God's condemning persons who adhere to non-Christian religions? I do not see that the very notion of hell is incompatible with a just and loving God. According to the New Testament, God does not want anyone to perish, but desires that all persons repent and be saved and come to know the truth (II Peter 3.9; I Timothy 2.4). He therefore seeks to draw all men to Himself. Those who make a well-informed and free decision to reject Christ are self-condemned, since they repudiate God's unique sacrifice for sin. By spurning God's prevenient grace and the solicitation of His Spirit, they shut out God's mercy and seal their own destiny. They, therefore, and not God, are responsible for their condemnation, and God deeply mourns their loss.

Nor does it seem to me that the problem can be simply reduced to the inconsistency of a loving and just God's condemning persons who are either un-, ill-, or misinformed concerning Christ and who therefore lack the opportunity to receive Him. For one could maintain that God graciously applies to such persons the benefits of Christ's atoning death without their conscious knowledge thereof on the basis of their response to the light of general revelation and the truth that they do have, even as He did in the case of Old Testament figures like Job who were outside the covenant of Israel.[12] The testimony of Scripture is that the mass of humanity do not even respond to the light that they do have, and God's condemnation of them is neither unloving nor unjust, since He judges them according to standards of general revelation vastly lower than those which are applied to persons who have been recipients of His special revelation.

Rather the real problem, it seems to me, involves certain counterfactuals of freedom concerning those who do not receive special revelation and so are lost. If we take Scripture seriously, we must admit that the vast majority of persons in the world are condemned and will be forever lost, even if in some relatively rare cases a person might be saved through his response to the light that he has apart from special revelation.[13] But then certain questions inevitably arise: Why did God not supply special revelation to persons who, while rejecting the general revelation they do have, would have responded to the gospel of Christ if they had been sufficiently well-informed concerning it? More fundamentally, Why did God create this world when He knew that so many persons would not receive Christ and would therefore be lost? Even more radically, why did God not create a world in which everyone freely receives Christ and so is saved?

Now all of these questions appear, at least, to presuppose that certain counterfactuals of freedom concerning people's response to God's gracious initiatives are true, and the last two seem to presuppose that God's omniscience embraces a species of knowledge known as middle knowledge (*scientia media*). For if there are no true counterfactuals of freedom, it is not true that certain persons would receive Christ if they were to hear the gospel, nor can God be held responsible for the number of the lost if He lacks middle knowledge, for without such knowledge He could only guess in the moment logically prior to His decree to create the world how many and, indeed, whether any persons would freely receive Christ (or whether He would even send Christ!) and be saved. Let us assume, then, that some such counterfactuals are true and that God has middle knowledge.[14]

For those who are unfamiliar with this species of knowledge and as considerable confusion exists concerning it, a few words about the concept of middle knowledge and its implications for providence and predestination might be helpful.

## SCIENTIA MEDIA

Largely the product of the creative genius of the Spanish Jesuit of the Counter-Reformation Luis Molina (1535–1600), the doctrine of middle knowledge proposes to furnish an analysis of divine knowledge in terms of three logical moments.[15] Although whatever God knows, He has known from eternity, so that there is no temporal succession in God's knowledge, nonetheless there does exist a sort of logical succession in God's knowledge in that His knowledge of certain propositions is conditionally or explanatorily prior to His knowledge of certain other propositions. That is to say, God's knowledge of a particular set of propositions depends asymmetrically on His knowledge of a certain other set of propositions and is in this sense posterior to it. In the first, unconditioned moment God knows all *possibilia,* not only all individual essences, but also all possible worlds. Molina calls such knowledge "natural knowledge" because the content of such knowledge is essential to God and in no way depends on the free decisions of His will. By means of His natural knowledge, then, God has knowledge of every contingent state of affairs which could possibly obtain and of what the exemplification of the individual essence of any free creature could freely choose to do in any such state of affairs that should be actual.

In the second moment, God possesses knowledge of all true counterfactual propositions, including counterfactuals of creaturely freedom. That is to say, He knows what contingent states of affairs would obtain if certain antecedent states of affairs were to obtain; whereas by His natural knowledge God knew what any free creature *could* do in any set of circumstances, now in this second moment God knows what any free creature *would* do in any set of circumstances. This is not because the circumstances causally determine the creature's choice, but simply because this is how the creature would freely choose. God thus knows that were He to actualize certain states of affairs, then certain other contingent states of affairs would obtain. Molina calls this counterfactual knowledge "middle knowledge" because it stands in between the first and third moment in divine knowledge. Middle knowledge is like natural knowledge in that such knowledge does not depend on any decision of the divine will; God does not determine which counterfactuals of creaturely freedom are true or false. Thus, if it is true that

> If some agent *S* were placed in circumstances *C*, then he would freely perform action *a*.

then even God in His omnipotence cannot bring it about that *S* would refrain from *a* if he were placed in *C*. On the other hand, middle knowledge is unlike natural knowledge in that the content of His middle knowledge is not essential to God. True counterfactuals of freedom are contingently true; *S* could freely decide to refrain from *a* in *C*, so that different counterfactuals could be true and be known by God than those that are. Hence, although it is essential to God that He have middle knowledge, it is not essential to Him to have middle knowledge of those particular propositions which He does in fact know.

Intervening between the second and third moments of divine knowledge stands God's free decree to actualize a world known by Him to be realizable on the basis of His middle knowledge. By His natural knowledge, God knows what is the entire range of logically possible worlds; by His middle knowledge He knows, in effect, what is the proper subset of those worlds which it is feasible for Him to actualize. By a free decision. God decrees to actualize one of those worlds known to Him through His middle knowledge. According to Molina, this decision is the result of a complete and unlimited deliberation by means of which God considers and weighs every possible circumstance and its ramifications and decides to settle on the particular world He desires. Hence, logically prior, if not chronologically prior, to God's creation of the world is the divine deliberation concerning which world to actualize.

Given God's free decision to actualize a world, in the third and final moment God possesses knowledge of all remaining propositions that are in fact true in the actual world. Such knowledge is denominated "free knowledge" by Molina because it is logically posterior to the decision of the divine will to actualize a world. The content of such knowledge is clearly not essential to God, since He could have decreed to actualize a different world. Had He done so, the content of His free knowledge would be different.

Molina saw clearly the profound implications a doctrine of middle knowledge could have for the notions of providence and predestination. God's providence is His ordering of things to their ends, either directly or mediately through secondary agents. Molina distinguishes between God's absolute and conditional intentions for creatures. It is, for example, God's absolute intention that no creature should sin and that all should reach beatitude. But it is not within the scope of God's power to control what free creatures would do if placed in any set of circumstances. In certain circumstances, then, creatures would freely sin, despite the fact that God does not will this. Should God then choose to actualize precisely those circumstances, He has no choice but to allow the creature to sin. God's absolute intentions can thus be frustrated by free creatures. But God's conditional intentions, which are based on His middle knowledge and thus take account of what free creatures would do, cannot be so frustrated. It is God's conditional intention to permit many actions on the part of free creatures which He does not absolutely will; but in His infinite wisdom God so orders which states of affairs obtain that His purposes are achieved despite and even through the sinful, free choices of creatures. God thus providentially arranges for everything that does happen by either willing or permitting it, and He causes everything to happen insofar as He concurs with the decisions of free creatures in producing their effects, yet He does so in such a way as to preserve freedom and contingency.

Middle knowledge also serves to reconcile predestination and human freedom. On Molina's view predestination is merely that aspect of providence pertaining to eternal salvation; it is the order and means by which God ensures that some free creature attains eternal life. Prior to the divine decree, God knows via His middle knowledge how any possible free creature would respond in any possible circumstances, which include the offer of certain gifts of prevenient grace which God might provide. In choosing a certain possible world, God commits Himself, out of His goodness, to offering various gifts of grace to every person which are sufficient for his salvation. Such grace is not intrinsically efficacious in that it of itself produces its effect; rather it is extrinsically efficacious in accomplishing its end in those who freely cooperate with it. God knows that many will freely reject His sufficient grace and be lost; but He knows that many others will assent to it, thereby rendering it efficacious in effecting their salvation. Given God's immutable decree to actualize a certain world, those whom God knew would respond to His grace are predestined to do so in the sense that it is absolutely certain that they will respond to and persevere in God's grace. There is no risk of their being lost: indeed, *in sensu composito* it is impossible for them to fall away. But *in sensu diviso* they are entirely free to reject God's grace; but were they to do so, God would have had different middle knowledge and they would not have been predestined.[16] Similarly those who are not predestined have no one to blame but themselves. It is up to God whether we find ourselves in a world in which we are predestined, but it is up to us whether we are predestined in the world in which we find ourselves.

## THE SOTERIOLOGICAL PROBLEM OF EVIL

Years ago when I first read Alvin Plantinga's basically Molinist formulation of the Free Will Defense against the problem of evil, it occurred to me that his reasoning might also help to resolve the problem of the exclusivity of salvation through Christ, and my own subsequent study of the notion of middle knowledge has convinced me that this is in fact so.[17] For the person who objects to the exclusivity of salvation through Christ is, in effect, posing what one might call the *soteriological* problem of evil, that is to say, he maintains that the proposition

1. God is omniscient, omnipotent, and omnibenevolent

is inconsistent with

2. Some persons do not receive Christ and are damned.

Since (1) is essential to theism, we must therefore deny (2).

The orthodox Christian will point out, however, that (1) and (2) are not explicitly contradictory, since one is not the negation of the other, nor are they logically contradictory, since a contradiction cannot be derived from them using first order logic. The objector, then, must mean that (1) and (2) are inconsistent in the broadly logical sense, that is, that there is no possible world in which both are true. Now in order to show this, the objector must supply some further premise(s) which meets the following conditions: (i) its conjunction with (1) and (2) formally entails a contradiction, (ii) it is either necessarily true, essential to theism, or a logical consequence of propositions that are, and (iii) its meeting conditions (i) and (ii) could not be rationally denied by a right-thinking person.[18]

I am not aware of anyone who has tried to supply the missing premise which meets these conditions, but let us try to find some such proposition. Perhaps it might be claimed that the following two propositions will suffice:

3. God is able to actualize a possible world in which all persons freely receive Christ.
4. God prefers a world in which no persons fail to receive Christ and are damned to a world in which some do.

It might be claimed that anyone who accepts (1) must also accept (3) and (4), since (3) is true in virtue of God's omniscience (which includes middle knowledge) and His omnipotence, and (4) is true in virtue of His omnibenevolence.

But is (3) necessarily true or incumbent upon the theist, who is a Molinist? This is far from clear. For although it is logically possible that God actualize any possible world (assuming that God exists in every possible world), it does not follow therefrom that it is feasible for God to actualize any possible world.[19] For God's ability to actualize worlds containing free creatures will be limited by which counterfactuals of creaturely freedom are true in the moment logically prior to the divine decree. In a world containing free creatures, God can strongly actualize only certain segments or states of affairs in that world, and the remainder He must weakly actualize, using His middle knowledge of what free creatures would do under any circumstances. Hence, there will be an infinite number of possible worlds known to God by His natural knowledge which are not realizable by Him because the counterfactuals of creaturely freedom which must be true in order for Him to weakly actualize such worlds are in fact false.[20] His middle knowledge serves to delimit, so to speak, the range of logically possible worlds to those which are feasible for Him to actualize. This might be thought to impugn divine omnipotence, but in fact such a restriction poses no non-logical limit to God's power.[21]

So the question is whether it is necessarily true or incumbent upon the Molinist to hold that within the range of possible worlds which are feasible to God there is at least one world in which everyone freely receives Christ and is saved. Now within Molinism there is a school known as Congruism which would appear to agree that such a position is mandatory for the theist.[22] According to Suarez, for any individual God might create there are gifts of prevenient grace which would be efficacious in winning the free consent of that individual to God's offer of salvation.[23] Such grace, which Suarez calls "congruent grace" (*gratia congrua*), consists in the divine gifts and aids which would be efficacious in eliciting the response desired by God, but without coercion. No grace is intrinsically efficacious, but congruent grace is always in fact efficacious because God knows via His middle knowledge that the creature would freely and affirmatively respond to it, were He to offer it. Accordingly, the Congruist might claim

5. God knows for any individual *S* under what circumstances *S* would freely receive Christ.

But why is it incumbent upon us to accept (5)? Given that persons are free, might there not be persons who would not receive Christ in any actual world in which they existed? Suarez himself seemed to vacillate at this point. When asked whether there is a congruent grace for every person God could create or whether some persons are so incorrigible that regardless of the grace accorded them by God, they would not repent, Suarez wants to say that God can win the free response of any creature He could create. But when pressed that it is logically possible that some person should resist every grace, Suarez concedes that this is true, but adds that God could still save such a person by overpowering his will.[24] But such coercive salvation is beside the point; so long as there might be individuals for whom no grace would be congruent, (5) cannot be regarded as necessary or essential to theism. On the contrary, the theist might hold that

6. For some individual *S*, there are no circumstances under which *S* would freely receive Christ.

In such a case, the theist could consistently maintain that there are no worlds feasible for God in which *S* exists and is saved.

The Congruist could, however, accept (6) and still insist that there are congruent graces for many other individuals and that God could actualize a world containing only such individuals, so that every one would receive Christ and be saved. But the Congruist must show more than that for certain (or even every) individual there are circumstances under which that person would freely receive Christ. He must show that the circumstances under which various individuals would freely receive Christ are compossible, so that all persons in some possible world would freely receive Christ and be saved. It is not even enough to show that the various circumstances are compossible; if he is to avoid the counterfactual fallacy of strengthening the antecedent, he must show that in the combined circumstances the consequent still follows. It might be that in circumstances $C_1$, individual $S_1$ would do action *a* and that in circumstances $C_2$ individual $S_2$ would do *b* and that $C_1$ and $C_2$ are compossible, but it does not follow that in $C_1 \cdot C_2$, $S_1$ would do *a* or that in $C_1 \cdot C_2$, $S_2$ would do *b*. Hence, even if it were the case that for any individual He might create, God could actualize a world in which that person is freely saved, it does not follow that there are worlds which are feasible for God in which all individuals are saved. Contrary to (3) the theist might hold that

7. There is no world feasible for God in which all persons would freely receive Christ.

Unless we have good reason to think that (7) is impossible or essentially incompatible with Christian theism, the objector has failed to show (1) and (2) to be inconsistent.

That leads to (4), which, it is said, is incumbent upon anyone who accepts God's omnibenevolence. Now I think that it is obvious that, all things being equal, an omnibenevolent God prefers a world in which all persons are saved to a world containing those same persons some of whom are lost. But (4) is stronger than this. It claims that God prefers *any* world in which all persons are saved to *any* world in which some persons are damned. But again, this is far from obvious. Suppose that the only worlds feasible for God in which all persons receive Christ and are saved are worlds containing only a handful of persons. Is it not at least possible that such a world is less preferable to God than a world in which great multitudes come to experience His salvation and a few are damned because they freely reject Christ? Not only does this seem to me possibly true, but I think that it probably is true. Why should the joy and blessedness of those who would receive God's grace and love be prevented on account of those who would freely spurn it? An omnibenevolent God might want as many creatures as possible to share salvation; but given certain true counterfactuals of creaturely freedom, God, in order to have a multitude in heaven, might have to accept a number in hell. Hence, contrary to (4) the theist might well hold that

8. God prefers certain worlds in which some persons fail to receive Christ and are damned to certain worlds in which all receive Christ and are saved.

So unless we have good reason to think that (8) is impossible or essentially incompatible with Christian theism, the objector has again failed to show (1) and (2) to be inconsistent.

Since we have no good grounds for believing (3) and (4) to be necessary or essential to theism, or for that matter even contingently true, the opponent of the traditional Christian view has not succeeded in demonstrating that there is no possible world in which God is omniscient, omnipotent, and omnibenevolent and yet in which some persons do not receive Christ and are damned.

But, on the pattern of the Free Will Defense, we can yet go further. For I believe that we can demonstrate not only that (1) and (2) have not been shown to be inconsistent, but also that they are, indeed, consistent. In order to show (1) and (2) to be consistent, the orthodox defender has to come up with a proposition which is consistent with (1) and which together with (1) entails (2). This proposition need not be plausible or even true; it need be only a possibly true proposition, even if it is contingently false.

Now we have seen that it is possible that God wants to maximize the number of the saved; He wants heaven to be as full as possible. Moreover, as a loving God, He wants to minimize the number of the lost; He wants hell to be as empty as possible. His goal, then, is to achieve an optimal balance between these, to create no more lost than is necessary to achieve a certain number of the saved.

But it is possible that the balance between saved and lost in the actual world is such an optimal balance. It is possible that in order to create the actual number of persons who will be saved, God had to create the actual number of persons who will be lost. It is possible that the terrible price of filling heaven is also filling hell and that in any other possible world which was feasible for God the balance between saved and lost was worse. It is possible that had God actualized a world in which there are less persons in hell, there would also have been less persons in heaven. It is possible that in order to achieve this much blessedness, God was forced to accept this much loss. Even if we grant that God could have achieved a better ratio between saved and lost, it is possible that in order to achieve such a ratio God would have had to so drastically reduce the number of the saved as to leave heaven deficient in population (say, by creating a world of only four people, three of whom go to heaven and one to hell). It is possible that in order to achieve a multitude of saints, God had to accept an even greater multitude of sinners.

It might be objected that necessarily a loving God would not create persons who He knew would be damned as a concomitant of His creating persons who He knew would be saved. Given His middle knowledge of such a prospect, He should have refrained from creation altogether. But this objection does not strike me as true, much less necessarily so. It is possible that God loves all persons and desires their salvation and furnishes sufficient grace for the salvation of all; indeed, some of the lost may receive even greater gifts of prevenient grace than some of the saved. It is of their own free will that people reject the grace of God and are damned. Their damnation is the result of their own choice and is contrary to God's perfect will, which is that all persons be saved, and their previsioned obduracy should not be allowed to preclude God's creating persons who would freely respond to His grace and be saved.

But it might be further objected that necessarily a loving God would not create persons who would be damned as a concomitant of His creating persons who would be saved if He knew that the former would under other circumstances have freely responded to His grace and been saved. Therefore, He should not have created at all. Now one might respond by denying the necessary truth of such a proposition; one could argue that so long as people receive sufficient grace for salvation in whatever circumstances they are, then they are responsible for their response in such circumstances and cannot complain that had they been in different circumstances, then their reaction would have been different. But even if we concede that the objector's principle is necessarily true, how do we know that its antecedent is fulfilled? We have seen that it is possible that some persons would not freely receive Christ under any circumstances. Suppose, then, that God has so ordered the world that all persons who are actually lost are such persons. In such a case, anyone who actually is lost would have been lost in any world in which God had created him. It is possible, then, that although God, in order to bring this many persons to salvation, had to pay the price of seeing this many persons lost, nevertheless He has providentially ordered the world such that those who are lost are persons who would not have been saved in any world feasible for God in which they exist. On the analogy of transworld depravity,[25] we may accordingly speak of the property of *transworld damnation,* which is possessed by any person who freely does not respond to God's grace and so is lost in every world feasible for God in which that person exists (this notion can, of course, be more accurately restated in terms of individual essences and instantiations thereof).

Therefore, we are now prepared to furnish a proposition which is consistent with (1) and entails (2):

9. God has actualized a world containing an optimal balance between saved and unsaved, and those who are unsaved suffer from transworld damnation.

So long as (9) is even possible, one is consistent in believing both (1) and (2).

On the basis of this analysis, we now seem to be equipped to provide *possible* answers to the three difficult questions which prompted our inquiry. (i) Why did God not create a world in which everyone freely receives Christ and so is saved? There is no such world which is feasible for God. He would have actualized such a world were this feasible, but in light of certain true counterfactuals of creaturely freedom every world realizable by God is a world in which some persons are lost. Given His will to create a world of free creatures, God must accept that some will be lost. (ii) Why did God create this world when He knew that so many persons would not receive Christ and would therefore be lost? God desired to incorporate as many persons as He could into the love and joy of divine fellowship while minimizing the number of persons whose final state is hell. He therefore chose a world having an optimal balance between the number of the saved and the number of the damned. Given the truth of certain counterfactuals of creaturely freedom, it was not feasible for God to actualize a world having as many saved as but with no more damned than the actual world. The happiness of the saved should not be precluded by the admittedly tragic circumstance that their salvation has as its concomitant the damnation of many others, for the fate of the damned is the result of their own free choice. (iii) Why did God not supply special revelation to persons who, while rejecting the general revelation they do have, would have responded to the gospel of Christ if they had been sufficiently well-informed concerning it? There are no such persons. In each world in which they exist God loves and wills the salvation of persons who in the actual world have only general revelation, and He graciously and preveniently solicits their response by His Holy Spirit, but in every world feasible for God they freely reject His grace and are lost. If there were anyone who would have responded to the gospel if he had heard it, then God in His love would have brought the gospel to such a person. Apart from miraculous intervention, "a single revelation to the whole earth has never in the past been possible, given the facts of geography and technology,"[26] but God in His providence has so arranged the world that as the gospel spread outward from its historical roots in first century Palestine, all who would respond to this gospel, were they to hear it, did and do hear it. Those who have only general revelation and do not respond to it would also not have responded to the gospel had they heard it. Hence, no one is lost because of lack of information due to historical or geographical accident. All who want or would want to be saved will be saved.

The above are only *possible* answers to the questions posed. We have been about a defense, not a theodicy, concerning the soteriological problem of evil. What I have shown is that the orthodox Christian is not inconsistent in affirming that an omniscient, omnipotent, and omnibenevolent God exists and that some people do not receive Christ and are damned. It might, of course, be countered that while the possibility of (9) shows the orthodox position to be consistent, still (9) is highly improbable, given the world in which we live, so that (2) still remains improbable, if not inconsistent, with regard to (1). But here the strength of the position I have been defending emerges beyond that of Plantinga's Free Will Defense. For while it seems fantastic to attribute all natural evil to the actions of demonic beings (e.g., earthquakes' being caused by the demons pushing about tectonic plates), (9) does not seem similarly implausible. On the contrary, I find the above account of the matter to be quite plausible not only as a defense, but also as a soteriological theodicy. Indeed, I think that it helps to put the proper perspective on Christian missions; it is our duty to proclaim the gospel to the whole world, trusting that God has so providentially ordered things that through us the good news will be brought to persons who God knew would respond if they heard it.

## CONCLUSION

In conclusion, then, I think that a middle knowledge perspective on the problem of the exclusivity of the Christian religion can be quite fruitful. Since all persons are in sin, all are in need of salvation. Since Christ is God's unique expiatory sacrifice for sin, salvation is only through Christ. Since Jesus and his work are historical in character, many persons as a result of historical and geographical accident will not be sufficiently well-informed concerning him and thus unable to respond to him in faith. Such persons who are not sufficiently well-informed about Christ's person and work will be judged on the basis of their response to general revelation and the light that they do have. Perhaps some will be saved through such a response; but on the basis of Scripture we must say that such "anonymous Christians" are relatively rare. Those who are judged and condemned on the basis of their failure to respond to the light of general revelation cannot legitimately complain of unfairness for their not also receiving the light of special revelation, since such persons would not have responded to special revelation had they received it. For God in His providence has so arranged the world that anyone who would receive

Christ has the opportunity to do so. Since God loves all persons and desires the salvation of all, He supplies sufficient grace for salvation to every individual, and nobody who would receive Christ if he were to hear the gospel will be denied that opportunity. As Molina puts it, our salvation is in our own hands.

Finally, I hope that no reader has been offended by what might appear to be a rather arid and dispassionate discussion of the salvation and damnation of people apart from Christ. But with such an emotionally explosive issue on the table, it seems to me that it is prudent to treat it with reserve. No orthodox Christian *likes* the doctrine of hell or delights in anyone's condemnation. I truly wish that universalism were true, but it is not. My compassion toward those in other world religions is therefore expressed, not in pretending that they are not lost and dying without Christ, but by my supporting and making every effort myself to communicate to them the life-giving message of salvation through Christ.[27]

## NOTES

1. On Jesus's self-understanding, see James D. G. Dunn, *Jesus and the Spirit* (London: SCM Press, 1975), pp. 11–92; Royce Gordon Gruenler, *New Approaches to Jesus and the Gospels* (Grand Rapids, Mich.: Baker, 1982), especially Pt. 1.

2. For arguments for the authenticity of this saying, see Dunn, *Jesus*, pp. 26–33, 371.

3. On the authenticity of this and other "Son of Man" sayings, see Seyoon Kim, *The Son of Man as the Son of God* (Grand Rapids, Mich.: Wm. B. Eerdmans, 1985), especially pp. 88–89, and the literature cited there.

4. The authenticity of this saying is supported by its multiple attestation (cf. Lk. 13:22–30), its Jewish milieu, and its coherence with Jesus's other teachings. The most plausible way to avoid the inference would be to deny the universal scope of the saying, restricting it to the Jews of Jesus's generation. But it hardly seems likely that Jesus believed that the majority of the Gentile world would respond to him in repentance and faith.

5. Augustine, *De vera religione* 3.5; 24.47; Augustine, *De civitate Dei* 20.5; Thomas Aquinas, *Summa contra gentiles* 1.6.

6. For a brief account, see my *The Historical Argument for the Resurrection of Jesus during the Deist Controversy*, Texts and Studies in Religion 23 (Lewiston, N.Y.: Edwin Mellen Press, 1985), pp. 82–92.

7. "Dogmatic Constitution on the Church" [*Lumen Gentium* 2.16], in *The Documents of Vatican II*, ed. W. M. Abbott (New York: Guild Press, 1966), p. 34.

8. "Declaration on Non-Christian Religions," in *Documents*, pp. 663–66.

9. "The Church" [*LG* 2.16], p. 35.

10. For example, the constitution on the Church also affirms that anyone who knows that Christ is the unique way of salvation and that the Church is his body and yet refuses to become a Catholic cannot be saved ("The Church" [*LG* 2.14], in *Documents*, pp. 32–33). The ambiguity and inconsistency of the documents probably reflects the struggle between traditionalists and modernists in the Council.

11. John Hick, "Jesus and the World Religions," in *The Myth of God Incarnate*, ed. John Hick (London: SCM Press, 1977), pp. 179–80.

12. For a defense of such a position, see Stuart C. Hackett, *The Reconstruction of the Christian Revelation Claim* (Grand Rapids, Mich.: Baker, 1985), pp. 242–46.

13. As we have seen, it is the testimony of Scripture that most persons who hear the gospel do not respond with saving faith and, moreover, that most of those without the light of the gospel do not even respond to the light of general revelation—a fact which sociological observations would seem to confirm. Hence, I would agree with Hick that attempts to resolve the difficulty by appeal to "anonymous Christians" or "implicit faith" or "the invisible church" are ultimately unavailing, but not because they are clinging to the husk of old theology, but precisely because they are incompatible with it.

14. Of course, this is a controversial assumption. But for a defense of the doctrine of middle knowledge see Alvin Plantinga, "Reply to Robert Adams," in *Alvin Plantinga*, ed. James Tomberlin and Peter van Inwagen, Profiles 5 (Dordrecht, Holland: D. Reidel, 1985), pp. 372–82; Jonathan L. Kvanvig, *The Possibility of an All-Know-*

*ing God* (New York: St. Martin's, 1986), pp. 121–48; Alfred J. Freddoso, "Introduction," in Luis Molina, *On Divine Foreknowledge,* trans. with notes by Alfred J. Freddoso (Ithaca: Cornell University Press, 1988), pp. 1–81; and my own *Divine Foreknowledge and Human Freedom* (Leiden, The Netherlands: E. J. Brill, 1991).

15. For Molina's doctrine, see Ludovici Molina, *De liberi arbitrii cum gratia donis, divina praescientia, providentia, praedestinationae et reprobatione concordia* 4. This section has been translated by Freddoso under the title in note 14. For Suarez's doctrine, see R. P. Francisci Suarez, *Opera omnia,* ed. Carolo Berton, vol. 11: *Opuscula theologica sex materiam de auxiliis gratiae absolventia quaestionesque de scientia, liberate et justitia Dei elucidantia: Opusculum II: De scientia Dei futurorum contingentium* 2.7.

16. In a proposition taken in the composite sense, the modal operator governs the proposition as a whole, e.g., "Necessarily, if God sees Socrates sitting, he is sitting." When the proposition is taken in the divided sense, the modal operator governs only a component of the proposition, e.g., "If God sees Socrates sitting, he is necessarily sitting." The distinction is analogous to the more familiar difference between necessity *de dicto* and *de re.* In the case at hand, the proposition "If God via His middle knowledge and decree has foreknown and chosen to actualize a world in which Peter will be saved, then necessarily Peter will be saved" is true *in sensu composito,* but false *in sensu diviso.*

17. For his reasoning, see Alvin Plantinga, *God and Other Minds* (Ithaca, N.Y.: Cornell University Press, 1967), pp. 115–55; Alvin Plantinga, *The Nature of Necessity,* Clarendon Library of Logic and Philosophy (Oxford: Clarendon Press, 1974), pp. 164–95; Alvin Plantinga, "Self-Profile," in *Plantinga,* pp. 36–55.

18. For an explanation of why each of these conditions must be met, see Plantinga, *God and Other Minds,* pp. 116–17, and Plantinga, "Self-Profile," pp. 39–40.

19. See Thomas P. Flint, "The Problem of Divine Freedom," *American Philosophical Quarterly* **20** (1983): 257. According to Flint, although all worlds are possible for God to actualize, a world is *feasible* for God to actualize if and only if it is a member of that proper subset of all possible worlds determined by the counterfactuals of creaturely freedom which God knows to be true.

20. See Plantinga, "Self-Profile," pp. 50–52.

21. See Thomas P. Flint and Alfred J. Freddoso, "Maximal Power," in *The Existence and Nature of God,* ed. Alfred J. Freddoso (Notre Dame, Ind.: University of Notre Dame Press, 1983), pp. 93–98.

22. On Congruism, see *Dictionnaire de théologie catholique,* ed. A. Vacant, E. Mangenot, E. Amann (Paris: E. Letouzey et ane, 1923), s.v. "Congruisme," by H. Quillet, vol. 3.1, cols. 1120–38; *Hastings' Encyclopedia of Religion and Ethics,* s.v. "Molinism," by Aelfred Whitacre; Th. de Régnon, *Bañes et Molina* (Paris: H. Oudin, 1883), pp. 122–60.

23. Suarez, *Opera,* vol. 11: *Opuscula* 1: *De concursu et effiicaci auxiilio Dei ad actus libri arbitrii necessario* 3.6, 14, 16, 17, 20; Suarez, *Opera,* vol. 10: Appendix prior: *Tractatus de vera intelligentia auxilii efficacis, ejusque concordia cum libertate voluntarii consensus* 1, 12, 13, 14.

24. Suarez, *De concursu et auxilio Dei* 3.14, 16; Suarez, *De scientia Dei* 2.6.9.

25. See Plantinga, *Nature of Necessity,* pp. 184–89.

26. Hick, "Jesus and World Religions," p. 180.

27. I am very grateful to Thomas Flint and Robert Gundry for helpful comments on the first draft of this paper.

CHAPTER 3

# Religious Pluralism and Salvation

JOHN HICK

Let us approach the problems of religious pluralism through the claims of the different traditions to offer salvation—generically, the transformation of human existence from self-centeredness to Reality-centeredness. This approach leads to a recognition of the great world faiths as spheres of salvation; and so far as we can tell, more or less equally so. Their different truth-claims express (a) their differing perceptions, through different religio-cultural "lenses," of the one ultimate divine Reality; (b) their different answers to the boundary questions of origin and destiny, true answers to which are however not necessary for salvation, and (c) their different historical memories.

## I

The fact that there is a plurality of religious traditions, each with its own distinctive beliefs, spiritual practices, ethical outlook, art forms, and cultural ethos, creates an obvious problem for those of us who see them, not simply as human phenomena, but as responses to the Divine. For each presents itself, implicitly or explicitly, as in some important sense absolute and unsurpassable and as rightly claiming a total allegiance. The problem of the relationship between these different streams of religious life has often been posed in terms of their divergent belief-systems. For whilst there are various overlaps between their teachings there are also radical differences: is the divine reality (let us refer to it as the Real) personal or non-personal; if personal, is it unitary or triune; is the universe created, or emanated, or itself eternal; do we live only once on this earth or are we repeatedly reborn? and so on and so on. When the problem of understanding religious plurality is approached through these rival truth-claims it appears particularly intractable.

I want to suggest, however, that it may more profitably be approached from a different direction, in terms of the claims of the various traditions to

From John Hick, "Religious Pluralism and Salvation," *Faith and Philosophy* **5** (October 1988): 365–77. Reprinted by permission from the author and *Faith and Philosophy*.

provide, or to be effective contexts of, salvation. "Salvation" is primarily a Christian term, though I shall use it here to include its functional analogues in the other major world traditions. In this broader sense we can say that both Christianity and these other faiths are paths of salvation. For whereas pre-axial religion was (and is) centrally concerned to keep life going on an even keel, the post-axial traditions, originating or rooted in the "axial age" of the first millenium B.C.E.—principally Hinduism, Judaism, Buddhism, Christianity, Islam—are centrally concerned with a radical transformation of the human situation.

It is of course possible, in an alternative approach, to define salvation in such a way that it becomes a necessary truth that only one particular tradition can provide it. If, for example, from within Christianity we define salvation as being forgiven by God because of Jesus' atoning death, and so becoming part of God's redeemed community, the church, then salvation is by definition Christian salvation. If on the other hand, from within Mahayana Buddhism, we define it as the attainment of *satori* or awakening, and so becoming an ego-free manifestation of the eternal Dharmakaya, then salvation is by definition Buddhist liberation. And so on. But if we stand back from these different conceptions to compare them, we can, I think, very naturally and properly see them as different forms of the more fundamental conception of a radical change from a profoundly unsatisfactory state to one that is limitlessly better because rightly related to the Real. Each tradition conceptualizes in its own way the wrongness of ordinary human existence—as a state of fallenness from paradisal virtue and happiness, or as a condition of moral weakness and alienation from God, or as the fragmentation of the infinite One into false individualities, or as a self-centeredness which pervasively poisons our involvement in the world process, making it to us an experience of anxious, unhappy unfulfillment. But each at the same time proclaims a limitlessly better possibility, again conceptualized in different ways—as the joy of conforming one's life to God's law; as giving oneself to God in Christ, so that "it is no longer I who live, but Christ who lives in me" (Galatians 2:20), leading to eternal life in God's presence; as a complete surrender (*islam*) to God, and hence peace with God, leading to the bliss of paradise; as transcending the ego and realizing oneness with the limitless being-consciousness-bliss (*satchitananda*) of Brahman; as overcoming the ego point of view and entering into the serene selflessness of nirvana. I suggest that these different conceptions of salvation are specifications of what, in a generic formula, is the transformation of human existence from self-centeredness to a new orientation, centered in the divine Reality. And in each case the good news that is proclaimed is that this limitlessly better possibility is actually available and can be entered upon, or begin to be entered upon, here and now. Each tradition sets forth the way to attain this great good: faithfulness to the Torah, discipleship to Jesus, obedient living out of the Qur'anic way of life, the Eightfold Path of the Buddhist dharma, or the three great Hindu *margas* of mystical insight, activity in the world, and self-giving devotion to God.

## II

The great world religions, then, are ways of salvation. Each claims to constitute an effective context within which the transformation of human existence can and does take place from self-centeredness to Reality-centeredness. How are we to judge such claims? We cannot directly observe the inner spiritual quality of a human relationship to the Real; but we can observe how that relationship, as one's deepest and most pervasive orientation, affects the moral and spiritual quality of a human personality and of a man's or woman's relationship to others. It would seem, then, that we can only assess these salvation-projects insofar as we are able to observe their fruits in human life. The inquiry has to be, in a broad sense, empirical. For the issue is one of fact, even though hard to define and difficult to measure fact, rather than being settleable by *a priori* stipulation.

The word "spiritual" which occurs above is notoriously vague; but I am using it to refer to a quality or, better, an orientation which we can discern in those individuals whom we call saints—a Christian term which I use here to cover such analogues as arahat, bodhisattva, jivanmukti, mahatma. In these cases the human self is variously described as becoming part of the life of God, being "to the Eternal Goodness what his own hand is to a man"; or being permeated from within by the infinite reality of Brahman; or becoming one with the eternal Buddha nature. There is a change in their deepest orientation from centeredness in the ego to a new centering in the Real as manifested in their own tradition. One is conscious in the presence of such a person that he or she is, to a startling extent, open to the transcendent, so as to be largely free from self-centered concerns and anxieties and empowered to live as an instrument of God/Truth/Reality.

It is to be noted that there are two main patterns of such a transformation. There are saints who withdraw from the world into prayer or meditation and saints who seek to change the world—in the medieval period a contemplative Julian of Norwich and a political Joan of Arc, or in our own century a mystical Sri Aurobindo and a political Mahatma Gandhi. In our present age of sociological consciousness, when we are aware that our inherited political and economic structures can be analyzed and purposefully changed, saintliness is more likely than in earlier times to take social and political forms. But, of whichever type, the saints are not a different species from the rest of us; they are simply much more advanced in the salvific transformation.

The ethical aspect of this salvific transformation consists in observable modes of behavior. But how do we identify the kind of behavior which, to the degree that it characterizes a life, reflects a corresponding degree of reorientation to the divine Reality? Should we use Christian ethical criteria, or Buddhist, or Muslim . . . ? The answer, I suggest, is that at the level of their most basic moral insights the great traditions use a common criterion. For they agree in giving a central and normative role to the unselfish regard for others that we call love or compassion. This is commonly expressed in the principle of valuing others as we value ourselves, and treating them accordingly. Thus in the ancient Hindu *Mahabharata* we read that "One should never do to another that which one would regard as injurious to oneself. This, in brief, is the rule of Righteousness" (*Anushana parva,* 113:7). Again, "He who . . . benefits persons of all orders, who is always devoted to the good of all beings, who does not feel aversion to anybody . . . succeeds in ascending to Heaven" (*Anushana parva,* 145:24). In the Buddhist *Sutta Nipata* we read, "As a mother cares for her son, all her days, so towards all living things a man's mind should be all-embracing" (149). In the Jain scriptures we are told that one should go about "treating all creatures in the world as he himself would be treated" (*Kitanga Sutra,* I.ii.33). Confucius, expounding humaneness (*jen*), said, "Do not do to others what you would not like yourself" (*Analects,* xxi, 2). In a Taoist scripture we read that the good man will "regard [others'] gains as if they were his own, and their losses in the same way" (*Thai Shang,* 3). The Zoroastrian scriptures declare, "That nature only is good when it shall not do unto another whatever is not good for its own self" (*Dadistan-i-dinik,* 94:5). We are all familiar with Jesus' teaching, "As ye would that men should do to you, do ye also to them likewise" (Luke 6:31). In the Jewish Talmud we read "What is hateful to yourself do not do to your fellow man. That is the whole of the Torah" (*Babylonian Talmud,* Shabbath 31a). And in the Hadith of Islam we read Muhammad's words, "No man is a true believer unless he desires for his brother that which he desires for himself" (*Ibn Madja,* Intro. 9). Clearly, if everyone acted on this basic principle, taught by all the major faiths, there would be no injustice, no avoidable suffering, and the human family would everywhere live in peace.

When we turn from this general principle of love/compassion to the actual behavior of people within the different traditions, wondering to what extent they live in this way, we realize how little research has been done on so important a question. We do not have much more to go on than general impressions, supplemented by travellers tales and anecdotal reports. We observe among our neighbors within our own community a great deal of practical loving-kindness; and we are told, for example, that a remarkable degree of self-giving love is to be found among the Hindu fishing families in the mud huts along the Madras shore; and we hear various other similar accounts from other lands. We read biographies, social histories, and novels of Muslim village life in Africa, Buddhist life in Thailand, Hindu life in India, Jewish life in New York, as well as Christian life around the world, both in the past and today, and we get the impression that the personal virtues (as well as vices) are basically much the same within these very different religio-cultural settings and that in all of them unselfish concern for others occurs and is highly valued. And, needless to say, as well as love and compassion we also see all-too-abundantly, and apparently spread more or less equally in every society, cruelty, greed, hatred, selfishness, and malice.

All this constitutes a haphazard and impressionistic body of data. Indeed I want to stress, not how easy it is, but on the contrary how difficult it is, to make responsible judgments in this area. For not only do we lack full information, but the fragmentary information that we have has to be interpreted in the light of the varying natural conditions of human life in different periods of history and in different economic and political circumstances. And I suggest that all that we can presently arrive at is the cautious and negative conclusion that we have no good reason to believe that any one of the great religious traditions has proved itself to be more productive of love/compassion than another.

The same is true when we turn to the large-scale social outworkings of the different salvation-projects. Here the units are not individual human lives, spanning a period of decades, but religious cultures spanning many centuries. For we can no more judge a civilization than a human life by confining our attention to a single temporal cross-section. Each of the great streams of religious life has had its times of flourishing and its times of deterioration. Each has produced its own distinctive kinds of good and its own distinctive kinds of evil. But to assess either the goods or the evils cross-culturally is difficult to say the least. How do we weigh, for example, the lack of economic progress, and consequent widespread poverty, in traditional Hindu and Buddhist cultures against the endemic violence and racism of Christian civilization, culminating in the twentieth century Holocaust? How do we weigh what the west regards as the hollowness of arranged marriages against what the east regards as the hollowness of a marriage system that leads to such a high proportion of divorces and broken families? From within each culture one can see clearly enough the defects of the others. But an objective ethical comparison of such vast and complex totalities is at present an unattainable ideal. And the result is that we are not in a position to claim an over-all moral superiority for any one of the great living religious traditions.

Let us now see where we have arrived. I have suggested that if we identify the central claim of each of the great religious traditions as the claim to provide, or to be an effective context of, salvation; and if we see salvation as an actual change in human beings from self-centeredness to a new orientation centered in the ultimate divine Reality; and if this new orientation has both a more elusive "spiritual" character and a more readily observable moral aspect—then we arrive at the modest and largely negative conclusion that, so far as we can tell, no one of the great world religions is salvifically superior to the rest.

## III

If this is so, what are we to make of the often contradictory doctrines of the different traditions? In order to make progress at this point, we must distinguish various kinds and levels of doctrinal conflict.

There are, first, conceptions of the ultimate as Jahweh, or the Holy Trinity, or Allah, or Shiva, or Vishnu, or as Brahman, or the Dharmakaya, the Tao, and so on.

If salvation is taking place, and taking place to about the same extent, within the religious systems presided over by these various deities and absolutes, this suggests that they are different manifestations to humanity of a yet more ultimate ground of all salvific transformation. Let us then consider the possibility that an infinite transcendent divine reality is being differently conceived, and therefore differently experienced, and therefore differently responded to from within our different religio-cultural ways of being human. This hypothesis makes sense of the fact that the salvific transformation seems to have been occurring in all the great traditions. Such a conception is, further, readily open to philosophical support. For we are familiar today with the ways in which human experience is partly formed by the conceptual and linguistic frameworks within which it occurs. The basically Kantian insight that the mind is active in perception, and that we are always aware of our environment as it appears to a consciousness operating with our particular conceptual resources and habits, has been amply confirmed by work in cognitive psychology and the sociology of knowledge and can now be extended with some confidence to the analysis of religious awareness. If, then, we proceed inductively from the phenomenon of religious experience around the world, adopting a religious as distinguished from a naturalistic interpretation of it, we are likely to find ourselves making two moves. The first is to postulate an ultimate transcendent divine reality (which I have been referring to as the Real) which, being beyond the scope of our human concepts, cannot be directly experienced by us as it is in itself but only as it appears through our various human thought-forms. And the second is to identify the thought-and-experienced deities and absolutes as different manifestations of the Real within different historical forms of human consciousness. In Kantian terms, the divine noumenon, the Real *an sich,* is experienced through different human receptivities as a range of divine phenomena, in the formation of which religious concepts have played an essential part.

These different "receptivities" consist of conceptual schemas within which various personal, communal, and historical factors have produced yet further variations. The most basic concepts in terms of which the Real is humanly thought-and-experienced are those of (personal) deity and of the (non-personal) absolute. But the Real is not actually experienced either as deity in general or as the absolute in general. Each basic concept becomes (in Kantian terminology) schematized in more concrete form. It is at this point that individual and cultural factors enter the process. The religious tradition of which we are a part, with its history and ethos and its great exemplars, its scriptures feeding our thoughts and emotions, and perhaps above all its devotional or meditative practices, constitutes an uniquely shaped and coloured "lens" through which we are concretely aware of the Real specifically as the personal Adonai, or as the Heavenly Father, or as Allah, or Vishnu, or Shiva . . . or again as the non-personal Brahman, or Dharmakaya, or the Void or the Ground. . . . Thus, one who uses the forms of Christian prayer and sacrament is thereby led to experience the Real as the divine Thou, whereas one who practices advaitic yoga or Buddhist zazen is thereby brought to experience the Real as the infinite being-consciousness-bliss of

Brahman, or as the limitless emptiness of *sunyata* which is at the same time the infinite fullness of immediate reality as "wondrous being."

Three explanatory comments at this point before turning to the next level of doctrinal disagreement. First, to suppose that the experienced deities and absolutes which are the intentional objects of worship or content of religious meditation, are appearances or manifestations of the Real, rather than each being itself the Real *an sich,* is not to suppose that they are illusions—any more than the varying ways in which a mountain may appear to a plurality of differently placed observers are illusory. That the same reality may be variously experienced and described is true even of physical objects. But in the case of the infinite, transcendent divine reality there may well be much greater scope for the use of varying human conceptual schemas producing varying modes of phenomenal experience. Whereas the concepts in terms of which we are aware of mountains and rivers and houses are largely (though by no means entirely) standard throughout the human race, the religious concepts in terms of which we become aware of the Real have developed in widely different ways within the different cultures of the earth.

As a second comment, to say that the Real is beyond the range of our human concepts is not intended to mean that it is beyond the scope of purely formal, logically generated concepts—such as the concept of being beyond the range of (other than purely formal) concepts. We would not be able to refer at all to that which cannot be conceptualized in any way, not even by the concept of being unconceptualizable! But the other than purely formal concepts by which our experience is structured must be presumed not to apply to its noumenal ground. The characteristics mapped in thought and language are those that are constitutive of human experience. We have no warrant to apply them to the noumenal ground of the phenomenal, i.e., experienced, realm. We should therefore not think of the Real *an sich* as singular or plural, substance or process, personal or non-personal, good or bad, purposive or non-purposive. This has long been a basic theme of religious thought. For example, within Christianity, Gregory of Nyssa declared that:

> The simplicity of the True Faith assumes God to be that which He is, namely, incapable of being grasped by any term, or any idea, or any other device of our apprehension, remaining beyond the reach not only of the human but of the angelic and all supramundane intelligence, unthinkable, unutterable, above all expression in words, having but one name that can represent His proper nature, the single name being "Above Every Name" (*Against Eunomius,* I, 42).

Augustine, continuing this tradition, said that "God transcends even the mind" (*True Religion,* 36:67), and Aquinas that "by its immensity, the divine substance surpasses every form that our intellect reaches" (*Contra Gentiles,* I, 14, 3). In Islam the Qur'an affirms that God is "beyond what they describe" (6:101). The Upanishads declare of Brahman, "There the eye goes not, speech goes not, nor the mind" (*Kena Up.,* 1, 3), and Shankara wrote that Brahman is that "before which words recoil, and to which no understanding has ever attained" (Otto, *Mysticism East and West,* E. T. 1932, p. 28).

But, third, we might well ask, why postulate an ineffable and unobservable divine-reality-in-itself? If we can say virtually nothing about it, why affirm its existence? The answer is that the reality or non-reality of the postulated noumenal ground of the experienced religious phenomena constitutes the difference between a religious and a naturalistic interpretation of religion. If there is no such transcendent ground, the various forms of religious experience have to be categorized as purely human projections. If on the other hand there is such a transcendent ground, then these phenomena may be joint products of the universal presence of the Real and of the varying sets of concepts and images that have crystallized within the religious traditions of the earth. To affirm the transcendent is thus to affirm that religious experience is not solely a construction of the human imagination but is a response—though always culturally conditioned—to the Real.

Those doctrinal conflicts, then, that embody different conceptions of the ultimate arise, according to the hypothesis I am presenting, from the variations between different sets of human conceptual schema and spiritual practice. And it seems that each of these varying ways of thinking-and-experiencing the Real has been able to mediate its transforming presence to human life. For the different major concepts of the ultimate do not seem—so far as we can tell—to result in one religious totality being soteriologically more effective than another.

## IV

The second level of doctrinal difference consists of metaphysical beliefs which cohere with although they are not exclusively linked to a particular conception of the ultimate. These are beliefs about the relation of the material universe to the Real: creation *ex nihilo,* emanation, an eternal universe, an unknown form of dependency . . . ? And about human destiny: reincarnation or a single life, eternal identity or transcendence of the self . . . ? Again, there are questions about the existence of heavens and hells and purgatories and angels and devils and many other subsidiary states and entities. Out of this mass of disputed religious issues let me pick two major examples: is the universe created *ex nihilo,* and do human beings reincarnate?

I suggest that we would do well to apply to such questions a principle that was taught by the Buddha two and a half millennia ago. He listed a series of "undetermined questions" (*avyakata*)—whether the universe is eternal, whether it is spatially infinite, whether (putting it in modern terms) mind and brain are identical, and what the state is of a completed project of human existence (a Tathagata) after bodily death. He refused to answer these questions, saying that we do not need to have knowledge of these things in order to attain liberation or awakening (nirvana); and indeed that to regard such information as soteriologically essential would only divert us from the single-minded quest for liberation. I think that we can at this point profitably learn from the Buddha, even extending his conception of the undetermined questions further than he did—for together with almost everyone else in his own culture he regarded one of our examples, reincarnation, as a matter of assured knowledge. Let us, then, accept that we do not *know* whether, e.g., the universe was created *ex nihilo,* nor whether human beings are reincarnated; and, further, that it is not necessary for salvation to hold a correct opinion on either matter.

I am not suggesting that such issues are unimportant. On their own level they are extremely important, being both of great interest to us and also having widely ramifying implications within our belief-systems and hence for our lives. The thought of being created out of nothing can nourish a salutary sense of absolute dependence. (But other conceptions can also nurture that sense.) The idea of reincarnation can offer the hope of future spiritual progress; though, combined with the principle of karma, it can also serve to validate the present inequalities of human circumstances. (But other eschatologies also have their problems, both theoretical and practical). Thus these—and other—disputed issues do have a genuine importance. Further, it is possible that some of them may one day be settled by empirical evidence. It might become established, for example, that the "big bang" of some fifteen billion years ago was an absolute beginning, thus ruling out the possibility that the universe is eternal. And again, it might become established, by an accumulation of evidence, that reincarnation does indeed occur in either some or all cases. On the other hand it is possible that we shall never achieve agreed knowledge in these areas. Certainly, at the present time, whilst we have theories, preferences, hunches, inherited convictions, we cannot honestly claim to have secure knowledge. And the same is true, I suggest, of the entire range of metaphysical issues about which the religions dispute. They are of intense interest, properly the subject of continuing research and discussion, but are not matters concerning which absolute dogmas are appropriate. Still less is it appropriate to maintain that salvation depends upon accepting some one particular opinion or dogma. We have seen that the transformation of human existence from self-centeredness to Reality-centeredness seems to be taking place within each of the great traditions despite their very different answers to these debated questions. It follows that a correct opinion concerning them is not required for salvation.

## V

The third level of doctrinal disagreement concerns historical questions. Each of the great traditions includes a larger or smaller body of historical beliefs. In the case of Judaism these include at least the main features of the history described in the Hebrew scriptures; in the case of Christianity, these plus the main features of the life, death, and resurrection of Jesus as described in the New Testament; in the case of Islam, the main features of the history described in the Qur'an; in the case of Vaishnavite Hinduism, the historicity of Krishna; in the case of Buddhism, the historicity of Guatama and his enlightenment at Bodh Gaya; and so on. But although each tradition thus has its own records of the past, there are rather few instances of direct disagreement between these. For the strands of history that are cherished in these different historical memories do not generally overlap; and where they do overlap they do not generally involve significant differences. The overlaps are mainly within the thread of ancient Near Eastern history that is common to the Jewish, Christian, and Muslim scriptures; and within this I can only locate two points of direct disagreement—the Torah's statement that Abraham nearly sacrificed his son Isaac at Mount Moriah (Genesis 22) versus the Muslim interpretation of the Qur'anic version (in Sura 37) that it was his other son Ishmael; and the New Testament witness that Jesus died on the cross versus the Qur'anic teaching that "they did not slay him, neither crucified him, only a likeness of that was shown them" (Sura 4:156). (This latter however would seem to be a conflict between an historical report, in the New Testament, and a theological inference—that God would not allow so great a prophet to be killed—in the Qur'an.)

All that one can say in general about such disagreements, whether between two traditions or between any one of them and the secular historians, is that they could only properly be settled by the weight of historical evidence. However, the events in question are usually so remote in time, and the evidence so slight or so uncertain, that the question cannot be definitively settled. We have to be content with different communal memories, enriched as they are by the mythic halo that surrounds all long-lived human memories of events of transcendent significance. Once again, then, I suggest that differences of historical judgment, although having their own proper importance, do not prevent the different traditions from being effective, and so far as we can tell equally effective, contexts of salvation. It is evidently not necessary for salvation to have correct historical information. (It is likewise not necessary for salvation, we may add, to have correct scientific information.)

## VI

Putting all this together, the picture that I am suggesting can be outlined as follows: our human religious experience, variously shaped as it is by our sets of religious concepts, is a cognitive response to the universal presence of the ultimate divine Reality that, in itself, exceeds human conceptuality. This Reality is however manifested to us in ways formed by a variety of human concepts, as the range of divine personae and metaphysical impersonae witnessed to in the history of religions. Each major tradition, built around its own distinctive way of thinking-and-experiencing the Real, has developed its own answers to the perennial questions of our origin and destiny, constituting more or less comprehensive and coherent cosmologies and eschatologies. These are human creations which have, by their association with living streams of religious experience, become invested with a sacred authority. However they cannot all be wholly true; quite possibly none is wholly true; perhaps all are partly true. But since the salvific process has been going on through the centuries despite this unknown distribution of truth and falsity in our cosmologies and eschatologies, it follows that it is not necessary for salvation to adopt any one of them. We would therefore do well to learn to tolerate unresolved, and at present unresolvable, differences concerning these ultimate mysteries.

One element, however, to be found in the belief-systems of most of the traditions raises a special problem, namely that which asserts the sole salvific efficacy of that tradition. I shall discuss this problem in terms of Christianity because it is particularly acute for those of us who are Christians. We are all familiar with such New Testament texts as "There is salvation in no one else [than Jesus Christ], for there is no other name under heaven given among men by which we must be saved" (Acts 4:12), and with the Catholic dogma *Extra ecclesiam nulla salus* (No salvation outside the church) and its Protestant equivalent—never formulated as an official dogma but nevertheless implicit within the eighteenth and nineteenth century Protestant missionary expansion—no salvation outside Christianity. Such a dogma differs from other elements of Christian belief in that it is not only a statement about the potential relationship of Christians to God but at the same time about the actual relationship of non-Christians to God. It says that the latter, in virtue of being non-Christians, lack salvation. Clearly such a dogma is incompatible with the insight that the salvific transformation of human existence is going on, and so far as we can tell going on to a more or less equal extent, within all the great traditions. Insofar, then, as we accept that salvation is not confined to Christianity we must reject the old exclusivist dogma.

This has in fact now been done by most thinking Christians, though exceptions remain, mostly within the extreme Protestant fundamentalist constituencies. The *Extra ecclesiam* dogma, although not explicitly repealed, has been outflanked by the work of such influential Catholic theologians as Karl Rahner, whose new approach was in effect endorsed by Vatican II. Rahner expressed his more inclusivist outlook by suggesting that devout people of other faiths are "anonymous Christians," within the invisible church even without knowing it, and thus within the sphere of salvation. The present Pope, in his Encyclical *Redemptor Hominis* (1979), has expressed this thought even more comprehensively by saying that "every man without exception has been redeemed by Christ" and "with every man without any exception whatever Christ is in a way united, even when man in unaware of it" (para. 14). And a number of Protestant theologians have advocated a comparable position.

The feature that particularly commends this kind of inclusivism to many Christians today is that it recognizes the spiritual values of other religions, and the occurrence of salvation within them, and yet at the same time preserves their conviction of the ultimate superiority of their own religion over all others. For it maintains that salvation, wherever it occurs, is Christian salvation; and Christians are accordingly those who alone know and preach the source of salvation, namely in the atoning death of Christ.

This again, like the old exclusivism, is a statement not only about the ground of salvation for Christians but also for Jews, Muslims, Hindus, Buddhists, and everyone else. But we have seen that it has to be acknowledged that the immediate ground of their transformation is the particular spiritual path along which they move. It is by living in accordance with the Torah or with the Qur'anic revelation that Jews and Muslims find a transforming peace with God; it is by one or other of their great *margas* that Hindus attain to *moksha;* it is by the Eightfold Path that Theravada Buddhists come to *nirvana;* it is by *zazen* that Zen Buddhists attain to *satori;* and so on. The Christian inclusivist is, then, by implication, declaring that these various spiritual paths are efficacious, and constitute authentic contexts of salvation, because Jesus died on the cross; and, by further implication, that if he had not died on the cross they would not be efficacious.

This is a novel and somewhat astonishing doctrine. How are we to make sense of the idea that the salvific power of the dharma taught five hundred years earlier by the Buddha is a consequence of the death of Jesus in approximately 30 C.E.? Such an apparently bizarre conception should only be affirmed for some very good reason. It was certainly not taught by Jesus or his apostles. It has emerged only in the thought of twentieth century Christians who have come to recognize that Jews are being salvifically transformed through the spirituality of Judaism, Muslims through that of Islam, Hindus and Buddhists through the paths mapped out by their respective traditions, and so on, but who nevertheless wish to retain their inherited sense of the unique superiority of Christianity. The only outlet left for this sense, when one has acknowledged the salvific efficacy of the various great spiritual ways, is the arbitrary and contrived notion of their metaphysical dependency upon the death of Christ. But the theologian who undertakes to spell out this invisible causality is not to be envied. The problem is not one of logical possibility—it only requires logical agility to cope with that—but one of religious or spiritual plausibility. It would be a better use of theological time and energy, in my opinion, to develop forms of trinitarian, christological, and soteriological doctrine which are compatible with our awareness of the independent salvific authenticity of the other great world faiths. Such forms are already available in principle in conceptions of the Trinity, not as ontologically three but as three ways in which the one God is humanly thought and experienced; conceptions of Christ as a man so fully open to and inspired by God as to be, in the ancient Hebrew metaphor, a "son of God"; and conceptions of salvation as an actual human transformation which has been powerfully elicited and shaped, among his disciples, by the influence of Jesus.

There may indeed well be a variety of ways in which Christian thought can develop in response to our acute late twentieth century awareness of the other world religions, as there were of responding to the nineteenth century awareness of the evolution of the forms of life and the historical character of the holy scriptures. And likewise there will no doubt be a variety of ways in which each of the other great traditions can rethink its inherited assumption of its own unique superiority. But it is not for us to tell people of other traditions how to do their own business. Rather, we should attend to our own.

## NOTES

This paper was originally delivered as the second Kegley Lecture at California State University, Bakersfield, on February 10th, 1988. For a fuller account of its proposals the reader is invited to see my *An Interpretation of Religion* (New Haven: Yale University Press and London: Macmillan, 1989).

CHAPTER 4

# The Philosophy of Religious Pluralism:

## *A Critical Appraisal of Hick and His Critics**

SUMNER B. TWISS

For well over a decade now, John Hick has been publishing important, illuminating, and provocative articles about the nature of religion and the meaning of religious diversity.[1] His main thesis is that there is an underlying unity to this diversity that is explicated as a set of differential responses to a transcendent reality conceived and perceived in alternative ways by different cultural and religious traditions. In effect, this is a thesis about the higher transcendental unity of all religions. This is an important thesis for a philosopher to propound at this time because there are signs that the philosophy of religion is becoming an increasingly comparative and cross-cultural discipline, with a concomitant need to make sense of the diversity of religions. Hick's thesis, the core of his emerging philosophy of religious pluralism, is one coherent response to this need.

Needless to say, Hick's work on the philosophy of religious pluralism has generated considerable critical response in the journal literature. Indeed, there are even alternative—some might say divergent or incompatible—critical readings of the conceptual and epistemological nature and significance of Hick's project. Griffiths and Lewis and Byrne, for example, see Hick as advancing a noncognitive, neo-Wittgensteinian position on the diversity of religious belief, while Netland and Corliss, respectively, see him as developing a cognitive metatheory and a nonevidentialist pragmatic position on religious belief.[2] And each of these readings argues—on different grounds, of course—that Hick's theory founders on issues of hermeneutical adequacy, internal conceptual coherence, and epistemic convincingness.

Such divergent readings of one theory, of course, raise the critical problem of its precise nature and import, as well as posing the question of whether the tensions and weakness identified, in fact, undercut the theory's

From Sumner B. Twiss, "The Philosophy of Religious Pluralism: A Critical Appraisal of Hick and His Critics," *The Journal of Religion* **70** (1990): 533–68. 

validity and coherence. In order to answer these questions, I propose first to offer my own reading of what Hick is saying. Then I will go on to analyze and discuss in some detail four areas of tension and weakness identified by Hick's critics, offering my own views of their nature, significance, and possible resolution. As will become clear, unlike most of his critics, I have a rather favorable view of Hick's theory and its prospects; this is in large part due to my belief that Hick's theory constitutes a rich organic web of more than one theoretical strand, giving it considerable resilience and subtlety in dealing with difficult philosophical challenges. The overarching issue, of course, is whether this organic web is finally coherent and satisfies criteria of economy, explanatory power, and the like. I believe it does. Let me now provide my reading of Hick's theory.

Hick's theory of religious pluralism advances and defends the hypothesis of a noumenal transcendent divine reality (in itself infinite and unknowable) underlying and serving as the ultimate referent of the diverse phenomenal religions (viewed as culturally shaped and differentiated conceptualizations of and responses to the divine noumenon). The development of the theory falls into four interconnected phases: philosophical presuppositions, methodological first steps, rational ontological postulate, and epistemological consequences. Let us sketch each of these phases in turn, keeping in mind that they constitute a web of mutually supportive and interactive beliefs and arguments.

**Philosophical Presuppositions.** Hick adopts a Wittgensteinian perspective on the nature of religions, conceiving of them as cultural–linguistic systems (language games) making possible corresponding forms of life, experience, and expression.[3] According to Hick, these systems are structured around the practical soteriological aim of encouraging and regulating transformation of the self in relation to differing conceptions of the ultimately real and valuable. Consonant with this perspective, Hick confers a degree of priority on religious practice (religious forms of life) as contrasted with doctrine and theory. Nonetheless, quite unlike other neo-Wittgensteinian philosophers of religion, he explicitly maintains that the practical language of worship and prayer presupposes the sincere user's belief in the independent reality of the divine ultimate reality. (At times he also characterizes this language as metaphoric and mythic but nonetheless referential in intention.)

There is, then, in the very "basement" of Hick's theory a striking tension. On the one hand, his theory adheres to a Wittgensteinian view of religious language and belief, which is usually understood to conceive of divine reality as internally related to practices and to construe religious discourse as grammatical rather than referential.[4] On the other hand, it also adheres to the view that religious language and belief are properly understood as presupposing an independent and ontologically real ultimate divine. One of Hick's problems, of course, is precisely how to put these two presuppositions (or theoretical strands) together into one coherent view that does justice to each and to the fact of the diversity of religions. We will need to return to this seeming tension or incompatibility; for now, however, let us just note these two presuppositions since together they explain much of the apparent structural duality in the subsequent phases of Hick's theory as well as offer one possible explanation of such different critical readings of the epistemology of Hick's project.

**Methodological First Steps.** Hick initiates the formal development of his theory by explicitly proposing a "revisionist" conception of, and approach to, religious diversity—involving the notion that the same soteriological process of human transformation takes place within the contexts of the different religious and cultural traditions—and then adopting as a methodological assumption the basic religious conviction that religious experience and thought mediate real contact with a higher reality (in-principled veridicality of religious experience and thought).[5] Defending the reasonability of this conviction for one's own religious experience and tradition, he then argues for the rationality of generalizing this conviction to other traditions and forms of religious experience (i.e., they, too, can in principle mediate real contact with a higher reality). He further proposes—in light of the prima facie rough equality of moral and spiritual fruits of major religious traditions—the conditional rationality of the pluralist hypothesis that all the major traditions are in fact veridical and mediate real contact with a higher reality (i.e., conditional on the coherence and plausibility of the following phases and the theory as a whole).

What is perhaps most striking about these first steps is that both may be conceived as paralleling Hick's two original philosophical presuppositions. Thus, the revisionist conception of religions continues the Wittgensteinian emphasis on conceiving religions as cultural–linguistic systems composed of soteriologically oriented forms of religious life and practice and adds the more controversial idea that there is not only structural similarity among these culturally differentiated forms of life but also substantive identity or overlap inasmuch as the same soteriological goal and process is at issue, taking "different forms all over the world." Moreover, the basic religious conviction (methodological assumption of veridicality) appears to continue and to build on the other basic commitment to the ontological realism of religious language and belief, now expanding this presupposition into a rational conviction about the veridicality of religious experience and thought. Again, these are controversial moves on Hick's part, and both lie behind a recurrent worry cited in all the critical readings of Hick: namely, do these methodological moves not lead to distorted understandings of the goals and claims advanced by religious traditions? We will have occasion to return to this question below.

**Ontological Postulate.** From Hick's point of view, the pluralist hypothesis rationally requires the postulation of a divine noumenal reality underlying and unifying the diverse phenomenal religions through a common ultimate referent for their different and humanly limited conceptions of the Real.[6] As a corollary to this postulate, Hick construes the epistemological relation between the divine noumenon and the phenomenal religions as the divine noumenon (never experienced directly in itself) coming to consciousness (indirectly) in terms of culturally differentiated conceptual schemes (e.g., dualistic–personalistic and monistic–impersonalistic) generated at the interface between divine noumenon and different patterns of human consciousness.

It is worth noting even at this early point a number of features of this ontological postulate. First, it is a postulate that is rationally required if the pluralist hypothesis is to be held; therefore, the only reasons supporting the postulate at this point are internal. Second, this postulate makes an ontological claim; it says that there is a (single) divine noumenon that is the ultimate referent of the major religions. Third, this postulate makes an epistemological claim: it says that the noumenon cannot be directly experienced or known in itself, and it says that it can, at best, be only indirectly known (which means that any knowledge about it can only be indirect and inferential). And in light of the different types of religious conceptual schemes, it says that the divine noumenon comes to consciousness in terms of radically different concepts of personality and impersonality.

**Epistemological Consequences.** According to Hick, the epistemological corollary of the ontological postulate entails the relative insignificance of differences in religious conceptualization and belief among traditions, for these traditions are viewed as alternative soteriological frameworks in relation to the same ultimate reality and value.[7] Moreover, he argues for (1) the deconstruction of absolute claims to truth as pride-inspired tribal and ethnic preferences given the arbitrary stamp of divine approval and (2) skepticism over the possibility of settling in any conclusive or satisfactory way differences over historical and metaphysical claims. For these reasons Hick recommends adopting a tolerant agnosticism regarding differences in truth-claims among religions. This, however, is not to gainsay the in-principled cognitive significance of religious claims and beliefs, since the central elements of religious interpretive schemes are still eschatologically verifiable, according to Hick. Nonetheless, in this life he suggests that the phenomenal religions can only be assessed for their pragmatic adequacy—in terms of, for example, moral authenticity of founders, saints, and ideals, internal consistency and coherence of intellectual systems (e.g., theologies), and, most importantly, soteriological efficacy of whole systems conceived as frameworks of transformation. Applying these criteria to elements of the major faiths, Hick concludes that, so far as anyone can tell, the world's religions are roughly equal in their moral authenticity, intellectual impressiveness, and soteriological success. Therefore, from Hick's perspective, these religions are equally valid or veridical, supporting the pluralist hypothesis proposed as a conditional claim in the "first-steps" phase above.

Once again, we need to observe that Hick has developed a complex epistemological position that, in its two main aspects, continues and concludes the outworking of his initial philosophical presuppositions. The ontological realism presupposition undergirds both his justification for adopting tolerant agnosticism—for example, while religious historical and metaphysical claims are in principle settleable, says Hick, most are not conclusively adjudicable in practice—and his use of the notion of eschatological verification to pin down the continuing cognitive significance of religious beliefs. The Wittgensteinian orientation to the importance and primacy of religious practice and forms of life appears to undergird Hick's attempt to develop a nascent epistemological pragmatism with respect to justifying and assessing religious systems. I believe that he sees these two epistemological threads as ultimately compatible: (1) in this life, the only sort of truth and justification we can attain with regard to religious beliefs and practices is that of pragmatic adequacy or authenticity; (2) nonetheless, it still remains possible that in the afterlife we will be able to see more exactly their ontological correspondence with reality; and (3) Hick seems to hold (not implausibly) that pragmatic adequacy or success is more likely than not to be an indication of ontological correspondence or truth.

It should be reasonably apparent from this reading that Hick's account of religious pluralism is composed of at least two different theoretical threads—cultural–linguistic and propositional–realist, respectively. Indeed, it is arguable that a number of others may be present as well.[8] The tendency to regard religious language and doctrine as metaphoric and mythic and to see all religions as expressions of a common core experience or soteriological orientation is suggestive of what Lindbeck would call an experiential–expressive thread, while the final development of a pragmatic epistemology of religious belief is reminiscent of William James and suggestive of a pragmatic theory of religion.[9] And, of course, there is no denying the fact that Hick's ontological postulate reflects a Kantian thread. By itself the recognition of such diverse theoretical threads should give pause to anyone contemplating the development or acceptance of a critical reading constructed around only one of these threads.

Furthermore, in light of the manifest fact that at least two of these threads—cultural–linguistic and propositional–realist—carry through the whole development of Hick's theory, one should be reasonably wary of any critical reading that emphasizes only one of these at the expense of the other. Thus, I want to suggest that my reading of Hick is distinguished from the other readings I mentioned by the fact that it at the very least does justice to the complexity of Hick's theory. Clearly, for example, in view of what I have already said, his theory is not properly represented as "noncognitive"—to be sure there is a grammatical or seemingly antirealist thread, but we cannot overlook Hick's commitment to ontological realism, the cognitive significance of religious discourse via eschatological verification, and so on. By the same token, it seems somewhat misleading to label his theory "cognitivist" *tout court* simply because the view connoted by this seems to be at some odds with Hick's skepticism about resolving truth-claims in this life as well as with his focus on nonevidential reasons in the justification and assessment of religious belief and practices. And, again, to view his theory as simply a pragmatic interpretation of religious belief seems to do an injustice to the realist, ontological, and eschatological elements in his account. We need, then, to examine Hick's theory apart from one-sided readings in order to be in a position to appreciate and assess the function, effect, and significance of its multidimensional theoretical strands. We need now to identify the principal critical issues or questions sighted in our reading of Hick's theory.

Each of the four phases of Hick's theory raises distinctive critical issues that have the potential of undermining the project as a whole. The first "presuppositional" phase, for example, seems composed of two very different—some would say incompatible—orientations to the epistemology of religious belief, the "grammatical" and the "realist." This naturally generates the question of how these can be held together and coherently pursued in one theory. The second "methodological" phase introduces a fundamental premise of substantial overlap or identity of soteriological goals among diverse religions that immediately raises a question of hermeneutical adequacy: can such a premise do justice to the self-understandings of traditions that seemingly see themselves as believing quite different things about the universe and as pursuing quite different ends relative to these beliefs. Furthermore, one may wonder whether Hick is being sufficiently critical in his adoption and generalization of the methodological assumption of the veridicality of religious experience and thought. The third "postulate" phase seems bedeviled by a fundamental dilemma—how can an essentially inaccessible and unknowable postulated noumenon be made relevant to the phenomenal religions without somehow modifying its epistemic status? And the fourth epistemological phase, in simultaneously proposing a this-worldly agnosticism and pragmatism together with an other-worldly confirmability, generates not only an issue of conceptual coherence but also a concern that this approach may beg the question about the supposed correlativity of pragmatic fruits, on the one hand, and religious truth, on the other.

As I have already mentioned, Hick's theory has generated considerable critical response, much of it oriented to or at least touching on many of the issues I have just identified. Two outstanding recent critical evaluations of Hick's position—Netland and Corliss—warrant special attention because they represent two very persuasive readings of Hick's theory as an explicit contribution to the philosophy of religion and because, between them, in building on past critical efforts as well as Hick's response to these, they appear to address, in a sophisticated and coherent manner, many of the critical issues seemingly endemic to Hick's position.[10]

In what follows I want to examine and appraise Netland's and Corliss's handling of four critical issues in an effort to determine whether their arguments (and these issues) significantly undermine Hick's theory. The issues are possible hermeneutical inadequacy of the revisionist approach, possible fallacy of the generalization of veridicality, possible incoherence in the postulate of a divine noumenon, and possible epistemic inadequacy of Hick's pragmatic justification and assessment of religious belief. I will argue that most, if not all, of their criticisms are inconclusive against Hick and that his theory represents a plausible account of religious diversity. Let me now turn to the four areas of critical concern addressed by Netland and Corliss, beginning with the issue of hermeneutical adequacy.

## APPRAISAL OF FOUR CRITICISMS

### *1. Hermeneutical Adequacy of Hick's Revisionist Conception of Religion(s)*

Hick begins the development of his theory by comparing and contrasting two views of religion and religious diversity—the standard view and an alternative revisionist view—both of which share the idea that religions are soteriological in aim, structure, and function but which diverge in interpreting the meaning of the diversity of religions.[11] The standard view conceives of religions as counterpoised rival systems of belief and practice whereby each system claims to have exclusive access to ultimate truth as well as the sole means of authentic salvation. The alternative revisionist view proposed and adopted by Hick, in contrast, sees religions as essentially related "kin" (rather than rival "strangers") that are concerned with the same vital process of moral and spiritual transformation (from ego- to reality-orientation) taking different forms in diverse cultural and historical settings. Particular religions, under this view, are working toward the same goal of human transformation in a mutually complementary rather than antagonistic way.

Now it is crucially important to realize that this revisionist conception entails a thesis much stronger than a more modest claim about a structural aim and pattern common to religions, for it incorporates the idea the same transformational process takes "different forms all over the world within the contexts of the different historical traditions."[12] This is a claim about substantive identity or overlap among diverse religious traditions, amounting to the adoption of "common core" or "unity" theory of religious pluralism, involving the claim of an underlying literal unity of some sort among all religions. The revisionist view, then, embodies a rather substantial thesis about the name of the world's religions, for it is, after all, a rather short step from claiming "the same transformational process" among different religions to claiming that these religions in fact refer in some important way to the "same ultimate reality."

It is not surprising to find critics challenging the propriety of this initial methodological move of Hick's theory, for with the revisionist conception Hick is taken considerably far in a particular theoretical direction—toward the transcendental unity of all religions. One immediate and pressing issue for these critics concerns precisely the hermeneutical adequacy of this move, especially considering the fact that its soteriological thesis seems to contradict the self-understanding of traditions about what they believe and practice.[13] And the issue is only made more exigent when one considers that, while many historians of religions might be willing to admit structural comparability in regard to cross-traditional soteriological aims, practices, and concepts, few seem willing to say that the data permit them to draw the conclusion of essential sameness or identity in soteriology cross traditionally. Indeed, most are likely to point to large differences in concept and practice that are in turn linked to equally large differences in meaning and reference. Thus, at the very outset of Hick's theory we need to record the serious—and some would say, decisive—reservation that it appears to overlook or discount what the religions say about themselves as well as what many historians of religions might say about how to understand properly religious beliefs and practices cross traditionally.

Perhaps the most explicit and pointed criticism of the hermeneutical adequacy of Hick's theory is that advanced by Netland.[14] Netland argues in a nutshell that Hick's theory is simply inadequate as a general second-order theory about religions precisely because it fails to take them on their own terms and reduces their central views and concepts (e.g., about soteriology) to understandings and terms unacceptable to the traditions themselves. Suggests Netland, a second-order theory such as Hick's must develop an account that can accommodate traditions' own orthodox understandings of doctrines, beliefs, and concepts without reinterpreting or reducing these (e.g., Incarnation) into other categories (e.g., mythological). With regard to the specific case at hand—soteriology—Netland claims that, in adopting "a lowest common denominator soteriology" (Netland's phrase for Hick's revisionist conception), Hick's theory is conceptually compelled to ignore or reinterpret the key soteriological concepts of various traditions in the form of minimizing their differences and claiming that they constitute one essential process (transition from ego- to reality-orientation) taking place in different contexts. Indeed, he even goes so far as to suggest that Hick's "lowest common denominator soteriology" simply reduces all religious soteriologies to the terms of ordinary morality (i.e., transition from egoism to altruism). At the very least, then, it appears to be Netland's contention that Hick's revisionist approach to religious diversity is unable to accommodate adequately the various soteriological claims internal to traditions as these claims are understood within the traditions themselves. Hick's approach is, in short, hermeneutically deficient in its handling of first-order religious traditions and their complexity. I believe that this fairly represents one of Netland's major objections to Hick's revisionist conception, and I believe that Netland's objection, in turn, is a fair statement of a common critical reaction to Hick's initial methodological move.

Now, I want to suggest that this common reaction—often regarded as a decisive objection to Hick's theory—in fact suffers from a crucial ambiguity in its own formulation as well as from a crucial misunderstanding about the structure and development of Hick's theory. Let me first address the ambiguity before turning to the misunderstanding of Hick. The ambiguity is best gotten at by reflecting on a crucial distinction most ably drawn by Wayne Proudfoot in his recent book on the philosophy of religious experience.[15]

Proudfoot argues (correctly I think) that much work in this field suffers from a failure to note that "interpretation" may refer to one or the other of two different tasks that are often confused, collapsed, or elided one with the other: (1) identifying and describing a religious belief or practice in terms of the concepts and rules employed by the tradition or culture in which that belief or practice is imbedded; (2) explaining that belief or practice (already identified and described as in 1) in terms of some higher-order scheme, framework, or theory in the effort to arrive at the best explanation of the belief or practice at issue. As Proudfoot suggests, these two tasks are very different, though both are necessary for a full and adequate interpretative account of a religious belief or practice. The first task is primarily descriptive, involving the identification of a belief or practice under the description by which a subject (person) or culture identifies it. To describe such a religious phenomenon in terms unacceptable to the subject or culture would be to misidentify it altogether and to alter the object of inquiry: this is the fallacy of descriptive reduction. The second task, by contrast, typically involves offering an explanation of an already identified and described belief or practice—in terms or categories of an explanatory scheme or framework that are not those of, or necessarily acceptable to, the subject or culture: this is explanatory reduction, but it is not a fallacy. Explanatory reduction constitutes a normal explanatory procedure that sets a properly identified and described belief or practice (à la the first task) within a new context or framework (e.g., scientific or philosophical theory).

Though task 2 presupposes the achievement of task 1, they are distinct, and, suggests Proudfoot, the failure to distinguish between the two kinds of reduction (one a fallacy and the other not) results in the overly parochial and protective view that an explanatory account of a belief or practice must be restricted to the perspective and terms of the subject or culture. But this is precisely to confuse different levels or senses of interpretation (and interpretive adequacy) in such a way as to block genuine inquiry and attempts at explanation and theory from a perspective different from that of a subject or culture. This seems at best myopic and at worst a confused antiintellectualism. We now need to apply this clarification to Netland's critique of Hick's hermeneutical inadequacy.

We need first to ask whether Netland's criticism means to charge Hick with (1) descriptive inadequacy (reduction) at the level of identification and description of diverse soteriological beliefs and practices, or (2) explanatory inadequacy at the level of theoretical explication and account. If the charge is descriptive reduction (and if Netland is right to so charge), then Hick's theory may have a problem at the ground level, so to speak. If the charge is explanatory reduction (because of a supposed failure to adopt the categories of traditions as being truly explanatory and to use instead those of another theory or framework), then Netland's criticism itself may suffer from a problem of its own—namely, the undue imposition of an unreasonable explanatory or theoretic requirement. Let us consider each possibility, in turn, in connection with Hick's methodology.

It seems to me that, in proposing a revisionist conception of religious and religious diversity—which it will be the burden of his full theory to defend—

Hick means to offer an explanatory hypothesis about how to account theoretically for the diversity of soteriological views and practices that are fully recognized by him to be quite different according to the viewpoints internal to the traditions themselves. Indeed, it is, from Hick's point of view, precisely the internal soteriological perspectives of religious traditions identified and understood in their own terms that generate the problem of the diversity of religions in the first place—for which he adopts the solution of the revisionist view. This implies, I think, that Hick must already have engaged in a prior step of identification and descriptive understanding from the viewpoints of the religious traditions themselves. Thus, if Netland's conclusion means to charge Hick with descriptive reduction, then this may be misguided since otherwise how is Hick so self-consciously aware of the diversity that needs to be explained and accounted for?

The possibility remains, of course, that Netland means to charge Hick with explanatory reduction, but this would seem myopic, for why should Hick at the level of theory and explanation be saddled with having to accept as adequate explanatory categories the conceptual schemes of the traditions themselves? Would this not simply generate competing explanatory accounts for which Hick (or someone else) would need to seek a higher-order explanation? At the level of explanation then, Hick seems perfectly within his rights as a scholar of (already identified and described) religious diversity to propose a theoretical–explanatory account that explains this diversity in terms of categories and concepts not fully acceptable to the traditions themselves (e.g., concepts of human transformation, common soteriological goal, contextual relativity, etc.). It is to be expected that a higher-order theoretical account would identify deeper (and perhaps common) explanatory factors that the more limited traditional perspectives would not have in view. On this reading, Hick simply takes (or assumes) first-order descriptions of soteriological processes and goals as the phenomena or data for which he now seeks an explanation in more comprehensive theoretical terms. That this might be seen as explanatory reduction is no objection at all.

As a consequence of the foregoing, I want to suggest that, on either interpretation of the charge of reductionism, Netland's criticism of Hick's theory as inappropriately reductionist seems to falter. I believe that Netland in fact simply fails to distinguish the two types of interpretive task—descriptive and explanatory—and then mistakenly conceives Hick's theoretical–explanatory account as being descriptively inaccurate. But this is a mistake, for why should we suppose that a theoretical–explanatory account must at that level simply replicate or be bound by traditional understandings and concepts? Netland writes, for example, "The traditional understanding of the Incarnation cannot be maintained on Hick's theory. Thus we are encouraged to reinterpret the Incarnation in mythological categories," or again, "The problem here is that Hick's theory cannot accommodate the Zen notion of satori as this is understood within the Zen tradition. Accordingly, Hick advocates a reinterpretation of satori . . . and this surely counts against his theory as a general theory."[16] Or yet again, "Can the great Pauline theme of justification, for example, . . . be reduced to transition from self-centeredness to Reality-centeredness?"[17] But the key question in all this is what Netland means by "adequately accounted for on Hick's analysis." Does he intend this in a descriptive–identification sense or an explanatory–theoretical sense? Netland does not say, but it does seem that the evidence he cites for a mistake on Hick's part involves claiming that Hick's theoretical–explanatory account is reductive. And one wants to say here: of course, the account is reductive, invoking nontraditional theoretical factors to explain in a systematic and comprehensive way what doctrines-as-they-are-understood-internally-to-traditions may really be all about. Is not this what a theory is supposed to do?

I think all of this justifies at least the claim that Netland's charge against Hick of hermeneutical inadequacy is inconclusive, though I am perfectly willing to concede that Hick himself could have been much clearer about the levels at which he works and which of two hats he is wearing when writing about religious pluralism. Sometimes, indeed, he speaks of writing as a Christian theologian to reinterpret in a first-order way the doctrine of the Incarnation because of the theory of religious pluralism he has developed in other places as a philosopher; knowing this about Hick sometimes encourages the confusion that Hick qua philosopher may be tampering reductively with the traditional understanding of doctrines.[18] But this is an illusion fostered by Hick's dual career. Qua philosopher, he accepts what traditions have to say about themselves (their doctrines and practices) and then asks, How can I qua philosopher account for this diversity, knowing what I do about philosophy and religious epistemology, and the like? The result of asking this question is a philosophical proposal that involves articulation and then elaboration, outworking, and defense of a revisionist conception of religions (contextual elaboration and differentiation of a process and goal held in common at the deepest level). If Hick really were to have committed the fallacy of descriptive reduction—thinking that all doctrinal schemes and practices obviously overlap, and so on—then I suggest Hick would have conducted his case in a different way, citing what he regarded as clear evidence of an essential core among religions and having no need to develop an argument of the sort that he does in fact develop. True descriptive reduction, I suggest, would be much more naive than Hick's evidently nonnaive argument, having no need to make methodological assumptions or to propose ontological postulates, and so forth. Hick is compelled to develop the elaborate defense that he does precisely because he is fully aware of diversity among traditions at the conceptual level of self-understanding.

## *2. Epistemic Adequacy of Hick's Basic Religious Conviction and Its Use*

In initiating his theory, Hick adopts as a crucially important methodological assumption a "basic religious conviction" about the veridicality of religious experience—"religious thought and experience is not, as such, a matter of delusion and projection but mediates a real contact with a higher reality."[19] He is well aware of the pivotal role of this assumption within his theory, for he himself points out in responding to his critics that it has the effects of putting "out of bounds" the challenges of various forms of religious skepticism as well as coming close to entailing the key postulate of his theory.[20] Though he forthrightly states that "it is not the purpose of a philosophy of religious pluralism to provide the safeguard against atheism," Hick does at least refer to a line of argument in defense of his basic conviction, involving the appeal to a rational principle of credulity with respect to perceptual and more broadly experiential claims.[21]

It has been cogently argued by many philosophers (including Hick himself in *Why Believe in God?*) that it is rational to trust one's epistemic seeming experience so long as one holds one's credulity open to defeating conditions—for example, evidence of abnormal physiological factors, evidence of the absence or nonexistence of the supposed perceptual object, and so on—that such a principle seems necessary for acquiring knowledge of our environment, and that, aside from skeptical prejudice, there is no reason to exclude its use in religious contexts.[22] Hick is also quick to point out that, "if it is rational for the Christian to believe in God on the basis of his or her distinctively Christian experience, it must by the same argument be rational for the Muslim . . . for the Hindu and the Buddhist . . . on the basis of their own distinctive forms of experience."[23] That is, he argues that one must play fair with regard to the use of a principle of credulity in different religious and cultural contexts—if we regard it as reasonable to appeal to it for our entitlement in making epistemic claims on the basis of our experience, then by the same token it must be reasonable for others (even in other cultures and traditions) to appeal to it for a similar entitlement with regard to grounding their epistemic claims.

Netland contends that, at this point, Hick waffles between drawing one of two conclusions: (1) "Since the veridicality of religious experience in general cannot be ruled out a priori, then religious experience for any given tradition can in principle be regarded as veridical," and (2) "if it is shown to be reasonable to accept as veridical religious experience for a particular tradition, then the religious experience of the other great traditions must also be accepted as veridical."[24] And Netland is quick to point out that, while 1 is valid, 2 is not, for the simple reason that religious experience must be evaluated on a case-by-case basis to ascertain whether or not defeating conditions apply. Claim 1 is simply a fair generalization to all religions of a principle of credulity. Claim 2, by contrast, attempts to generalize a claim about actual veridicality to all traditions without taking into account the need to be epistemically responsible in using a principle of credulity.

Now, while Netland's distinction between claims 1 and 2 is certainly valid in itself, and while his objection to claim 2 as it stands is certainly correct, I believe that he is quite wrong in suggesting that Hick's "basic religious conviction" argument is ambiguous between claims 1 and 2 or that he even tries to advance claim 2 on the basis of simply "generalizing" a principle of credulity. My reason for saying this is quite simple: Hick does want to argue for something like claim 2—the equal veridicality of the major religious traditions—and in order to do this, he explicitly develops a whole theory of religious pluralism to support the contention. That is to say, Hick seems fully cognizant that the argument for claim 1 is insufficient to establish a version of claim 2; this is precisely why he leaves that argument and its conclusion (claim 1) behind in further proposing a pluralist hypothesis, for which he then goes on to develop a whole supporting framework of postulate, argument, and assessment of data that results finally in a pragmatic case for the equal authenticity (and hence veridicality) of the major traditions.

Hick is quite clear about the logic of his position when, after he has established the general in-principled applicability of a principle of credulity to religious experience, he goes on to suggest that this principle has its limits. He writes, "Treating one's own form of religious experience, then, as veridical . . . one then has to take account of the fact that there are other great streams of religious experience which take different forms."[25] And, asks Hick, What account is reasonable to develop here in light of the fact that these other traditions might well invoke a principle of credulity and from their points of view come to judge their forms of experience and their traditions as veridically as one judges one's own experience and tradition? How are we to adjudicate the challenge posed by this situation—what is the most reasonable response? Hick goes on to suggest three possible answers to this challenge, two of which he regards as flawed, with the third being the most reasonable, permitting us finally to hold that the major traditions are equally veridical.[26]

The first answer is that of exclusivism, which holds that only one's own form of religious experience is properly regarded as veridical, while all others are delusory. According to Hick, this exclusivist claim is unreasonably arbitrary. The second answer is that of inclusivism, which holds that religious experience in general is veridical, though this is most clear and effective in the case of one's own form of religious experience. According to Hick, the reasonability of this claim is belied by the fact of significant moral and spiritual transformations in other religious traditions. The argument here is that, assuming the premise of a strong correlation between veridicality and moral–spiritual fruits (actual transformation in people's lives), it is by no means clear that religious traditions differ greatly in either the quality of their fruits or, by implication, the degree of clarity of their veridicality. Finally, the third answer is that of pluralism, which holds that all forms of religious experience across traditions are properly regarded as being veridical (equally). And, according to Hick, this is the most reasonable position to adopt, for it avoids the flaws of the other two answers and is supported by a consistent line of reasoning as well as by evident facts. That is, assuming a strong correlation between veridicality and moral–spiritual fruits, this answer recognizes the equality of transformational fruits across traditions and, by implication, the equal authenticity or veridicality of these traditions.

Now it seems clear enough that, on the terms laid out by Hick, this third pluralist position can be regarded as reasonable only if there are good reasons to think that (1) there is a strong correlation between veridicality, on the one hand, and transformational moral and religious fruits, on the other, such that the latter fruits inductively support the former claim; and (2) the moral and spiritual fruits of the major traditions are equal. The premise represented by 1 needs support because for all we know these fruits can be had entirely apart from veridical religious experiences. The claim represented by 2 needs support not merely because it is not obviously true (and therefore requires convincing data) but also because the criteria for identifying and assessing moral and spiritual fruits are not self-evident (and therefore require articulation and defense). Since there is no reason at this point to accept the pluralist solution as the most reasonable response to Hick's challenge, we should expect Hick to develop a set of considerations bearing on the above premise and claim. And this I suggest is precisely the goal and burden of the remainder of his theory of religious pluralism. His theory is intended to provide us with a set of good reasons for accepting the pluralist hypothesis and its implications for equal veridicality. Thus, as I suggested in my original précis of Hick's theory, at this point Hick is proposing only the *conditional rationality* of the pluralist hypothesis that all the major religious traditions are in fact veridical and mediate real contact with a higher reality—that is to say, "conditional" on his subsequent adducement of good reasons.

It is precisely this "practical" turn in Hick's theory toward consideration of moral and spiritual authenticity that prompts Corliss's objection to Hick's basic religious conviction and its experience.[27] Whereas Netland challenges the way that Hick uses this conviction, Corliss objects to its use at all. He claims that Hick's basic conviction wrongly assumes that the primary cognitive content of religions is found in veridical religious experiences, and he claims further that Hick's contextual–linguistic thesis about such experience being shaped by traditional concepts and categories (imbedded in language games) undercuts the need for Hick's adopting such a conviction in the first place. From Corliss's perspective the cognitive content of religions resides in their views of life and the claims that they make, not in the experiences to which they give rise; to think otherwise illegitimately analogizes the role of religious experience in religions to the role of sense experience in dealing with the world around us. Therefore, Corliss would encourage Hick to put aside his basic religious conviction and concern for veridical religious experiences in order to focus exclusively on the validity of religious views of life.

There is something right about Corliss's complaint against Hick and also something wrong about it. Where Corliss goes wrong, I think, is in his flat-out rejection of any cognitive role for religious experience in religions analogous to the cognitive role of sense (e.g., perceptual) experience in dealing with the environment. It seems that the reason he gives for this rejection has to do with the fact that religious experiences are shaped and filtered by background concepts and categories. But this seems no less true of perceptual experiences, which anthropologists, psychologists, and linguists tell us are shaped and filtered by background conceptual and linguistic conditions. Furthermore, Corliss's rejection of a cognitive role for religious experiences appears to discount without clear and convincing reasons those cognitive practices internal to religious traditions involving adherents' appeals to religious experiences as a way to warrant their cognitive claims. Finally, it is not clear to me that Corliss has given any thought to a possible role for the principle of credulity (together with defeating conditions) in relation to religious experience; I wonder if the admission of such a principle might ease the need to draw a strong distinction between a cognitive role for perceptual experience and no cognitive role for religious experience at all.

What seems right about Corliss's complaint against Hick is this: Hick does in fact hold a conceptual–linguistic thesis about religious experience, and this does encourage us to wonder why he begins with an apparent methodological focus on the veridicality of religious experience.[28] And this puzzlement is heightened by Hick's own need to turn to other considerations (e.g., moral and spiritual fruits) as a way to assess issues of veridicality. Why not start with these other considerations in appraising background religious frameworks and views of life? Some of this puzzlement is dissipated, I think, by the realization that "religious experience" for Hick is a category intended by him to be equivalent to religious forms of life.[29] Thus, in speaking of veridical religious experience and thought, he is referring to the belief on the part of participants in religious forms of life (practices) that they are somehow in touch with, praying to, worshipping, and so forth, something that is real and not illusory. Hick does not mean "religious experience" to denote narrowly a religious sense percept. A second point to be made is that, in one sense, Hick agrees with Corliss—yes, it is important to assess the background religious framework for its cognitive content in religious experience—while at the same time disagreeing that this is somehow incompatible with an interest in the veridicality of religious experience and, of course, disagreeing that the focus ought to be truth-claims as contrasted with moral and spiritual fruits of religious practice (the latter represents another issue to which we will return). Indeed, we might ask, why cannot cognitive assessment have two foci (e.g., experience and belief), especially if these are seen to be conceptually related?

As in the case of Hick's "revisionist conception of religion," we are, I think, compelled to conclude that criticisms of his "basic religious conviction" are at best inconclusive (in the case of Corliss) or at worst simply wrong (in the case of Netland). Thus, it seems entirely legitimate for Hick to propose as the conclusion to the methodological phase of his argument a "pluralist hypothesis" about the deeper unity that may underlie the diversity of religions. We need now to consider what Hick has to say about the nature and implications of this hypothesis that is here only proposed as being conditionally rational and that will be the burden of his theory to defend more conclusively.

## 3. Coherence of Hick's Postulate of a Divine Noumenon

From Hick's perspective, the pluralist hypothesis can only make sense on the assumption of "a divine reality which is itself limitless, exceeding the scope of human conceptuality and language, but which is humanly thought and experienced in various conditioned and limited ways."[30] That is to say, in order to be coherently proposed and maintained, the pluralist hypothesis rationally requires the postulation of a divine noumenal reality (in itself infinite and unknowable) underlying and serving as the common ultimate referent of phenomenal religious systems, which in turn involve culturally shaped conceptualizations and experiences of the real. According to Hick, this postulation permits us to acknowledge in a consistent and coherent manner the diversity of forms of religious experience together with their mutual conditional veridicality—for though diverse they are all finally "about" (or better, "focused on") the same transcendent ultimate.

This postulation of a divine noumenon rests on an important distinction between the Real *an sich* and the Real-for-us that Hick sees as drawn by all religious traditions in their (structurally) common affirmations of a higher reality-in-itself exceeding human conceptualization and as lying beyond or behind the higher-reality-as-humanly-experienced-and-thought in their traditions. The fact that all the major traditions draw this distinction encourages Hick to propose the idea that the Real *an sich* is one cross-traditional reality in fact, though it is humanly experienced only in very limited culturally bound ways within the diverse religions. In other words, at the core of Hick's pluralist hypothesis is the postulated notion that the Real *an sich* of the different religions is one and the same reality in all cases and further that the Real-for-us (of each tradition) is the way that the tradition experiences and conceptualizes for itself the Real *an sich.* As Hick himself says, "this thought lies at the heart of the pluralist hypothesis," and it clearly constitutes a very substantive claim indeed.[31] It behooves us, therefore, to be clear about its conceptual content and logical function within his theory.

To begin with, we need to recognize that Hick's postulate has both ontological and epistemological dimensions—that is, it makes an ontological claim with an epistemological corollary. Ontologically speaking, Hick's postulate proposes that there is a Real *an sich* that is the unifying ground of the foci (Real-for-us) of the various traditions. This ground is the deeper source and object of all religious soteriologies and thus ontologically unifies them such that essentially the same process of moral and spiritual transformation is involved in all cases, for, in a significant sense, the process in each tradition has the same ultimate aim in the deepest sense. Epistemologically, Hick sees his Real *an sich* (divine noumenon) as the ground of religious experience and thought, making forms of religious experience across traditions veridical inasmuch as they all constitute our conditioned and limited access to the Real *an sich.* Hick elaborates on this epistemological dimension by suggesting, in conformity with his understanding of the conceptual–linguistic nature of religious experience, that the Real *an sich* impinges on culturally conditioned human consciousness, which for its part responds to and becomes aware of this impingement indirectly though the mediating lenses of culturally diverse conceptual schemes. Thus, the noumenon is not directly experienced or known but rather only indirectly encountered in terms of concepts, structures, and images "generated at the interface between the Real and different patterns of human consciousness."[32]

In this way, Hick manages to integrate the ontological and epistemological dimensions of his postulate: though the Real *an sich* is postulated as an ontological reality, it is known only through the mediating conceptual schemes of religious traditions that in turn are shaped by diverse cultural histories. Hick, of course, is well aware that conceptual schemes are very different—in fact, he identifies two clearly divergent types (personalist and impersonalist)—but he nonetheless holds that they all ultimately refer to the same divine noumenon or Real *an sich.* He explains how this can be conceived to be possible by developing an analogy to an application of the complementarity principle in physics: the personal and impersonal conceptual schemes of religion are to the divine noumenon in itself as the wave and particle conceptualizations of electromagnetic radiation are to light in itself.[33] In both cases, though the conceptualizations—personal/impersonal, wave/particle—are radically different, they still refer ultimately to the same logical subject (noumenon and light, respectively).

As might be expected, Hick's postulate of a divine noumenon has been the focus of considerable critical attention. Netland's discussion represents a particularly forceful and sustained critique of the postulate's coherence and its ability to succeed in the unifying and referential role cast for it by Hick.[34] The basic problem, according to Netland, resides precisely in Hick's distinction between the Real *an sich* and the Real-as-humanly-experienced and in the way he interprets their relation. Netland suggests that there are two possible interpretations of their relation, both of which are advanced by Hick in his writings. The first interpretation focuses on the element of continuity between the Real *an sich* and its various manifestations in phenomenal religious conceptions of the Real. In order for Hick to maintain that these latter conceptions are in fact manifestations or images of the divine noumenon, he must, suggests Netland, posit significant continuity (ontological and epistemological) between them—else why represent them as "manifestations or images" and why posit the divine noumenon as their unifying ontological ground and source? This continuity view, however, runs into a serious problem because of the great diversity—indeed seeming incompatibility—among conceptions or images of the divine (e.g., personal deity vs. impersonal principle or goal), yet it seems crucial to Hick's thesis that the Real *an sich* be ontologically and epistemological continuous with all conceptions. This seems to imply, however, that the noumenon must actually itself be (e.g.) both personal and nonpersonal at the same time, suggesting that it may suffer from an internal incoherence of some sort. The only way to avoid this consequence, suggests Netland, is to draw a distinction between the direct/penultimate referents of the phenomenal religious conceptions (e.g., "God" vs. "Nirvana") and their indirect/ultimate referents (e.g., Real *an sich*), which, of course, Hick regards as the same in all cases. But there is a problem here, according to Netland: given the great differences in the meanings of such phenomenal terms as "God," "Nirvana," and so on, it does not seem plausible to maintain that they all denote (ultimately) the same reality. What reason can be given for claiming that the ultimate referent of each is the same? The emphasis on continuity, then, from Netland's point of view runs smack up against the problem of radical phenomenal discontinuity of so-called manifestations or images with seemingly incompatible entailments that undermine the plausibility of claiming "same ultimate referent nonetheless." Netland suggests that the burden of proof is on Hick to come up with good reasons for "claiming that the ultimate referent of each is the same."

The second interpretation of the relation between the Real *an sich* and phenomenal religious conceptions focuses on their element of discontinuity. This interpretation, suggests Netland, highlights the strong Kantian implications of Hick's postulate of a divine noumenon that is never itself directly experienced, but rather "is posited in order to make sense of the fact of religious experience in general." Religious experience and thought, under this interpretation, is limited to culturally conditioned experience of phenomenal religious images and manifestations. But, argues Netland, this element of discontinuity, while avoiding the sort of problem addressed above in connection with the continuity view, raises problems of its own, stemming from the lack of knowledge of the divine noumenon. If this noumenon cannot be known in itself, then is it at all informative, asks Netland, to refer to phenomenal religious conceptions as images or manifestations of it? And, again, given the lack of knowledge about this Real *an sich,* on what grounds is it posited as a single divine reality rather than as a plurality of noumena? In short, suggests Netland, under this discontinuity view, the ontological status of the divine noumenon becomes very unclear in light of its epistemic obscurity. Indeed, Netland goes so far as to suggest that the reasons for postulating the existence of a divine noumenon are obscure: is it, he asks, anything more than an elaborate hypothesis developed to avoid concluding that perhaps all religions are not in touch with the same divine reality?

In a nutshell, then, Netland is arguing the following points against Hick's postulate of a divine noumenon. First, given the great differences—indeed, seeming incompatibilities—among phenomenal religious conceptions, it is not plausible for Hick to maintain that they all refer to the same ultimate reality. Furthermore, given the claim about the inaccessibility of this ultimate, it is not plausible for Hick to think that it can function adequately as a unifying referent for phenomenal religious conceptions. In the first case, the data of religious diversity suggest more plausibly the diversity of ultimate referents. In the second case, the epistemic gap between the noumenon and phenomenal religions undercuts the ability of the former to serve as unifying referent at all.

Now, despite the initial cogency of these criticisms, I believe their destructive force can be mitigated considerably by elements in Hick's position that Netland has either overlooked or discounted. The two principal ideas that Netland appears to miss are (1) the analogy that Hick draws between his postulate and the complementarity principle in physics and (2) the precise role that Hick casts for his postulate within the pluralist hypothesis and what this implies regarding the postulate's justification. The analogy with the complementarity principle addresses Netland's first point about compatibility and reference, while the postulate's role appears to address his second point about the destructiveness of the epistemic gap. Let me take each of these points in turn, beginning with the analogy.

Hick analogizes the ontological status and referential function of the divine noumenon (in relation to divergent phenomenal religious conceptions) to the ontological status and referential function of light (in relation to the divergent conceptions of wave and particle).[35] On the side of the analogical object, the analogy suggests that, when experimented on in different ways, light exhibits apparently divergent, contradictory behavioral properties, while at the same time in itself being such as to be capable of yielding these results or conceptualizations. On the side of the principal object, the analogy suggests that, when "experimented" on in different ways via the practices of different religious traditions, the divine noumenon exhibits apparently divergent, if not contradictory, qualities, while at the same time in itself being such as to be capable of yielding these results or conceptualizations. That is, the ontological status and nature of both light and divine noumenon are such that, under certain conditions, they exhibit what appear to be incompatible properties. Now for this force of the analogy: since the apparently incompatible properties in first case do not incline us to deny the plausibility of light's referential function in relation to these properties, so too, suggests Hick, the apparent incompatibilities in the second case ought not to undermine the plausibility of the divine noumenon's referential function in relation to these apparent incompatibilities. If in at least one important case—light—we accept the idea of one and the same referent for the incompatible conceptualizations of wave and particle, then it is not implausible to accept the idea in another case—divine noumenon—as well. It seems to me that Hick's analogy does in fact address the first of Netland's criticisms, mitigating its force or at least making its objection inconclusive.[36]

This analogy does not, however, address Netland's other concerns about Hick's postulate—that is, the positive justification for positing one ultimate referent and, further, the justification for thinking that such an inaccessible noumenon can in concept function referentially. Netland's concern about positive justification is met, I think, by emphasizing the "postulate" status and internal role of the divine noumenon within Hick's pluralist hypothesis. The "positive" reason justifying Hick's positing of the noumenon is that the postulate is rationally necessary for the internal consistency of the pluralist hypothesis, and this seems to be a strong enough justification at this point. Of course, we will want eventually to have reasons for adopting less conditionally the hypothesis as a whole, and when Hick undertakes to supply these reasons, then the justification for the postulate will also be stronger than internal rational necessity. But it seems a bit premature (and unfair) to require this fuller justification before accepting that the postulate is at least conditionally justified by its role within the pluralist hypothesis. And the latter is all that Hick means to claim in this phase of his theory: a divine noumenal reality is rationally needed to "complete" (so to speak) the pluralist hypothesis. That is, the divine noumenon as ultimate referent is, from Hick's point of view, the only way to reconcile religious diversity with conditional mutual veridicality.

But, at this point, Netland's remaining concern seems to rear its head—for he wants to know why Hick (or anyone) should think that such an epistemically inaccessible ultimate should be able conceptually to function as a referent for phenomenal religious conceptions. Does not the very lack of knowledge about this ultimate undermine its capacity to serve as a unifying referent in any serious sense? Despite the seeming cogency of this complaint, however, I think that Hick has answered it precisely by arguing that the postulate of a divine noumenon is both rationally necessary (for the hypothesis of mutual veridicality) and not implausible (by analogy with the principle of complementarity). Together, these two prongs of Hick's thinking about his postulate imply that an epistemically inaccessible noumenon can serve as a ultimate unifying referent. If Netland is requiring more reasons at this point, then he is requiring too much at this stage. What Hick is proposing in this phase is perfectly conceivable and coherent, and what he is proposing seems justified (internally) from the perspective of the pluralist hypothesis. Other and stronger reasons must, again, await Hick's defense of his hypothesis as a whole.[37]

It would not be amiss to mention that, unlike Netland, Corliss does apparently conceive of Hick's theory as referentially coherent in principle, though in arguing this he does think of himself as adding to or clarifying Hick's position. Thus, for example, in asking whether different divine phenomenal realities can be rooted in experience of the same ultimate, Corliss (also apparently unaware of Hick's complementarity analogy) argues that, inasmuch as value-contextualism is possible (e.g., same commitment to the importance of life underlying, in different contexts, strategies of nonviolence and proportionate use of force), so too is it possible for the same ultimate reality to underlie, in different contexts, diverse phenomenal conceptions of the divine embodying apparently different values.[38] This point seems to function logically very much like Hick's own complementarity analogy. And in asking whether it is consistent both to claim no knowledge of the noumenon itself and at the same time to claim that the One is beyond knowledge, Corliss (apparently discounting Hick's own representation of his position) answers that Hick needs to adopt the consistent approach of considering his theory an hypothesis for which knowledge is not attainable, but evidence and reasons appropriate.[39] But this is just what Hick does by conditionally proposing the pluralist hypothesis along with a postulate of a divine noumenon for which he later proposes to adduce evidence and reasons. This point on Corliss's part simply seems to recapitulate the logic of Hick's position.

## *4. Epistemic Adequacy of Hick's Justification for Adopting the Pluralist Hypothesis*

In the final phase of the development of his theory, Hick proposes three mutually complementary lines of argument for adopting as valid the pluralist hypothesis (up to this point advanced only as a conditional claim).[40] The first line of argument advances a set of considerations supporting the adoption of an attitude of tolerant agnosticism in this life regarding differences and disagreements in belief among religious traditions. The second line of argument introduces the notion of afterlife verification in order to assure, nonetheless, the in-principled cognitivity of religious belief and discourse. And the third line of argument proposes and deploys a this-life pragmatic justification for the independent and equal veridicality of the diverse perceptions of and salvific routes to the Real as represented by the major faiths.

Hick initiates the first line of argument by drawing a distinction between the "goods"(salvation, liberation) conveyed by a religious system and the "claims" (salvation-claim, truth-claim) that it might make about these goods and related states of affairs.[41] According to Hick, the "goods" represent the valuable, essential, and primary content of religious traditions, while their "claims" and "doctrines" represent just so much secondary "packaging and labelling," though Hick concedes that these are nevertheless "essential" to transmitting the "vital" contents.[42] It seems clear that, in this weighting of goods over claims, Hick is reaffirming one of the logical consequences of his initial methodological preference for the revisionist conception of religion(s) as well as his Wittgensteinian perspective on the nature of religions.

In keeping with this methodological commitment, Hick then deconstructs those absolute claims often advanced by religions in the effort to assert their respective salvific superiority and truth over other traditions. Hick maintains that these claims simply represent in the context of religion an extension of the common social–psychological phenomenon of ethnic pride in one's heritage and tradition. Absolute claims, he suggests, are no more than instances of natural pride "elevated to the level of absolute truth and built into the belief system of a religious community," instances where, in short, "a natural human tribal preference . . . receives the stamp of divine approval."[43] Thus does Hick manage to introduce a note of skepticism about the truth value of claims to religious exclusivity.[44]

This modest skeptical point about religious belief is developed more extensively by Hick in his examination and assessment of differences in three principal types of beliefs advanced by religious traditions—historical, metaphysical, and ultimate.[45] In each case, Hick proposes reasons for being skeptical about whether differences in these beliefs can be conclusively settled in this life. Differences in historical belief among traditions, while in principle settleable by historical evidence, usually are not settled because of the paucity of data about many crucial founding events. Thus, Hick expresses considerable skepticism about whether many important differences in historical belief will ever be actually settled. Metaphysical differences, presumably settleable in principle by reference to actual states of affairs, tend to involve the interaction of conceptual, empirical, and ontological issues so complex that it is extremely difficult to resolve conclusively matters of their verification and truth. Again, Hick expresses much skepticism about the actual resolution in this life of such issues, suggesting that they will be debated until the end of human history. Finally, differences in ultimate belief, while presumably veridical in some important sense (compare Hick's basic religious conviction), nonetheless are embodied within complex and elusive mythic and metaphoric (rather than literal) formulations, making it difficult to settle conclusively which aspects of traditions might be veridical about the ultimate reality.

The upshot, then, of Hick's first line of argument is a rather skeptical view about the prospect of resolving in this life many disagreements in belief (at these various levels) among religious traditions. Thus, Hick recommends the adoption of an attitude of tolerant agnosticism regarding these differences in belief, suggesting—in conformity with his opening point about the priority of goods over claims—that while these might be of "philosophical importance as elements within respective theories about the universe they are not of great 'religious,' i.e., soteriological, importance."[46]

Despite his skepticism about settling differences in belief in this life, Hick nonetheless stalwartly defends in his second line of argument the in-principled cognitivity of religious belief. He does this by appealing to the notion of eschatological verification, which involves the concept of an ultimate afterlife situation capable of verifying (at long last) the truth of religious claims about the nature of reality.[47] Hick argues that such a situation—understood to include a transformed human existence involving a powerful sense of being in ultimate relation with an ultimate reality—could in principle confirm the truth of religious interpretations of the deep structure and process of the universe. Furthermore, suggests Hick, the very possibility of such future confirmation (or better, confirmability) means now that present religious accounts of the universe are factual in character, intending to claim that a given state of affairs (involving a transcendent reality) does in fact obtain. In effect, Hick conceives of eschatological verification as a post mortem experiential confirmation of religious convictions that are held now largely on the basis of faith and, further, as an expectation built into the structure of religious convictions having the logical function of making these convictions cognitive in principle.

As Hick himself observes, this notion is "not directly relevant to the assessment of the conflicting truth-claims of the various traditions" since subsequent eschatological confirmations (if any) are not available to us in the present.[48] Thus, from the vantage of those now living, Hick's appeal to eschatological verification amounts to a hypothesis unverifiable to us now but possibly verifiable to us post mortem (if there is an afterlife). And, maintains Hick, this implies that, despite a justified agnosticism about them in this life, religious beliefs are nonetheless in principle confirmable in another.

With the results of his first two lines of argument behind him, Hick is now faced with the difficult task of trying to provide justifying reasons for adopting the pluralist hypothesis as valid. In light of his argument for tolerant agnosticism regarding differences in religious beliefs, these reasons presumably cannot be evidential ones that somehow demonstrate conclusively the truth of the central claims of the diverse traditions. And it will hardly do for Hick to rely on his position of eschatological verification since that would only support the view that the pluralist hypothesis is cognitive in principle because it is eschatologically verifiable. Hick needs now to supply positive reasons for us to accept now, in this life, the actual validity of the pluralist hypothesis as contrasted with other possible hypotheses attempting to account for religious diversity. That is to say, the cogency of Hick's theory finally rests on his being able to cash out his earlier promissory note on supplying reasons for why his hypothesis is the stronger and more acceptable position.

Hick's third line of argument proposes that, in light of the soteriological aim and structure of religions, it may be most appropriate to develop a pragmatic justification and assessment of religious frameworks of belief and practice, focusing precisely on the issue of their effectiveness in accomplishing their avowed aim of transforming persons from ego-centeredness to Reality-centeredness.[49] He further proposes that the appropriate sorts of criteria for such appraisal and justification can be gleaned from the religious context itself—most particularly from the initial positive responses to great religious figures who founded new religious traditions. Suggests Hick, "human discriminative capacities must . . . have been at work, operating in accordance with at least implicit criteria" in the acceptance of these founders.[50] Furthermore, he continues, such criteria were (and are) presumably operative in subsequent phases of development of these traditions. What criteria exactly? Here Hick offers three sorts of related criteria, concerned, respectively, with the moral authenticity of the founder's teaching and personal character taken together as a unity; the combined intelligibility, plausibility, and attractiveness of the vision or reality he articulates; and, finally, the soteriological efficacy of his message and vision (i.e., capacity to evoke actual change in people in relation to the Real).

With these originary moral and spiritual pragmatic criteria identified, Hick then goes on to ascertain how they might be applied in the assessment and justification of religious–cultural phenomena. With regard to forms of religious experience as well as basic visions of reality (conceived as "maps" designed to lead people to the Real), he argues that the most appropriate question is whether they are, respectively, veridical and accurate and that this is best assessed by whether the total systems built up around them are soteriologically effective and actually put people in touch with the Real. With regard to the explicit interpretive schemes of religions (i.e., their theologies or philosophies), Hick argues that these may be rationally assessed in terms of their internal consistency and coherence as well as their adequacy to the root experiences and basic visions of their traditions. And with respect to the historical results or outworkings of religious soteriological systems, Hick argues that the most appropriate assessment is a moral one that focuses on the quality of the religions' actual and ideal fruits.

When he goes on to apply these criteria in assessing religious phenomena and traditions, Hick makes the following observations. First, to the extent that the interpretive schemes of different religions are compatible, they appear to be "equally massive and powerful systemizations of different basic visions."[51] Second, inasmuch as they involve transformation of the self composed of respect for persons and love of others, the ideal ways of life associated with the major traditions appear equally impressive from a moral point of view. Third, the historical records of the actual virtues and vices of the major traditions are so complex and diverse that it is not possible to render a defensible comparative judgment. Fourth, to the extent that we can ascertain soteriological efficacy in this life—in terms of, for example, whether people are made happier, lead more fulfilling lives, and are enabled to become better persons—it appears that the main historical streams of religious experience and life constitute equally impressive and successful soteriological frameworks for hundreds of millions for centuries. In light of all this, Hick concludes that, so far as we can tell, the major traditions are equally efficacious soteriologically and therefore possess equally valid (veridical) perceptions of the Real. Therefore, from Hick's perspective, the pragmatic assessment of religious traditions yields a pragmatic justification for accepting the pluralist hypothesis as valid.

Not surprisingly, the epistemic adequacy of Hick's justification for his pluralist hypothesis has been challenged on a number of grounds, most notably for its apparent denial of the significance of truth-claims in religion and for its seeming preference for the language of authenticity rather than truth in relation to the justification and assessment of religious beliefs and practices. Perhaps the two most vigorous criticisms along these lines have been those of Griffiths and Lewis and Byrne.[52] Griffiths and Lewis, for example, interpret Hick as explicitly developing a noncognitivist position on the nature and justification of religious belief, and they expend particular effort on challenging the hermeneutical adequacy of such a position in dealing with the beliefs and claims of diverse traditions. They argue against Hick that (1) since historically it is clear that religious spokesmen "really did think they were making claims about the nature of things," therefore, (2) any position that presupposes that the "creators and systematizers of religious worldviews were actually doing something other than what they thought they were doing" must be hermeneutically inadequate because (3) it fails to "take the tradition seriously on its own terms and . . . is almost certain to lead to a serious distortion of the tradition."[53]

This charge against Hick is not only unfounded but is also itself methodologically flawed. Clearly, from all that we have said about his position, Hick does not deny that religious spokesmen intend to make truth-claims about the nature of reality. Quite the reverse: he presupposes at the very outset of his study and reiterates throughout his position that they do intend to advance truth-claims. (And indeed, his own positions of tolerant agnosticism and eschatological verification entail the maintenance of an underlying commitment to the in-principled cognitivity of religious belief.) So, the charge against Hick appears unfounded. Furthermore, it appears to be methodologically flawed as well, inasmuch as it (like Netland's critique of Hick's claim about "same soteriological process") fails to take account of the distinction between descriptive reduction (a fallacy that is not committed by Hick) and explanatory reduction (which is no fallacy at all). Thus, for Hick to argue at the level of (second-order) theory an agnosticism about differences in (first-order) truth-claims among religious traditions appears to take adequate descriptive account of these latter claims—precisely in order to mount a higher claim about their lack of conclusive adjudicability, verification, and so on, in this life.

Byrne, while not necessarily agreeing with Griffiths and Lewis's interpretation of Hick as an explicit noncognitivist, argues nonetheless that Hick's position, in emphasizing notions of genuineness, authenticity, and practical appropriateness, and the like, borders on the abandonment of truth in religion. Byrne claims that Hick's "tolerant agnostic[ism] about different and even conflicting accounts which can all have an equal degree of truth akin to map projections of the earth" simply violates what he (Byrne) calls the "logic of truth," reducing cognitive appraisal to mere "terms of usefulness or clarity."[54] This criticism, however, seems quite inconclusive in light of its apparent failure to acknowledge an important turn in Hick's argument. Hick is clearly interested in epistemically relating his pragmatic assessment to claims about veridicality and truth: if, for example, a religious system proves to be soteriologically effective, then this, according to Hick, has some bearing on whether the system is veridical (i.e., whether its root religious experience is about something real and whether its basic vision actually corresponds to the way reality is structured). Such an interest indicates that Hick is inclined toward developing some sort of pragmatic epistemology in relation to the justification and assessment of religious belief and practice. And, if this is so, then Byrne cannot simply dismiss Hick's move here by asserting that it violates the "logic of truth" since it is precisely the nature of this truth that is at issue: is religious truth merely a matter of propositions that somehow correspond with reality (as Byrne seems to presuppose), or is it also a matter of personal being in relation to the ultimate (as Hick seems to propose)?

With the work of Corliss and Netland, the criticisms of the epistemic adequacy of Hick's position take a more sympathetic turn, for both appear to be fully aware of the cognitive intentions of Hick's theory, and, in the case of Corliss especially, there is considerable sensitivity to the way that Hick develops his justificatory position in light of the soteriological aim and structure of religions. This is not to suggest, however, that Hick's position somehow escapes unscathed. Quite the reverse, for Corliss expends considerable effort in trying the delineate the shortcomings of Hick's pragmatic approach to the justification of religious belief.

While he agrees with Hick that religions ought to be assessed in terms relating to their soteriological function, Corliss nevertheless sees Hick as having an overly narrow view of the criteria appropriate for assessing their fulfillment of this function—that is, pragmatic success in resolving individual unhappiness and advancing individual happiness.[55] According to Corliss, this perspective tends to discount the equally (if not more) important rational–moral appraisal of ends and ideals imbedded in traditions as well as their "spiritual hypotheticals" (complex combinations of moral–spiritual values and personal goods—for example, if one follows the Noble Eightfold Path, then he or she will resolve personal suffering and achieve Nirvana). From Corliss's perspective, religious views of life have validity to the extent that they embody or entail true or reasonable claims, and therefore the validity of such views is determined largely by the validity and reasonability of the value-claims and spiritual hypotheticals contained within them. This approach, suggests Corliss, permits a degree of agnosticism about the ultimate reality and yet permits the development of a rational faith filtered through a critique of moral–spiritual values and hypotheticals. By contrast, presumably, Hick's approach falls somewhat short of a "rational faith" precisely because, according to Corliss, it focuses only on some of the values pertinent to the soteriological process (i.e., those pertaining to personal happiness and fulfillment), while denying that others can also be assessed in a rational manner (moral–spiritual values, ideals, and hypotheticals).

The simple response to this critique of Hick's position is that it takes a rather limited view of what Hick intends to cover by the notion of pragmatic assessment or justification. From our reconstruction of Hick's arguments and proposals, it seems fairly clear that Hick includes rational–moral appraisal of values and ideals in what he intends by pragmatic assessment—how else to explain his criteria of moral authenticity and internal coherence as well as his concern with ideal ways of life and historical records of virtues and vices, in addition to soteriological efficacy of total religious systems? Furthermore, it seems fairly clear that what Hick means by soteriological efficacy includes a bit more than achievement of personal happiness or resolution of personal suffering since he appears to construe transformation of the self as a transition from egocentricity to Reality orientation involving respect and love for others. That is to say, Hick's notion of soteriological efficacy is properly conceived in large part as being moral and spiritual in nature, not narrowly hedonic and egoistic. Thus, I think that Hick can easily accommodate Corliss's criticism by simply arguing that it is another way to state his (Hick's) own understanding of pragmatic justification of religious belief and practice.

None of this quite addresses the deep epistemic issue raised by Byrne about Hick's view of knowledge and truth in religion. Though he fails to argue a counterposition against Hick's nascent pragmatic epistemology, Byrne's reaction does raise an important question about the adequacy of such an approach. Corliss, by contrast, while critical of what he (wrongly) perceives to be Hick's narrow concern with pragmatic success, nevertheless seems to accept without argument the adequacy of a (broadly) pragmatic approach to the nature of religious justification. So, despite the inconclusiveness of objections raised against Hick's pragmatic justification of his pluralist hypothesis, we still seem to be left with an important outstanding issue about the adequacy of his general underlying position on the epistemology of religious belief.

Nevertheless, I want now to contend that, despite appearances, Hick has in fact addressed this issue by developing a justificatory position resting on a two-tiered understanding of religious truth and a double-phased analysis of the epistemology of religious belief.[56] From Hick's point of view, religious truth is a complex epistemic category coordinating propositional truth with what he calls personalistic truth. Propositional truth refers to the correspondence between, on the one hand, a belief or claim purporting to describe reality (here including the Real) and, on the other, the reality itself. Personalistic truth refers to the "moral truthfulness of a person's life"—that is, the existential coherence between propositional beliefs and the sort of life and character developed in light of these beliefs.[57] For Hick, religious truth involves both propositional and personalistic truth such that the life a person leads coheres with beliefs or truth-claims that correspond to the way that reality is.

Now, corresponding to this analysis of religious truth and taking into account the arguments for tolerant agnosticism, Hick develops a two-phased epistemology of religious belief that undercuts any simple (strict) disjunction between a realist approach (Byrne) and a pragmatic approach (Corliss). On the one hand, he advances a notion of eschatological verification that not only sustains the cognitivity in principle of religious belief but also spells out (loosely, to be sure) a procedure for confirming in a conclusive way the propositional truth-claims associated with religious beliefs. On the other hand, he also advances a pragmatic justification for these beliefs inasmuch as they are associated with distinctive sorts of lives and self-development (oriented around human transformation), suggesting that beliefs thus justified are more likely than not to be in harmony with reality as it is. This latter point, of course, is hardly conclusive evidence for the propositional truth of religious beliefs; nonetheless, suggests Hick, pragmatic assessment (in the broad sense) of a set of religious beliefs may provide some indication—the best possible in this life—of their fuller correspondence with reality as it is. This, I believe, would be Hick's answer to both Byrne and Corliss: a proposal of two sorts of justificatory procedure—one for this life and a second for the afterlife—together with a wager about their correlation.[58]

## CONCLUSION

Hick's theory of religious pluralism is a sustained attempt to account for the diversity of religions by combining elements from two views of and approaches to religious belief and practice: a Wittgensteinian–grammatical view, on the one hand, and a more traditional propositional–realist view, on the other. In this hybrid account, the diverse religions are conceptualized as cultural–linguistic grammars or idioms for engaging in soteriologically oriented forms of religious life that ultimately refer to one radically transcendent reality. From first to last, the various phases of the development of

Hick's theory may be viewed as a grand attempt to mediate or synthesize these two views of religious belief. The methodological phase of the theory involves the adoption of precisely the two views in question, the revisionist conception of religions encapsulates a grammatical view of religions as cultural traditions, while the basic religious conviction incorporates the commitment to an ontologically real divine. The postulate phase puts those two philosophical commitments together by positing a radically transcendent ontological reality that can be encountered only indirectly through "grammatical" conceptual schemes or lenses. And the justification phase completes this integration by proposing a two-tiered epistemology of religious belief: a this-life pragmatic justification oriented to the authenticity of religious forms of life combined with an eschatological confirmability-in-principle of their implicit central truth-claims about the nature of reality. Thus does it seem that Hick's theory represents a deepening and extension of his initial philosophical presuppositions involving the simultaneous commitment to a grammatical view of religion as well as to an ontological realism about the meaning and reference of religious language.

It has been suggested by more than one philosopher that these two approaches to religious belief and to practice constitute rival epistemologies that show little, if any, common ground. Thus, it might be theorized that it would be difficult if not impossible to integrate them into one coherent theory or account. Stuart Brown, for example, in contrasting the views of a neo-Wittgensteinian theorist (Peter Winch) with the views of a traditional realist (Michael Durrant) has written of "the yawning gulf between the philosophical traditions from which Winch and Durrant write": "fundamentally different views about meaning . . . imply[ing] further differences in the kind of theology they think possible."[59] Suggests Brown, the grammatical view "seems to yield a radically anti-metaphysical conception of religion" (i.e., theology as regulative grammar), while the traditional view "sees the loss of a metaphysical element . . . as the loss of something essential to religion." In view of such differences in orientation and implication, it is not surprising that many scholars understand these approaches as constituting rival and incompatible theories of religion. Even Hick himself notes the strong contrast between the standard conception of religions as rival and competing sets of propositional beliefs and the revisionist conception that he himself prefers. Nonetheless, he means for his pluralist theory to integrate these two approaches since each has, from his point of view, a contribution to make to the development of an adequate and unified theory of religious diversity. The grammatical view permits Hick to emphasize the elements of cultural conditioning and contextualization in working out his understanding of religious epistemology, while the realist view permits him to nonetheless hold together these diverse contexts at the deeper ontological level.

In view of these different theoretical strands in Hick's account of religious pluralism, it is perhaps not so surprising that critics have been able to interpret his project in radically different ways—for example, as akin to a neo-Wittgensteinian noncognitivism (Griffiths and Lewis) and as akin to traditional cognitivism (Netland). It is also not surprising that they would focus their critical attention on issues of meaning and reference and epistemology since these identify crucial points in Hick's theory where the successes or failures of his integrative effort would be most evident. Despite the initial theoretical implausibility of putting together elements from two such different views of religious language and belief, I believe that the success or failure of Hick's integrative effort needs to be assessed in light of the actual arguments and counterarguments about the theory rather than simply in terms of what one might, in the abstract, consider to be theoretically feasible. And, I suggest, when we look at the actual arguments pro and con the crucial points of theoretical tension in Hick's account, we will find that Hick's views fare pretty well and are not in any obvious way either incoherent or implausible. Indeed, as I have suggested in my review of the critical concerns raised by Netland and Corliss, major challenges to Hick's integrative effort can either be rebutted or at least be shown to be quite inconclusive. Therefore, I think we need to conclude on the basis of our critical scrutiny of Hick and his critics that Hick's theory of religious pluralism constitutes one coherent and not implausible account of the diversity of the world's religious traditions.

## NOTES

*I want to express my gratitude to colleagues who read and commented on drafts of this essay: Wendell S. Dietrich (Brown University), Mark J. Franklin (Reed College), John P. Kenny (Reed College), and most especially John P. Reeder, Jr. (Brown University).

1. For example, John Hick "The Outcome: Dialogue into Truth," in *Truth and Dialogue in World Religions,* ed. John Hick (Philadelphia: Westminster, 1974), pp. 114–15, *God Has Many Names* (Philadelphia: Westminster, 1982), *Problems of Religious Pluralism* (New York: St. Martin's, 1985) (hereafter cited as *Problems*), *An Interpretation of Religion* (New Haven, Conn.: Yale University Press, 1989).

2. See Paul Griffiths and Delmas Lewis, "On Grading Religions, Seeking Truth, and Being Nice to People—A Reply to Professor Hick," *Religious Studies* **19** (1983): 75–80; Peter Byrne, "John Hick's Philosophy of World Religions," *Scottish Journal of Theology* **35** (1982): 289–301; George A. Netland, "Professor Hick on Religious Pluralism," *Religious Studies* **22** (1986): 249–61; Richard Corliss, "Redemption and the Divine Realities: A Study of Hick and an Alternative," *Religious Studies* **22** (1986): 235–48.

3. See Hick, *Problems,* Chapter 2.

4. See, e.g., Peter Winch, "Meaning and Religious Language," in *Reason and Religion,* ed. Stuart Brown (Ithaca, N.Y.: Cornell University Press, 1977), pp. 193–221.

5. See Hick, *Problems,* Chapters 3, 6, and 7.

6. *Ibid.*

7. *Ibid.,* Chapters 4, 5, and 6.

8. For this typology of theories of religion, see George Lindbeck, *The Nature of Doctrine* (Philadelphia: Westminster, 1984), Chapters 1 and 2.

9. See William James, *The Will to Believe and Other Essays in Popular Philosophy* (New York: Dover Library reprint, 1956), and *The Varieties of Religious Experience,* ed. John Smith (Cambridge, Mass.: Harvard University Press, 1985).

10. See Note 2.

11. See Hick, *Problems,* Chapter 3 (Note 1).

12. *Ibid.,* p. 29.

13. See the particularly trenchant comment by Griffiths and Lewis: "The goal at which religions direct their practitioners—tellingly described by Professor Hick as salvation/liberation (the use of "/" is usually a sign of a philosopher's rather uneasy attempt to combine two notions which really cannot be combined)—is single, universal, in all cases the same" (Griffith and Lewis, Note 2, p. 76).

14. Netland (Note 2), pp. 255–57.

15. See Wayne Proudfoot, *Religious Experience* (Berkeley and Los Angeles: University of California Press, 1985), Chapters 2 and 5.

16. Netland, p. 255.

17. *Ibid.*, p. 256.

18. See, e.g., Hick, *Problems*, Chapter 4.

19. *Ibid.*, pp. 102–3.

20. *Ibid.*, p. 106.

21. *Ibid.*, p. 103. Hick makes this point against Byrne's vigorous efforts to argue that Hick must deal more fully with the position of the rational skeptic, especially of the ilk of Feuerbach; see Byrne (Note 2), pp. 299–300. I agree wholeheartedly with Byrne on this score. Perhaps this is the place to remark on the great importance of Hick's basic religious conviction in preventing him from taking seriously the possibility of a completely projectionist account of religious diversity, i.e., the possibility that the conceptual schemes of cultural traditions might simply "constitute" the corresponding forms of religious experience entirely apart from any ultimate ontological reality. Though I do not discuss the issue in this article, I do believe that Hick needs to consider more fully and carefully the major alternatives to his theory of religious experience and thought purely as forms of projection and nothing more.

22. See, e.g., Richard Swinburne, *The Existence of God* (Oxford: Clarendon, 1979), Chapter 13; George I. Mavrodes, *Belief in God* (New York: Random House, 1970), Chapter 3; John Hick, "Mystical Experience as Cognition," reprinted in *Understanding Mysticism*, ed. Richard Woods (Garden City, N.J.: Doubleday, 1980), pp. 422–37 (see esp. pp. 433–36); Michael Goulder and John Hick, *Why Believe in God?* (London: SCM, 1983), Chapter 2. Swinburne is particularly persuasive on the principle of credulity and its proper formulation. There are problems pertinent to the application of this principle that Hick does not consider. For example, Proudfoot has recently suggested that the noetic component of religious experience embeds or encodes a hypothesis about the perceptual object of the experience also being its cause, and this suggestion, if true, "ups the ante" with regard to critical evaluation of the truth of this hypothesis as contrasted with other possible explanations of the experience (e.g., projectionist accounts); see Proudfoot, Chapter 5.

23. Hick, *Problems* (Note 1), p. 103.

24. Netland (Note 2), p. 257, Note 1.

25. Hick, *Problems*, p. 37.

26. See esp. *ibid.*, Chapter 3.

27. Corliss (Note 2), p. 247.

28. See esp. Hick, *Problems*, Chapter 2.

29. Hick's opening move in his analysis of religious experience is to suggest that Wittgenstein was right to affirm the primacy of religious experience and practice over conventional religious organization and doctrine. Thus, according to Hick, students of religion must understand and investigate religious experience within the context of religious forms of life (experiential–dispositional–behavioral–linguistic "packages" of first-order religious life and practice) rather than theological doctrines and formal religious regulations. Hick goes on to apply Wittgenstein's discussion of the interpretive nature of perception to the religious context, suggesting in rough outline that religious experience is best understood as being aware of situations-in-the-world in terms of background systems of religious concepts associated with particular traditions and being disposed both to see these situations as (e.g.) manifesting divine presence and to act accordingly. In effect, the thesis is that religious experience must be understood as being shaped conceptually by background social–linguistic–contextual religious conditioning and learning. All religious experience is properly understood as experiencing-as, in which the experiencer is conditioned by his or her background religious language games and forms of life. For further elaboration, see *ibid.*, Chapter 2.

30. *Ibid.*, Chapters 3, 6, and 7; quote is from p. 104.

31. *Ibid.*, p. 40.

32. *Ibid.*, p. 32.

33. Hick develops his complementarity analogy in response to some criticisms made by Almond; see Philip Almond, "John Hick's Copernican Theology," *Theology* **86** (1983): 36–41.

34. Netland (Note 2), pp. 258–61.

35. Hick, *Problems* (Note 1), pp. 98–99.

36. In contrast, this analogy may seem less convincing for the simple reason that light is directly experienced and then indirectly conceptualized, while the divine noumenon is never directly experienced but only indirectly conceptualized and known. So, in the case of light, we can be confident that the apparently contradictory properties inhere in one reality. In the case of the divine noumenon, however, we cannot have the same degree of confidence, for it seems possible that at least two (and perhaps more) Realities *an sich* might be involved; and if so, then it would be improper to speak of the personal and impersonal as different faces of one Real *an sich*.

37. There are a couple of history-of-religions type of criticisms that occur to me but which I do not feel competent to pursue. The first is this: Do all religious traditions really mean to refer to an ultimate ontological reality? Hick seems to claim this, but I wonder if it is true. Such a claim seems to fit best the theistic religions, but one wonders whether (e.g.) the goal-state of Nirvana is properly characterized as an ontologically ultimate Real *an sich*. To think of this transformed state of being—which looks past illusions, including those of a metaphysical variety—as an ontologically ultimate Real *an sich* seems to do some injustice to what Theravadin tradition (e.g.) is all about. And a recognition of the possible ill-fittingness between Hick's claim and some religious traditions suggests the possibility that his claim might well be theistically loaded and at best applicable only to those theistic traditions that are historically related (e.g., Judaism, Christianity, Islam). This suspicion of a theistic orientation or bias seems to gain some support from a second consideration: By what right does Hick claim an ultimate ontological unity rather than a plurality? This question presses the critical issue of why Hick prefers the claim of unity (oneness) when it seems that, logically speaking, it is possible to square religious diversity and equal veridicality by postulating a plurality of ontological ultimates, with each serving as the referent for a corresponding phenomenal religious system. Again, it seems possible that Hick's preference for an ontological unity might indicate a (mono)theistic loading.

38. Corliss (Note 2), pp. 245–46.

39. *Ibid.*, pp. 246–47.

40. See Hick, *Problems*, Chapters 3, 6, and 7.

41. *Ibid.*, Chapter 4.

42. *Ibid.*, p. 46.

43. *Ibid.*, p. 50.

44. In proposing this deconstructive account and introducing this note of skepticism about absolute claims, Hick seems perilously close to committing the genetic fallacy, i.e., the fallacy of thinking that a causal account of the genesis of a statement or belief settles the question as to its truth or falsity. Even if it were the case that a given absolute claim were to have arisen in the way Hick suggests, it seems to be another sort of question entirely as to whether the claim is true or false—the latter is an issue to be settled by an epistemic appraisal of the claim's presuppositions, the adequacy of evidence pertinent to its truth, the consistency of supporting arguments, etc. Hick seems to assume that his social–psychological account addresses these matters or somehow obviates the need to address them, but this is just not so. As it turns out, of course, Hick does offer a deeper and more extensive critique of the epistemology of religious beliefs; so there is no need to pursue this point any further.

45. See Hick, *Problems* (Note 1), Chapter 6.

46. *Ibid.*, pp. 93–94. Despite Hick's pessimism about our ability to find "conclusive" grounds for the acceptance or rejection of historical and metaphysical truth-claims, it is not clear that he is completely justified in his extreme pessimism. After all, some stable consensuses do seem to emerge on past historical events (e.g., about religious founders) and even on controversial metaphysical issues (e.g., the unlikelihood of a great chain of being). Thus, Hick's push toward an attitude of agnosticism may be somewhat premature. Nevertheless, I have to admit that it strikes me that Hick's attitude together with his subsequent pragmatism are steps in the right direction.

47. *Ibid.*, Chapter 8.

48. *Ibid.*, p. 125.

49. *Ibid.*, Chapter 5.

50. *Ibid.*, p. 74.

51. *Ibid.*, p. 81.

52. See Note 2.

53. Griffiths and Lewis (Note 2), pp. 78–79.

54. Byrne (Note 2), p. 296.

55. Corliss (Note 2), pp. 237–39, 248.

56. See esp. Hick, "The Outcome: Dialogue into Truth" (Note 1), pp. 140–55. For a helpful discussion and analysis of various views of religious truth, see Donald Wiebe, *Religion and Truth* (The Hague: Mouton, 1981), esp. Chapters 10–12. Wiebe refers briefly to Hick's view in connection with his (Wiebe's) critical appraisal of W. C. Smith's position (see pp. 213–14). See also Lindbeck's illuminating, "Excursus on Religion and Truth" in his *The Nature of Doctrine* (Note 8), pp. 63–69.

57. Hick, "The Outcome: Dialogue into Truth," p. 144.

58. My colleague Jock Reeder has suggested to me that Hick's epistemology may be fruitfully characterized as attempting to combine a pragmatist theory of the justification of religious belief with a correspondence theory of religious truth. Reeder goes on to ask whether Hick is a coherentist and pragmatist in this life while being a covert foundationalist in the next, or whether he is a thoroughgoing pragmatist in both this life and the next. The textual evidence bearing on this question is somewhat ambiguous, though I believe finally that Hick means to plumb for a thoroughgoing pragmatist epistemology. On the one hand, in developing his notion of eschatological verification, Hick speaks explicitly of the gradual and holistic confirmation of a reli-

gious (e.g., theistic) interpretation of the process of the universe, thereby suggesting a broadly coherentist and pragmatist account of such confirmation: "What we are seeking to verify is the truth of the theistic interpretation of the process of the universe. . . . Thus an eschatological situation which is to verify the truth of the theistic interpretation of the universe . . . will . . . have . . . the more limited task of confirming to the full that the history of the universe has led to an end-state in which the postulated divine purpose for humanity can be seen to be fulfilled" (Hick, *Problems,* Note 1, pp. 115–17). On the other hand, Hick also speaks occasionally of a maximal God-consciousness in the afterlife and of "living in continuous awareness of the divine presence" (*ibid.,* p. 117)—phrases that suggest shades of a more direct, experiential, and perhaps foundationalist understanding of the confirmation of religious belief. On balance, however, Hick appears to advance a coherentist and pragmatist interpretation of eschatological verification, for, from his point of view, this confirmation involves principally the "progressive awareness of humanity perfected" (*ibid.,* p. 119), and this understanding of confirmation appears to be an extension into the afterlife of Hick's earlier position: "an understanding of religious dogma and doctrines as not, for the most part, straightforward assertions of fact but as complex mixtures of the mythical, the symbolic, the philosophical, and the empirical. They are, therefore . . . to be judged . . . by the extent to which, as conceptual systems, they provide a framework within which the transformation of human existence from self-centredness to reality-centredness can take place" (*ibid.,* p. 207). For an illuminating discussion of recent changes in Hick's position on eschatological verification, see Myra B. Mackie, "Concerning 'Eschatological Verification Reconsidered,'" *Religious Studies* **23** (1987): 129–35.

59. Stuart Brown, "Religion and the Limits of Language," in his *Reason and Religion* (Note 4), pp. 233–55; the quotes in this paragraph are from pp. 240–41.

CHAPTER 5

# A Contemplation of Absolutes

NINIAN SMART

John Hick's well-known doctrine of the Real and its phenomenal manifestations invites us to consider differing ways of conceiving the distinction. More especially, we are drawn to think through the problems posed by the style of language we use for the Real. For, in using Kantian or quasi-Kantian vocabulary (for instance, John Hick refers to the Real *an sich*), we are inevitably left exposed to some of the classical critiques of the *ding an sich.* By contemplating these we may stimulate some further thoughts about the ultimate referent or referents of religious language.

It was always, of course, a problem of whether we are right to think of the Real as singular. Again, there is the issue of ontology: should we be thinking at all of some kind of substantive Real? Or would it be better to think of process or energy or some dynamic notion to characterise the ultimate? And again, should not the ultimate be a mere placeholder, with no lineaments at all, but just providing the space, so to speak, to lodge whatever each religious tradition takes as ultimate? Though these are abstract-sounding questions, they have some practical meaning.

For if we take the Real *an sich* to be a substantive entity for which the various religions have differing names, then the moral might be that it does not in the long run matter which faith you adopt, though there might be relatively minor disputes as to which set of values you practically espouse: religions might be critical of each others' practical behaviour up to a point, but beyond this there would be little point in disputation. Most missionary activity could be phased out, with profit, since people would not be misled into thinking that their own Real was not the same as that of others. Undoubtedly such a conclusion would be irenic, and part of the intention of perennial philosophers, including John Hick, is undoubtedly peaceful and ecumenical.

I wish to argue in the first place that a Buddhist notion of an Empty or completely open "Absolute" may be what is called for. I shall then proceed from there to comment on the variety of shapes of the ultimate.

The first point to note is that a main problem of the language of "the Real" is that it inevitably suggests that there is a single something which lies in back of all the phenomenal deities and so forth, from Śiva to Christ and from the Tao to Brahman, projected by the varied traditions upon it. All these phenomenal deities and the like are so many representations of the one Real. But if we are to continue using Kantian language, then it follows that we should not be using either the singular or the plural of that which is noumenal.

But it may be responded that it is natural to think of the Real as singular because the phenomenal ultimates are singular. That is to say, Judaism looks to one God, and Śaivism does too, and there is but one Tao and one Brahman in their respective traditions. It becomes easy to think that somehow Śaivites and Jews are worshipping the same God, and behind that the same Real. Well, it may indeed be that many great religions have a single Focus. But it does not follow that the various Foci refer behind themselves to One Reality. We might put this point in a different way by saying that the abstractness of the idea of the noumenon means that we can infer no resemblance between what lies behind and what is phenomenal. Or we might otherwise say that if the ultimate Focus is plural (perhaps the Trinity is plural or maybe we should think of some plural emanationist theology such as that of Neoplatonism), then, insofar as it refers behind, it refers to a plural entity, and if it is singular, then the Real is singular. But strictly the Real should be neither singular nor plural, since it lies in an inaccessible realm beyond numbers. It is ineluctably beyond space and time, the framework for applying numbers.

But what about those notions that there is an aspect of the divine known as *nirguṇam* Brahman? Is not this somehow affirming the existence of a Real? But John Hick is clear about this, and I here note from his article in the *Encyclopedia of Religion:*

> At this point . . . one might object that in Hindu and Buddhist thought *brahman* and *nirvāṇa* and *śūnyatā* are not forms under which the Real is humanly known but are the Real itself, directly experienced in a unitive awareness in which the distinction between knower and known has been overcome. The gods may be forms in which the Real appears to particular human groups; but *brahman,* or *śūnyatā,* is reality itself directly apprehended. Nevertheless, this claim is called into question by the plurality of experienced absolutes with their differing characters—for the *brahman* of Advaita Vedanta is markedly different from the *nirvāṇa* of Theravada Buddhism and from the *śūnyatā* of the Mahāyāna, and this very variety suggests a human contribution to these forms of mystical experience. . . .[1]

So it is clear that the absolutes, however clothed in the negative way, are themselves phenomenal Foci of aspiration. It is muddled to think of them as directly being the Real. They are still conceptualised and experienced as phenomenal, albeit at a very high and interior level of phenomena. The fact that the subject–object distinction does not typically apply to this kind of non-dual experience in no way detracts from its experiential character. We may note in passing that usually the negative path is prominent in those phases of religion which emphasise the interior, mystical experience (rather than prophetic visions and devotional encounters with the personal Other, i.e., the world of what Otto calls the numinous).

It would seem, then, that the Real is neither one nor many. It can by the same token be questioned as to whether it is Real, as we have already indicated. That is, why should we take it as being a sort of substance? Some writers, such as Tillich, have perhaps brought out the point that it is not exactly a thing, because it is not in space and time or space–time, by using the phrase "being itself." But even *being* as a notion contains something like the ghost of thingness. We could use the concept *becoming,* for instance, which is equally empty, but does not suggest substantiality. Or we might turn to such alternatives as *process* or *energy.* Why not?

Indeed, there are philosophical thoughts which might turn one away from being. They are various. First, some religious philosophies are not substance-bound, such as Theravāda Buddhism, which does not make out that *nibbāna* is some kind of thing. Second, there are forms of cosmology which are hooked to the notion of events or processes rather than substances, such as Whitehead's metaphysics. Since these event-philosophies can be used to express religious ideas, they postulate non-substantial religious absolutes. Third, there are languages such as Chinese where the difference, at least in classical forms, between substances and processes is fluid. In such languages the sky skies and the tree trees.

So far we conclude that the ultimate is neither singular nor plural and is neither being nor becoming. That is, it is unwise, not to say contradictory, to look on the ultimate as belonging to categories that essentially belong to the world of phenomena. This, of course, poses a problem in relation to the categories used in a religion. For instance, in the Christian tradition, however much it might be affirmed that God is not to be described as this or that, She or He is worshipped as being personal. It is hard or impossible in the last resort to think of God, in that tradition, as non-personal. And so we assume that the properties of the Focus are projected back upon the entity or whatever lying behind. Still, let us pursue the path to that noumenal ultimate which is neither being nor becoming and neither singular nor plural; does this not remind us of Emptiness or *śūnyatā* in the Mahāyāna tradition?

There would be interesting consequences of identifying the noumenal with Emptiness. It would be easy enough, no doubt, to generate a Nāgārjuna-like dialectic which would show that the noumenal is the Empty, or the Open.[2] The argument would go as follows. First, the non-cosmic, not belonging to space–time where entities are identifiable and re-identifiable,[3] is such that it is transcendentally oblivious to numbers and counting. It is, of course, not difficult to conceive the uncountable: for instance, it does not make sense to say that love is one or many, or at least not serious sense. It is true, of course, that there are many lovers and many acts of love: but love is something observable in the world which yet is neither many things nor one thing. It is an aspect of life, I guess, but this hardly means that it is one thing.

Moreover, the notion of being or becoming as lying "behind" what is presented phenomenally in human experience relies on a metaphor, that of "behind" (or "beneath" or "beyond," etc.). Figuratively it is visualised by us perhaps as lying on the far side of a screen of phenomena. Such a metaphor or analogy happens to be quite common in religion. It is part of the meaning of transcendence which, after all, is simply a latinised extension of the idea of being *beyond* as in *trans.* It is an intelligible notion, but it is not a literal one. Obviously what lies beyond the cosmos, as a Real or *ding an sich,* cannot be literally on the other side of the phenomenal, since the latter is embedded in space–time, and so the conception of what lies on the other side of space has to be a metaphor. "To be on the other side of" means to be in a part of space different from that of which it is on the other side. To be in a different area of space from space makes no literal sense. Consequently the Real or *ding an sich* is only metaphorically beyond or behind what is phenomenal.

So what does the idea amount to that the Focus of worship or mystical experience, or whatever—that is, the presentation of the ultimate in human thought and experience—refers back to the Real behind? Is there some lingering notion left over from Kant's things in themselves that they somehow give rise to phenomena? This, however, does not make sense. Or at least it does not from a strictly Kantian perspective. Causation applies to phenomena: it does not apply to what lies beyond phenomena. So noumena cannot give rise to anything. They are a feeble set of anchors thrown out in order to suggest that phenomena really have something to do with what lies "out there." But, strictly speaking, and to extend Gertrude Stein, there is no "out there out there."

We would conclude here that if there is going to be room for some ghostly space beyond space into which we project the Foci of religion, that space is best described as Emptiness. This bypasses concepts both of Reality and of Process.

Such a noumenon does not do much, however, towards the thesis that all the representations of the Divine point to the same Real. It leaves that thesis on one side. If you want to hold, after all, that all gods are the same (to speak roughly), then that is your Focus. It is in no way guaranteed by the concept of a space beyond. Emptiness can neither guarantee sameness nor difference, for the simple reason that it is neither singular nor plural. If you want to align yourself with *smārta* thought in India, with Aldous Huxley, with Swami Vivekananda, or with John Hick, then you have to devise a phenomenal representation of the Divine which affirms this. This is not at all a bad thing to do, and I almost believe it myself (though I draw back because of *nirvāṇa*), nor do I wish here to be critical of that thesis. It has great plausibility, though probably for epistemological rather than ontological reasons. Its plausibility stems from the fact that you cannot deduce the falsity of one tradition or the non-existence of one Focus simply from the standpoint of another tradition or Focus. On the other hand, the criteria of truth as between religions are soft, to put it no more strongly. Let us put it in a sharper form. Either traditions are hermetically sealed from one another, in which case none can judge any other, and all are relative; or we can rise above traditions as human beings and excogitate criteria for judging different traditions. But, in the latter case, there can be no doubt that the criteria or tests are soft ones. We might judge traditions by fruits, but that is a pretty squashy criterion. Or by religious experience: but here too we have no sharpness. Or by metaphysics, but, notoriously, metaphysical judgements differ and allegedly logical arguments move in different directions. And so either we can make no judgements or, if we can, they are soft ones. Now in the light of these epistemological observations, which amount to saying that no point of view or worldview can be proved, it is not implausible to fuse the great traditions together and to see them as so many fingers pointing at the same moon. But even this thesis cannot be proved, and we must have some sympathy for those who, frightened by softness, involve themselves in particularist backlashes. But we cannot preempt discussion by our philosophical apparatus. If we affirm a single Real, we have already taken a step inside the cosmos: we have stepped into the Perennial Philosophy thesis. This may well be the truth.

Another thought, however, is a rather differing one, namely, the notion that all Foci point to Emptiness, which implies nothing. It is true that this would seem to favour the Focus of that form of Mahāyāna which argues for Emptiness. This is not so: for in an important way the question of the Focus remains. If it is meant to be real Emptiness—that is to say, a kind of conscious blankness as manifested in the higher states of meditation and in the philosophy of Emptiness—then it has no more nor less connection with the transcendental Emptiness than does any other Focus. If the Beyond is, so to say, a blank, then it has no connections at all with anything, however minimally, characterised as lying on the hither side. A blank noumenon represents no phenomenon and is just there, in effect, as a placeholder.

All this, of course, bypasses the argument that we are and should be experiencing a Copernican revolution. It seems less epicyclical to postulate a Real to which all religions point than to wrestle with problems of Christian or Buddhist interpretations of all other religious traditions. I am not here wishing to confront this argument directly. But there is another way of looking at traditions.

This is to hold that the differing traditions point at a placeholder. That is, we can talk of the ultimate as lying beyond them, but that placeholder is a space for alternatives, not the point at which differing paths meet (though it might *per accidens* be that). In other words, the differing religions may overlap somewhat but really have differing, and no doubt complementary, messages. We do not need to suppose that God is really *nirvāṇa* or that the Tao is *brahman.* Such equations can, of course, be argued for and could be true. But the Focus of Theravāda Buddhism remains very remarkably different from that of the Hebrew Bible. It is not so easy to see them both pointing to the same Real: and even if they do, many of the divergences stay in place. Maybe it is better to think of the various religions as overlapping, and yet being different, and often complementary. Complementarity is probably a better model than that of unity. In the long run, perhaps, not too much difference is generated by the alternative models. The desirable effect of the idea of unity is that different traditions should honour one another and cooperate. On the other hand, the desirable effect of the complementarity model is that differing traditions should not merely honour one another but also provide friendly criticism and advice. Complementary religions can instruct one another and render critiques in a positive and caring manner. So it may turn out that the fruits of the models will resemble one another quite a lot.

Complementarity suggests the possibility, but by no means the certainty, of convergence. Since nothing about world-views and value systems can ever be sure, there can be no way of answering the question as to whether there will be a single world religion or ideology. I doubt it, for several reasons. First, every merger produces a backlash, and every friendship an enmity. So where two religions begin to merge, there are backlashes in both traditions, reacting against what can be seen as a weakening of each tradition. Second, the rather radical distinctions between some theistic traditions and non-theistic faiths, notably Theravāda Buddhism, seems to be unbridgeable. Thus, Theravāda Buddhism believes essentially in no Creator, while Islam and Christianity have faith in a Creator. The Theravāda believes in rebirth or reincarnation; most of Christianity and Judaism do not. And so on. Third, the progress of science and human creativity involves diversity. The critical mind is vital. The human race therefore has a vested interest in pluralism, and so world-views should be somewhat encouraged to differ (no doubt in a friendly way: courtesy is often the oil which lubricates mutual criticism).

Paradoxically, however, there is a feature of Hick's Kantianism which may point in the opposite direction and reinforce his general position. In invoking the categorical structure of the human mind as having input into knowledge as the mind filters the phenomena, he is, in the case of religions, postulating something much weaker than the *a priori*. After all, it is the traditions which mould the minds which experience the Absolute. In the quotation I cited above he obviously thinks of contingent traditions, such as the Theravāda or Advaita Vedānta, as providing the structures which people bring to their meditation. It is because of them that mysticism appears different. I am, of course, highly sympathetic with this account ("of course," because the major conflicts between differing writers on mysticism concern, after all, the question of how many types there are—few go to the extreme of supposing that there are radically different and separately contextualised mysticisms wherever you look—in short radically different forms to the same number as individuals engaged in mystical practices. Such extreme particularism becomes self-defeating since it precludes cross-cultural studies and cross-cultural uses of language).

Now the differing traditions, while they soak into the minds and hearts and social structures of the people and realms over which they hold sway, are contingent. A Chinese does not have to remain Chinese. It is true that once we have been raised in one tradition we may be so heavily influenced by it that we can never fight our way out of it. But it is not an iron paper bag: we can in fact in some degree struggle out of our cultures. Many people come to have two or more cultural milieus. So even if I may think like a Britisher and a Scot in particular, this does not prevent me thinking somewhat like an American, since I have lived much of my life in the United States. I have also been much influenced by the fact that I have an Italian wife, and have been involved a lot in Sri Lankan and Indian cultures. So I am now a bit of a cultural mishmash. I regard that as a good thing, as it happens. But it is clear that the filters through which I experience the world have altered. So it is not as if I possess a fixed *a priori*. Now as traditions influence one another so they may come to converge and generate a more unified view of the ultimate. In other words, because the concepts which different folk bring to bear in interpreting their experience are contingent or accidental, they can influence one another. In this way the ground may be prepared for a Perennial Philosophy. It could be, despite the arguments which I used above in the opposite direction, that the developing world civilisation will tend to generate a Perennial Philosophy which is not unlike Hick's. Though this unity might breed boring agreement, it would not in itself be at all disagreeable, for the main trouble in the past has been senseless hostilities between differing traditions.

There might, of course, be aspects of the traditions whose shape is not contingent. For instance, the divergence between the mystical path, culminating in the non-dual experience which abolishes the duality between subject and object, and the numinous encounter with the Other, is something entrenched in religions. There are, in addition, other major forms of religious experience, such as the panenhenic. These three begin to account for Theravāda Buddhism (which emphasises the mystical strand), prophetic Judaism (emphasising the numinous), and early Taoism (emphasising the panenhenic)—and so forth. This is admittedly a crude way of characterising differences, but is not without truth. We could look to deeper structures of religion than the brute particularity of the traditions. So there could be a way of looking at religious patterns which underlies traditionalism. Even so, what we would be revealing by such a phenomenological analysis is patterns of religiosity, and it is a further step to try to establish that these are *a priori*. In brief, the notion advanced by John Hick, quite correctly, that experience is affected and channelled by traditional expectations and background differs from the classical Kantian view. It harbours contingency of traditions. As critical beings we can surely suppose that traditions are neither immutable nor unchallengeable. There is possibly what may be called a "traditionalist positivism" in his position. This would not be unnatural, since all of us in the field of the study of religion tend to be emerging from a period of (Christian) theological excessivism and so want to accentuate what is positive in "other" faiths. But even so we should not forget the critical mode. From the standpoint of criticism, the positivist mode of emphasising the actual traditions in filtering experience needs to be sceptically considered. In brief, we do not need to accept any one traditional view of the ultimate. And this already means that our schematism is not truly Kantianism. We might dub it "contingent Kantianism." This is, of course, different from the classical notion that certain categories are built into our minds and we filter phenomena through such categories. In short, the way we filter religious experience and so on is culturally contingent.

All this means that we are a long way from Kant. Does this matter? In one way it does not. He was a great philosopher, but he is long dead. Who do these dead men think they are? The upshot is that we cannot pretend that there is anything necessary in the way we interpret religious experience. Given such a critical attitude to religious experience, then we are embarked on a much more broadly based set of criticisms of religious traditions. We are now in a different age, and we have started to live without authority. "We" are, of course, those who live in a relatively open society, such as the United States, the United Kingdom, India, and Germany. In the open society we, as individuals, make our choices, as individuals.

It seems inevitable to conclude that we are entering upon an age of eclecticism. This is increasingly true of the democracies of America and Europe, not to mention Australasia and even India. I say "even India" to exhibit the fact that that great democracy is subject to some of the same forces that operate elsewhere. In short, individualism is spreading. Of course, it encourages individuals to make significant choices in religion (as elsewhere). It is not unnatural that this situation should breed not just individualism, but eclecticism too. This increases the pluralism of modern societies. But so what? How does all this affect the argument about Hick?

It affects it because we can no longer make any assumptions about the stability of traditions. With a certain strength in the continuity of older religions we might suppose that there is less contingency in the way we approach experiences. That is, we might think somehow that there are deep patterns underlying the way we come to see our absolute. But individualism amplifies the contingency of traditions. Eclecticism fragments and dissolves rigid traditions from the ages which we look back to. As traditions crumble, we are more prone to pick and choose. Even where a tradition still retains its appeal, its pattern can be changed and its rigidities can be sapped. Thus, while about 50 per cent or a little under of North Italians are Catholic in behaviour, there is about the lowest birthrate in the world. The people are relatively loyal to the tradition, but they thumb their noses at papal teaching about birth control. They are vigorously displaying an eclectic attitude. Now if all this is so—and if this kind of shift of loyalty be realistic—then it follows that holistic traditions are not as vital as we once may have thought. And all this saps the foundations of what we have taken to be traditions. Those traditions are continuously weakened. Whether this be a good or a bad thing is a question I leave on one side. But we are undoubtedly witnessing great changes in the West concerning world-views. We do not need to suppose that they are much more, in democratic societies, than lobbies and associations, and they are sustained by the loyalty of those who support the activities of church leadership.

In brief, the notion that there are deep categories underlying the church and Saṅgha, etc., traditions which help to inform and shape our experience, is one which needs to be questioned. Traditions crumble and soften, and we are seeing it happen in front of our eyes as we swivel them across the world. That gaze, sweeping across cultural frontiers, takes in changes across the spiritual horizon. There are no longer genuine fixed points and horizons. Nor are there Crosses and Bodhi Trees and sacred shrines we can easily cling to, as if there were sure means of salvation in today's world or even in yesterday's world, seeing that our world-views are so diverse and uncertain.

So what are we to conclude from all the foregoing arguments? First, it may not be necessary to postulate a single Real as though there is a single point towards which the various Foci of the world's religions are supposed to point. As we have argued, there are problems about the noumenal. There is not a single Beyond, nor yet a plural Beyond, for number does not apply outside space–time. This makes the model of Buddhist Emptiness attractive. But it does not mean that Emptiness becomes our absolute. Second, we have noted that the *via negativa* typically arises in connection with the mystical path. Such negative language does not mean that we somehow through it reach beyond experience. Rather it is that minimalist description of experience is registered. The mystic's experience, even if it may be non-dual, that is, with no subject–object duality, is still phenomenal. Third, we do not at all resolve the problem of the diversity of Foci by postulating a single Real. One cannot establish the identity of Focus A and Focus B on the basis of their both referring to a single Real: rather the claim that they both refer to the same Real is another way of affirming the identity, which has to be argued on other grounds.

The plausibility of the affirmation of a single Real is high in general, but problematic in particular. For instance, the fact that the Theravāda does not have a substantive Absolute is a stumbling-block in the theory of transcendental unity; but yet the idea is attractive to those who have generous views about other traditions.

There is another way of affirming unity, however, which may not have the problems associated with the notion of a single Real. This is the eschatological way. That is, we notice that differing traditions have evolved quite a lot over time. However much a latter-day liberal Protestant may wish to think that his or her world-view is firmly rooted in that of the New Testament, it is plain that considerable changes have occurred between then and now. For one thing, the major features of our world were absent from the New Testament era. Let me list a few: the industrial revolution and its aftermath; capitalism; modern democracy; birth control; modern psychology and psychotherapy; the global world-order; the abolition of slavery; the feminist revolution; and electronic systems of communication. All these features of our life have large and subtle effects upon faith. Given, then, that of necessity traditions have changed, why should they not continue to be transformed? It is conceivable, therefore, that the great traditions, today in contradiction, may evolve patterns which converge. And so while a single Real here and now may not be easy to establish, we might look towards a future Real. The Empty is also open, as we have remarked earlier.

An advantage of this future convergence theory is that it lets us regard the present traditions as being complementary to one another. They can teach each other lessons. Thus a Christian might wish to hold that the Spirit works in all cultures, and the rivalry of religions is designed by the Divine to keep them honest so far as possible. Universal agreement often breeds corruption, since it certainly engenders complacency. This theory of the complementary roles of religions makes it important, by the way, for education to include learning about the various important spiritual cultures of the world, since they can help to correct one another and at the same time enrich one another. At the same time the theory suggests that we should all take a self-critical stance towards our own traditions. Looking backward in a rigid manner and failing to recognise the transformation of the past are undesirable attitudes. Still, the fluidity of our situation in world society, with its many challenges to traditions, is bound to multiply backlashes against the open and irenic outlooks I am here advocating, and which follow too from John Hick's position. So we would be very foolish to expect agreement. Still, a world-view of world-views which looks to a future convergence will probably become more and more influential as the globe reflects upon its close texture, made dense by instantaneous communications and rapid travel.

## NOTES

1. John Hick, "Religious Pluralism," in Mircea Eliade (ed.), *The Encyclopedia of Religion* (New York: Macmillan, 1988), Vol. 12, pp. 332–33.

2. Nancy McCagney, *Nagarjuna Then and Now* (Santa Barbara: University of California doctoral dissertation, 1991).

3. Peter F. Strawson, *Individuals: An Essay in Descriptive Metaphysics* (London: Methuen, 1959).

CHAPTER 6

# Truth and the Diversity of Religions

KEITH WARD

I will be concerned with only one problem about truth which is raised by the diversity of religions which exist in the world. The problem is this: many religions claim to state truths about the nature of the universe and human destiny which are important or even necessary for human salvation and ultimate well-being. Many of these truths seem to be incompatible; yet there is no agreed method for deciding which are to be accepted; and equally intelligent, informed, virtuous and holy people belong to different faiths. It seems, therefore, that a believing member of any one tradition is compelled to regard all other traditions as holding false beliefs and therefore as not leading to salvation. Since each faith forms a minority of the world's population, all religious believers thus seem committed to saying that most intelligent, virtuous and spiritually devoted people cannot know the truth or attain salvation. This is a problem, because it is in tension with the belief, held by many traditions, that the supremely real being is concerned for the salvation of all rational creatures. How can this be so if, through no fault of their own, most creatures cannot come to know the truth and thereby attain salvation?

Among those who have seen this as a problem and have proposed a philosophical defence of one solution to it, John Hick must take a foremost place. His book, *An Interpretation of Religion* (London, 1989), is a statement of the position which has come to be known as religious pluralism. This major work, filled with illuminating discussions of the phenomena of religious belief and with fresh and lucid insights, is meant to be, not the end of the debate, but an opening up of discussion which might clarify the problem and its solutions further, and might establish a coherent framework for developing inter-faith dialogue and for a credible religious faith held in full awareness of and with full respect for the beliefs of others. My aim is to contribute to this discussion; and I shall do it by using the time-honoured philosophical technique of niggling and irritating criticism of various theses Hick presents. My argument will be that Hick's position is philosophically unacceptable as

From Keith Ward, "Truth and the Diversity of Religions," *Religious Studies* **26,** 1 (March 1990): 1–18. 

it stands, though it would be unwise simply to reject it wholesale; and I hope that my attack, such as it is, will be taken as a tribute to the force of the issues Hick places before us.

The pluralistic hypothesis is that religions provide different valid but culturally conditioned responses to a transcendent reality, and offer ways of transcending self and achieving a limitlessly better state centred on that reality. Thus no one tradition possesses a set of absolute and exclusive truths, while all others are delusory and ineffective for salvation. All will, or at least can be, saved by adhering to their own traditions, which purvey differing, but authentic, responses to the ultimately real. All can know the truth and attain salvation in their own traditions; so believers no longer have to condemn all others as mistaken, and no longer have to wonder why their God leaves the majority of creatures in mortal error. Here is an elegant and morally attractive solution of the problem of error in religion; and it is one that has great appeal for those who are reluctant to say that they alone are right and everyone else is wrong.

Nevertheless the hypothesis is riddled with difficulties; and the most obvious one can be put very forthrightly. To believe a proposition is to think that it is true. To think that it is true is to affirm that reality is as it is described by that proposition. Insofar as our affirmations are fallible, it is always possible that reality is not as some proposition asserts it to be. Thus an affirmation by its nature excludes some possible state of affairs; namely, one which would render the proposition false. If an assertion excludes nothing, it affirms nothing. In that sense, all truth-claims are necessarily exclusive.

It immediately follows that, where any truth-claim is made, it is logically possible to make another truth-claim which the first claim excludes. It is logically impossible for all possible truth-claims to be compatible. So it is possible for religious traditions to contain incompatible truth-claims, claims which exclude one another. Since this is a matter of logical possibility, it is a necessary truth that not all possible religious traditions can be equally true, authentic or valid. One can easily construct traditions which are strictly incompatible and of them, at least, pluralism must be false. That is, they will not consist of equally valid concepts of ultimate reality. One does not even need to invent such traditions, since, for example, Satanism and Christianity are fundamentally opposed both morally and factually.

But if this version of pluralism, which we might call "extreme pluralism," is incoherent, it might nevertheless be the case that many religious traditions, and maybe all the major ones that exist on our planet, do not contain mutually exclusive beliefs, but are equally valid paths of salvation and of authentic experience of the Real. This is "hard pluralism"; and it is a contingent hypothesis; whether or not it is true will be a matter for careful investigation. But it certainly looks as though many claims exclude one another. The Buddhist assertion that there is no creator god excludes the Christian assertion that there is one all-perfect creator. The Muslim assertion that Allah has no son excludes the Christian assertion that God has an only-begotten Son. What is the pluralist to do about these *prima facie* incompatible claims?

Hick's strategy is to retreat from discussing particular religious beliefs and to talk instead of "religion"; to retreat from discussing specific truth-claims and to talk instead of "religious traditions." This may seem innocuous, but it can be, and turns out to be, very misleading. It is well-known that definitions of religion are hard to find; and Hick proposes that we regard "religion" as a family-resemblance concept, so that there is no essential core definition. Yet he is concerned with only one sort of religion or one feature of religious beliefs. He characterizes the central strand of religion with which he is chiefly concerned as "awareness of and response to a reality that transcends ourselves and our world."[1] Fairly rapidly, he nominalizes the verb "transcends," and speaks of "belief in the transcendent," saying that "most forms of religion have affirmed a salvific reality that transcends human beings and the world" (6). What he is doing is to pick out one class of religious beliefs, or one set of religious phenomena which can be defined in terms of belief in a transcendent salvific reality. There is nothing wrong with that; but it should be noted that it picks out one area of agreement in truth-claims by definition. Faiths which lack that central belief are not going to be counted; conversely, faiths which are counted are assured of a minimal degree of agreement to begin with. They will all agree on something, so they will not be incompatible in all respects. But, so far, this is not really pluralism (the acceptance of very different beliefs as equally valid); it is exclusivism at a relatively abstract and general level (those are excluded who do not believe in one transcendent salvific reality). It is also an acceptance of some truth-claim—the claim that there is such a reality which can bring creatures to a limitlessly good state—as "absolute," or true for everyone, regardless of their point of view or cultural situation.

Even when this area of agreement has been defined, however, there remain many incompatible truth-claims, which notoriously divide religions from each other. Hick's strategy now is to direct our focus of attention away from such particular truth-claims, which he regards as unsettlable and therefore (we shall have to look again at this "therefore") not necessary for salvation; and to look instead at the "religious traditions" as totalities "which mediate the Real" and within which the "salvific process occurs" (370). The point about a "religious tradition" is that it is not just a collection of truth-claims. Ninian Smart's well-known six-dimensional analysis of religion emphasizes that considerations of truth and falsity concern only one dimension of a much more complex social phenomenon, which includes stories, law codes, social and personal ethical recommendations, ritual practices and techniques of mental training. My own pastoral experience suggests that issues of truth do not loom very large in the life of the average believer, and that one may participate in a tradition for many reasons, including the sort of social relations one finds in it, varieties of aesthetic satisfaction it provides, and the moral and psychological support it provides in times of crisis. Anthropologists and sociologists can provide illuminating accounts of religion and reasons for religious belief without ever raising the issue of truth. Moreover, identical religious assertions can be interpreted in many ways, as conversation with any two Anglican priests soon shows. Thus if one asks the question, "Can people find resources to help them love others and find meaning in life more or less equally in many traditions?," the answer is obviously going to be affirmative.

Viewed as social phenomena, religious traditions are forms of life which are culturally and ethnically differentiated. Since they contain many possibilities of diverse interpretation, and many dimensions of significance, it becomes apparent that a person will usually belong to such a tradition by birth, and can find within it many resources of meaning and moral teaching. As it seems absurd to say that one culture is "true" and all others "false," so the use of the expression "religious tradition" subtly leads one to say that one cannot compare such traditions for truth; and that therefore one is not to be preferred to the others, except as an expression of cultural imperialism.

It is indeed odd to speak of a whole religious tradition as being true or false, especially when one remembers that people as diverse as Quakers and Tridentine Catholics presumably exist within "the Christian tradition." Yet in the end the traditions that exist in the world today go back to particular individuals, known or unknown, who did propound particular beliefs. The "great traditions" are Scriptural traditions; and the scriptures contain, among many other things, teachings about the nature of reality and the way to salvation. There are particular truth-claims; and even though they can be interpreted variously, one can isolate a particular interpretation and ask of it whether it is true or false. Though the ascension of Jesus into heaven can be interpreted variously, one can ask whether it is true that he physically rose in the air; and there is a correct and precise answer to the question, however hard it is for us to know that answer.

Having isolated traditions which might plausibly be said to believe in one transcendent salvific reality, the hard pluralist then stresses the cultural totality and complexity of such traditions, and suggests that "we always perceive the transcendent through the lens of a particular religious culture" (8). Since whole cultures cannot reasonably be compared for truth and falsity, recognition of this fact should lead each tradition to "de-emphasise its own absolute and exclusive claim" (3), and accept that it is one among many ways to knowledge of and union with the transcendent. The correct response to this claim is to refrain from speaking of religio-cultural traditions, with all the problems of boundary-definition that brings with it, and to insist on focusing on particular truth-claims, and on particular interpretations of them, which can be properly assessed for truth and falsity. Then the question is not whether all traditions constitute different responses to the transcendent, which covers so many possibilities that it is almost bound to be true in some sense, but whether all specific truth-claims are equally warranted by the facts. When the question is put like that, it is obvious that they are not.

The hard pluralist response must now be to accept that disputes about truth, both of historical fact and about human origins and destiny, do exist, both within and between specific parts of diverse religions; but to assert that this is irrelevant both to knowledge of the Real itself and to the completion of the salvific process of moving from selfish egoism to the limit lessly better state of "Reality-centredness." There are two parts to this claim, one to do with knowledge of the Real and one to do with the nature and possibility of salvation. I shall consider each in turn, beginning with the claim that, though disputes about events in the past and future of the world are real enough, when it comes to speaking of the ultimately Real, different beliefs "constitute different ways in which the same ultimate Reality has impinged upon human life" (373). Moreover, these different ways of impinging are equally veridical for different observers.

Many religious beliefs do speak of a transcendent reality; and they do say that this reality is ineffable, or beyond the grasp of human thought. If this is so, it may seem that no humanly formulated truth-claim can apply to it as it really is; so that all claims must be inadequate finite attempts to characterize an infinite reality, and none will be markedly better than any others. But three major difficulties at once arise: if the Real is ineffable, how can one know that it exists? If no truth-claim can apply to it, how can one be entitled to say anything of it? And if this reality is unknowable, how can we know that all claims about it are equally valid, except in the sense that all are completely mistaken? Hick quotes a number of authoritative sources from a range of religions to show that ineffability is a common characteristic of the ultimately Real. "The Tao that can be expressed is not the eternal Tao" (*Tao Te Ching*); God is "incapable of being grasped by any term" (Gregory of Nyssa); Nirguna Brahman is such that all words fall back from attaining it (Sankara). Inexpressibility by any human concepts is certainly a feature of the ultimate object of devotion or striving in many religious traditions. And it may seem a short move from saying that two ideas are of an ineffable reality to saying that they are of the same reality; for what could distinguish two ineffables?

It can easily be seen that this argument is invalid, however. If *X* is indescribable by me, and *Y* is indescribable by me, it does not follow that *X* is identical with *Y*. On the contrary, there is no way in which *X* could be identified with *Y*, since there are no criteria of identity to apply. It is rather like saying, "I do not know what *X* is; and I do not know what *Y* is; therefore *X* must be the same as *Y*." If I do not know what either is, I *ipso facto* do not know whether they are the same or different. To assert identity is thus to commit the quantifier-shift fallacy, of moving from "Many religions believe in an ineffable Real" to "There is an ineffable Real in which many religions believe."

The principle of economy may be appealed to; to identify *X* and *Y*, and so have one unknown, is simpler than to keep them distinct. But how do I know that ultimate reality is simple and not complex? The blunt truth is that I am not entitled to assert identity or difference of ineffable objects. Hick says, "It (the Real *an sich*) cannot be said to be one or many, person or thing, substance or process, good or evil, purposive or non-purposive" (246). But if it cannot be said to be one or many, one is not even entitled to use the singular term "it." There may be many unknowns beyond the universe. Hick uses the singular because, he says, "there cannot be a plurality of ultimates"; but he says in the same paragraph, that there is "no reason *a priori* why the closest approximation that there is to a truly ultimate reality" may not consist in "an unrelated plurality." So I think we must either remain truly agnostic, or confess that the Real can be said to be one; and that is a piece of real and definite knowledge, opposed to all forms of simple polytheism. It is also opposed to at least some forms of Buddhism; as Paul Williams writes of Tibetan Buddhism, which he espouses, "There is no Being, no Absolute at all." Many Christians, too, of course, explicitly reject the apophatic doctrine that God is ultimately unknowable, supposing that he is truly known in Christ. So there does not seem to be much hope of uniting all traditions around even the rather short creed of one ineffable reality. They may say there is no such reality; or that there is more than one; or that it is not ineffable.

Suppose, however, one considers those strands of thought which do speak of one transcendent ineffable reality. It is not at all clear that different religions think of that which they say to be ineffable as the same in each case. It is unlikely in the extreme that they simply mean to say, "As well as everything I have said, there are some things I do not know about, which exist beyond the universe." This very statement would be self-contradictory, in asserting, "I know *X* exists," which entails, "I know at least one thing about *X* (that it exists beyond the universe)," at the same time as, "I know nothing about *X*." But ineffability cannot in any case be sensibly interpreted to mean, "Lack of knowledge." What I know absolutely nothing about must be, one feels, hardly worth mentioning. One finds a much more positive characterization in, for instance, Aquinas' notion of Divine simplicity, in many ways the key concept for his interpretation of the Divine. Simplicity is an ontological, not an epistemic, property, for Aquinas. That is, it is not that I do not know what God is; I *do* know that the being of God is such that it contains no distinctions, no parts, no complexity which human concepts could grasp. The Divine being is unlimited, and therefore beyond human comprehension. It is not just unknowable by us—in which case, it might well be internally complex for all we know. On the contrary, we know—thinks Aquinas—that the Divine being is utterly simple; and we know this by an argument from the nature of the world to its ultimately self-sufficient cause.

Now it would seem to follow that if two beings were both simple in this sense, containing no parts or distinctions or properties at all, they would have to be identical. If they were distinct, there would have to be some property, minimally the property of "not being the same as *Y*," in virtue of which they were distinct. *Ex hypothesi,* there are no such properties. It might, however, be said in reply that this reality must in any case at least possess the property of "being identical with itself," of being one and not many, as well as the property of existing—if that is a property. Aquinas perceives this, and it causes him trouble. One possibility is to say that God possesses no property which entails real internal distinctions. But then one could have many simple substances, as atoms were once thought to be; distinguished by some sorts of external relation, as atoms are distinguished by spatial location. Aquinas eliminates this possibility by holding that God is infinite, not being limited by an external relation. And I think it is true that infinity and simplicity together entail that any two beings possessing those properties are identical; i.e., there is only one such possible being.

For Aquinas, then, it is true to say of God that he exists, is one, simple and unlimited in reality. It is Divine simplicity and infinity which renders human concepts, fitted to deal with complex finite objects, incapable of expressing the Divine nature. The essential Divine nature will forever be beyond the grasp of human understanding— that is what ineffability means in the Thomist Christian tradition. It does not mean that nothing at all is known of, or can be truly said of, God. Aquinas asserts that many things can truly, and literally (though analogically) be said of God—that he is good, powerful, knowing and wise, for example (Cf. *Summa Theologiae;* 1a, 13, 2 & 3). What we cannot understand is what his knowledge is like, or what it is like to experience as God experiences. We cannot in this life comprehend the Divine being or be acquainted with it as it essentially is. This is rather like saying that I cannot imagine how bees perceive things, though I know very well that they do. The manner of their perception is beyond my experience or imagination. And, with God, the manner of his essential being will forever be so. We can know that God knows, though we cannot know how he knows, or what it is like for him to know. The traditional doctrine of divine ineffability, as classically formulated by Aquinas, is not that we can know nothing of God; it is that we cannot comprehend what God's essential nature is in itself.

Hick quotes Gregory of Nyssa as saying that God remains "beyond the reach not only of the human but of the angelic and all supramundane intelligence, unthinkable, unutterable" (*Against Eunomius,* 1: 42). What is significant here is that God is *beyond* or above all human concepts. His proper nature is not just totally other; it is greater than our concepts can reach, not less or such as to render them wholly inappropriate. It is as if we say, "I know that God is good and wise; but since I also know that he is infinite and simple, I do not know what it is in God's essential nature that makes these terms appropriate."

How do I know these terms apply to God? For Aquinas, it is by a causal argument from the nature of finite beings to their only wholly adequate cause and foundation. We must say of God that as cause of all, he contains in himself in a greater manner all the perfections to be found in things. The theistic perception, as Mascall puts it, is "a genuine apprehension of God as present by immensity at the ontological root of finite beings" (E. L. Mascall, *He Who Is,* 1966: 197). Whatever we think of Aquinas' arguments, he is not portraying the existence of some thing or things of which nothing can be said. He is portraying a being of whom it can truly be said that it is the one perfect cause of all finite things; though if we go on to ask what that being is like outside any relation to us, no adequate description can be given. There is that in God which makes the ascription of goodness to him appropriate; we cannot imagine or describe what it is, for we can only say how it causes God to seem to us (correctly) from our limited viewpoint. I think this is what Aquinas means by saying that terms denoting positive perfections apply properly to God, though not in the sense in which we understand them, i.e., in which we apply them to finite things. We have a positive reason for claiming that we do not know just how these terms apply; the reason is that God, as the adequate cause of all finite things, is simple and infinite. But we also have a positive reason for applying them; namely, that God relates to us as a supremely desirable being who brings us to good by uniting us to himself. We can thus interpret the much-disputed Thomistic *aporia* by saying that what we do not know is the nature of God, as it exists out of any relation to human cognition, though we do know there is such an ineffable nature. We can know that God is not limited in any way, so that finite properties do not, *qua* finite, properly apply to him (we can know "what he is not"). And we can know what difference the existence of God makes to the experiences and destinies of finite creatures ("how other things are related to him").

I would not wish to be committed to asserting the coherence of Thomas' remarks on ineffability. What I want to bring out is that when he speaks of ineffability, he is not saying that God is such that no terms can be truly affirmed of him—he takes Maimonides to task on this very point (though of course Maimonides too is in no doubt that the assertions of the Hebrew Bible about God are unequivocally true). Thomas is saying that, though we cannot comprehend *how* terms apply to God, because of his simplicity, we can know that they do apply; so that God truly is the omniscient creator of all finite things. Now when Japanese Buddhists in the tradition of Asvaghosa say that Reality is non-dual, they precisely do not mean that this reality can be regarded as personal creator of all. Something is said to be ineffable in both cases; but in Aquinas' case it is the nature of a reality which is quite distinct from that of the finite world; in Asvaghosa's case it is the ultimate nature of the finite world itself. In the Indian philosopher Sankara, we may have yet a different view, that what is ineffable, *nirguna Brahman,* is both different from this illusory finite realm (Nirvana is *not* Samsara) and yet not a substantially distinct reality. In each case, something is said to be ineffable; but that it is *not* precisely the same thing is shown by the disputes on the point between Aquinas and Maimonides, Ramanuja and Sankara, and the followers of Asvaghosa and Nagarjuna, respectively.

So the traditional theistic doctrine of ineffability arises from the exploration of the greatness and infinity of God. It presupposes the truth of many descriptive statements; indeed, it entails at least one descriptive statement, namely, that God is ineffable (a proposition which is not self-evident). It can consistently point out the inadequacy of such statements to give anything like a full understanding of God, and their possible misleadingness, if we do take them as implying that God is just like finite cases where such descriptions normally apply. We are aware of our limitations and partialities, of the superficiality of our knowledge, the inadequacy of our grasp of the reality of things. We seek for something unlimited, impartial, with a secure reality and perfection. The Real is not the dependent and transient; it is the wholly independent and enduring; upon it, in some sense, all things depend. The idea of the transcendent is the idea of supreme reality and value, a reality supremely valuable and a value supremely real. We can postulate that there is such a being, without being able to describe it in any detail. Indeed, the postulate requires that it is beyond our conceptual grasp; we cannot envisage just what or how it is; but we envisage something when we claim that it is supremely real and perfect.

Seeking to defend his view that the Real is radically unknowable, Hick dismisses as "logical pedantry" the logical point that the Real must at least have the property of "being able to be referred to" (239). But there is more meat to the point than he admits. For if *X* has the property of being able to be referred to, this reference must be accomplished either by ostentation or description. Ostentation is ruled out by definition, for an object which transcends the universe. So any reference must be made by description; *X* must be identified as "the *X* which. . . ." Further, if an identifying reference is to have any hope of succeeding, one must be able to pick out *X* as some sort of substance, process or stuff. It is not enough to say, "the *X* which exists beyond the universe," if there may be many such things. One will need to say, "*X* is the one and only thing which satisfies the properties. . . ." Hick gives the game away by using the term "the Real." For him, *X* is the one and only thing which is real in the fullest sense (i.e., independent, self-existent, unchanging in its essential nature, unlimited by anything else . . .). This is a description which could only apply to one thing, if it could apply at all. The object is identified descriptively by constructing a notion of a unique sort of reality upon which all others depend. Whether such a reference could ever succeed is another question; but for it even to have meaning, it is apparent that quite a lot of our concepts do need to apply to *X*.

But these, says Hick, are "purely formal and logically generated properties"; they are not "substantial properties," like being good, powerful or wise. Now, he says, the claim to ineffability is that substantial properties do not apply to the being of God beyond the range of human experience. Does this distinction between formal and substantial properties hold? The distinction between form and substance might most naturally be taken as a distinction between what is said and the form in which it is said. Thus the substance, or content, of "The cat sat on the mat" is whatever is asserted by the utterance of those words. The form is the syntax or grammatical structure of English; noun, verb and predicate; a structure which enables me to say anything at all. Study of the structure will give me no particular content; it is like doing Logic with nothing but ps and qs; I can go on for pages without knowing what I am talking about (perhaps that is not well put; I can set out possible argument-forms without actually uttering an argument).

Now if I say, "*X* is to be used as a noun" that could be called a formal property of *X*; it tells me what sort of term *X* is, without telling me what real thing *X* might be. But if I say, "*X* is the referent of some noun," I am talking about some actual object, not a term. And I am saying what sort of thing it is; a thing which could be referred to by description, by someone with human conceptual equipment. I am saying, "This object is such that it can be identified by some human language user." That may not tell me much about it, but it does have content; it is a synthetic proposition, though it is obvious, in the sense that I would hardly be speaking of the object if it could not be identified, at least in thought. And of course it invites further questions about how it can be identified. We must conclude that the statement "*X* is an identifiable object" attributes a substantial property to *X*, the property of being identifiable; and the more one spells out the manner of identifying it, the more one will say about *X*. In fact, Hick includes as a formal property the property of being that than which nothing greater can be conceived (246). Far from being purely formal, that property entails (in the concept of "greatness") the idea of value, of the rationally desirable, and thus of goodness, which he admits to being a substantial property, in at least one clear sense.

Moreover, this is an absolute truth about God. For if it is true from our viewpoint that God is maximally great, then it is true of God that, from our viewpoint, he is maximally great. The distinction which is often made between absolute truths and relative truths is insupportable. An absolute truth is supposed to be one which states what is the case independent of any particular person believing it. A relative truth states what is the case, from the point of view of a particular person; that is, it states what truly appears to be the case to some observer. But if *A* will truly appear as *B* to *P*, then it is true of *A* that it will appear as *B* to *P*. And this truth is absolute; it does not depend upon anybody knowing or believing it, since it may be true even though *P* never exists. So we know many true things about God, but we also know that much of God transcends our thoughts.

I propose that Hick has seized upon some very difficult and disputed statements of major religious intellectuals and has taken the doctrine of the *via negativa* out of relation to its complementary doctrine of the *via eminentia,* to produce a new doctrine that the Real *an sich* is wholly unknowable. Then he argues that, since one unknowable is indistinguishable from another, they are all the same. Since all human concepts are bound to be inadequate to the Real, if it is unknowable, and since we have no way of choosing between different descriptions, we must say that all the "great world faiths embody different perceptions and conceptions of, and correspondingly different responses to, the Real" (240).

When Kant foisted the doctrine of the noumenal realm upon the philosophical world, it was in the form of an undigested remnant of his pre-Critical view that the noumenal, or intelligible world, was the real world, and was knowable by pure intellect, whereas the senses give a confused appearance of this realm of rational spirits. In his Critical doctrine, he confined the intellect strictly to the realm of the senses, and justified the categories as necessary and universal preconditions of the possibility of scientific knowledge. The noumenal lost its theoretical role entirely. It has often been pointed out that a residual inconsistency vitiates Kant's idea of the noumenal, since to say that it exists as the cause of the phenomenal applies the categories beyond the permissible range of cognitive meaning. When this inconsistency is cleared away, Kant can be interpreted as proposing that Reason necessarily constructs an Ideal of a perfect value and reality, to be used as a regulative idea in our practical conduct of life. It has no theoretical validity, and is to be judged by its efficacy in enabling us to live a moral life, or to conceive of the rationality of such a life.

Hick makes a similar move, revealing that the real focus of his concern is not with theoretical truth, but with the "salvific efficacy" of religions. When he comes to state criteria of assessing religious phenomena, he says that "the basic criterion is soteriological" (14); that is, efficacy in leading humans from self-centredness to Reality-centredness, most readily observable by growth in love or compassion. Yet, like Kant, he is unable to renounce theoretical claims entirely. This is hardly surprising, since even to say that a limitlessly better state is possible for all is a factual statement about the future, which is presumably experientially accessible in principle. Thus the theistic picture of the universe sees it as "a creative process leading to a limitlessly good end state in conscious communion with God" (179). This picture can be confirmed beyond rational doubt by conscious experience of that end state. Now there are certainly views which would refute this picture. Any atheistic view or any non-realist religious view would deny the existence of such an end state; so there is no question that some religious views deny precisely what traditional theism asserts. As Hick says, non-realism in religion offers "a radically different vision" (208) of things, which leaves no place for ultimate cosmic optimism. Samkhya Yogins, Advaitic Vedantins and many Buddhists, both Theravadin and Mahayana, would also deny that the universe is a creative process leading to an end state; they see the world as an illusory cycle of ills, without beginning or end. And even if the individual can achieve a limitlessly good end state, it will not be one of conscious communion with a perfect creator; it will be entry into the quiescent state of desirelessness, far beyond personhood as we understand it. Assertions made about the nature of the universe and about ultimate human destiny are very different. Is it not obvious that at most one set of such views can be true? And if Hick does not hesitate to exclude non-realist religious views and atheistic views of the world, why should he hesitate to exclude views which take a different view of human destiny, even though they might agree on the existence of a perfect supreme reality?

I think that he has increasingly come to feel, and argues at length in *An Interpretation of Religion,* that we cannot reasonably claim "that our own form of religious experience . . . is veridical whilst the others are not" (235). He allows that virtually every religious tradition has done so, but then proposes the following argument:

(1) By something akin to Swinburne's Principle of Credulity, *A* is justified in thinking that what seems to be the case probably is the case, in the absence of strong countervailing reasons. So if *A* seems to apprehend God's presence, she is justified in thinking that God is in fact present, and therefore that God exists.

(2) By the principle of universalizability, however, *B* is similarly justified in believing that reality is non-dual, on the basis of her experiences of *samadi* or enlightenment.

(3) Since the fact that "*A* is me" is not a relevant reason for giving *A*'s views greater force than *B*'s, it seems that *A* and *B* are equally justified in believing contradictory things.

(4) Therefore, it is implausible to believe that all religious experience is delusory except one's own.

(5) This suggests the Pluralistic Hypothesis, that different types of religious experience are veridical but partial responses to a reality which cannot be adequately described by any set of beliefs alone.

This argument is plainly invalid. The trouble lies with step (4). A sharp distinction is to be made between justification and truth. I can be justified in believing something false (e.g., that the earth is flat) due to imperfect knowledge. In complex situations, given rather different initial information, people may be justified in believing contradictory things. But contradictory beliefs cannot both be true; so all that follows is that at least one person is justified in believing something false. Hick has already argued that both atheists and theists can be rationally justified in adopting the views of the world they do adopt, given the ambiguous nature of that world. But it does not follow that each must accept the other's view as equally true. The very reverse is the case. If I am rationally justified in believing *X*, and you are rationally justified in believing not-*X*, then we are both justified in believing the other to be deluded, or in some other way mistaken.

Now something *does* follow from this about the character of such beliefs. I must admit other believers may have reasons which seem just as strong to them to accept their views as I have to accept mine. Therefore, I cannot claim that they are obviously or detectably mistaken. And I cannot seriously claim that my view is obviously or clearly true. So I must admit the equal right of others to exist and hold the views they do. And I must admit the fallibility and theoretical uncertainty of my view. To accept this might in itself be a great advance in religion, but it does not constitute a reason for accepting hard pluralism. It could be a reason for denying any right to believe any view in this area. However, one can argue, as Hick does, that the matter is so important that I am justified in making some choice. It may even be that I *must* believe something in this area, though it is hard to say how detailed my beliefs must be. In fact Hick vacillates, sometimes saying that, because conflicting views have so little to choose between them, it is not important to hold such views, and one should concentrate simply on the practical matter of salvation. But at other times (e.g., as between realist and non-realist religious views) he says that it is important to choose a realist and cosmically optimistic view, because only that offers good news to all.

Whichever he says, it *is* reasonable to claim that our own experiences are veridical whilst all others are not. It is unreasonable to claim anything else. But the situation does not have to have this all-or-nothing character. Surely we do not wish to say that centuries of prayer, meditation, sanctity and devotion in other traditions are founded on illusion? Surely they must be putting people in touch with the real spiritual reality, whatever it is? Hick himself gives the answer: "There seems to me to be no difficulty in principle in the thought that a person may be correctly experiencing some aspects of reality whilst falsely experiencing others" (220). That is, there may well be something veridical in what great religious traditions experience, but also (very often) something false. He even tells us how to discriminate: we accept some belief as veridical "because it evokes a confirming echo within our own experience" (220). We reject others because they clash with our experience. There are many echoes of our experience in the religious experiences of others; and we may take these to be veridical. By parity of reasoning, we may think that our own tradition, even our own present experience within that tradition, is liable to contain many mistakes, though we will not know what they are. Humility is certainly in order; it does sound arrogant to say "my religious experience is perfectly correct; all others are totally false." But we can say: "My religious experience is correct in important respects, though it may contain many errors. The experiences of others may contain many veridical elements; but there are important misinterpretations, too." The veridical elements will be those which seem to echo my own; the errors those which clash with my own; nor will I be able to identify the errors in my own. I can be on the lookout for such errors, and look to other traditions to help me identify them. And I can look for elements other traditions have which may complement, rather than contradict, my own. Thus my beliefs are always revisable; and others may always be capable of disclosing new insights. Yet those beliefs which lie near the core of my belief-system must be given preference over competing beliefs.

Hick does precisely this, of course. He identifies many errors in the Christian tradition—belief in Hell and literal belief in incarnation are just two which he takes to be morally undesirable and rationally insupportable. His core-beliefs are that one should turn from selfish egoism to attain a limitlessly good end-state by some sort of relation to a reality of supreme value; and he is only prepared to accept beliefs which are compatible with these. The suggestion is that any set of beliefs which result in such an end-state is likely to be true; others are not. The trouble is that this criterion is quite unusable, as Hick's discussion makes very clear. Some of the most obviously deluded, restrictive and exclusive belief-systems produce astonishing commitment, assurance, love and self-sacrifice. On the other hand, as Hick points out, the great Scriptural traditions have histories replete with hatred, intolerance and violence; so that none of them emerges as much better than any others, in the long sad history of human fanaticism. It seems, then, that either the suggested criteria of adequacy do not enable us to choose between many different beliefs, or that they are in tension with the criterion of consistency with other well-established knowledge. In this situation, might it not be better to abandon the Kantian *noumenon,* say that we do know something about the Real—namely, that it is an ultimate unity of reality and value—and thus that criteria of adequacy, at this abstract level, are metaphysical criteria of providing the most intelligible account of the genesis of the universe from an ultimately real and perfect source? Hick tends to dismiss metaphysical speculations, together with particular historical claims, as unsettlable and unnecessary to salvation. But of course his whole book is a metaphysical exploration of what can be intelligibly said about the object of religious faith; and the fact that his version of pluralistic religious realism is unsettlable and highly disputable does not stop him from asserting both its truth and its importance for a correct (non-exclusive) understanding of salvation.

This brings us back to the question, which I deferred earlier, of whether unsettlable beliefs can be necessary for salvation. Hick finds this "implausible" (369), but it is rendered immediately more plausible by the consideration that the very concept of what salvation is involves beliefs which are theoretically unsettlable in practice. If one asks what is necessary for salvation, one might be asking whether any beliefs are requisite for the final attainment of wholly fulfilled human life. Atheists, of course, will deny that there is any such final attainment, or even any such possible notion as that of a wholly fulfilled life; "do your own thing" might better be their motto. So the mere acceptance of the concept of a wholly fulfilled life presupposes the very contestable belief that there is a proper goal of human activity. If there is such a consciously attained goal, then one cannot achieve it without having the correct belief about what it is, and how one has come to achieve it. In this sense the possession of some particular beliefs is necessary to salvation. People without those beliefs will not attain salvation, for the simple reason that salvation consists in attaining a state which entails possessing such beliefs; i.e., it entails that one knows what salvation is and that one has attained it. At such a point, of course, one may suppose that religious disputes will finally be settled. As Hick says, "To participate knowingly in fulfilment would confirm the reality of God beyond the possibility of rational doubt" (179). In other words, at least some important metaphysical claims about the existence and nature of God are settlable by experience in principle.

But one might also ask whether any beliefs are requisite *now* if one is to have a reasonable hope of attaining salvation later, or if one is to be on the right path towards salvation. Different views exist on this question, but Hick seems to me correct in thinking that if there is a God of universal love, he will not make our loss of eternal life dependent merely upon making an honest mistake. So one might suppose that a positive response to whatever seems to be good and true, by a conscience as informed as one can reasonably expect, and a commitment to seek truth and realize goodness, is sufficient to dispose one rightly to salvation. Some beliefs are requisite, but they will depend on particular circumstances, since what one is justified in believing at one time may well be different from what one is justified in believing at another. Nevertheless, if one believes in such a God of love, one will also think that he will eventually bring rational creatures to know what he truly is, so that the search for truth will issue in a specific set of true beliefs sometime. Thus it is misleading, though in one sense true, to say that no metaphysical beliefs are essential to salvation. It may not be essential to your eventual salvation that you hold them now, but it is essential to your actual salvation that you come to hold them. Metaphysics, however difficult and disputable, is important to faith (I don't mean anything very grand by this, just beliefs about the nature of what is ultimately real).

In a recent paper, Hick refers to the "novel," "astonishing," and "bizarre" doctrine that "the salvific power of the dharma taught five hundred years earlier by the Buddha is a consequence of the death of Jesus." But one need not deny that the dharma is an effective way of overcoming egoism and attaining inner peace and compassion, when one asserts that it does not bring one into a conscious loving relationship with a personal God. Nor is it bizarre to hold that one can be brought into such a relationship only by the saving activity of God uniting human nature to himself in the life and death of Jesus, and subsequently in those who come to accept Jesus as Lord and Saviour. It is not that Buddhists attain salvation by the Middle Way, though somehow the efficacy of this way depends on something that had not yet happened. Buddhists do not attain Christian salvation, since their Way does not lead to that personal relationship with God which is salvation. They attain a high degree of compassion and inner peace, and their unselfish devotion to the truth as they see it will surely fit them to receive salvation from a personal God when his saving activity becomes clear to them. There is a salutary reminder here that metaphysics is not what saves us; for Christians, the act of God, establishing creatures in knowledge and love of him, does that. But metaphysics is needed to set out the coherence of the concept of a God who can so act in a world like this.

It may help at this point if we distinguish what we may call soft pluralism from hard pluralism. Soft pluralism is the view that the Real can manifest in many traditions, and humans can respond to it appropriately in them. I think this view is defensible and important, and it is certainly different from the view, held by many, that there is only one God, who only reveals himself in one tradition and only saves those who belong to that tradition—the restrictive interpretation of the decree of the Council of Florence, "Outside the Church there is no salvation." It is coherent to hold that there is a God who is infinite and beyond human comprehension in his essential nature, who discloses something of that nature, as it stands in relation to us, in many religious traditions. It is coherent to hold that in many (though not all) religious traditions, believers aim to overcome selfish desire in relation to a supreme objective value which promises bliss, knowledge and freedom, and that this does constitute a positive and appropriate response to God, as disclosed to them. It is also coherent to hold that no tradition has the completeness of truth about God, that all contain many revisable and corrigible beliefs, and that we should look to other traditions to complement, correct or reshape our own. This is certainly part of Hick's thesis.

But another form of the thesis is also at work, a thesis both more intolerant of virtually all actual religious traditions and sliding at times into incoherence. The intolerance surfaces in many stringent remarks about the bizarre, primitive and astonishing beliefs held by orthodox believers. The incoherence appears in the claim of hard pluralism that all (or at least all "great") traditions are equally valid paths to salvation and equally authentic modes of experience of a Real which is a completely unknowable postulate of the religious life. It is the stress on equal validity, equal authenticity and complete unknowability which is incoherent. These three claims constitute an inconsistent triad of propositions, since one cannot assert all of: (1) There is something wholly unknowable; (2) all experiences of it are equally authentic; and (3) all paths to fuller experience of it are equally valid. If (1) is true, (2) and (3) cannot be asserted. Not only is there no way of knowing if they are true; they cannot be true, if they entail (as they do) experiential knowledge of the wholly unknowable. If there are any criteria of authenticity at all, it must be possible to distinguish more and less authentic experiences. But this can only be done by means of some concept of the Real which can be described more or less adequately. Once one has such a concept, there may indeed be experiences which give equally authentic knowledge of it, but that can only be so if those experiences are complementary, not contradictory. That means (as is the case with the often quoted wave–particle duality of light) that competent observers must agree that both of two descriptions of an object can be true, in different conditions of observation. Unfortunately, most Buddhists will not agree that it is true that there is an omnipotent personal agent who brings about changes in history; and most Christians will not agree that the idea of God is an imaginative projection which needs to be overcome in the recognition of one non-dual reality. Hard pluralism is as strongly falsified as any contingent hypothesis is ever likely to be.

Yet it might be insisted that this situation must be changed. There is another version of pluralism, which might be termed "revisionist pluralism," which asserts that all the Scriptural traditions need to be radically revised, in consequence of the rise of the natural sciences, of Biblical scholarship and of post-Enlightenment critical thinking in general. The idea of an infallible Scriptural revelation will need to be discarded, and many particular beliefs revised in the light of new knowledge of the world and of human psychology. Now if this is done in all the great Scriptural traditions, one will be much less clear about which beliefs are essential or even central to each tradition; and the revised beliefs may well turn out to be compatible with similarly revised beliefs in other traditions.

If a Buddhist is prepared to regard belief in reincarnation as a myth, a Christian thinks of the Incarnation as a mistaken fourth-century doctrine, and a Muslim agrees that the Koran is a fallible and morally imperfect document, they might well be able to agree much more than they used to. One can see the Scriptural faiths, defined by their acceptance of infallible revelation (and even the Buddhist scriptures are regarded in that way by many orthodox believers), as belonging to past history just as surely as their tribal predecessors do. Religion can move to a more universal phase, in which insights are selected from many traditions, while most of their differences are relegated to the museum of dead beliefs. I suspect that Hick wishes to commend revisionist pluralism, too. There is much to be said for it, but it cannot be said that it sees all existing traditions as equally valid perceptions of truth. On the contrary, most existing traditions have to be radically purged of error, in the light of the more adequate views of a post-Critical age. It is ironic that this view, which sees the great traditions as "earlier stages in an evolution of which it is the culmination" is precisely of the type which Hick earlier characterises as unacceptably arrogant (2). Revisionist pluralism makes its own absolute and exclusive claim—it is just true that there is one Reality of supreme value which will bring all creatures to good; and anything which denies this or tries to restrict the ways in which this may happen is false.

Revisionist pluralism is incompatible with hard pluralism, since it denies that unrevised traditions are equally adequate forms of religious truth. It is compatible with soft pluralism, but not entailed by it, since it is possible that one existing tradition characterizes the Real most adequately; that is, that its central truth-claims are more adequately descriptive of the Real than competing alternatives. To the extent that the Real is a personal and active self-disclosing agent, one might think that an existing tradition which claims to have witnessed the self-disclosing acts of this agent is more likely to be adequate than the conclusions of a highly abstract and speculative philosophical hypothesis. But that is a question of the acceptability and coherence of particular conceptions of ultimate reality, which needs to be argued out in detail. One thing is certain, that revisionist pluralism is not in a position to assert moral superiority, greater tolerance or greater impartiality over any particular tradition as such, when traditions are taken as not excluding ultimate salvation for others, since the claims each must make for itself are logically on a par.

Religious believers do not have to suppose that the majority of the human race are excluded from salvation, as long as they have a view which allows for a development of knowledge after death. They are, however, committed to thinking that most people are mistaken in their beliefs about the ultimate nature of reality. That is, after all, not a very surprising thought, though it is a sad one. It should lead to a keen sense of one's own fallibility, a deeper appreciation of the attempts of others to understand human nature and destiny, and a firm stress on the primacy of moral and spiritual practice in religion. These are the leading themes of John Hick's recent work, which he formulates in the pluralist hypothesis. I have suggested that in at least one sense (soft pluralism) his case is persuasive. There are other senses, however, which, if I am right, are not sustainable. On this, at least, truth is exclusive, and one of us must be wrong.

## NOTES

1. John Hick, *An Interpretation of Religion: Human Responses to the Transcendent* (New Haven and London: Yale University Press, 1989), p. 3. Subsequently in this chapter page references to this book will be made parenthetically in the body of the text.

CHAPTER 7

# Religious Pluralism and the Divine: *Another Look at John Hick's Neo-Kantian Proposal*

PAUL R. EDDY

John Hick offers one of the most sophisticated and influential pluralistic philosophies of world religions currently available. It is the purpose of this study to examine the heart of Hick's model—namely, his answer to the problem of conflicting human conceptions of the divine. In the end, I contend that Hick's neo-Kantian subjectivist moment ultimately undermines his religious realism.

In barest terms, Hick's pluralistic hypothesis proposes that

> the great world faiths embody different perceptions and conceptions of, and correspondingly different responses to, the Real from within the major variant ways of being human; and that within each of them the transformation of human existence from self-centeredness to Reality-centeredness is taking place.[1]

The most critical conceptual problem facing this hypothesis involves the *de facto* existence of the often radically conflicting conceptions of divine reality throughout the world religions. The heart of the problem is this. Given Hick's pluralistic model, one would *prima facie* expect human perceptions of the single divine Reality to be relatively similar, or at least not mutually exclusive, in nature. Phenomenologically, of course, this is anything but the case. The most obvious—and problematic—of these differences is the radical conceptual dichotomy between those religions that view the Real as a personal Being, and those that view it in terms of a non-personal principle, force, or "absolute." Thus, to survive the day, it is clear that Hick's pluralistic philosophy of religions must include a viable solution to this problem of apparently contradictory conceptions of the divine.

From Paul R. Eddy, "Religious Pluralism and the Divine: Another Look at John Hick's Neo-Kantian Proposal," *Religious Studies* **30,** 4 (December 1994): 467–78. 

## I. JOHN HICK'S NEO-KANTIAN PROPOSAL[2]

The broad outline of Hick's current solution to the conflicting conceptions problem made its public début in the mid-1970s.[3] By the early 1980s it was being developed in earnest.[4] One must turn to Hick's much-acclaimed work, *An Interpretation of Religion,* to find its most comprehensive exposition and defence to date. Here, his response functions as the central apologetic pillar of his pluralistic hypothesis. Hick's proposal is constructed from the two primary strands of thought that have informed his religious worldview throughout the last four decades: the primacy of religious experience and a Kantian epistemology.[5] In its simplest terms, his proposal is an attempt to combine a realist understanding of religious experience that is, at the same time, seriously qualified by a critical subjectivizing element.

Hick begins with the "highly generalized" Kantian insight that the human mind actively interprets sensory information in terms of its inherent mental concepts.[6] More specifically, Hick focuses on the noumenal–phenomenal distinction that allowed Kant to distinguish between an entity as it is in itself and as it appears in the act of human perception. By taking this Kantian epistemological principle and applying it—in a decidedly un-Kantian fashion—to human religious experience, Hick arrives at a synthesis that forms the foundation for his response to the conflicting conceptions problem. In fact, given Hick's proposal, conflicting images of the divine are not merely understandable, but are even to be expected. In Hick's words,

> I want to say that the noumenal Real is experienced and thought by different human mentalities . . . as the range of gods and absolutes which the phenomenology of religions reports. And these divine [phenomenal manifestations] are not illusory but are empirically, that is experientially, real as authentic manifestations of the Real.[7]

In this manner, Hick's model seeks to maintain a realist core, i.e., the noumenal Real, while nonetheless anticipating radically diverse understandings of It within the various religions. According to Hick, the key to preserving parity between the variety of religious conceptions of the divine is the fundamental insistence that absolutely *nothing* can be said or known about the divine in and of itself. As Hick clearly states:

> [The divine Reality in itself] cannot be said to be one or many, person or thing, substance or process, good or bad, purposive or non-purposive. None of the concrete descriptions that apply within the realm of human experience can apply literally to the unexperienceable ground of that realm. . . . We cannot even speak of this as a thing or an entity.[8]

Clearly then—if Hick is right—on the one hand, the divine in itself is neither personal nor non-personal; on the other, *both* personal and non-personal conceptions can represent authentic manifestations of the divine as perceived in the various religions. In this manner, he offers a religious realist—as opposed to a naturalistic—interpretation of religion, while at the same time allowing the subjectivist component to create the space for radically divergent human understandings of the divine Reality.

In *An Interpretation of Religion,* Hick fleshes out this basic proposal in two critical sections.[9] The first represents an attempt to locate the rudimentary essence of his model, in terms of a distinction between the divine in itself and as humanly experienced, within the various religious traditions. The second explicitly develops the neo-Kantian proposal itself. The remainder of this paper will examine the critical elements of Hick's model, as discussed in these two sections, from a generally philosophical vantage point.

## II. THE DIVINE IN ITSELF *VS.* THE DIVINE AS HUMANLY EXPERIENCED

Hick claims that his neo-Kantian proposal is essentially a complex philosophical articulation of a more general religious observation—namely, that an inherent epistemological rift exists between the divine Reality as it exists in itself and as it is humanly experienced. He supports this claim by offering evidence of this awareness in such diverse religious traditions as Hinduism, Mahayana and Pure Land Buddhism, Taoism, Kabbalist Judaism, and Islam, both in its traditional and Sufist forms. Within Christianity, he detects this insight in the traditional distinction between God *a se* and God *pro nobis,* as well as in Eckhart's mysticism, and the progressive ventures of such modern theologians as Paul Tillich, Ninian Smart, and Gordon Kaufmann.[10]

Hick identifies the root of this "basic [inter-religious] assumption" as the conviction that divine reality is

> unlimited and therefore may not be equated without remainder with anything that can be humanly experienced and defined. Unlimitedness, or infinity, is a negative concept, the denial of limitation.[11]

Such a notion, Hick suggests, is logically entailed by the claim to divine ultimacy. For if the divine is limitable in some external mode, this would render it, by definition, non-ultimate. Part and parcel with the concept of unlimitedness is

> the equally natural and reasonable assumption that the Ultimate, in its unlimitedness, exceeds all positive characterizations in human thought and language.[12]

Hick garners support for this notion of divine ineffability—based on infinity—from a gamut of Christian theologians including Gregory of Nyssa, Augustine, Aquinas, Eckhart, and St. John of the Cross, as well as from Hindu and Islamic traditions. He derails the criticism that making such a claim to ineffability is itself an application of a human concept to the Infinite by drawing the distinction between formal and substantive properties. While he allows that "purely formal and logically generated properties such as 'being a referent of a term'" can legitimately be predicated of the divine, it nonetheless "makes perfectly good sense to say that our *substantial* concepts do not apply to the Ultimate."[13] In this manner, Hick baptizes his radical neo-Kantian subjectivism in the pure waters of the classical Christian tradition.[14]

In response to this line of argument, one must begin by noting that the classical notion of divine infinity entails nothing like the type of radical epistemological rift embodied in Hick's model. It is clear from its use—at least within orthodox Christian tradition—that the idea of divine infinity does allow for some positive characterizations of the divine. Here, infinity is generally taken to mean not a radical and complete "denial of limitation" in every sense of the term,[15] but rather (for example) "that [the divine] possesses the fullness of all possible perfections."[16] In fact, within the Christian tradition—including those very theologians that Hick appeals to for support—limitation of the divine, both inherent (e.g., the inability to sin) and self-imposed (e.g., the creation of the finite world and free creatures in relation to which the divine is delimited), is admitted without question.

It is important to note here that even the more minimalist views of religious language—such as a fairly agnostic reading of Aquinas's analogical predication or, more so, the Areopagite's *via negativa*—still deal in the production of knowledge concerning the divine.[17] Hick's attempt to correlate his proposal with the Thomistic model of analogy by offering the latter as a "thought model" suggestive of his own hypothesis must finally be regarded as an apologetic failure. Certainly, arguments have been made for relatively agnostic readings of analogy in general, and Aquinas's model of it in particular.[18] However, even amongst those who interpret Aquinas in such a fashion, virtually no one would suggest that his understanding of analogy, or his dictum—"Things known are in the knower according to the mode of the knower," imply anything like the type of radical subjectivity and agnosticism called for by Hick's model.[19] And on the other side of the interpretive field, there are those who see predication in general and/or Aquinas's analogical view in particular, as offering the possibility of a significant linguistic/conceptual correspondence between the human and divine.[20]

To return to the idea of infinity, one can argue that the implications of applying this notion to the divine are anything but obvious, contrary to Hick's specific and radical claims.[21] First, even if the notion of infinity is unproblematically applicable to the divine in a literalistic, philosophical sense, it is far from self-evident that the *concepts* of a finite being are then rendered *a priori* incommensurable with it. Only by positing further undemonstrated assumptions—e.g., that a finite being is limited to finite concepts, and/or that the concepts associated with an infinite being are themselves infinite—does this argument follow.[22]

Secondly, even among those who recognize some type of serious incommensurability based on divine infinity (and here, Hick merely represents one example from the radical end of the spectrum), there is little agreement on either the degree of incommensurability or its specific effects on predication potential. In this light, it would appear that "infinity" predicated of the divine refers figuratively (vis-à-vis the mathematical infinite) to Its mystery and transcendence rather than literally to any particular unlimitable quality that would *a priori* preclude some degree of conceptual commensurability.[23] And if this is the case, then "divine infinity" becomes not a *cause of or reason for* incommensurability, but, at most—though not necessarily—an *expression of* such.[24] Again, all of this is not to deny that the concept of divine infinity entails both mystery and transcendence. However, the most this would suggest, contrary to Hick, is that the divine can never be *exhaustively* known. To admit that we can never know *all* of the divine is a far cry from claiming that we can never know *anything* of the divine.[25]

Third and finally, a proper understanding of infinity also reveals the confusion inherent in Hick's view of divine ultimacy, a view which *a priori* disallows the divine the possibility of co-existence with any delimiting state of affairs. Paradoxically, such a view only gains ultimacy at the expense of divine sovereignty and flexibility. Moreover, it is difficult to see just what meaning it can have given the obvious existence of a finite cosmos, which—unless one opts for a pan- (or panen-)theistic notion of the divine—entails an external (if self-imposed) delimiting of the Real. All of this goes to show that Hick's model, rather than merely representing a recognition of the relative epistemological humility that is called for by the various religions, exemplifies instead a hyper-subjectivism that outstrips any parallels in the religions by postulating a complete conceptual incommensurability between the human and divine.

In light of the above, one is forced to question even the one remaining manner in which Hick himself aspires to speak of the noumenal Real. He suggests that by retreating from a "strong ineffability" position, one can still make formal, logically-generated (versus substantive) statements concerning the divine. Apart from the pressing question of whether in fact Hick's model *can* escape a "strong" notion of ineffability, a serious problem remains: namely, the fact that Hick's expressed instances of supposedly formal properties betray definite signs of a smuggled foreign substance. To speak of purely formal properties is to speak solely in terms of relation, with absolutely no substantive content whatsoever. But clearly to say that *X* has the property of "being a referent of a term" *does* deliver some amount of substantive content. If nothing else, it reveals that *X* "can be identified by some human language user," and such a property breaks the bound of the purely formal.[26] Hick's confusion of logical and substantive claims is even more apparent when he describes the Anselmian definition of God—"that which no greater can be conceived"—as a formal statement.[27] As Keith Ward notes, "greater" carries with it such connotations as value, being rationally desirable, etc., all of which are substantial properties.[28]

Thus we are left wondering if Hick's model is justified in saying *anything* about the divine worth saying. Such a position serves to raise the spectre of the Feuerbachian challenge:

> To deny all the qualities of a being is equivalent to denying the being himself. . . . The denial of determinate, positive predicates concerning the divine nature is nothing else than a denial of religion, with, however, an appearance of religion in its favor, so that it is not recognized as a denial; it is simply a subtle disguised atheism. . . . Dread of limitation is dread of existence.[29]

Hick faces a dilemma here. If, in reaction to Feuerbach's challenge, he allows for *some* substantive knowledge of the Real, the heart of his pluralistic programme is betrayed. Thus, Hick is destined to walk that neo-Kantian no-man's land that lies somewhere in an imaginary space between religious realism and a thoroughly subjectivized anti-realism.

## III. KANT AND HICK'S NEO-KANTIAN PROPOSAL

It is only with an examination of Hick's modified Kantian epistemology that the full force of his proposal's radical subjectivism is revealed. Hick spends a significant amount of time delineating the exact nature of his hypothesis' relation to Kant's own epistemology. Here, both detailed explication and qualification are critical to his thesis. A distinct, oscillating pattern emerges as Hick alternatively links—and then distances—himself from Kant. One can identify four important strands of continuity:

1. First, there is the use of Kant's noumenal–phenomenal distinction, which, when transposed from the realm of sensory to religious experience, allows Hick to "postulate" a single divine noumenon as the common source of the various, often conflicting, human experiences of the divine.[30]
2. Secondly, there is the employment of Kantian-like "category-analogues."[31] Here, Hick suggests that the conceptions of the Real as personal *vs.* non-personal function analogously to Kant's categories of the understanding. Fleshing out this neo-Kantian parallel, Hick claims that, similar to the role played by *time* in Kant's system, the range of human cultures serves as the particularizing factor by which the two larger categories are schematized, thus resulting in the range of human conceptions of the divine.[32]
3. Thirdly, like Kant, Hick maintains that his use of the noumenal category is a *negative* one. That is, he does not mean to make any positive claims regarding the unknowable divine noumenon—a charge with which he is often faced. Rather, he wants to refer to it only as a necessary postulate—one required by his broader religious philosophy—by way of formal categories. Thus, as in his reading of Kant, Hick emphatically declares that the noumenal exists independently of our experience of it, and, accordingly he stresses that "the phenomenal world is that same noumenal world as it appears to our human consciousness."[33]

4. Finally, Hick strengthens his association with Kant by offering corroborating evidence for the general Kantian model derived from several modern disciplines. Specifically, he states that the basic Kantian epistemological programme has been

> massively confirmed as an empirical thesis by modern work in cognitive and social psychology and in the sociology of knowledge.[34]

There are, however, specific junctures at which Hick wants to distance himself from Kant. This explicit distancing actually serves as a preemptive apologetic for his proposal. It provides the context within which he can respond to two critical types of attack on his model: first, to those that criticize him for particular aspects of his model that conflict with Kant's ideas, and, second, to those that criticize him on the basis of problems endemic to Kant's philosophy. As noted above, he makes it abundantly clear throughout his discussion that the general distinction upon which his model rests—i.e., between the Real in itself and as humanly experienced—in no way *depends* upon Kant's philosophical insights. Rather, Kant is merely the one to have developed this general observation in the most philosophically detailed manner. Hick claims that Aquinas' similar dictum, that "Things known are in the knower according to the mode of the knower," could just as easily form the departure point for a pluralistic hypothesis.[35] Hick goes on to broaden his appeal by pointing out that every human being can arrive at the same basic insight via reflection on their own empirical experience. We all know that the *same* object can appear quite *differently* depending on a particular human observer's spatial location, the condition of their sensory organs, and their own unique recognition and interpretive abilities.

On this basis, Hick does not hesitate to acknowledge those features of his model that are quite distinct from—even conflictive with—Kant's own philosophy. He notes two specific instances:

1. First, his decidedly un-Kantian shift of the noumenal–phenomenal distinction from the realm of sensory epistemology to the realm of religious epistemology, and the fundamental contrast between their respective understandings of religious experience that such a move evinces. As far as Hick is concerned, this presents no problem whatsoever. Simply because Kant did not choose to relate his insights regarding sensory experience to the realm of religious epistemology, this should not "bar others" from making such a move.[36] In fact, Hick's general apologetic response to those who bring Kantian-related criticisms against his model is that they do not apply given his transposition of Kant's ideas to the realm of religious epistemology. Based on this distinction, Hick feels that he can safely refuse to enter into the sticky nest of problems associated with modern Kantian interpretation.[37]

2. The second acknowledged divergence from Kant involves the nature of Hick's category-analogues. Specifically, while Kant's forms and categories are *a priori,* and are thus universal and necessary in nature,[38] Hick's analogues are both culture-relative and contingent.[39]

And so, Hick's neo-Kantian proposal represents a complex attempt to allow for a pluralistic interpretation of religions, while still safeguarding his realist core belief that religious experience, ultimately, is a non-illusory experience of transcendent Reality. I suggest that his particular nuanced use of Kant, far from side-stepping common Kantian criticisms, only serves to magnify them: specifically, his proposal represents an intensification of Kantian subjectivity—transposed to the religious realm—and thus threatens any realist core with immanent collapse.[40] Four lines of critique can be mentioned here.

1. First, those disciplines from which Hick garners supporting evidence—particularly the sociology of knowledge school—in and of themselves suggest a fully constructivist/anti-realist interpretation of religion. While Hick makes use of such thought in one sector of his theory—i.e., in his relativization of phenomenal manifestations, he arbitrarily refuses it admission into those quarters of his model where it could do some serious anti-realist damage—i.e., the insular sanctum that safely houses his postulated noumenal Real. Thus, Hick is found walking a thin, imaginary tight-rope, with threats to his religious realism, or pluralism, on either side.
2. Secondly, Hick's various attempts to distance himself from Kant serve to heighten, rather than dampen, the subjectivist menace. The general transposition of Kant's schema from sensory to religious experience is not merely "very non-Kantian" in a benign sort of way.[41] Rather, it is a transfer to an experiential realm where there is significantly less "empirical" consensus or control. Thus, from the outset, one can expect that Hick's religious project will justly be exposed to subjectivist suspicions even beyond those directed at Kant's sensory-centred programme.[42]
3. A third critical problem involves Hick's category-analogues. As J. William Forgie has shown, "hyper-Kantian" readings of religious experience such as Hick's serve to intensify the already present Kantian subjectivist threat in at least two ways. As noted earlier, while Kant's categories—as *a priori* knowledge—are by definition strictly universal and necessary, applying to all persons of all places and times, Hick's analogues are entirely culture-relative and contingent in nature. Hick explicitly acknowledges this first prong of Forgie's critique, but his only response is that such a deviation constitutes no rival system to Kant, since it is applied in a different experiential realm. Here he seems to miss the damaging subjectivist implications at the heart of the charge.[43] Forgie's observation can be further devel-

oped through the additional insight that, given our "age of eclecticism," fuelled by the modern spirit of individualism, religious "traditions" themselves have been rendered unstable and contingent.[44] Thus a second level of contingency reveals itself in Hick's category-analogues. Add to all of this the phenomenological observation that—even within the *very same religio-culture system*—one can often witness radically *different* experiences of the divine, just where Hick's model would seem to suggest a similar schematization. Each of these observations serves to implicate further Hick's proposal with a radical subjectivism, and hence scepticism.

Another—and potentially more devastating—observation of Forgie's goes unaddressed by Hick. Forgie notes that in Kant's model, the categories "shape" experience and thus ensure that it will take certain forms. But the categories themselves do not provide the *content* of the experiences they form.[45] In "hyper-Kantian" models, however, the subject-based category-analogues (and one could add "form-analogues") *do* contribute to the phenomenological content of the experience.[46] And when it comes to Hick's model in particular, the contribution is clearly significant. This hyper-Kantian twist forces the conclusion that the human subject's religious category-analogues, schematized by their religio-cultural systems, *can* account for both the form and content of religious experience. And thus one is forced to ask what, in fact, differentiates Hick's neo-Kantian constructivism from the essentially identical reductionist, anti-realist models?[47]

**4.** Fourth and finally, considering the complexity—many would add internal inconsistency—of Kant's "things in themselves" *vs.* "appearances" schema, and the various interpretations, counter-interpretations, and accusations with which one finds it embroiled, anyone seeking to make use of it today must be prepared to enter the philosophical fray.[48] As suggested above, Hick's relocation of the schema to the religious realm does not safeguard him from such questions, but rather actually exacerbates them. Thus, Hick's claim to immunity from having to enter into the thicket of Kantian interpretation debate is unconvincing.

One way in which Hick has attempted to avoid the radical subjectivist threat is by maintaining—as does his reading of Kant—that "the phenomenal world *is* [the noumenal world] as it appears to our human consciousness."[49] Such an emphasis is characteristic of a "one world" or "double aspect"—as opposed to a "two worlds"—reading of Kant. (I.e., the noumenal/phenomenal distinction signifies not two ontologically independent realms or "worlds," but rather merely the one objective world considered from two *perspectives:* as it is in itself, *vs.* as it appears to human consciousness.) Clearly Hick does (and must) associate himself with such a perspectival understanding of the noumenal/phenomenal schema, given the nature and claims of his model.

The problem is, however, that his specific restructuring of the Kantian programme (which itself already stands in a questionable relation to a pure and simple "one world" interpretation)[50] exhibits just the type of developments that would serve to render such an interpretation implausible. Specifically, in a perspectival interpretation, to speak of the unknowability of the noumenal is simply to speak tautologically: it is to consider an object of a subject's knowledge as *apart* from that knowledge, and so—by definition—as unknowable.[51] What, then, leads Kant to postulate the real existence of such a noumenon behind the phenomenal apprehension when, in fact, it is strictly unknowable? In large part, the answer to this question is that aside from such a postulation,

> it would be impossible to give any plausible account of the source of "the empirical differences in shapes and sizes" of the objects of everyday experience. . . . Only what is common to all representations is, for Kant, supplied a priori by the subject in the act of representing. So the thing in itself must be posited and assumed to determine in some sense the raw material for any possible object of knowledge.[52]

But when a similar question is asked of Hick's neo-Kantian model—namely, upon what basis he can make a realist claim concerning the divine noumenal Real—a comparable defence is not available. The simple reason for this is that, unlike Kant, Hick's subject-based categories themselves—as discussed earlier—contribute significantly to the supposed "raw material" of religious experience. Thus, virtually *everything* of content—including the specific and varied "shapes and sizes" so to speak—of the religious phenomenal manifestations can be accounted for by those religious concepts and sentiments found in the religio-cultural systems and/or in the individuals themselves. In Hick's hypothesis—again, unlike Kant's—there is *nothing* residual that *requires* the postulation of an "unknowable" (divine) noumenon; everything can be adequately explained, via the human form/category-analogues, apart from and without the noumenon.

Hick would no doubt respond that such a charge ignores his claim that a transcendent source of "information" is always an essential constitutive element of religious experience. But a counter-question reveals the practical insignificance of this claim: what "information," given the complete incommensurability between human conceptual capacities and the divine, could ever make a distinguishable—and thus practical—difference? Or, again, upon what basis should one ever suspect that "religious experience" includes an irreducibly extra-subjective element when, in fact, it can already be accounted for *in its entirety* as a purely projective exercise? Even on his own terms, the most Hick can allow for from the divine side of the experience is an undefinable apprehension "at some deep level" of the human psyche, which is, of course, always then "expressed in forms supplied by his or her mind."[53] Such non-informative "information" hardly offers hard data in the religious experience. And thus, Hick's appeal to a non-human, transcendently derived component in religious experience does not vitiate the radical subjectivism of his proposal.

In conclusion, it would appear that the noumenal Real in Hick's system is rendered a purely unnecessary and unjustifiable construct. While it *may* exist, like almost anything in the realm of the "conceivably possible," there is certainly no reason to think that it *does*. Clearly Gavin D'Costa's characterization of Hick's position as a "transcendental agnosticism" is more than accurate.[54] It is critical to see here that there is virtually nothing that Hick can do to remedy this unfortunate situation; he is precariously situated between the proverbial Scylla and Charybdis. For the only way out of the jaws of the anti-realist constructivism implied in this critique is to reinvest the noumenal Real with the ability to deliver a decisive—and identifiable—amount of raw experiential content, above and beyond any human-based contributions. But this is exactly what Hick cannot do if his neo-Kantian model is to serve and protect his pluralistic agenda. And so, with Don Cupitt, one may rightly ask in regard to Hick's "thin-line" religious realism, what, really, prevents him from taking "just one more step and [saying] that religion is wholly human."[55] Again—and this is critically important—Hick's typical response to this challenge, that *religious experience* provides the basis for such realist hopes, has been shown to be effectively undermined by the implications of his own neo-Kantian proposal.[56]

## NOTES

1. John Hick, *An Interpretation of Religion: Human Responses to the Transcendent* (New Haven/London: Yale University Press, 1989), p. 240. This work is henceforth noted as *IR*.

2. The term "neo-Kantian" is used throughout this essay in a very general sense; it implies no connection to the German philosophical movement of the late nineteenth and early twentieth centuries.

3. Hick, "Mystical Experience as Cognition," in Harold Coward and Terence Penelhum (eds.), *Mystics and Scholars: The Calgary Conference on Mysticism, 1976* (Calgary: Canadian Corp. for Studies in Religion, 1977), pp. 41–61.

4. See, for instance, the essays comprising Chapters 3, 5, and 6 in Hick, *God Has Many Names* (Philadelphia: Westminster, 1980).

5. See Hick, *Faith and Knowledge* (2nd ed.; London: Collins-Fontana, 1974 [1957]), p. viii.

6. *IR*, p. 240.

7. *Ibid.*, p. 242.

8. *Ibid.*, p. 246.

9. See (1) "The Real in Itself and as Humanly Experienced," pp. 236–40; and (2) "Kant's Epistemological Model," pp. 240–46.

10. *IR*, pp. 236–37.

11. *Ibid.*, p. 237.

12. *Ibid.*, p. 238.

13. *Ibid.*, p. 239 (emphasis added).

14. While Hick ("The Philosophy of World Religions," *Scottish Journal of Theology*, XXXVII [1984], 232) has denied that his model owes anything significant to the notion of divine infinity, the fact that he nonetheless continues to devote a significant amount of space to it in the explication of his pluralist hypothesis (see *IR*, pp. 237–39) suggests that he is still gaining currency from this connection.

15. *Ibid.*, p. 237.

16. Thomas Finger, *Christian Theology: An Eschatological Approach* (Scottsdale, PA: Herald, 1985, 1989), vol. II, p. 502. See also Stephen Davis, "Why God Must be Unlimited," in Linda J. Tessier (ed.), *Concepts of the Ultimate* (New York: St. Martin's Press, 1989), pp. 4–6.

17. See especially Raoul Mortley, *From Word to Silence*, vol. 2: *The Way of Negation, Christian and Greek* (Bonn: Hanstein, 1986), pp. 242–54. See also Keith Ward, "Truth and the Diversity of Religions," *Religious Studies*, XXVI (1990), 6–11 [see pp. 114–18 in Chapter 6 of this volume]; *idem*. "Divine Ineffability," in Arvind Sharma (ed.) *God, Truth and Reality: Essays in Honour of John Hick* (New York: St. Martin's Press, 1993), pp. 210–220; Alvin Plantinga, *Does God Have a Nature?* (Milwaukee: Marquette University Press, 1980), pp. 18–20.

18. E.g., see, respectively, Humphrey Palmer, *Analogy: A Study of Qualification and Argument in Theology* (New York: St. Martin's Press, 1973), esp. Chapter 13; David Burrell, *Aquinas, God and Action* (London: Routledge and Kegan, 1979).

19. E.g., see Gerard J. Hughes, "Aquinas and the Limits of Agnosticism," in G. Hughes (ed.), *The Philosophical Assessment of Theology: Essays in Honour of Frederick C. Copleston* (Washington D.C.: Georgetown University Press, 1987), pp. 37–63; Gregory P. Rocca, "Aquinas on God-Talk: Hovering Over the Abyss," *Theological Studies*, LIV (1993), 641–61; George Lindbeck, "The *A Priori* in St. Thomas' Theory of Knowledge," in R. E. Cushman and E. Grislis (eds.), *The Heritage of Christian Thought: Essays in Honor of Robert Lowry Calhoun* (New York: Harper & Row, 1965), pp. 41–63.

20. E.g., see Richard Swinburne, *The Coherence of Theism* (rev. ed.; Oxford Clarendon, 1993), Chapters 4 and 5; *idem*. "Analogy and Metaphor," in *Philosophical Assessment of Theology*, pp. 65–84; Patrick J. Sherry, "Analogy Today," *Philosophy* LI (1976), 431–46; Barry Miller, "Analogy Sans Portrait: God-Talk as Literal but Non-Anthropomorphic," *Faith and Philosophy*, VII (1990), 63–71.

21. E.g., see Timothy J. Pennings, "Infinity and the Absolute: Insights into Our World, Our Faith and Ourselves," *Christian Scholar's Review*, XXIII/2 (1993), 159–80.

22. See Palmer's (*Analogy*, pp. 26–27) discussion in this regard. I am indebted at several points here to Peter Byrne's ("John Hick's Philosophy of World Religions," *Scottish Journal of Theology*, XXXV [1982], 296–99) critique of Hick's use of the concept of divine infinity.

23. For an excellent discussion of these matters, see Jill Le Blanc, "Infinity in Theology and Mathematics," *Religious Studies*, XXIX (1993), 51–62.

24. See *Ibid.*, pp. 59–62.

25. In this regard see Frederick Ferre, "In Praise of Anthropomorphism," in Robert P. Scharlemann and Gilbert E. M. Ogutu (eds.), *God in Language* (New York: Paragon, 1987), p. 192.

26. Ward, "Truth and the Diversity of Religions," p. 10 [see p. 117 in Chapter 6 of this volume].

27. *IR*, p. 246.

28. Ward, "Truth and the Diversity of Religions," p. 10 [see p. 118 in Chapter 6 of this volume].

29. Ludwig Feuerbach, *The Essence of Christianity* (trans. George Elliot; New York: Harper & Row, 1957 [1841]), pp. 14–15. See the similar challenge of David Hume, *Dialogues Concerning Natural Religion* (Indianapolis/New York: Bobbs-Merrill, 1947 [1779]), Pt. IV, p. 158.

30. Hick was not the first to view religious experience in light of these specific Kantian categories; e.g., see Rudolf Otto, *Naturalism and Religion* (New York: Putnam's Sons, 1907); Robert A. Oakes, "Noumena, Phenomena, and God," *International Journal for Philosophy of Religion*, IV (1973), 30–38.

31. This term derives from William Forgie's "Hyper-Kantianism in Recent Discussions of Mystical Experience," *Religious Studies*, XXI (1985), 208. Forgie does not, however, apply his critique to Hick.

32. *IR*, p. 245.

33. *Ibid.*, p. 241.

34. *Ibid.*, p. 240. Here important sources for Hick include Peter Berger and Thomas Luckmann, *The Social Construction of Reality* (Garden City: Doubleday, 1966); Michael Arbib and Mary Hesse, *The Construction of Reality* (Cambridge: Cambridge University Press, 1986); and the work of Clifford Geertz.

35. Cited in *IR*, pp. 240–41. Here, Hick also claims the same vis-à-vis the Muslim thinker al Junaid's maxim: "The colour of the water is the same as that of its container."

36. *Ibid.*, p. 244.

37. *Ibid.*, pp. 240, 244.

38. See Immanuel Kant, *The Critique of Pure Reason* (abr. ed.; trans. Norman Kemp Smith; London: Macmillan, 1952), pp. 26–27, 72.

39. *IR*, pp. 243–44.

40. For readings of Kant's noumenal/phenomenal distinction in an antirealist vein, see Hilary Putnam, *Reason, Truth, and History* (Cambridge: Cambridge University Press, 1981), Chapter 3; Carl Posy, "Dancing to the Antinomy: A Proposal for Transcendental Idealism," *American Philosophical Quarterly*, XX (1983), 81–94.

41. Hick, *God Has Many Names*, p. 105.

42. E.g., see L. Philip Barnes, "Relativism, Ineffability, and the Appeal to Experience: A Reply to the Myth Makers," *Modern Theology*, VII (1990), 101–14.

43. *IR*, p. 244.

44. See Ninian Smart, "A Contemplation of Absolutes," in *God, Truth and Reality*, pp. 184–85 [see p. 106 in Chapter 5 of this volume].

45. For Kant, "the *a priori,* then, is merely relational, without inherent content" (Norman Kemp Smith, *A Commentary to Kant's "Critique of Pure Reason"* [rev. ed.; Atlantic Highlands, NJ: Humanities, 1992], p. xxxvi).

46. Forgie, "Hyper-Kantianism," p. 208.

47. In this general regard, see Michael Stoeber, "Constructivist Epistemologies of Mysticism: A Critique and Revision," *Religious Studies,* XXVIII (1992), 107–16.

48. In regard to the various interpretations and criticisms of Kant at this point, see Karl Ameriks, "Recent Work on Kant's Theoretical Philosophy," *American Philosophical Quarterly,* XIX (1982), 1–24; Richard E. Aquila, "Things in Themselves and Appearances: Intentionality and Reality in Kant," *Archiv für Geschichte Der Philosophie,* LXI (1979), esp. pp. 293–95.

49. *IR,* p. 241 (emphasis added).

50. See the surveys cited at Note 48 for problematic aspects of reading Kant in a purely "one world"/perspectival manner. See also Philip Rossi, "The Final End of All Things: The Highest Good as the Unity of Nature and Freedom," in P. Rossi and M. Wreen (eds.), *Kant's Philosophy of Religion Reconsidered* (Bloomington/Indianapolis: Indiana University Press, 1991), pp. 133–64.

51. Stephen R. Palmquist, *Kant's System of Perspectives: An Architectonic Interpretation of the Critical Philosophy* (Lanham: University Press of America, 1993), pp. 169–70, 176–77; see also Appendix 5: "The Radical Unknowability of the Thing In Itself."

52. *Ibid.,* p. 178.

53. *IR,* p. 166.

54. D'Costa, "John Hick and Religious Pluralism: Yet Another Revolution," in Harold Hewitt (ed.), *Problems in the Philosophy of Religion: Critical Studies of the Work of John Hick* (New York: St. Martin's Press, 1991), pp. 3–18.

55. Don Cupitt, "Thin-Line Theism," *The Times Literary Supplement,* 8 August 1980, p. 902.

56. Many thanks to Professor Hick, as well as Michael Barnes, Gavin D'Costa, Brad Hinze, Harold Netland, Bruce Reichenbach, Philip Rossi, and John Sanders, for helpful comments on earlier drafts of this paper.

CHAPTER 8

# Polytheism

George I. Mavrodes

*Ben-hadad had sent out scouts, and they reported to him, "Men have come out from Samaria." He said, "If they have come out for peace, take them alive; if they have come out for war, take them alive."*

*But these had already come out of the city: the young men who serve the district governors, and the army that followed them. Each killed his man; the Arameans fled and Israel pursued them, but King Ben-hadad of Aram escaped on a horse with the cavalry. The king of Israel went out, attacked the horses and chariots, and defeated the Arameans with a great slaughter. . . .*

*The servants of the king of Aram said to him, "Their gods are gods of the hills, and so they were stronger than we; but let us fight against them in the plain, and surely we shall be stronger than they."*[1]

Almost all philosophy of religion in the West has assumed that any religion worth thinking about seriously is either monotheistic or else the nontheistic analogue of monotheism, a religion oriented toward a single impersonal ultimate. Polytheism has not gotten a fair shake in the philosophical casino; indeed, it has hardly gotten any shake at all, at least in the West. But perhaps that neglect is being remedied, to some small extent, now at the end of the twentieth century. I am thinking primarily of John Hick's published Gifford Lectures.[2] Hick is (in my opinion, at least) probably the most important philosophical defender of polytheism in the history of Western philosophy. But I think he does not much care for that description himself. In any case, my own interest in polytheism has been largely stimulated by Hick's work, and his book provides a lot of material for philosophical rumination on that topic. In this essay I intend to explore some of the possibilities, and also some of the problems, associated with polytheism, with considerable reference to some of Hick's claims. But I have begun with an ancient reference to actual polytheistic religious thought (and practice?), an account from the Hebrew scriptures in the Bible.

The Aramean polytheists who figure in this passage were not, I suppose, philosophers in any profound sense. They were practitioners of their own religion but probably not deep reflectors on it. And the person who here described them—a Hebrew scribe—probably was not a philosopher either. I suppose the philosophical reflection and analysis must largely be ours, but some of the religions, and the religious thought, on which we are reflecting are theirs (and their neighbors'). I begin by trying to identify and clarify several prominent characteristics of the religious views of these ancient Arameans, as they are suggested in this text.

1. *Realism.* The Arameans of this story are evidently realists with regard to the gods. That is, they think of the gods as belonging to the order of reality, as being real entities (rather than, say, hallucinations, imaginary beings, or fictions). I suppose they think that the gods are at least as real as they themselves are, and at least as real as ordinary physical objects, animals, and so on. A good clue to their realism is the fact that they evidently expect the gods to have effects in the ordinary world, in such a way that some happenings in the world can be explained by reference to the actions of the gods. They account for their own military defeat by citing the fact that they were foolish enough to fight in the hills, the home turf of the Hebrew gods. Naturally, they lost. And so they resolve not to make that mistake again. Next time they will fight on the plains, where presumably their own gods are at home and the Hebrew gods are strangers, and they expect to win there.

In this essay I adopt what I take to be the expectation of the Arameans as a minimal working account of a sufficient condition for something's being *real.* If some putative entity, *x*, can *itself* have a causal effect in the ordinary world, then *x* is real (or at least real enough for what I want to say here). But I stress the "itself" above. The fact that a belief in *x*, for example, or some other intentional attitude toward *x*, can generate effects in the world is not sufficient to make *x* real. Atheists deny the existence and reality of God (or the gods). So they do not suppose that God created the world; they do not expect the miraculous cure of a disease or the reversal of a tide of battle by an infusion of divine power. But they do not characteristically deny that *belief* in God, the *worship* of God, and so on have real effects in the world. On the contrary, they often bemoan those effects and sometimes praise them. I think such atheists have a grip on the notion of reality, and I am adopting it here.

2. *Pure Descriptivism.* These Arameans appear to be pure descriptivists in their use of the term "god." That is, when they use this term, they presumably intend to identify and refer to a being of a certain kind, but they do not, merely by using this term, express any particular attitude of their own toward that being. In particular, they do not imply that they themselves worship the god to whom they refer, or that they are committed to serve or obey that god, or that they have any loyalty to him or her, and so on. This seems clear from the fact that they refer

> to the Hebrew deities ("their gods") even while plotting a way of defeating these gods and their Hebrew protegés.

No doubt the Arameans had gods to whom they did have some commitments of loyalty and obedience, whom they worshiped, and so on. Following the suggestion in this text, I use possessive pronouns ("my," "their," etc.) and similar locutions when I wish to indicate the gods who are linked to certain persons by relations such as worship and commitment, and use "god" without such indicators as a descriptive term without any implication of such relations.

Many, at least, of the attitudes and actions that link people with their gods are *intentional.* It isn't easy to define intentionality precisely. But perhaps we are familiar enough with it in statements such as "Debbie is looking for a perfect man." If I were to assert that, I would *not* be committing *myself* to the belief that there is such a thing as a perfect man, or even that there could be. (Nor, for that matter, would I commit myself to the view that there is no perfect man.) But I might well be describing Debbie's project in a way that she could recognize and accept. And what I would be saying about her could well be true even if there is no such thing as a perfect man. If I were to say, however, that Debbie had *found* a perfect man, then (in its ordinary interpretation) what I said could not be true unless there were in fact a perfect man. *Looking for* is an intentional notion, and it does not require that its object exist. *Finding,* on the other hand, is nonintentional, and it requires an existing object. And so I say that the Arameans worshiped gods of the plains, while remaining neutral myself about whether there really are any gods of the plains. The intentional objects of their worship are the gods of the plains, even if in fact there are no gods of the plains.

I say that the Arameans use "god" as a descriptive term, but nothing in the text indicates just what description they may have had in mind. They might be willing to accept a description suggested by Richard Swinburne, "a very powerful non-embodied rational agent."[3] At any rate, I begin with this as a sort of working description, and I will say something more later on about the possible attributes of a polytheistic god.

3. *Pluralism.* I think these Arameans are pluralist about the gods in the sense that they think there really are *distinct* gods. It doesn't seem that they would have any enthusiasm at all for the suggestion that these various gods might really all be the very same god, going by different names. For they evidently think that these gods might be in conflict with one another, some of them backing the Hebrews and others supporting the Arameans. These people would take seriously the "poly" in "polytheist."
4. *Descriptive Polytheism vs. Cultic Polytheism.* The Arameans evidently recognize some gods whom they do not worship or serve. But probably they were religious people themselves, worshiping and serving one or more gods. That fact suggests a distinction that is especially

important in thinking about polytheism. A person who is both a realist and a pluralist about the gods is a *descriptive* polytheist. She thinks there are several distinct entities that fit some appropriate description, perhaps the description I suggested above. (And if she is also a pure descriptivist, she may use the term "god" for all these entities.)[4] If she herself worships and serves more than one distinct god, then she is a *cultic* polytheist. The Arameans were probably cultic polytheists (though nothing is said specifically about that in this text). But their cultic polytheism was not as broad as their descriptive polytheism, since they recognized the Hebrew gods[5] but did not worship or serve them.

Once we recognize this distinction, we can see that there are several other possible combinations of these two elements. One of the more interesting is that of combining descriptive polytheism with cultic monotheism.[6] Such a person would recognize the reality of several gods but would give his heart to only one of them. As we shall see below, John Hick might be just such a person. And I suppose there might be someone who was a descriptive polytheist (or a descriptive monotheist, for that matter) and a cultic atheist, recognizing several gods (or one) but worshiping and serving none at all.[7]

Might there be a person who is a descriptive atheist and a cultic monotheist (or polytheist)? I return to this question later, in connection with one of Hick's suggestions.

The distinction we have just been considering is closely related to a distinction that can be put in somewhat different terms, that between polytheism in *religion* and polytheism in *religious thought.* A person who worships and serves a single god might plausibly be said to be practicing a monotheistic religion, regardless of how many other gods she recognizes. But I suppose that a person who recognizes several gods would be a polytheist in her religious thought—or, perhaps better, in her thought about religion—regardless of how many gods (if any) she serves. In this essay I shall have occasion to comment on both polytheistic religion and polytheistic religious thought, but most of the discussion focuses on the latter.

5. *Finitism.* The Arameans evidently considered the gods, both their own and those of the Hebrews, to be finite entities, limited in important ways. The most prominent version of this feature in the story at hand involves the way in which the Arameans believed the gods to be associated with various geographical regions. Other versions of polytheism limit the gods in other ways; for example, the polytheists of classical Greece and Rome assigned the various gods a particular influence and hegemony over various and distinct areas of human life and interest.
6. *A Common World.* Though the gods, as the Arameans construed them, were finite and distinct, they were not isolated from one another. They shared a common world as at least one focus of their actions.

> They could collide with one another. Perhaps there could be direct, unmediated collisions and conflicts, though nothing is clearly said about that possibility here. It does seem pretty clear, however, that they could collide in a mediated way, through their effects on elements of the ordinary world, particularly through their sponsorship of, or actions against, various human beings and human groups. The Arameans and the Hebrews shared a common world (even if it was mostly a common border between the hill country and the lowlands), and so their gods, if they were to have effects in the world of their protegés, must also share that same common world.

So much, for the time being, about these characteristics of Aramean polytheism. How might they bear on polytheism now, especially philosophical polytheism?

I don't have much of an idea, in any detail anyway, about why the Arameans of this story believed in their own gods. But they probably did not make up the Hebrew gods out of whole cloth. They probably knew that the Hebrews had a religion, that they had ceremonies of worship, sacrifice, prayer, and so on. Perhaps they were even familiar with some Hebrew claims about their god or gods. Since they thought of their own gods in a rather limited and parochial way, it may have seemed natural to them to suppose that there must be other gods who had a similar parochial relation to other nations. And maybe they were generous enough to accept, more or less at face value, those other people's accounts of their own deities.

However that may be, we find ourselves in a somewhat similar situation, whether or not we have a religion of our own. For we too know that other people are religious, that (in the intentional sense, at least) they worship gods or contemplate impersonal absolutes, and so on. And so the question may arise for us too, as to how we are to think of the gods and absolutes that are not our own. One might say that in addition to the celebrated problem of other minds, there is, in a vaguely analogous way, a problem of other gods.

The hard-nosed (descriptive) atheist, I suppose, will not have much trouble with this question. Such a person has a single, all-purpose attitude toward the whole menagerie of divinities. They are all unreal. They do not exist, neither the Holy Trinity, or Allah, nor Shiva, nor . . . They do not belong to the order of the world.

The situation may be somewhat more complex for people who are themselves religious believers. Christians, for example, generally profess to be cultic monotheists. So they do not reject gods out of hand or universally. What are they descriptively? Many of them would also, I think, profess to being descriptive monotheists. And where does that leave the gods of the other religions? Here there seem to be two alternatives.

The first is that of saying that the gods of the other religions are real too, just as real as the god of Christianity. And how can that answer cohere with descriptive monotheism? It's easy. On this view the gods of the other religions are simply *identical* with the god of Christianity. And this is sometimes put by the slogan that God has many names. Of course, to be consistent, this view has to accept the consequence that some theologies—some bodies of belief that are integral to one religion or another—must be pretty badly mistaken. It doesn't seem possible, for example, that Muslims and Christians can both be right about the doctrine of the Trinity. But perhaps this consequence can be accepted, especially if we remember that saying that a certain theology is badly mistaken need not be the same thing as saying that the corresponding religion is evil, or useless, or anything of the sort.

I suspect, however, that rather few Christians have accepted the whole-hog view just described. More of them have been attracted to a somewhat weakened version of it, to the effect that the gods of *some* other religions are identical with the god of Christianity. The other religions usually turn out to be monotheisms themselves, and indeed monotheisms that seem to be rather like Christianity in some important ways.[8] In any case, this watered-down version leaves us with the question of what to do with the remaining gods.

The second option for those who want to be both cultic and descriptive monotheists is that of denying the reality of the other gods (or of some of them). Those Christians will be, one might say, theists with respect to the Holy Trinity and atheists with respect to the other gods.[9] So far as I can see, there is nothing radically incoherent in such a position, though it may strike some observers as ungenerous, chauvinistic, or the like. This position, however, might give rise to some penetrating and disturbing questions, questions about how so many people in the other religious traditions could be deluded into worshiping nonexistent entities, and into building whole lives, sometimes lives of remarkable devotion and sacrifice, around gross unrealities. Such questions may be disturbing to the cultic monotheist because they (or their answers) tend to generate doubts about *her own* religious commitments. She, after all, does not write off the *whole* religious program as the atheist does. She will want to maintain the reality of her own god, even as she denies the reality of the others. But her denial of the reality of what *seems* real to so many other people of high intelligence and evident goodness may generate, in her own mind, doubts about the correctness of her judgment of her own religion and her own god. I say that such doubts may be generated, and that there is the potential for "disturbance" in such questions. But, of course, one or another monotheist of this general sort may find a way to resolve such doubts and to lay such disturbances to rest, at least to his or her own satisfaction.

Some Christians, however (and some other cultic monotheists, I suppose), are descriptive polytheists. That is, they are descriptive polytheists in fact, if not in name. A comparatively straightforward position of this sort is that of Christians who have held that the gods of other religions are devils. Of course, saying that the god of another religion is a devil seems to imply a strongly negative judgment, and no doubt that is what was usually intended. But that need not prevent this view from being a genuine descriptive polytheism. Possibly, the attitude of worship requires a judgment on the part of the worshiper that the object of his worship is good and/or holy. But *descriptive* polytheism does not imply an attitude of worship on the part of the descriptivist. And it is worth noting that the description of a god that I culled earlier from Richard Swinburne makes no mention of goodness or any similar value or virtue. A devil would seem to fit Swinburne's description perfectly well. And so it seems quite possible that some one entity should be both a god and a devil—a god in Swinburne's sense and a devil in some expanded sense that includes (negative) valuational elements. Furthermore, those Christians who think that the gods of other religions are devils are likely to think also that devils are real beings, at least as real as cantaloupes and giraffes. That is, they think that devils are actual creatures (on some views, angelic creatures who "fell"), created by the same divine power that created the rest of the existing universe.[10]

There are still other ways of being simultaneously a cultic monotheist and a descriptive polytheist. I mentioned John Hick as a distinguished modern defender of polytheism. Hick's position will be of special interest to philosophers, I think, because it is attached to a prominent, though highly controversial, philosophical tradition, that of Kantian epistemology and metaphysics. I turn now to a consideration of Hick's proposal as it was developed in his series of Gifford Lectures, exploring some of its promise and also some of its problems.

I begin with a quotation:

> Within each tradition we regard as real the object of our worship or contemplation. If, as I have already argued, it is also proper to regard as real the objects of worship or contemplation within the other traditions, we are led to postulate the Real *an sich* as the presupposition of the veridical character of this range of forms of religious experience. Without this postulate we should be left with a plurality of *personae* and *impersonae* each of which claimed to be the Ultimate, but no one of which alone can be. We should have either to regard all the reported experiences as illusory or else return to the confessional position in which we affirm the authenticity of our own stream of religious experience whilst dismissing as illusory those occurring within other traditions. But for those to whom neither of these options seems realistic the pluralistic affirmation becomes inevitable, and with it the postulation of the Real *an sich*, which is variously experienced and thought as the range of divine phenomena described by the history of religion. (p. 249)

In this paragraph, as indeed throughout the book, a monistic element is interwoven with the pluralistic strand of Hick's thinking. If for the moment we leave out that monistic element—that is, the references to the Real *an sich*—then we get a view that seems, to me at least, strongly suggestive of the Aramean picture with which this essay began. We regard as real the gods and absolutes of our own religion, *and we are to regard the gods and absolutes of the other religions also as real.* We may or may not be cultic monotheists, depending on the architecture of our own religion, but Hick argues that the only religiously proper and justified *descriptive* stance is that of polytheism.

I say that on Hick's view this is the "religiously" proper stance because Hick professes to give us here a *religious* interpretation of religion. His interpretation, that is, is not one that is intended to reduce religion to something else, accounting for it in terms of purely natural factors. Rather, he intends to understand religion as a "human response to a transcendent reality or realities" (p. 1). The reductionistic, naturalistic mode of interpretation would yield the conclusion that *all* the gods were unreal or illusory.[11] From the religious standpoint, however, we come to regard them all as real.

I have already mentioned a view sometimes casually affirmed by religious ecumenists which readily yields the conclusion that all the gods are real, or at least that they are as real as our own god. This is the view that all the gods of the various religions are really just one and the same god, the view sometimes put by saying that God has many names. But Hick seems to reject this view, on the grounds that the various gods are described, within the various corresponding religions, in mutually incompatible ways. "Surely these reported ultimates, personal and impersonal, are mutually exclusive" (p. 234). And if they are mutually exclusive, then, I suppose, they could not be identical.

It would be possible to reject this argument by holding that the enthusiasts of most religions—or all of them, for that matter—are substantially mistaken about their gods. They attribute to their gods properties they do not actually have, and it is these properties that generate the apparent incompatibility among the divine beings. So we might hold that the Muslim God and the Christian God are one and the same being after all, but that either the Muslims are mistaken in thinking that Allah is not a trinity or else the Christians are mistaken in thinking that there are three divine persons in the Godhead. And we might hold, perhaps even more radically, that the Holy Trinity is identical with Nirvana, but that Buddhists generally are mistaken in believing that Nirvana is nonpersonal, and so on. But maybe Hick thinks that the supposition that religious people could be so wildly mistaken about their own deities is too implausible to be taken seriously.

Comparing Hick's views with those I identified earlier in connection with the Arameans, we get (so far) the following results:

1. Hick, like the Arameans, seems to be both a realist and a pluralist about the various gods.
2. Again like the Arameans, Hick seems to be a pure descriptivist in his use of the term "god." He recognizes a wide variety of gods, and he calls them "gods," but he also makes clear (at least in conversation) that he intends his own religious commitments, worship, and so on, to find their place within the Christian tradition. In recognizing the reality of the Hindu gods, he does not become a Hindu.
3. Hick therefore, like the Arameans, seems to be a descriptive polytheist, but (probably unlike the Arameans) he is a cultic monotheist.
4. Is Hick, like the Arameans, a finitist with respect to the gods? Perhaps that question can be better answered after we consider the monistic strand in Hick's thinking.

Hick is pluralistic about the gods of the world's religions, but he declares himself to be monist about something else, something that is more ultimate in some final way, and hence metaphysically more basic, than any of these religious *personae* and *impersonae.* This item is what Hick calls "the Real." But though the Real appears to be on a different metaphysical level from that of the gods, it is not unrelated to them. I suppose it would not be far amiss to say that, on Hick's view, the Real is the ground and source of the gods.

Hick's own way of putting the point makes use of Kantian terminology and appeals to Kantian epistemology and metaphysics. Hick says, for example:

> In developing this thesis our chief philosophical resource will be one of Kant's most basic epistemological insights, namely that the mind actively interprets sensory information in terms of concepts. . . . For Kant God is postulated, not experienced. In partial agreement but also partial disagreement with him, I want to say that the Real *an sich* is postulated by us as a pre-supposition, not of the moral life, but of religious experience and the religious life, whilst the gods, as also the mystically known Brahman, Sunyata and so on, are phenomenal manifestations of the Real occurring within the realm of religious experience. Conflating these two theses one can say that the Real is experienced by human beings, but experienced in a manner analogous to that in which, according to Kant, we experience the world: namely by informational input from external reality being interpreted by the mind in terms of its own categorical scheme and thus coming to consciousness as a meaningful phenomenal experience. All that we are entitled to say about the noumenal source of this information is that it is the reality whose influence produces, in collaboration with the human mind, the phenomenal world of our experience. (pp. 240, 243)

This is not, of course, Kant's own account of religious experience or of divine beings. Hick has here taken Kant's way of treating our sensory experience of the ordinary world and has adapted it to serve as a way of understanding religious experience and its special objects, especially the gods and the impersonal absolutes. And he has broadened Kant's idea of the categorical machinery the mind brings to experience by allowing it to include elements that are not innate and universal but that are instead culturally conditioned and variable. And, according to Hick, the fact that different religious traditions provide their adherents with differing categories for conceptualizing the divine is what accounts for the diversity of divine beings that appear in these different religions.

This account, it seems to me, adds some further substance to my earlier claim that Hick can be thought of as a *realist* with respect to the gods and so on of the various religions.[12] For we can say that, on Hick's view, all the gods are real *in the same sense that cantaloupes are real on the Kantian view.* And, of course, on the Kantian view of things, ordinary cantaloupes such as one may buy in the supermarket are real in an important sense. They are not imaginary cantaloupes, they are not fictional melons, not hallucinations, and so on. They coexist with us and other things in the physical world, where they are causally significant. But, of course, Kantian cantaloupes are not metaphysically ultimate—they are not *Dingen an sich.* And neither are Hickian gods.

Is that a *religiously* satisfactory view? Probably that question has no single answer. Some people will certainly not find Hick's view satisfactory. They want their gods to be *more real* than cantaloupes—and not merely bigger or more powerful than cantaloupes. A watermelon, or even an elephant, would come no closer to filling the bill. And if those people cannot find gods who do seem to fill that bill, then they will give up on religion altogether. On the other hand, there have apparently been people who have built a religious and spiritual life around gods whose warrant (they believed) ended with the first line of hills, not twenty miles away, or with gods who took care of agriculture but had nothing to do with seafaring. Perhaps those people would not have found Hick's phenomenal gods all that unsatisfactory. (After all, those gods are thought to be at least a real as cantaloupes. And a cantaloupe is a real entity, a force to be reckoned with, something to be sought for the enrichment of human life.) For all I know, there may be people like that still.

There is, however, a deep ambiguity in Hick's way of thinking about the relation of the Real to the gods, an ambiguity that has an important bearing on the logical viability of any polytheism. And this ambiguity may be the reflection of a similar ambiguity in Kant's own discussions of the phenomenal world and the noumenal reality that is supposed to underlie it. It involves the difference between, on the one hand, thinking (or saying) that the phenomenon *is the noumenon* as experienced, as it appears, and so on, and, on the other hand, thinking (or saying) that the phenomenon *is a human creation* in reaction to some influence, input, or the like from the noumenon. I call these two ways of thinking about the phenomenon/noumenon relation the "disguise model" and the "construct model," respectively.

The difference between these models may perhaps be made plainer by thinking of two analogies. One of these is suggested by Hick himself. He says that we need not work through Kant's "complex philosophical architectonic" to arrive at the distinction between noumena and phenomena. "For it arises out of elementary reflection upon our experience. We quickly realise that the same thing appears in either slightly or considerably different ways to different people owing both to their varying spatial locations in relation to it and to differences in their sensory and mental equipment and interpretive habits" (p. 242). And, of course, Hick must be right about that. Things are not always what they appear to be, and they appear differently to one person and another. Thus we distinguish, early on, between appearance and reality.

The prince, let us suppose, wants to get an undistorted idea of what the lives of his people are like, what they are thinking, and so on. So he decides to visit the various provinces, but not openly as prince. He appears, therefore, in the marketplace of one town as an itinerant monk—that is, he comes barefooted, wearing a dark and shapeless gown made of rough cloth, cinched around the waist by a frayed robe, a cowl over his head, a wooden cross as a pendant upon his breast, perhaps a rosary in his hand. He does not appear to be a prince; he appears to be a monk. Of course, he might not appear to everyone to be a monk. There might be an ignorant person in the market that day, a person who has no knowledge at all of the monastic orders, who has never heard of monks, a person who has no idea at all, either accurate or stereotypical, of what a monk would wear. To that person the prince probably does not appear as a monk. To him, lacking in the appropriate interpretive categories, the prince may look simply like someone wearing funny clothes. But to the others who have the appropriate categories, the prince appears as a monk.

The prince need not always appear as a monk, even when not appearing as prince. In another province he may come to the Spring Fair as, say, a journeyman stonemason. He is wearing the heavy leather apron and openly carrying the tools of his purported trade. Perhaps he has even sprinkled stone dust into his beard. And thus (again to those who have the appropriate interpretive categories) he appears as neither prince nor monk but stonemason.

So much, for the moment, for the first analogy. I will come back to it. But here let us turn to a second analogy. Imagine several artists who sit, side by side, looking at a landscape. There is a country church there, a few tombstones beside it, trees nearby and a small stream, sheep on the hill beyond. The artists paint, looking back and forth from their easels to the landscape. And when the paintings are finished, we look at them.

We may imagine that these artists, or most of them at any rate, paint in the abstract and nonrepresentational manner. So the paintings do not strike us as looking much like the landscape itself. (If a stranger in the area told us he was looking for that church, we would not immediately think of giving him one of these paintings, and saying, "Take this. It will help you recognize the church when you come to it.") Furthermore, the paintings do not look much like one another. If we saw them hanging together on a gallery wall, we would not immediately suspect that they had been painted from the same location. Nevertheless, each artist assures us that his or her painting was indeed inspired by the actual landscape. And each is confident that if there had been a McDonald's restaurant there instead of the church, or perhaps even camels grazing instead of the sheep, then the painting would also have been noticeably different. So the landscape has contributed something to each painting. There is a real input there, and some sort of dependence. In some way, each painting is the way it is because the landscape is the way it is.

But, of course, the landscape does not provide the only input; it is not the only factor that goes into making the painting what it is. There is also the aesthetic creativity of the artist, his or her artistic interpretation, and so on. The painting itself is a construct, a humanly constructed entity, the product of an artistic reaction to, and interaction with, a (largely) natural landscape.

So we have two stories, the prince and the painters, and the corresponding two models for the phenomenon/noumenon distinction. But these models are not compatible. Which shall we use, if we are attracted by the Kantian project at all?

A crucial difference between these models, in the present connection, is this. In the disguise model there is an identity relation that holds among the various appearances. The (apparent) monk is identical with the prince, and the (apparent) stonemason is identical with the prince, and therefore the monk is identical with the stonemason. Hick recognizes this identity relation when he says, in the last passage I quoted above, "We quickly realise that *the same thing* appears in either slightly or considerably different ways to different people" (p. 242, italics mine). In this model there may be many appearances, but there is a single entity that has these appearances, a single entity that is experienced in these various ways. This identity is the basis for many hypotheticals. If the monk walks barefoot in the marketplace, then the prince must endure the hot cobblestones beneath his feet. And if the stonemason drinks too much at the fair and drowns in the nearby river, then the life of the prince also ends in that river.

But may not the stonemason appear to be a middle-aged man, while the prince is a vibrant youth? Certainly. The stonemason may appear to have properties the prince does not have. But if the stonemason *is* the prince (in disguise), then the stonemason must *be* the same age as the prince. He can *appear* to be older, but that must be merely an appearance, and those who take it at face value are misled by an appearance.

The construct model, on the other hand, does not postulate an identity between the construct and its source, input, and so on, and consequently it does not support similar hypotheticals. The landscape is an important factor in making the painting what it is, but the painting is not identical with the landscape. The painting is not *the same thing* as the landscape. Therefore, a vandal who burns the painting does not thereby burn the church, and if he slashes the painting, he does not thereby kill a sheep.[13]

It is fairly common, I think, for philosophers to interpret the Kantian metaphysics along the lines of the construct model. We think, that is, that the ordinary world of Kantian metaphysics—the world of sense-experience as Kant construes it—is a human construct, the product of human cognitive operations reacting to some "kick" provided by an unknown and unexperienced noumenal reality. And the entities of the ordinary world, the cantaloupes, are phenomenal entities. On this interpretation, a cantaloupe is not a noumenon wearing a disguise, and when we take it to be a cantaloupe, we are not being misled by its appearance. It really is just what it appears to be. We *construct* the objects of our experience, and the only objects we experience are the objects we construct. These constructs belong to a different metaphysical level from that of the noumena, which are not human constructs at all and therefore cannot be identical with them.

Thinking of the gods in accordance with this model yields a genuine polytheism. The various gods are real—at least as real as the more ordinary furniture of the world, and possibly more real—and they are distinct from one another, again as the more ordinary entities of the world are distinct. The disguise model, however, when applied to the gods, does not yield a polytheism at all. Or at most it yields a polytheism only of names. For according to this model, there is just one god who appears in all the various religions.

As I said above, Hick himself seems deeply ambivalent at this point. Often he speaks as though he adopted the disguise model both in understanding Kant and in adapting the Kantian machinery to his own purposes. So he says, for example, that "Kant distinguished between noumenon and phenomenon, or between a *Ding an sich* and that thing as it appears to human consciousness" (p. 241). And, speaking for himself, he says that "the divine Reality is not directly known *an sich.* But when human beings relate themselves to it in the mode of I–Thou encounter, they experience it as personal. Indeed in the context of that relationship it *is* personal, not It but He or She. When human beings relate themselves to the Real in the mode of non-personal awareness they experience it as non-personal, and in the context of this relationship it *is* non-personal" (p. 245; Hick's italics). In the first of these quotations the phrase "that thing" must refer to the *Ding an sich,* and so the *Ding an sich* is the thing that appears to human consciousness. In a similar way, the repeated "it" of the second quotation refers to the previously mentioned divine Reality, which Hick here treats as a single entity. And, in a quotation I cited earlier, Hick tries to make Kant's views plausible by observing that "*the same thing* appears in either slightly or considerably different ways to different people" (p. 242; my italics).

Understood in this way, Hick is not a polytheist at all. His view turns out to be very much like that of those who say that God has many names. God has many appearances, many disguises. The divine reality can adopt many different *personae.* And the divine reality can appear without a *persona* at all, appearing instead as an *impersona,* a non-personal object of contemplation.

Sometimes, however, Hick speaks in a way that fits much better with the construct model, both in explaining Kant's views and in applying them for his own purposes. He says, for example, that "all that we are entitled to say about the noumenal source of this information is that it is the reality whose influence produces, in collaboration with the human mind, the phenomenal world of our experience" (p. 243). In this passage the phenomenal world is not "the same thing" as the noumenal world. It is rather something *produced* by the joint influence, the collaboration, of a noumenal reality and a human mind. And this is exactly the construct interpretation of Kantian metaphysics.

In addition, some of Hick's arguments make sense on the construct interpretation but not on the disguise interpretation. He argues, for example, that not all the intentional gods and impersonal absolutes could possibly exist, since they are described in ways that exclude one another. He says "The gods of the monotheistic faiths are thought of in each case as the one and only God, so that it is impossible for there to be more than one instantiation of this concept" (p. 234). But there is nothing impossible about there *appearing* to be more than one instantiation of a concept, even if it is impossible that it be instantiated more than once. There would be nothing impossible about a noumenon appearing to be the one and only god, Jahweh, and also appearing to be the one and only god, Allah. For something can appear to have a property without having it, and consequently to appear to instantiate a concept, even if it does not instantiate it. If we are to construe the reality and existence of the gods along Kantian or quasi-Kantian lines, and if we are to interpret Kant in terms of the disguise model, then Hick's line of argument here would fail entirely. But if phenomenal entities are construed not as noumena in disguise but as constructs generated by the joint action of noumena and human minds, then indeed no two such contructs could instantiate a concept that is intrinsically limited to a single instantiation. And so Hick's argument for the mutual exclusivity of some of the Gods would succeed.

Well, so much for this rather extended account of Hick's position, at least as I understand it. I turn again to a more general discussion of descriptive polytheism, with only occasional references to Hick. And I propose to discuss what reasons we may have for either accepting or denying descriptive polytheism. But I'm looking here for reasons particularly relevant to *polytheism.* For better or worse, I ignore reasons for theism in general, along with reasons for general atheism.

What reasons might we have for asserting the existence of *more than one* god? The reason Hick gives (p. 235) seems to me fallacious. He argues that "persons living within other traditions, then, are equally justified [as justified as we are] in trusting their own distinctive religious experience and in forming their beliefs on the basis of it." And he apparently wants to draw from this the conclusion that we cannot reasonably "claim that our own form of religious experience, together with that of the tradition of which we are a part, is veridical whilst the others are not." And so, since we assert the reality of our God, we must also accept the analogous assertions of others. This is fallacious because it confuses the notions of justification and truth or veridicality. Other people may be as justified as I am in relying on what seems to us to be our divergent experience. But that justification is largely independent of the veridicality of those experiences, and of the truth of the beliefs that they generate. As Hick himself says, "A proposition believed can be true or false: it is the believing of it that is rational or irrational" (p. 212). And the rationality of a belief, unlike the truth of what is believed, is sensitive to the epistemic situation of the believer. So, contrary to what Hick seems to argue, there is nothing unreasonable in a person's asserting that someone else is justified in relying on a certain experience, but that nevertheless the experience is nonveridical.[14]

I don't know of any other attempt to provide a sort of general or philosophical reason in support of *poly*theism. I know of one religious or confessional reason, from within Christianity. And it is the reason for my saying earlier in this essay that I am now a sort of descriptive polytheist. The Christian tradition, both in the New Testament documents and in later theological developments, seems to me to take seriously the idea that human beings are not the only rational creatures in the realm of existence. And in particular it seems to countenance the existence of powerful and nonembodied intelligences. At least, that is how I understand the references to angels and devils within the Christian tradition. I don't take this to be a really central doctrine in Christianity, but for what it is worth it inclines me to think that there are many beings who satisfy Swinburne's definition of a god. And so in Swinburne's sense I am (even if a little tentatively) a descriptive polytheist.

Are any of these beings—could any of them be—the gods of some actual religion? Now that I come to think of it (and my thinking of it is very recent),

I don't think of any strong reason for returning a negative answer. Playing such a role might, of course, be a usurpation of divine prerogatives. But I think that the possibility of such a usurpation is not entirely foreign to Christian thought. On the other hand, could such a role be divinely *assigned,* a service provided by the condescension of divine grace for the redemption of the world? The idea strikes me as strange, perhaps vaguely unsettling. But I do not now rule it out.

We can also divide objections to polytheism into two rough and nonexclusive categories: primarily religious objections and more general philosophical objections.

The primarily religious objections usually arise within a particular religion and are embedded in the theological or confessional apparatus of the religion. They can be prohibitions against polytheistic practice, as in "I am the Lord your God, who brought you forth out of the land of Egypt, out of the house of bondage. You shall have no other gods before me" (Exod. 20:2, 3). Or they can be ringing declarations of the monotheistic nature of the religion in which they appear, the insistence that "our" god is singular, not plural. One of the best-known examples of this is the *Shema,* "Hear, O Israel: The Lord our God is one Lord" (Deu. 6:4).

Such injunctions and declarations, however, are for the most part directed toward cultic polytheism, and do not seem to deny the thesis of descriptive polytheism—that is, they do not deny that there are other real gods who are, perhaps, the gods of other religions. Of course, there might be a religion that included such a denial in its theology. But (at least if we think of a god along Swinburne's lines) Christianity does not seem to be a strong candidate for such a religion.

Another sort of religious objection to polytheism, perhaps not dependent on the theology of a particular religion, would be the claim that polytheism is religiously unsatisfactory, religiously defective. This too, I suppose, would be a thesis about cultic polytheism, and even if true would not show that descriptive polytheism was mistaken. But perhaps some versions of this objection are closely related to some of the more general and philosophical objections, to which I now turn.

It has sometimes been supposed that descriptive polytheism must be mistaken because there could not possibly be more than one god. And why not? Because a god must have properties that cannot possibly (logically?) have more than one instantiation. Now, in the case of the unabashedly finite gods who are apparently the intentional objects of worship in some actual and historical religions, this objection seems to have very little force. The properties that are, or were, ascribed to them probably were no more incapable of multiple instantiation than the properties many Christians ascribe to angels and devils.

The objection might be pressed, however, by insisting that there is something profoundly unsatisfactory about religions of that sort. And here the objection connects with the second type of religious objection noted above. The finite gods, confined to the hill country or interested only in wine making, are not big enough to satisfy the fully developed and reflective religious impulse. We are not satisfied with Swinburne's minimalist definition. A god must have more than that, he must *be* more than that! And it might be suspected that gods described in such a way as to make them suitable religious principals will be so strongly endowed that they cannot possibly coexist.

It is certainly true that the theologies of the "high" religions tend to ascribe to their divinities extreme and unlimited versions of various attributes. (Cf. the "omni-" attributes that are stock items in Christian theologies.) And probably that does represent a genuine religious impulse. But is it clear that the divinities thus endowed must be incapable of coexistence?

No doubt that will depend on just what the unlimited attributes are. What seems initially most obvious is that not every unlimited attribute is intrinsically incapable of multiple instantiation. Think, for example, of perfect goodness, or of perfect love. I, at any rate, cannot think of any way at all of starting on an argument to show that there could not be more than one being who had these properties. In these cases, one instantiation does not seem to generate any special difficulty for a second. The same seems to be the case for omniscience and omnipresence. If it is coherent to suppose that some one being knows every truth, then why should it be impossible that there be a second being who also knows every truth? And if there is some being who, in some sense, is present everywhere (even in places that are also occupied by other objects), then why should not a second being also be omnipresent in that same sense? To me, at any rate, these properties, though they figure in the theology of my own religion, do not seem to be such as to belong *necessarily* to no more than one being.[15]

There is an "omni-" attribute, however, that seems to have more promise along this line. It is, of course, omnipotence. Here there seems to be more room, initially at least, for the suspicion that we have hit upon an "instantiation-exclusive" property. And, of course, it is the "omni-," the unlimitedness, that generates the exclusivity. Limited powers can be instantiated in distinct agents, and perhaps an unlimited power in one agent is compatible with limited powers elsewhere. But could there be two (or more) centers of *unlimited* power?

Well, why not? Intuitively, the attractive line of argument is captured in the hoary conundrum, What happens when an irresistible force meets an immovable object? If the force is thwarted, then it was not irresistible after all, and if the object is moved, then it was not immovable. In a similar way, one is to imagine the two putative omnipotent powers colliding, and then it will be seen that one of them was not omnipotent after all.[16] (If their contest ends in a draw, then I suppose we should think that neither was omnipotent.)

Though this argument is superficially attractive, I think that we cannot make it work. Ever since the time of Thomas, at least, Christian theologians have, for the most part, held that the power of God extends over what is logically possible, and *only* over what is logically possible. It has been surprisingly difficult to specify this version of omnipotence in a fully clear and satisfactory way. But suppose for the moment that the general idea of this version is correct and that this is how we should think of omnipotence. Then we could hold that God is omnipotent, even if we were to admit that He cannot create a mountain whose slopes run uphill only (the anathema of skiers). On this view of omnipotence, such "failures" as these do not damage an agent's claim to omnipotence.

Now let us assume, as the hypothesis that is to be explored, that there are two omnipotent agents, A and B. And let them be *essentially* omnipotent, so that they cannot survive the loss of power. And suppose they collide. Might A overpower B? Well, it certainly seems logically impossible that an essentially omnipotent agent should be overpowered. If that is so, then (given the Thomistic idea of omnipotence) A cannot overpower B. But it also follows that his inability to overpower B does not damage his omnipotence, any more than does his inability to create the mountain whose slopes run only uphill.

Might we have been mistaken in supposing that it is logically impossible for an essentially omnipotent agent to be overpowered? Maybe (though I cannot generate much doubt about it myself). But if we were mistaken in that, then being overpowered must be compatible with essential omnipotence. In that case, A might indeed overpower B, but this "defeat" would not damage B's omnipotence. In neither case, then, do we get the conclusion that one (or both) of these agents fails of omnipotence.

The situation between A and B is symmetrical, and we could have posed our questions in terms of B's thwarting A, rather than in terms of A's overpowering B. The results, however, are the same.[17]

This argument has been conducted on the assumption that the Thomistic idea of omnipotence is on the right track. A minority of philosophical theologians (Descartes perhaps) seem to reject the Thomistic restriction and to hold that omnipotence ought to be construed as encompassing even what is logically impossible. How does the collision fare under this assumption? It would seem that A could then overpower B, even though it is logically impossible for B (in virtue of his omnipotence) to be overpowered. In the same way, B could, in virtue of his omnipotence, also thwart A, and B could overpower A while A thwarted B. Indeed, so far as I can see, all these outcomes could be the result of a single collision. Of course, it seems logically impossible that it could be true *both* that A overpowers B and that B thwarts A. It certainly strikes me as logically impossible. But, *under the assumption with which we are now working,* that is just what omnipotent beings are supposed to be able to do. They can actualize impossible states of affairs. Under this assumption, therefore, the fact that a collision of omnipotent agents would result in an impossible outcome should not be taken to show that there cannot be a multiplicity of omnipotent beings.

Regardless, then, of whether we take omnipotence to be limited to the realm of the logically possible, it seems that there is no barrier to the multiple instantiation of this attribute.

I suppose that we could generate an instantiation-exclusive property out of just about any property by adding to it some restriction such as "the one and only." So even if more than one being could be perfectly loving, it seems plausible to suppose that no more than one could be *the one and only perfectly loving being.* And so if two or more distinct divinities were required to have this property, then I would suppose that no more than one of them could actually exist. But properties specified in this way have something of an ad hoc flavor about them. I don't know whether there are examples in actual religions of divinities that would exclude each other in this way.

There are, however, some closely related properties that do figure in actual theologies and that would seem to have that effect. I am thinking of exclusive relations, in which the divinity is said to bear a unique relation to some particular thing. Examples (taken primarily from Christian thought) are relational properties such as *being the creator of the world* and *being the judge of all the earth.* In such expressions it is rather natural to understand the definite article to mean "the one and only," and no doubt that is how it is usually taken by the theologians who attribute these relational properties to God. And so, if the Holy Trinity is the creator of the world, then no divinity who is distinct from the Holy Trinity could also be the creator of the world. And if it is required of a god that he (or she) be the creator of the world, then there could be at most only one god.

Christian theology certainly seems to involve relational properties with this feature, and I suppose that some other theologies do also. Probably there are cases in which one such property is ascribed (in different religions) to apparently distinct deities. At any rate, I would not be surprised if it were so. Would that show, or at least give one strong reason to suppose, that those two gods could not both exist?

I can think of only two ways of avoiding that conclusion. Both of them are of some interest, though neither in the end seems attractive to me. And both of them are suggested by Hick, in one way or another.

At one point Hick refers to "two alternative models for the status of the divine *personae*" (p. 272), both of which he says are compatible with his general hypothesis. One of these models is radically realist, and it is hard to imagine what more a person would have to assert to be taken to be a polytheist. According to the other one, however, the gods are

> projections of the religious imagination. . . . Applied to the divine *personae* this would mean that Jahweh, the heavenly Father, Allah, Shiva, Vishnu and so on are not objectively existent personal individuals with their own distinctive powers and characteristics. . . . They would be analogous to what have been called in the literature of parapsychology, "veridical hallucinations". . . . This experience is not caused by a particular invisible person—Jahweh or Vishnu, for example. It does however constitute a transformation of authentic information of which the Real is the ultimate source. (p. 273)

According to this model, the gods of the various religions are imaginary entities.[18] But they are *veridical* imaginary entities, in the sense that these imaginary entities are appropriate ways in which some genuine information derived from the Real can be represented and expressed by human beings.

Perhaps the idea here is analogous to what we may have in mind when we say that a certain work of literature is "true to life," although every character and setting in it is purely fictional.

Now in fictional works, and perhaps in the realm of the imagination generally, it seems to be the case that distinct entities (fictional entities, of course) can bear exclusive relations to (what at least seems to be) a single object. There can be two novels in each of which there is a character identified as "the last king of France" and in which these two characters are otherwise described in wildly different ways. This need not involve an incoherence in either novel, nor is there any incoherence in the existence of the two novels (perhaps even written by the same author). And it is possible that we might find both these novels "true to life," expressive of deep truths about the human situation.

If the various gods—the Holy Trinity, say, and Allah—are really imaginary entities, then perhaps both of them can be, individually and distinctly, the sole creator of the world, in the same sense that two fictional characters can be, individually and distinctly, the last king of France. And so not even the occurrence of exclusive relations in the various theologies would rule out the plurality of gods.

I said that this option did not seem attractive to me. That is because, though it may salvage the element of plurality, it gives up what seems to me to be even deeper in any genuine theism—indeed, in any genuine religion—whether it be of the mono- or the poly- variety. That element is what I called "realism" in describing the Aramean view. Any theism at all, if it is to have a deep religious significance, will construe its god or gods as belonging to the order of reality, as being (at the very least) as real as the ordinary furniture of the world. Hick himself says that "within each tradition we regard as real the objects of our worship or contemplation" (p. 249). That sounds exactly right to me. And if we cease to think of those objects as real—if we come to regard them as hallucinations, fictions, projections of our imaginations, or something of the sort—then we have abandoned that tradition. Maybe we have moved to another religion, or perhaps to no religion at all. And maybe we were right to make that move. Maybe the old gods were fictions after all. But what we ourselves take to be a fiction, rightly or wrongly, will not sustain our religious life and cannot be the central object in it.

In comparing cultic and descriptive versions of polytheism and monotheism, I posed the question whether one could be a cultic monotheist (or polytheist) and a descriptive atheist. The model we have just been discussing seems to me to be a descriptive atheism with respect to the gods (and absolutes) of the actual religions. And any view about religion that is compatible with this model must be compatible with atheism about these gods. Persons whose religious thought is compatible in that way could be worshipers of one of those gods, it seems to me, only by an extraordinary separation of their thinking from their religious life. But, of course, a person who counted all the old gods as fictions could be realist about something else, some new god or absolute. And if so, then that new divinity might be the ground of her religious life. That would be a new religion.

Well, I said that there might be two ways in which one could avoid the threat that exclusive relations pose for the plurality of gods. The second way turns on a problem (as I see it) in Kantian metaphysics, a problem Hick perhaps inherits. It would indeed seem that no two gods could be, individually and distinctly, the sole creator of the world, *provided that the world is a single entity.* But if there is a plurality of worlds, and gods are matched to worlds, then various gods may be the creators of the various corresponding worlds. In thinking of a phrase such as "the creator of the world," then, we should have to think of the referential force of "the world" as being tied to the referential force of "the creator," so that the whole phrase refers successfully only if there is an appropriate match between these two included references.

I say that this is connected with a problem in Kantian metaphysics for the following reason. In that metaphysics (interpreted in terms of the construct model) the phenomenal objects of my experience are constructs related in some way to some noumenal reality and also to a categorical scheme that I supply. The "I think" that accompanies all my mental life unifies all the phenomenal objects of my experience into a single interrelated whole—one phenomenal world. But it is hard to see what, in the Kantian metaphysics, could account for, or even permit, a phenomenal world that was *common* to two or more perceivers. Rather, it looks as though each such perceiver must construct, and perceive, his or her own world. These worlds might be similar to one another (but how could any perceiver compare one world with another?), but they would be distinct worlds. Think, for example, of the situation in which I am initially alone in a melon patch, and I am the sole percipient of a cantaloupe there. It would seem, on the Kantian view, that this cantaloupe must be constituted by the categories I supply. When a second observer arrives, how could she observe *that very same* cantaloupe? Must she not rather observe a cantaloupe that is constituted by her own categorical contribution, and that is integrated into a world by *her* "I think" and not by mine? But then it would be her cantaloupe, in her world, and not mine.

For me, at any rate, the existence of a genuinely common world is one of the facts for which any satisfactory metaphysics must account, or which at least it must permit. The Kantian approach, therefore, does not seem likely to be satisfactory.

There is an analogue of this difficulty in the hypothesis we are considering here. We do sometimes talk loosely about the Hindu world-view and the Hindu world, the Christian world-view and the Christian world, and so forth. And if we could take seriously the idea of there being distinct worlds associated with the various religions, then possibly we could also take seriously the idea that the various gods are the creators of the various worlds. But the fact seems to be that there is no distinctly Christian world or Hindu world. All of us—Hindus, Christians, atheists, Buddhists, and all the rest—live in one single and shared world. In that world we love one another and hate one another, help one another and kill one another, do business with one another and cheat one another, and so on down the line. If my god is real—if he can have an effect in my world—then he must also have an effect in the world of the Hindu, because (if for no other reason) I am a part of the Hindu's world. And mutatis mutandis for the Hindu god and my world. And (as for Kantian metaphysics in general) I can hardly imagine what an argument could have in it that would override the conviction that the world is in fact a single reality shared by many observers and participants.

What I have been calling the "exclusive relations," therefore, seems to set a limit to the plurality of gods. If the Holy Trinity is the creator of the world, then either Allah is identical with the Holy Trinity or else Allah is not the creator of the world. It is not possible that just any old set of intentional religious objects should be both real and distinct, and it is quite possible that some of the intentional objects, the gods or absolutes, of the world's actual religions are mutually exclusive in this way. But though these relations may rule out some putative polytheisms, they will not rule out all of them. For not all the candidate gods will be burdened with such relations.

Well, no doubt there is much more that could be said about this topic. In particular, I think, it would be worthwhile if we could find more incisive and conclusive arguments either for or against the reality of particular gods other than our own, and some usable criterion for determining the identity or non-identity of the objects of worship. But I don't now know how to do that. Let me therefore close with just one suggestion. In the absence of strong reasons to the contrary, it might be wise to proceed on the assumption that we need not say the *same* thing about every case. We ought, for example, to allow the possibility that there may be distinct religions that have the very same god, and others that really do have distinct gods. There might be religions whose gods are purely fictional and imaginary entities, others whose gods are phenomenal beings in some Kantian or quasi-Kantian sense, still others whose gods are substantial creaturely beings, and still others whose god is the Real, the rock-bottom reality who gives the gift of being to everything else that exists. At least, assumptions such as these would provide a benchmark from which we might measure our progress in considering the possibility of polytheism.

## NOTES

1. 1 Kings 20:17–21, 23. All the biblical quotations in this essay are taken from the New Revised Standard Version.

2. John Hick, *An Interpretation of Religion* (New Haven: Yale University Press, 1989). This book is based on the Gifford Lectures for 1986–1987. Page references appear in the parentheses in the text.

3. Richard Swinburne, *The Concept of Miracle* (London: Macmillan, 1970), p. 53. Possibly, Swinburne meant merely to attribute this definition to David Hume. Someone may wish to add that a god must be the god of some actual religion, must actually be worshiped by some people, or something of the sort. The addition of such a clause will, I think, not make much difference to what is said here.

4. But there may now be strong cultural reasons for even a pure descriptivist to avoid using "god" (or "God") in this way. I am myself a descriptivist polytheist, but I characteristically use the term "God" in my first-order utterances—i.e., when I am expressing my own religious convictions and not merely reporting other people's religion, etc.—to refer only to a single entity. This point becomes clearer, I hope, in the subsequent discussion.

5. I use the plural here, since that is how the Aramean view of Hebrew religion is put in the text, but without prejudice to the question of whether the Hebrews themselves were monotheists or polytheists at the time.

6. This combination is sometimes called "henotheism."

7. Perhaps this is the position ascribed to the devils in James 2:19.

8. Some who profess to worship the same god as do modern Jews, and even the god of the Hebrew prophets, may find the Jahweh of earlier Hebrew religion too bloodthirsty for their tastes.

9. This gives rise to the jibe that Christians are not much different from atheists after all—it is just a matter of one god. I suppose Christians might reply that there is a lot of difference between one and none, as, for example, with respect to having a wife.

10. Whether devils (and angels) are *supernatural* creatures, as distinguished from natural creatures, is an obscure and difficult question. I set it aside, largely because I don't know much to say about it.

11. "The naturalistic response is to see all these systems of belief as factually false" (p. 234).

12. But, at least in some moods, Hick seems ambivalent about this. On pp. 272–75 he suggests that two models, one strongly realist about the gods and one strongly nonrealist, are both compatible with his position. I discuss his nonrealist model below.

13. It is not the nonrepresentational style of painting that cuts off these hypotheticals. Even if some of the artists in the story are representational painters, and their paintings are easily recognizable depictions of that particular landscape, it would nevertheless remain true that one would not destroy the church or injure a sheep simply by vandalizing the painting.

14. I have discussed this point somewhat more at length, and developed some other criticisms of Hick's views, in "The God above the Gods," in Eleonore Stump, ed., *Reasoned Faith* (Ithaca: Cornell University Press, 1993), pp. 179–203.

15. I am, of course, ignoring arguments to the effect that these alleged attributes are internally incoherent. That, if it were true, would show that *nothing* had such attributes. It would have no *special* relevance to polytheism.

16. Hick seems to appeal to this line of argument (p. 79).

17. Someone may still feel unsatisfied with this result, because no definitive answer has been given to the question of what the outcome of such a collision would be. For what it is worth, my own view about that is that the outcome would not be determined by *force*. But an outcome might be generated in some other way—by love, perhaps, or justice, or chance (the flipping of a cosmic coin?), or. . . . What is relevant to the present discussion, however, is the conclusion that omnipotence is not intrinsically an instantiation-exclusive attribute.

18. On the other model, by way of contrast, the gods are "objectively existing, supramundane and subtle beings . . . real personal beings, independent centres of consciousness, will, thought, and emotion" (p. 274).

CHAPTER 9

# Hick's Religious Pluralism and "Reformed Epistemology": *A Middle Ground*

DAVID BASINGER

*The purpose of this discussion is to analyze comparatively the influential argument for religious pluralism offered by John Hick and the argument for religious exclusivism (sectarianism) which can be generated by proponents of what has come to be labeled "Reformed Epistemology." I argue that while Hick and the Reformed exclusivist appear to be giving us incompatible responses to the same question about the true nature of "religious" reality, they are actually responding to related, but distinct questions, each of which must be considered by those desiring to give a religious explanation for the phenomenon of religious diversity. Moreover, I conclude that the insights of neither ought to be emphasized at the expense of the other.*

No one denies that the basic tenets of many religious perspectives are, if taken literally, quite incompatible. The salvific claims of some forms of Judeo-Christian thought, for example, condemn the proponents of all other perspectives to hell, while the incompatible salvific claims of some forms of Islamic thought do the same.

Such incompatibility is normally explained in one of three basic ways. The nontheist argues that all religious claims are false, the product perhaps of wish fulfillment. The religious pluralist argues that the basic claims of at least all of the major world religions are more or less accurate descriptions of the same reality. Finally, the religious exclusivist argues that the tenets of only one religion (or some limited number of religions) are to any significant degree accurate descriptions of reality.[1]

The purpose of this discussion is to analyze comparatively the influential argument for religious pluralism offered by John Hick and the argument for religious exclusivism which can be (and perhaps has been) generated by proponents of what has come to be labeled "Reformed Epistemology." I shall

From David Basinger, "Hick's Pluralism and 'Reformed Epistemology': A Middle Ground," *Faith and Philosophy*, 5 (October 1988): 421–33. Reprinted by permission of the author and *Faith and Philosophy*.

argue that while Hick and the Reformed epistemologist appear to be giving us incompatible responses to the same question about the true nature of "religious" reality, they are actually responding to related, but distinct questions, each of which must be considered by those desiring to give a religious explanation for the phenomenon of religious diversity. Moreover, I shall conclude that the insights offered by both Hick and the Reformed epistemologist are of value and, accordingly, that those of neither ought to be emphasized at the expense of the other.

## JOHN HICK'S THEOLOGICAL PLURALISM

Hick's contention is not that different religions make no conflicting truth claims. In fact, he believes that "the differences of belief between (and within) the traditions are legion," and has often in great detail discussed them.[2] His basic claim, rather, is that such differences are best seen as "different ways of conceiving and experiencing the one ultimate divine Reality."[3]

However, if the various religions are really "responses to a single ultimate transcendent Reality," how then do we account for such significant differences?[4] The best explanation, we are told, is the assumption that "the limitless divine reality has been thought and experienced by different human mentalities forming and formed by different intellectual frameworks and devotional techniques."[5] Or, as Hick has stated the point elsewhere, the best explanation is the assumption that the correspondingly different ways of responding to divine reality "owe their differences to the modes of thinking, perceiving and feeling which have developed within the different patterns of human existence embodied in the various cultures of the earth." Each "constitutes a valid context of salvation/liberation; but none constitutes the one and only such context."[6]

But why accept such a pluralistic explanation? Why not hold, rather, that there is no higher Reality beyond us and thus that all religious claims are false—i.e., why not opt for naturalism? Or why not adopt the exclusivistic contention that the religious claims of only one perspective are true?

Hick does not reject naturalism because he sees it to be an untenable position. It is certainly *possible,* he tells us, that the "entire realm of [religious] experience is delusory or hallucinatory, simply a human projection, and not in any way or degree a result of the presence of a greater divine reality."[7] In fact, since the "universe of which we are part is religiously ambiguous," it is not even *unreasonable or implausible* "to interpret any aspect of it, including our religious experience, in non-religious as well as religious ways."[8]

However, he is quick to add, "it is perfectly reasonable and sane for us to trust our experience"—including our religious experience— "as generally cognitive of reality except when we have some reason to doubt it."[9] Moreover, "the mere theoretical possibility that any or all [religious experience] may be illusory does not count as a reason to doubt it." Nor is religious experience overturned by the fact that the great religious figures of the past, including Jesus, held a number of beliefs which we today reject as arising from the now outmoded science of their day, or by the fact that some people find "it impossible to accept that the profound dimension of pain and suffering is the measure of the cost of creation through creaturely freedom."[10]

He acknowledges that those who have "no positive ground for religious belief within their own experience" often do see such factors as "insuperable barriers" to religious belief.[11] But given the ambiguous nature of the evidence, he argues, it cannot be demonstrated that all rational people must see it this way. That is, belief in a supernatural realm can't be shown to be any less plausible than disbelief. Accordingly, he concludes, "those who actually participate in this field of religious experience are fully entitled, as sane and rational persons, to take the risk of trusting their own experience together with that of their tradition, and of proceeding to live and to believe on the basis of it, rather than taking the alternative risk of distrusting it and so—for the time being at least—turning their backs on God."[12]

But why choose pluralism as the best religious hypothesis? Why does Hick believe we ought not be exclusivists? It is not because he sees exclusivism as incoherent. It is certainly possible, he grants, that "one particular 'Ptolomaic' religious vision does correspond uniquely with how things are."[13] Nor does Hick claim to have some privileged "cosmic vantage point from which [he can] observe both the divine reality in itself and the different partial human awarenesses of that reality."[14] But when we individually consider the evidence in the case, he argues, the result is less ambiguous. When "we start from the phenomenological fact of the various forms of religious experience, and we seek an hypothesis which will make sense of this realm of phenomena" from a religious point of view, "the theory that most naturally suggests itself postulates a divine Reality which is itself limitless, exceeding the scope of human conceptuality and language, but which is humanly thought and experienced in various conditioned and limited ways."[15]

What is this evidence which makes the pluralistic hypothesis so "considerably more probable" than exclusivism? For one thing, Hick informs us, a credible religious hypothesis must account for the fact, "evident to ordinary people (even though not always taken into account by theologians) that in the great majority of cases—say 98 to 99 percent—the religion in which a person believes and to which he adheres depends upon where he was born."[16] Moreover, a credible hypothesis must account for the fact that within all of the major religious traditions, "basically the same salvific process is taking place, namely the transformation of human existence from self-centeredness to Reality-centeredness."[17] And while pluralism "illuminates" these otherwise baffling facts, the strict exclusivist's view "has come to seem increasingly implausible and unrealistic."[18]

But even more importantly, he maintains, a credible religious hypothesis must account for the fact, of which "we have become irreversibly aware in the present century, as the result of anthropological, sociological and psychological studies and of work in the philosophy of language, that there is no one universal and invariable" pattern for interpreting human experience, but rather a range of significantly different patterns or conceptual schemes "which have developed within the major cultural streams." And when considered in light of this, Hick concludes, a "pluralistic theory becomes inevitable."[19]

## THE REFORMED OBJECTION

There are two basic ways in which Hick's pluralistic position can be critiqued. One "appropriate critical response," according to Hick himself, "would be to offer a better [religious] hypothesis."[20] That is, one way to challenge Hick is to claim that the evidence he cites is better explained by some form of exclusivism.

But there is another, potentially more powerful type of objection, one which finds its roots in the currently popular "Reformed Epistemology" being championed by philosophers such as Alvin Plantinga. I will first briefly outline Plantinga's latest version of this epistemological approach and then discuss its impact on Hick's position.

According to Plantinga, it has been widely held since the Enlightenment that if theistic beliefs—e.g., religious hypotheses—are to be considered rational, they must be based on propositional evidence. It is not enough for the theist just to refute objections to any such belief. The theist "must also have something like an argument for the belief, or some positive reason to think that the belief is true."[21] But this is incorrect, Plantinga maintains. There are beliefs which acquire their warrant propositionally—i.e., have warrant conferred on them by an evidential line of reasoning from other beliefs. And for such beliefs, it may well be true that proponents need something like an argument for their veridicality.

However, there are also, he tells us, *basic* beliefs which are not based on propositional evidence and, thus, do not require propositional warrant. In fact, *if* such beliefs can be affirmed "without either violating an epistemic duty or displaying some kind of noetic defect," they can be considered *properly basic.*[22] And, according to Plantinga, many theistic beliefs can be properly basic: "Under widely realized conditions it is perfectly rational, reasonable, intellectually respectable and acceptable to believe [certain theistic tenets] without believing [them] on the basis of [propositional] evidence."[23]

But what are such conditions? Under what conditions can a belief have positive epistemic status if it is not conferred by other propositions whose epistemic status is not in question? The answer, Plantinga informs us, lies in an analysis of belief formation.

> [We have] cognitive faculties designed to enable us to achieve true beliefs with respect to a wide variety of propositions—propositions about our immediate environment, about our interior lives, about the thoughts and experiences of other persons, about our universe at large, about right and wrong, about the

> whole realm of *abstracta*—numbers, properties, propositions, states of affairs, possible worlds and their like, about modality—what is necessary and possible—and about [ourselves]. These faculties work in such a way that under the appropriate circumstances we form the appropriate belief. More exactly, the appropriate belief is *formed in us;* in the typical case we do not *decide* to hold or form the belief in question, but simply find ourselves with it. Upon considering an instance of *modus ponens,* I find myself believing its corresponding conditional; upon being appeared to in the familiar way, I find myself holding the belief that there is a large tree before me; upon being asked what I had for breakfast, I reflect for a moment and find myself with the belief that what I had was eggs on toast. In these and other cases I do not *decide* what to believe; I don't total up the evidence (I'm being appeared to redly; on most occasions when thus appeared to I am in the presence of something red, so most probably in this case I am) and make a decision as to what seems best supported; I simply find myself believing.[24]

And from a theistic point of view, Plantinga continues, the same is true in the religious realm. Just as it is true that when our senses or memory is functioning properly, "appropriate belief is formed in us," so it is that God has created us with faculties which will, "when they are working the way they were designed to work by the being who designed and created us and them," produce true theistic beliefs.[25] Moreover, if these faculties are functioning properly, a basic belief thus formed has "positive epistemic status to the degree [the individual in question finds herself] inclined to accept it."[26]

What, though, of the alleged counter-evidence to such theistic beliefs? What, for example, of all the arguments the conclusion of which is that God does not exist? Can they all be dismissed as irrelevant? Not immediately, answers Plantinga. We must seriously consider potential defeaters of our basic beliefs. With respect to the belief that God exists, for example, we must seriously consider the claim that religious belief is mere wish fulfillment and the claim that God's existence is incompatible with (or at least improbable given) the amount of evil in the world.

But to undercut such defeaters, he continues, we need not engage in positive apologetics: produce propositional evidence for our beliefs. We need only engage in *negative* apologetics: refute such arguments.[27] Moreover, it is Plantinga's conviction that such defeaters do normally exist. "The non-propositional warrant enjoyed by [a person's] belief in God, for example, [seems] itself sufficient to turn back the challenge offered by some alleged defeaters"—e.g., the claim that theistic belief is mere wish fulfillment. And other defeaters such as the "problem of evil," he tells us, can be undercut by identifying validity or soundness problems or even by appealing to the fact that "experts think it unsound or that the experts are evenly divided as to its soundness."[28]

Thus, not surprisingly, he concludes that, even considering all the alleged counter-evidence, there is little reason to believe that many theistic beliefs cannot be considered properly basic for most adult theists—even intellectually sophisticated adult theists.

Do Plantinga or other proponents of this Reformed epistemology maintain that their exclusivistic religious hypotheses are properly basic and can thus be "defended" in the manner just outlined? I am not *certain* that they do. However, when Plantinga, for example, claims that "God exists" is for most adult theists properly basic, he appears to have in mind a classical Christian conception of the divine—i.e., a being who is the triune, omnipotent, omniscient, perfectly good, *ex nihilo* creator of the universe. In fact, given his recent claim that "the internal testimony of the Holy Spirit . . . is a source of reliable and perfectly acceptable beliefs about what is communicated [by God] in Scripture," and the manner in which most who make such a claim view the truth claims of the other world religions, it would appear that Plantinga's "basic" conception of God is quite exclusive.[29]

However, even if no Reformed epistemologist actually does affirm an exclusivistic hypothesis she claims is properly basic, it is obvious that the Reformed analysis of belief justification can be used to critique Hick's line of reasoning. Hick claims that an objective inductive assessment of the relevant evidence makes his pluralistic thesis a more plausible religious explanation than any of the competing exclusivistic hypotheses. But a Reformed exclusivist could easily argue that this approach to the issue is misguided. My affirmation of an exclusivistic Christian perspective, such an argument might begin, is not evidential in nature. It is, rather, simply a belief I have found formed in me, much like the belief that I am seeing a tree in front of me or the belief that killing innocent children is wrong.

Now, of course, I must seriously consider the allegedly formidable defeaters with which pluralists such as Hick have presented me. I must consider the fact, for example, that the exclusive beliefs simply formed in most people are not similar to mine, but rather tend to mirror those beliefs found in the cultures in which such people have been raised. But I do not agree with Hick that this fact is best explained by a pluralistic hypothesis. I attribute this phenomenon to other factors such as the epistemic blindness with which much of humanity has been plagued since the fall.[30]

Moreover, to defend my position—to maintain justifiably (rationally) that I am right and Hick is wrong—I need not, as Hick seems to suggest, produce objective "proof" that his hypothesis is weaker than mine. That is, I need not produce "evidence" that would lead most rational people to agree with me. That would be to involve myself in Classical Foundationalism, which is increasingly being recognized as a bankrupt epistemological methodology. All I need do is undercut Hick's defeaters—i.e., show that his challenge does not require me to abandon my exclusivity thesis. And this I can easily do. For Hick has not demonstrated that my thesis is self-contradictory. And it is extremely doubtful that there exists any other non-question-begging criterion for plausibility by which he could even attempt to demonstrate that my thesis is less plausible (less probable) than his.

Hick, of course, believes firmly that his hypothesis makes the most sense. But why should this bother me? By his own admission, many individuals firmly believe that, given the amount of seemingly gratuitous evil in the world, God's nonexistence is by far most plausible. Yet this does not keep him from affirming theism. He simply reserves the right to see things differently and continues to believe. And there is no reason why I cannot do the same.

Moreover, even if what others believed were relevant, by Hick's own admission, the majority of theists doubt that his thesis is true.[31] Or, at the very least, I could rightly maintain that "the experts are evenly divided as to its soundness." Thus, given the criteria for defeater assessment which we Reformed exclusivists affirm, Hick's defeaters are clearly undercut. And, accordingly, I remain perfectly justified in continuing to hold that my exclusivity thesis is correct and, therefore, that all incompatible competing hypotheses are false.

## A MIDDLE GROUND

It is tempting to see Hick and the Reformed exclusivist as espousing incompatible approaches to the question of religious diversity. If Hick is correct—if the issue is primarily evidential in nature—then the Reformed exclusivist is misguided and vice versa. But this, I believe, is an inaccurate assessment of the situation. There are two equally important, but distinct, questions which arise in this context, and Hick and the Reformed exclusivist, it seems to me, each *primarily* address only one.

The Reformed exclusivist is primarily interested in the following question:

> Q1: Under what conditions is an individual within her epistemic rights (is she rational) in affirming one of the many mutually exclusive religious diversity hypotheses?

In response, as we have seen, the Reformed exclusivist argues (or at least could argue) that a person need not grant that her religious hypothesis (belief) requires propositional (evidential) warrant. She is within her epistemic rights in maintaining that it is a *basic* belief. And if she does so, then to preserve rationality, she is not required to "prove" in some objective manner that her hypothesis is most plausible. She is fulfilling all epistemic requirements solely by defending her hypothesis against claims that it is less plausible than competitors.

It seems to me that the Reformed exclusivist is basically right on this point. I do believe, for reasons mentioned later in this essay, that attempts by any knowledgeable exclusivist to defend her hypothesis will ultimately require her to enter the realm of positive apologetics—i.e., will require her to engage in a comparative analysis of her exclusivistic beliefs. But I wholeheartedly agree with the Reformed exclusivist's contention that to preserve rationality, she need not actually demonstrate that her hypothesis is most plausible. She need ultimately only defend herself against the claim that a thoughtful assessment of the matter makes the affirmation of some incompatible perspective—i.e., pluralism or some incompatible exclusivistic perspective—the only rational option. And this, I believe, she can clearly do.

What this means, of course, is that if Hick is actually arguing that pluralism is the only rational option, then I think he is wrong. And his claim that pluralism "is considerably more probable" than exclusivism does, it must be granted, make it appear as if he believes pluralism to be the only hypothesis a knowledgeable theist can justifiably affirm.

But Hick never actually calls his opponents irrational in this context. That is, while Hick clearly believes that sincere, knowledgeable exclusivists are *wrong,* he has never to my knowledge claimed that they are guilty of violating the basic epistemic rules governing rational belief. Accordingly, it seems best to assume that Q1—a concern with what can be rationally affirmed—is not Hick's primary interest in this context.

But what then is it with which Hick is concerned? As we have seen, Q1 is defensive in nature. It asks for identification of conditions under which we can justifiably continue to affirm a belief we *already* hold. But *why* hold the specific religious beliefs we desire to defend? Why, specifically, choose to defend religious pluralism rather than exclusivism or vice versa? Or, to state this question of "belief origin" more formally:

> Q2: Given that an individual can be within her epistemic rights (can be rational) in affirming either exclusivism or pluralism, upon what basis should her actual choice be made?

This is the type of question in which I believe Hick is primarily interested.

Now, it might be tempting for a Reformed exclusivist to contend that she is exempt from the consideration of Q2. As I see it, she might begin, this question is based on the assumption that individuals consciously choose their religious belief systems. But the exclusivistic hypothesis which I affirm was not the result of a conscious attempt to choose the most plausible option. I have simply discovered this exclusivistic hypothesis formed in me in much the same fashion I find my visual and moral beliefs just formed in me. And thus Hick's question is simply irrelevant to my position.

But such a response will not do. There is no reason to deny that Reformed exclusivists do have, let's say, a Calvinistic religious hypothesis just formed in them. However, although almost everyone in every culture does in the appropriate context have similar "tree-beliefs" just formed in them, there is no such unanimity within the religious realm. As Hick rightly points out, the religious belief that the overwhelming majority of people in any given culture find just formed in them is the dominant hypothesis of that culture or subculture. Moreover, the dominant religious hypotheses in most of these cultures are exclusivistic—i.e., incompatible with one another.

Accordingly, it seems to me that Hick can rightly be interpreted as offering the following challenge to the knowledgeable Reformed exclusivist (the exclusivist aware of pervasive religious diversity): I will grant that your exclusivistic beliefs were not originally the product of conscious deliberation.

But given that most sincere theists initially go through a type of religious belief-forming process similar to yours and yet usually find formed in themselves the dominant exclusivistic hypotheses of their own culture, upon what basis can you justifiably continue to claim that the hypothesis you affirm has some special status just because you found it formed in you? Or, to state the question somewhat differently, Hick's analysis of religious diversity challenges knowledgeable Reformed exclusivists to ask themselves why they now believe that their religious belief-forming mechanisms are functioning properly while the analogous mechanisms in all others are faulty.

Some Reformed exclusivists, as we have seen, have a ready response. Because of "the fall," they maintain, most individuals suffer from religious epistemic blindness—i.e., do not possess properly functioning religious belief-forming mechanisms. Only our mechanisms are trustworthy. However, every exclusivistic religious tradition can—and many do—make such claims. Hence, an analogous Hickian question again faces knowledgeable Reformed exclusivists: Why do you believe that only those religious belief-forming mechanisms which produce exclusivistic beliefs compatible with yours do not suffer from epistemic blindness?

Reformed exclusivists cannot at this point argue that they have found this belief just formed in them for it is *now* the reliability of the belief-forming mechanism, itself, which is being questioned. Nor, since they are anti-foundationalists, can Reformed exclusivists argue that the evidence demonstrates conclusively that their position is correct. So upon what then can they base their crucial belief that their religious belief-forming mechanisms *alone* produce true beliefs?

They must, it seems to me, ultimately fall back on the contention that their belief-forming mechanisms can alone be trusted because that set of beliefs thus generated appears to them to form the most plausible religious explanatory hypothesis available. But to respond in this fashion brings them into basic methodological agreement with Hick's position on Q2. That is, it appears that knowledgeable Reformed exclusivists must ultimately maintain with Hick that when attempting to discover which of the many self-consistent hypotheses that *can* rationally be affirmed is the one that *ought* to be affirmed, a person must finally decide which hypothesis she believes best explains the phenomena. Or, to state this important point differently yet, what Hick's analysis of religious diversity demonstrates, I believe, is that even for those knowledgeable Reformed exclusivists who claim to find their religious perspectives just formed in them, a conscious choice among competing religious hypotheses is ultimately called for.

This is not to say, it must again be emphasized, that such Reformed exclusivists must attempt to "prove" their choice is best. But, given the culturally relative nature of religious belief-forming mechanisms, a simple appeal to such a mechanism seems inadequate as a basis for such exclusivists to continue to affirm their perspective. It seems rather that knowledgeable exclusivists must ultimately make a conscious decision whether to retain the religious hypothesis that has been formed in them or choose another. And it further appears that they should feel some prima facie obligation to consider the available options—consciously consider the nature of the various religious hypotheses formed in people—before doing so.

Now, of course, to agree that such a comparative analysis should be undertaken is not to say that Hick's pluralistic hypothesis is, in fact, the most plausible alternative. I agree with the Reformed exclusivist that "plausibility" is a very subjective concept. Thus, I doubt that the serious consideration of the competing explanatory hypotheses for religious phenomena, even by knowledgeable, open-minded individuals, will produce consensus.

However, I do not see this as in any sense diminishing the importance of engaging in the type of comparative analysis suggested. For even if such comparative assessment will not lead to consensus, it will produce two significant benefits. First, only by such assessment, I feel, can a person acquire "ownership" of her religious hypothesis. That is, only by such an assessment can she insure herself that her belief is not solely the product of environmental conditioning. Second, such an assessment should lead all concerned to be more tolerant of those with which they ultimately disagree. And in an age where radical religious exclusivism again threatens world peace, I believe such tolerance to be of inestimable value.

This does not mean, let me again emphasize in closing, that the consideration of Q1—the consideration of the conditions under which a religious hypothesis can be rationally affirmed—is unimportant or even less important than the consideration of Q2. It is crucial that we recognize who must actually shoulder the "burden of proof" in this context. And we need to thank Reformed exclusivists for helping us think more clearly about this matter. But I fear that a preoccupation with Q1 can keep us from seeing the importance of Q2—the consideration of the basis upon which we choose the hypothesis to be defended—and the comparative assessment of hypotheses to which such consideration leads us. And we need to thank pluralists such as Hick for drawing our attention to this fact.

## NOTES

1. This terminology basically comes from John Hick, "On Conflicting Religious Truth-Claims," *Religious Studies* **19** (1983): 487.

2. *Ibid.*, p. 491.

3. John Hick, "The Philosophy of World Religions," *Scottish Journal of Theology* **37:** 229.

4. *Ibid.*

5. John Hick, "The Theology of Religious Pluralism," *Theology* (1983): 335.

6. Hick, *Scottish Journal of Theology*, pp. 229, 231.

7. John Hick, *Why Believe in God?* (London: SCM Press, Ltd., 1983), pp. 43–44.

8. *Ibid.*, p. 67.

9. *Ibid.*, p. 34.

10. *Ibid.*, pp. 64, 100.

11. *Ibid.*, p. 100.

12. *Ibid.*, p. 67.

13. Hick, *Theology*, p. 338.
14. *Ibid.*, p. 336.
15. Hick, *Scottish Journal of Theology*, p. 231.
16. John Hick, *God Has Many Names* (London: The Macmillan Press, Ltd., 1980), p. 44.
17. Hick, *Scottish Journal of Theology*, p. 231.
18. Hick, *God Has Many Names*, p. 49.
19. Hick, *Scottish Journal of Theology*, p. 232.
20. Hick, *Theology*, p. 336.
21. Alvin Plantinga, "The Foundations of Theism: A Reply," *Faith and Philosophy* **3** (July, 1986): 307.
22. *Ibid.*, p. 300.
23. Alvin Plantinga, "On Taking Belief in God as Basic," Wheaton College Philosophy Conference (Oct. 23–25, 1986), Lecture 1 handout, p. 1.
24. Alvin Plantinga, "Justification and Theism," *Faith and Philosophy* **4** (October, 1987): 405–406.
25. *Ibid.*, p. 411.
26. *Ibid.*, p. 410.
27. Plantinga, "The Foundations of Theism," p. 313, n. 11.
28. *Ibid.*, p. 312.
29. Alvin Plantinga, "Sheehan's Shenanigans," *The Reformed Journal*, April, 1987, p. 25.
30. Mark Talbot, "On Christian Philosophy," *The Reformed Journal*, September, 1984.
31. John Hick, *Scottish Journal of Theology*, p. 236.

CHAPTER 10

# Pluralism:
## *A Defense of Religious Exclusivism*

Alvin Plantinga

When I was a graduate student at Yale, the philosophy department prided itself on diversity: and it was indeed diverse. There were idealists, pragmatists, phenomenologists, existentialists, Whiteheadians, historians of philosophy, a token positivist, and what could only be described as observers of the passing intellectual scene. In some ways, this was indeed something to take pride in; a student could behold and encounter real live representatives of many of the main traditions in philosophy. It also had an unintended and unhappy side effect, however. If anyone raised a philosophical question inside, but particularly outside, class, the typical response would be a catalog of some of the various different answers the world has seen: there is the Aristotelian answer, the existentialist answer, the Cartesian answer, Heidegger's answer, perhaps the Buddhist answer, and so on. But the question "what is the truth about this matter?" was often greeted with disdain as unduly naive. There are all these different answers, all endorsed by people of great intellectual power and great dedication to philosophy; for every argument *for* one of these positions, there is another *against* it; would it not be excessively naive, or perhaps arbitrary, to suppose that one of these is in fact *true,* the others being false? Or, if there really is a truth of the matter, so that one of them is true and conflicting ones false, wouldn't it be merely arbitrary, in the face of this embarrassment of riches, to *endorse* one of them as the truth, consigning the others to falsehood? How could you possibly know which was true?

Some urge a similar attitude with respect to the impressive variety of religions the world displays. There are theistic religions but also at least some nontheistic religions (or perhaps nontheistic strands of religion) among the enormous variety of religions going under the names "Hinduism" and "Buddhism"; among the theistic religions, there are strands of Hinduism and Buddhism and American Indian religion as well as Islam, Judaism, and Christianity; and all these differ significantly from one another. Isn't it somehow arbitrary, or irrational, or unjustified, or unwarranted, or even oppressive and imperialistic to endorse one of these as opposed to all the others? According to Jean Bodin, "each is refuted by all"[1]; must we not agree? It is in this neighborhood that the so-called problem of pluralism arises. Of course, many concerns and problems can come under this rubric; the specific problem I mean to discuss can be thought of as follows. To put it in an internal and personal way, I find myself with religious beliefs, and religious beliefs that I realize aren't shared by nearly everyone else. For example, I believe both

(1) The world was created by God, an almighty, all-knowing, and perfectly good personal being (one that holds beliefs; has aims, plans, and intentions; and can act to accomplish these aims)

and

(2) Human beings require salvation, and God has provided a unique way of salvation through the incarnation, life, sacrificial death, and resurrection of his divine son.

Now there are many who do not believe these things. First, there are those who agree with me on (1) but not (2): there are non-Christian theistic religions. Second, there are those who don't accept either (1) or (2) but nonetheless do believe that there is something beyond the natural world, a something such that human well-being and salvation depend upon standing in a right relation to it. And third, in the West and since the Enlightenment, anyway, there are people—*naturalists,* we may call them—who don't believe any of these three things. And my problem is this: when I become really aware of these other ways of looking at the world, these other ways of responding religiously to the world, what must or should I do? What is the right sort of attitude to take? What sort of impact should this awareness have on the beliefs I hold and the strength with which I hold them? My question is this: how should I think about the great religious diversity the world in fact displays? Can I sensibly remain an adherent of just one of these religions, rejecting the others? And here I am thinking specifically of *beliefs.* Of course, there is a great deal more to any religion or religious practice than just belief, and I don't for a moment mean to deny it. But belief is a crucially important part of most religions; it is a crucially important part of *my* religion; and the question I mean to ask here is what the awareness of religious diversity means or should mean for my religious beliefs.

Some speak here of a *new* awareness of religious diversity, and speak of this new awareness as constituting (for us in the West) a crisis, a revolution, an intellectual development of the same magnitude as the Copernican revolution of the sixteenth century and the alleged discovery of evolution and our animal origins in the nineteenth.[2] No doubt there is at least some truth to this. Of course, the fact is all along many Western Christians and Jews have known that there are other religions and that not nearly everyone shares *their* religion.[3] The ancient Israelites—some of the prophets, say—were clearly aware of Canaanitish religion; and the apostle Paul said that he preached "Christ crucified, a stumbling block to Jews and folly to the Greeks" (I Cor. 1:23). Other early Christians, the Christian martyrs, say, must have suspected that not everyone believed as they did. The church fathers, in offering defenses of Christianity, were certainly apprised of this fact; Origen, indeed, wrote an eight-volume reply to Celsus, who urged an argument similar to those put forward by contemporary pluralists. Aquinas, again, was clearly aware of those to whom he addressed the *Summa contra gentiles,* and the fact that there are non-Christian religions would have come as no surprise to the Jesuit missionaries of the sixteenth and seventeenth centuries or to the Methodist missionaries of the nineteenth. In more recent times, when I was a child, *The Banner,* the official publication of the Christian Reformed Church, contained a small column for children; it was written by "Uncle Dick," who exhorted us to save our nickels and send them to our Indian cousins at the Navaho mission in New Mexico. Both we and our elders knew that the Navahos had or had had a religion different from Christianity, and part of the point of sending the nickels was to try to rectify that situation.

Still, in recent years probably more of us Western Christians have become aware of the world's religious diversity; we have probably learned more about people of other religious persuasions, and we have come to see more clearly that they display what looks like real piety, devoutness, and spirituality. What is new, perhaps, is a more widespread sympathy for other religions, a tendency to see them as more valuable, as containing more by way of truth, and a new feeling of solidarity with their practitioners.

There are several possible reactions to awareness of religious diversity. One is to continue to believe what you have all along believed; you learn about this diversity but continue to believe, that is, take to be true, such propositions as (1) and (2) above, consequently taking to be false any beliefs, religious or otherwise, that are incompatible with (1) and (2). Following current practice, I call this *exclusivism;* the exclusivist holds that the tenets or some of the tenets of *one* religion—Christianity, let's say—are in fact true; he adds, naturally enough, that any propositions, including other religious beliefs, that are incompatible with those tenets are false. Now there is a fairly widespread belief that there is something seriously wrong with exclusivism. It is irrational, or egotistical and unjustified,[4] or intellectually arrogant,[5] or elitist,[6] or a manifestation of harmful pride,[7] or even oppressive and imperialistic.[8] The claim is that exclusivism as such is or involves a vice of some sort: it is wrong or deplorable; and it is this claim I want to examine. I propose to argue that exclusivism need not involve either epistemic or moral failure and that furthermore something like it is wholly unavoidable, given our human condition.

These objections are not to the *truth* of (1) or (2) or any other proposition someone might accept in this exclusivist way (although, of course, objections of that sort are also put forward); they are instead directed to the *propriety* or *rightness* of exclusivism. And there are initially two different kinds of indictments of exclusivism: broadly moral or ethical indictments and broadly intellectual or epistemic indictments. These overlap in interesting ways, as we shall see below. But initially, anyway, we can take some of the complaints about exclusivism as *intellectual* criticisms: it is *irrational* or *unjustified* to think in an exclusivistic way. And the other large body of complaint is moral: there is something *morally* suspect about exclusivism: it is arbitrary, or intellectually arrogant, or imperialistic. As Joseph Runzo suggests, exclusivism is "neither tolerable nor any longer intellectually honest in the context of our contemporary knowledge of other faiths."[9] I want to consider both kinds of claims or criticisms; I propose to argue that the exclusivist is not as such necessarily guilty of any of these charges.

## MORAL OBJECTIONS TO EXCLUSIVISM

I first turn to the moral complaints: that the exclusivist is intellectually arrogant, or egotistical, or self-servingly arbitrary, or dishonest, or imperialistic, or oppressive. But first three qualifications. An exclusivist, like anyone else, will probably be guilty of some or all of these things to at least some degree, perhaps particularly the first two; the question is, however, whether she is guilty of these things just by virtue of being an exclusivist. Second, I shall use the term "exclusivism" in such a way that you don't count as an exclusivist unless you are rather fully aware of other faiths, have had their existence and their claims called to your attention with some force and perhaps fairly frequently, and have to some degree reflected on the problem of pluralism, asking yourself such questions as whether it is or could be really true that the Lord has revealed himself and his programs to us Christians, say, in a way in which he hasn't revealed himself to those of other faiths. Thus my grandmother, for example, would not have counted as an exclusivist. She had, of course, *heard* of the heathen, as she called them, but the idea that perhaps Christians could learn from them, and learn from them with respect to religious matters, had not so much as entered her head; and the fact that it *hadn't* entered her head, I take it, was not a matter of moral dereliction on her part. The same would go for a Buddhist or Hindu peasant. These people are not, I think, plausibly charged with arrogance or other moral flaws in believing as they do.

Third, suppose I am an exclusivist with respect to (1), for example, but nonculpably believe, like Thomas Aquinas, say, that I have a knock-down, drag-out argument, a demonstration or conclusive proof of the proposition that there is such a person as God; and suppose I think further (and nonculpably) that if those who don't believe (1) were to be apprised of this argument (and had the ability and training necessary to grasp it, and were to think about the argument fairly and reflectively), they too would come to believe (1). Then I could hardly be charged with these moral faults. My condition would be like that of Gödel, let's say, upon having recognized that he had a proof for the incompleteness of arithmetic. True, many of his colleagues and peers didn't believe that arithmetic was incomplete, and some believed that it *was* complete; but presumably Gödel wasn't arbitrary or egotistical in believing that arithmetic is in fact incomplete. Furthermore, he would not have been at fault had he nonculpably but *mistakenly* believed that he had found such a proof. Accordingly, I shall use the term "exclusivist" in such a way that you don't count as an exclusivist if you nonculpably think you know of a demonstration or conclusive argument for the beliefs with respect to which you are an exclusivist, or even if you nonculpably think you know of an argument that would convince all or most intelligent and honest people of the truth of that proposition. So an exclusivist, as I use the term, not only believes something like (1) or (2) and thinks false any proposition incompatible with it; she also meets a further condition C that is hard to state precisely and in detail (and in fact any attempt to do so would involve a long and at present irrelevant discussion of ceteris paribus clauses). Suffice it to say that C includes (1) being rather fully aware of other religions, (2) knowing that there is much that at the least looks like genuine piety and devoutness in them, and (3) believing that you know of no arguments that would necessarily convince all or most honest and intelligent dissenters of your own religious allegiances.

Given these qualifications, then, why should we think that an exclusivist is properly charged with these moral faults? I shall deal first and most briefly with charges of oppression and imperialism: I think we must say that they are on the face of it wholly implausible. I daresay there are some among you who reject some of the things I believe; I do not believe that you are thereby oppressing me, even if you do not believe you have an argument that would convince me. It is conceivable that exclusivism might in some way *contribute to* oppression, but it isn't in itself oppressive.

The important moral charge is that there is a sort of self-serving arbitrariness, an arrogance or egotism, in accepting such propositions as (1) or (2) under condition C; exclusivism is guilty of some serious moral fault or flaw. According to Wilfred Cantwell Smith, "except at the cost of insensitivity or delinquency, it is morally not possible actually to go out into the world and say to devout, intelligent, fellow human beings: '. . . we believe that we know God and we are right; you believe that you know God, and you are totally wrong.'"[10]

So what can the exclusivist have to say for herself? Well, it must be conceded immediately that if she believes (1) or (2), then she must also believe that those who believe something incompatible with them are mistaken and believe what is false. That's no more than simple logic. Furthermore, she must also believe that those who do not believe as she does—those who believe neither (1) nor (2), whether or not they believe their negations—*fail* to believe something that is true, deep, and important, and that she *does* believe. She must therefore see herself as *privileged* with respect to those others—those others of both kinds. There is something of great value, she must think, that *she* has and *they* lack. They are ignorant of something—something of great importance—of which she has knowledge. But does this make her properly subject to the above censure?

I think the answer must be no. Or if the answer is yes, then I think we have here a genuine moral dilemma; for in our earthly life here below, as my Sunday School teacher used to say, there is no real alternative; there is no reflective attitude that is not open to the same strictures. These charges of arrogance are a philosophical tar baby: get close enough to them to use them against the exclusivist, and you are likely to find them stuck fast to yourself. How so? Well, as an exclusivist, I realize I can't convince others that they should believe as I do, but I nonetheless continue to believe as I do: and the charge is that I am as a result arrogant or egotistical, arbitrarily preferring my way of doing things to other ways.[11] But what are my alternatives with respect to a proposition like (1)? There seem to be three choices.[12] I can continue to hold it; I can withhold it, in Roderick Chisholm's sense, believing neither it nor its denial; and I can accept its denial. Consider the third way, a way taken by those pluralists who, like John Hick, hold that such propositions as (1) and (2) and their colleagues from other faiths are literally false although in some way still valid responses to the Real. This seems to me to be no advance at all with respect to the arrogance or egotism problem; this is not a way out. For if I do this, I will then be in the very same condition as I am now: I will believe many propositions others don't believe and will be in condition C with respect to those propositions. For I will then believe the denials of (1) and (2) (as well as the denials of many other propositions explicitly accepted by those of other faiths). Many others, of course, do not believe the denials of (1) and (2), and in fact believe (1) and (2). Further, I will not know of any arguments that can be counted on to persuade those who do believe (1) and (2) (or propositions accepted by the adherents of other religions). I am therefore in the condition of believing propositions that many others do not believe and furthermore am in condition C. If, in the case of those who believe (1) and (2), that is sufficient for intellectual arrogance or egotism, the same goes for those who believe their denials.

So consider the second option: I can instead *withhold* the proposition in question. I can say to myself: "the right course here, given that I can't or couldn't convince these others of what *I* believe, is to believe neither these propositions nor their denials." The pluralist objector to exclusivism can say that the right course under condition C is to *abstain* from believing the offending proposition and also abstain from believing its denial; call him, therefore, "the abstemious pluralist." But does he thus really avoid the condition that, on the part of the exclusivist, leads to the charges of egotism and arrogance? Think, for a moment, about disagreement. Disagreement, fundamentally, is a matter of adopting conflicting propositional attitudes with respect to a given proposition. In the simplest and most familiar case, I disagree with you if there is some proposition $p$ such that I believe $p$ and you believe $-p$. But that's just the simplest case: there are also others. The one that is at present of interest is this: I believe $p$ and you withhold it, fail to believe it. Call the first kind of disagreement "contradicting"; call the second "dissenting."

My claim is that if contradicting others (under the condition C spelled out above) is arrogant and egotistical, so is dissenting (under that same condition). For suppose you believe some proposition *p* but I don't: perhaps you believe it is wrong to discriminate against people simply on the grounds of race, but I, recognizing that there are many people who disagree with you, do not believe this proposition. I don't disbelieve it either, of course, but in the circumstances I think the right thing to do is to abstain from belief. Then am I not implicitly condemning your attitude, your *believing* the proposition, as somehow improper—naive, perhaps, or unjustified, or in some other way less than optimal? I am implicitly saying that my attitude is the superior one; I think my course of action here is the right one and yours somehow wrong, inadequate, improper, in the circumstances at best second-rate. Also, I realize that there is no question, here, of *showing* you that your attitude is wrong or improper or naive; so am I not guilty of intellectual arrogance? Of a sort of egotism, thinking I know better than you, arrogating to myself a privileged status with respect to you? The problem for the exclusivist was that she was obliged to think she possessed a truth missed by many others; the problem for the abstemious pluralist is that he is obliged to think he possesses a virtue others don't, or acts rightly where others don't. If, in condition C, one is arrogant by way of believing a proposition others don't, isn't one equally, under those reflective conditions, arrogant by way of withholding a proposition others don't?

Perhaps you will respond by saying that the abstemious pluralist gets into trouble, falls into arrogance, by way of implicitly saying or believing that his way of proceeding is *better* or *wiser* than other ways pursued by other people, and perhaps he can escape by abstaining from *that* view as well. Can't he escape the problem by refraining from believing that racial bigotry is wrong, and also refraining from holding the view that it is *better,* under the conditions that obtain, to withhold that proposition than to assert and believe it? Well, yes, he can; then he has no *reason* for his abstention; he doesn't believe that abstention is better or more appropriate; he simply does abstain. Does this get him off the egotistical hook? Perhaps. But then, of course, he can't, in consistency, also hold that there is something wrong with *not* abstaining, with coming right out and *believing* that bigotry is wrong; he loses his objection to the exclusivist. Accordingly, this way out is not available for the abstemious pluralist who accuses the exclusivist of arrogance and egotism.

Indeed, I think we can show that the abstemious pluralist who brings charges of intellectual arrogance against exclusivism is hoist with his own petard, holds a position that in a certain way is self-referentially inconsistent in the circumstances. For he believes

> (3) If S knows that others don't believe *p* and that he is in condition C with respect to *p*, then S should not believe *p*;

this or something like it is the ground of the charges he brings against the exclusivist. But, the abstemious pluralist realizes that many do not accept (3); and I suppose he also realizes that it is unlikely that he can find arguments for (3) that will convince them; hence he knows that he is in condition C.

Given his acceptance of (3), therefore, the right course for him is to abstain from believing (3). Under the conditions that do in fact obtain—namely, his knowledge that others don't accept it and that condition C obtains—he can't properly accept it.

I am therefore inclined to think that one can't, in the circumstances, properly hold (3) or any other proposition that will do the job. One can't find here some principle on the basis of which to hold that the exclusivist is doing the wrong thing, suffers from some moral fault—that is, one can't find such a principle that doesn't, as we might put it, fall victim to itself.

So the abstemious pluralist is hoist with his own petard; but even apart from this dialectical argument (which in any event some will think unduly cute), aren't the charges unconvincing and implausible? I must concede that there are a variety of ways in which I can be and have been intellectually arrogant and egotistic; I have certainly fallen into this vice in the past and no doubt am not free of it now. But am I really arrogant and egotistic just by virtue of believing what I know others don't believe, where I can't show them that I am right? Suppose I think the matter over, consider the objections as carefully as I can, realize that I am finite and furthermore a sinner, certainly no better than those with whom I disagree, and indeed inferior both morally and intellectually to many who do not believe what I do; but suppose it *still* seems clear to me that the proposition in question is true: can I really be behaving immorally in continuing to believe it? I am dead sure that it is wrong to try to advance my career by telling lies about my colleagues; I realize there are those who disagree; I also realize that in all likelihood there is no way I can find to show them that they are wrong; nonetheless, I think they *are* wrong. If I think this after careful reflection—if I consider the claims of those who disagree as sympathetically as I can, if I try level best to ascertain the truth here—and it *still* seems to me sleazy, wrong, and despicable to lie about my colleagues to advance my career, could I really be doing something immoral in continuing to believe as before? I can't see how. If, after careful reflection and thought, you find yourself convinced that the right propositional attitude to take to (1) and (2) in the face of the facts of religious pluralism is abstention from belief, how could you properly be taxed with egotism, either for so believing or for so abstaining? Even if you knew others did not agree with you? So I can't see how the moral charge against exclusivism can be sustained.

## EPISTEMIC OBJECTIONS TO EXCLUSIVISM

I turn now to *epistemic* objections to exclusivism. There are many different specifically epistemic virtues, and a corresponding plethora of epistemic vices; the ones with which the exclusivist is most frequently charged, however, are *irrationality* and *lack of justification* in holding his exclusivist beliefs. The claim is that as an exclusivist, he holds unjustified beliefs and/or irrational beliefs. Better, *he* is unjustified or irrational in holding these beliefs. I shall therefore consider those two claims, and I shall argue that the exclusivistic views need not be either unjustified or irrational. I shall then turn to the question whether his beliefs could have *warrant:* that property, whatever precisely it is, that distinguishes knowledge from mere true belief, and whether they could have enough warrant for knowledge.

## Justification

The pluralist objector sometimes claims that to hold exclusivist views, in condition C, is *unjustified—epistemically* unjustified. Is this true? And what does he mean when he makes this claim? As even a brief glance at the contemporary epistemological literature shows, justification is a protean and multifarious notion.[13] There are, I think, substantially two possibilities as to what he means. The central core of the notion, its beating heart, the paradigmatic center to which most of the myriad contemporary variations are related by way of analogical extension and family resemblance, is the notion of *being within one's intellectual rights,* having violated no intellectual or cognitive duties or obligations in the formation and sustenance of the belief in question. This is the palimpsest, going back to Descartes and especially Locke, that underlies the multitudinous battery of contemporary inscriptions. There is no space to argue that point here; but chances are when the pluralist objector to exclusivism claims that the latter is unjustified, it is some notion lying in this neighborhood that he has in mind. (And, here we should note the very close connection between the moral objections to exclusivism and the objection that exclusivism is epistemically unjustified.)

The duties involved, naturally enough, would be specifically *epistemic* duties: perhaps a duty to proportion degree of belief to (propositional) evidence from what is *certain,* that is, self-evident or incorrigible, as with Locke, or perhaps to try one's best to get into and stay in the right relation to the truth, as with Roderick Chisholm,[14] the leading contemporary champion of the justificationist tradition with respect to knowledge. But at present there is widespread (and, as I see it, correct) agreement that there is no duty of the Lockean kind. Perhaps there is one of the Chisholmian kind,[15] but isn't the exclusivist conforming to that duty if, after the sort of careful, indeed prayerful, consideration I mentioned in the response to the moral objection, it still seems to him strongly that (1), say, is true and he accordingly still believes it? It is therefore hard to see that the exclusivist is necessarily unjustified in this way.

The second possibility for understanding the charge—the charge that exclusivism is epistemically unjustified—has to do with the oft-repeated claim that exclusivism is intellectually *arbitrary.* Perhaps the idea is that there is an intellectual duty to treat similar cases similarly; the exclusivist violates this duty by arbitrarily choosing to believe (for the moment going along with the fiction that we *choose* beliefs of this sort) (1) and (2) in the face of the plurality of conflicting religious beliefs the world presents. But suppose there is such a duty. Clearly, you do not violate it if you nonculpably think the beliefs in question are *not* on a par. And, as an exclusivist, I *do* think (nonculpably, I hope) that they are not on a par: I think (1) and (2) *true* and those incompatible with either of them *false.*

The rejoinder, of course, will be that it is not *alethic* parity (their having the same truth value) that is at issue: it is *epistemic* parity that counts. What kind of epistemic parity? What would be relevant here, I should think, would be *internal* or internalist epistemic parity: parity with respect to what is internally available to the believer. What is internally available to the believer includes, for example, detectable relationships between the belief in question and other beliefs you hold; so internal parity would include parity of propositional evidence. What is internally available to the believer also includes the *phenomenology* that goes with the beliefs in question: the *sensuous* phenomenology, but also the nonsensuous phenomenology involved, for example, in the belief's just having the feel of being *right.* But once more, then, (1) and (2) are not on an internal par, for the exclusivist, with beliefs that are incompatible with them. (1) and (2), after all, seem to me to be true; they have for me the phenomenology that accompanies that seeming. The same cannot be said for propositions incompatible with them. If, furthermore, John Calvin is right in thinking that there is such a thing as the Sensus Divinitatis and the Internal Testimony of the Holy Spirit, then perhaps (1) and (2) are produced in me by those belief-producing processes, and have for me the phenomenology that goes with them; the same is not true for propositions incompatible with them.

But then the next rejoinder: isn't it probably true that those who reject (1) and (2) in favor of other beliefs have propositional evidence for their beliefs that is on a par with mine for my beliefs; and isn't it also probably true that the same or similar phenomenology accompanies their beliefs as accompanies mine? So that those beliefs really are epistemically and internally on a par with (1) and (2), and the exclusivist is still treating like cases differently? I don't think so: I think there really are arguments available for (1), at least, that are not available for its competitors. And as for similar phenomenology, this is not easy to say; it is not easy to look into the breast of another; the secrets of the human heart are hard to fathom; it is hard indeed to discover this sort of thing even with respect to someone you know really well. But I am prepared to stipulate both sorts of parity. Let's agree for purposes of argument that these beliefs are on an epistemic par in the sense that those of a different religious tradition have the same sort of internally available markers—evidence, phenomenology, and the like—for their beliefs as I have for (1) and (2). What follows?

Return to the case of moral belief. King David took Bathsheba, made her pregnant, and then, after the failure of various stratagems to get her husband Uriah to think the baby was his, arranged for Uriah to be killed. The prophet Nathan came to David and told him a story about a rich man and a poor man. The rich man had many flocks and herds; the poor man had only a single ewe lamb, which grew up with his children, "ate at his table, drank from his cup, lay in his bosom, and was like a daughter to him." The rich man had unexpected guests. Instead of slaughtering one of his own sheep, he took the poor man's single ewe lamb, slaughtered it, and served it to his guests. David exploded in anger: "The man who did this deserves to die!" Then, in one of the most riveting passages in all the Bible, Nathan turns to David, stretches out his arm and points to him, and declares, "*You are that man!*" And David sees what he has done.

My interest here is in David's reaction to the story. I agree with David: such injustice is utterly and despicably wrong; there are really no words for it. I believe that such an action is wrong, and I believe that the proposition that it *isn't* wrong—either because really *nothing* is wrong, or because even if *some* things are wrong, *this* isn't—is false. As a matter of fact, there isn't a lot I believe more strongly. I recognize, however, that there are those who disagree with me; and once more, I doubt that I could find an argument to show them that I am right and they wrong. Further, for all I know, their conflicting beliefs have for them the same internally available epistemic markers, the same phenomenology, as mine have for me. Am I then being arbitrary, treating similar cases differently in continuing to hold, as I do, that in fact that kind of behavior *is* dreadfully wrong? I don't think so. Am I wrong in thinking racial bigotry despicable, even though I know there are others who disagree, and even if I think they have the same internal markers for their beliefs as I have for mine? I don't think so. I believe in Serious Actualism, the view that no objects have properties in worlds in which they do not exist, not even nonexistence. Others do not believe this, and perhaps the internal markers of their dissenting views have for them the same quality as my views have for me. Am I being arbitrary in continuing to think as I do? I can't see how.

And the reason here is this: in each of these cases, the believer in question doesn't really think the beliefs in question *are* on a relevant epistemic par. She may agree that she and those who dissent are equally convinced of the truth of their belief, and even that they are internally on a par, that the internally available markers are similar, or relevantly similar. But she must still think that there is an important epistemic difference: she thinks that somehow the other person has *made a mistake,* or *has a blind spot,* or hasn't been wholly attentive, or hasn't received some grace she has, or is in some way epistemically less fortunate. And, of course, the pluralist critic is in no better case. He thinks the thing to do when there is internal epistemic parity is to withhold judgment; he knows there are others who don't think so, and for all he knows, that belief has internal parity with his; if he continues in that belief, therefore, he will be in the same condition as the exclusivist; and if he doesn't continue in this belief, he no longer has an objection to the exclusivist.

But couldn't I be wrong? Of course I could! But I don't avoid that risk by withholding all religious (or philosophical or moral) beliefs; I can go wrong that way as well as any other, treating all religions, or all philosophical thoughts, or all moral views, as on a par. Again, there is no safe haven here, no way to avoid risk. In particular, you won't reach safe haven by trying to take the same attitude toward all the historically available patterns of belief and withholding: for in so doing, you adopt a particular pattern of belief and withholding, one incompatible with some adopted by others. You pays your money and you takes your choice, realizing that you, like anyone else, can be desperately wrong. But what else can you do? You don't really have an alternative. And how can you do better than believe and withhold according to what, after serious and responsible consideration, seems to you to be the right pattern of belief and withholding?

## *Irrationality*

I therefore can't see how it can be sensibly maintained that the exclusivist is unjustified in his exclusivistic views; but perhaps, as is sometimes claimed, he or his view is *irrational.* Irrationality, however, is many things to many people; so there is a prior question: what is it to be irrational? More exactly: precisely what quality is it that the objector is attributing to the exclusivist (in condition C) when the former says the latter's exclusivist beliefs are irrational? Since the charge is never developed at all fully, it isn't easy to say. So suppose we simply consider the main varieties of irrationality (or, if you prefer, the main senses of "irrational") and ask whether any of them attach to the exclusivist just by virtue of being an exclusivist. I believe there are substantially five varieties of rationality, five distinct but analogically[16] connected senses of the term "rational"; fortunately, not all of them require detailed consideration.

1. *Aristotelian Rationality.* This is the sense in which man is a rational animal, one that has *ratio,* one that can look before and after, can hold beliefs, make inferences, and is capable of knowledge. This is perhaps the basic sense, the one of which the others are analogical extensions. It is also, presumably, irrelevant in the present context; at any rate, I hope the objector does not mean to hold that an exclusivist will by that token no longer be a rational animal.
2. *The Deliverances of Reason.* To be rational in the Aristotelian sense is to possess reason: the power of thinking, believing, inferring, reasoning, knowing. Aristotelian rationality is thus *generic.* But there is an important more specific sense lurking in the neighborhood; this is the sense that goes with reason taken more narrowly, as the source of a priori knowledge and belief.[17] An important use of "rational" analogically connected with the first has to do with reason taken in this more narrow way. It is by reason thus construed that we know *self-evident* beliefs—beliefs so obvious that you can't so much as grasp them without seeing that they couldn't be false. These are among the *deliverances of reason.* Of course, there are other beliefs—*38 × 39 = 1482,* for example—that are not self-evident but are a consequence of self-evident beliefs by way of arguments that are self-evidently valid; these too are among the deliverances of reason. So say that the deliverances

of reason are the set of those propositions that are self-evident for us human beings, closed under self-evident consequence. This yields another sense of rationality: a belief is *rational* if it is among the deliverances of reason and *irrational* if it is contrary to the deliverances of reason. (A belief can therefore be neither rational nor irrational, in this sense.) This sense of "rational" is an analogical extension of the fundamental sense, but it is itself extended by analogy to still other senses. Thus we can broaden the category of reason to include memory, experience, induction, probability, and whatever else goes into science; this is the sense of the term when reason is sometimes contrasted with faith. And we can also soften the requirement for self-evidence, recognizing both that self-evidence or a priori warrant is a matter of degree, and that there are many propositions that have a priori warrant but are not such that no one who understands them can fail to believe them.[18]

Is the exclusivist irrational in *these* senses? I think not; or at any rate the question whether he is isn't the question at issue. For his exclusivist beliefs are irrational in these senses only if there is a good argument from the deliverances of reason (taken broadly) to the denials of what he believes. I myself do not believe there are any such arguments. Presumably, the same goes for the pluralist objector; at any rate his objection is not that (1) and (2) are demonstrably false or even that there are good arguments against them from the deliverances of reason; his objection is instead that there is something wrong or subpar with believing them in condition C. This sense too, then, is irrelevant to our present concerns.

3. *The Deontological Sense*. This sense of the term has to do with intellectual *requirement*, or *duty*, or *obligation:* a person's belief is irrational in this sense if in forming or holding it she violates such a duty. This is the sense of "irrational" in which, according to many contemporary evidentialist objectors to theistic belief, those who believe in God without propositional evidence are irrational.[19] Irrationality in this sense is a matter of failing to conform to intellectual or epistemic duties; and the analogical connection with the first, Aristotelian sense is that these duties are thought to be among the deliverances of reason (and hence among the deliverances of the power by virtue of which human beings are rational in the Aristotelian sense). But we have already considered whether the exclusivist is flouting duties; we need say no more about the matter here. As we saw, the exclusivist is not necessarily irrational in this sense either.
4. *Zweckrationalität*. A common and very important notion of rationality is *means–end* rationality—what our Continental cousins, following Max Weber, sometimes call *Zweckrationalität,* the sort of rationality displayed by your actions if they are well calculated to achieve your goals. (Again, the analogical connection with the first sense is clear:

the calculation in question requires the power by virtue of which we are rational in Aristotle's sense.) Clearly, there is a whole constellation of notions lurking in the nearby bushes: what would *in fact* contribute to your goals, what you *take* it would contribute to your goals, what you *would* take it would contribute to your goals if you were sufficiently acute, or knew enough, or weren't distracted by lust, greed, pride, ambition, and the like, what you would take it would contribute to your goals if you weren't thus distracted and were also to reflect sufficiently, and so on. This notion of rationality has assumed enormous importance in the last one hundred fifty years or so. (Among its laurels, for example, is the complete domination of the development of the discipline of economics.) Rationality thus construed is a matter of knowing how to get what you want; it is the cunning of reason. Is the exclusivist properly charged with irrationality in this sense? Does his believing in the way he does interfere with his attaining some of his goals, or is it a markedly inferior way of attaining those goals?

An initial caveat: it isn't clear that this notion of rationality applies to belief at all. It isn't clear that in *believing* something, I am acting to achieve some goal. If believing is an action at all, it is very far from being the paradigmatic kind of action taken to achieve some end; we don't have a choice as to whether to have beliefs, and we don't have a lot of choice with respect to which beliefs we have. But suppose we set this caveat aside and stipulate for purposes of argument that we have sufficient control over our beliefs for them to qualify as actions: would the exclusivist's beliefs then be irrational in this sense? Well, that depends upon what his goals *are;* if among his goals for religious belief is, for example, not believing anything not believed by someone else, then indeed it would be. But, of course, he needn't have *that* goal. If I do have an end or goal in holding such beliefs as (1) and (2), it would presumably be that of believing the truth on this exceedingly important matter, or perhaps that of trying to get in touch as adequately as possible with God, or more broadly with the deepest reality. And if (1) and (2) are *true,* believing them will be a way of doing exactly that. It is only if they are *not* true, then, that believing them could sensibly be thought to be irrational in this means–ends sense. Since the objector does not propose to take as a premise the proposition that (1) and (2) are false—he holds only that there is some flaw involved in *believing* them—this also is presumably not what he means.

**5.** *Rationality as Sanity and Proper Function*. One in the grip of pathological confusion, or flight of ideas, or certain kinds of agnosia, or the manic phase of manic–depressive psychosis will often be said to be irrational; the episode may pass, after which he regains rationality. Here "rationality" means absence of dysfunction, disorder, impairment, pathology with respect to rational faculties. So this variety of rationality is again analogically related to Aristotelian rationality; a person is rational in this sense when no malfunction obstructs her use of the faculties by virtue of the possession of which she is rational in the Aristotelian sense. Rationality as sanity does not require possession of particularly exalted rational faculties; it requires only normality (in the nonstatistical sense), or health, or proper function. This use of the term, naturally enough, is prominent in psychiatric discussions—Oliver Sacks's man who mistook his wife for a hat,[20] for example, was thus irrational.[21] This fifth and final sense of rationality is itself a family of analogically related senses. The fundamental sense here is that of sanity and proper function, but there are other closely related senses. Thus we may say that a belief (in certain circumstances) is irrational not because no sane person would hold it, but because no person who was sane and had also undergone a certain course of education would hold it, or because no person who was sane and furthermore was as intelligent as we and our friends would hold it; alternatively and more briefly, the idea is not merely that no one who was functioning properly in those circumstances would hold it but rather no one who was functioning *optimally,* as well or nearly as well as human beings ordinarily do (leaving aside the occasional great genius), would hold it. And this sense of rationality leads directly to the notion of *warrant;* I turn now to that notion; in treating it we also treat *ambulando* this fifth kind of irrationality.

## Warrant

So the third version of the epistemic objection: that at any rate the exclusivist doesn't have warrant, or anyway *much* warrant (enough warrant for knowledge), for his exclusivistic views. Many pluralists—for example, Hick, Runzo, and Wilfred Cantwell Smith—unite in declaring that at any rate the exclusivist certainly can't *know* that his exclusivistic views are true.[22] But is this really true? I shall argue briefly that it is not. At any rate from the perspective of each of the major contemporary accounts of knowledge, it may very well be that the exclusivist knows (1) or (2) or both. First, consider the two main internalistic accounts of knowledge: the justified true belief account(s) and the coherentist account(s). As I have already argued, it seems clear that a theist, a believer in (1), could certainly be *justified* (in the primary sense) in believing as she does: she could be flouting no intellectual or cognitive duties or obligations. But then on the most straightforward justified true belief account of knowledge, she can also *know* that it is true—if, that is, it *can* be true. More exactly, what must be possible is that both the exclusivist is justified in believing (1) and/or (2) and they be true. Presumably, the pluralist does not mean to dispute this possibility.

For concreteness, consider the account of justification given by the classical Chisholm.[23] On this view, a belief has warrant for me to the extent that accepting it is apt for the fulfillment of my epistemic duty, which (roughly speaking) is that of trying to get and remain in the right relation to the truth. But if after the most careful, thorough, thoughtful, open, and prayerful consideration, it still seems to me—perhaps more strongly than ever—that (1) and (2) are true, then clearly accepting them has great aptness for the fulfillment of that duty.[24]

A similarly brief argument can be given with respect to coherentism, the view that what constitutes warrant is coherence with some body of belief. We must distinguish two varieties of coherentism. On the one hand, it might be held that what is required is coherence with some or all of the other beliefs I actually hold; on the other, that what is required is coherence with my *verific* noetic structure (Keith Lehrer's term): the set of beliefs that remains when all the false ones are deleted or replaced by their contradictories. But surely a coherent set of beliefs could include both (1) and (2) together with the beliefs involved in being in condition C; what would be required, perhaps, would be that the set of beliefs contain some explanation of why it is that others do not believe as I do. And if (1) and (2) *are* true, then surely (and a fortiori) there can be coherent verific noetic structures that include them. Hence neither of these versions of coherentism rules out the possibility that the exclusivist in condition C could know (1) and/or (2).

And now consider the main externalist accounts. The most popular externalist account at present would be one or another version of *reliabilism.* And there is an oft-repeated pluralistic argument (an argument that goes back at least to John Stuart Mill's *On Liberty* and possibly all the way back to the third century) that seems to be designed to appeal to reliabilist intuitions. The conclusion of this argument is not always clear, but here is its premise, in John Hick's words:

> For it is evident that in some ninety-nine percent of cases the religion which an individual professes and to which he or she adheres depends upon the accidents of birth. Someone born to Buddhist parents in Thailand is very likely to be a Buddhist, someone born to Muslim parents in Saudi Arabia to be a Muslim, someone born to Christian parents in Mexico to be a Christian, and so on.[25]

As a matter of sociological fact, this may be right. Furthermore, it can certainly produce a sense of intellectual vertigo. But what is one to do with this fact, if fact it is, and what follows from it? Does it follow, for example, that I ought not to accept the religious views that I have been brought up to accept, or the ones that I find myself inclined to accept, or the ones that seem to me to be true? Or that the belief-producing processes that have produced those beliefs in me are unreliable? Surely not. Furthermore, self-referential problems once more loom; this argument is another philosophical tar baby.

For suppose we concede that if I had been born in Madagascar rather than Michigan, my beliefs would have been quite different.[26] (For one thing, I probably wouldn't believe that I was born in Michigan.) But, of course, the same goes for the pluralist. Pluralism isn't and hasn't been widely popular in the world at large; if the pluralist had been born in Madagascar, or medieval France, he probably wouldn't have been a pluralist. Does it follow that he shouldn't be a pluralist or that his pluralistic beliefs are produced in him by an unreliable belief-producing process? I doubt it. Suppose I hold

> (4) If S's religious or philosophical beliefs are such that if S had been born elsewhere and elsewhen, she wouldn't have held them, then those beliefs are produced by unreliable belief-producing mechanisms and hence have no warrant;

or something similar: then once more I will be hoist with my own petard. For in all probability, someone born in Mexico to Christian parents wouldn't believe (4) itself. No matter what philosophical and religious beliefs we hold and withhold (so it seems), there are places and times such that if we had been born there and then, then we would not have displayed the pattern of holding and withholding of religious and philosophical beliefs we *do* display. As I said, this can indeed be vertiginous; but what can we make of it? What can we infer from it about what has warrant and how we should conduct our intellectual lives? That's not easy to say. Can we infer *anything at all* about what has warrant or how we should conduct our intellectual lives? Not obviously.

To return to reliabilism, then: for simplicity, let's take the version of reliabilism according to which S knows *p* iff the belief that *p* is produced in S by a reliable belief-producing mechanism or process. I don't have the space, here, to go into this matter in sufficient detail: but it seems pretty clear that if (1) and (2) are true, then it *could be* that the beliefs that (1) and (2) be produced in me by a reliable belief-producing process. For either we are thinking of *concrete* belief-producing processes, like your memory or John's powers of a priori reasoning (*tokens* as opposed to types), or else we are thinking of *types* of belief-producing processes (type reliabilism). The problem with the latter is that there are an enormous number of *different* types of belief-producing processes for any given belief, some of which are reliable and some of which are not; the problem (and a horrifying problem it is[27]) is to say which of these is the type the reliability of which determines whether the belief in question has warrant. So the first (token reliabilism) is the better way of stating reliabilism. But then, clearly enough, if (1) or (2) *is* true, it could be produced in me by a reliable belief-producing process. Calvin's Sensus Divinitatis, for example, could be working in the exclusivist in such a way as reliably to produce the belief that (1); Calvin's Internal Testimony of the Holy Spirit could do the same for (2). If (1) and (2) are true, therefore, then from a reliabilist perspective there is no reason whatever to think that the exclusivist might not know that they are true.

There is another brand of externalism that seems to me to be closer to the truth than reliabilism: call it (faute de mieux) "proper functionalism." This view can be stated to a first approximation as follows: S knows *p* iff (1) the belief that *p* is produced in S by cognitive faculties that are functioning properly (working as they ought to work, suffering from no dysfunction), (2) the cognitive environment in which *p* is produced is appropriate for those faculties, (3) the purpose of the module of the epistemic faculties producing the belief in question is to produce true beliefs (alternatively: the module of the design plan governing the production of *p* is aimed at the production of true beliefs), and (4) the objective probability of a belief's being true, given that it is produced under those conditions, is high.[28] All this needs explanation, of course; for present purposes, perhaps, we can collapse the account into the first condition. But then clearly it *could* be, if (1) and (2) are true, that they are produced in me by cognitive faculties functioning properly under condition C. For suppose (1) is true. Then it is surely possible that God has created us human beings with something like Calvin's Sensus Divinitatis, a belief-producing process that in a wide variety of circumstances functions properly to produce (1) or some very similar belief. Furthermore, it is also possible that in response to the human condition of sin and misery, God has provided for us human beings a means of salvation, which he has revealed in the Bible. Still further, perhaps he has arranged for us to come to believe what he means to teach there by way of the operation of something like the Internal Testimony of the Holy Spirit of which Calvin speaks. So on this view, too, if (1) and (2) are true, it is certainly possible that the exclusivist *know* that they are. We can be sure that the exclusivist's views lack warrant and are irrational in this sense, then, only if they are false; but the pluralist objector does not mean to claim that they *are* false; this version of the objection, therefore, also fails. The exclusivist isn't necessarily irrational, and indeed might *know* that (1) and (2) are true, if indeed they *are* true.

All this seems right. But don't the realities of religious pluralism count for anything at all? Is there nothing at all to the claims of the pluralists?[29] Could that really be right? Of course not. For many or most exclusivists, I think, an awareness of the enormous variety of human religious response serves as a *defeater* for such beliefs as (1) and (2)—an *undercutting* defeater, as opposed to a *rebutting* defeater. It calls into question, to some degree or other, the sources of one's belief in (1) or (2). It doesn't or needn't do so by way of an *argument;* and indeed, there isn't a very powerful argument from the proposition that many apparently devout people around the world dissent from (1) and (2) to the conclusion that (1) and (2) are false. Instead, it works more directly; it directly reduces the level of confidence or degree of belief in the proposition in question. From a Christian perspective, this situation of religious pluralism and our awareness of it is itself a manifestation of our miserable human condition; and it may deprive us of some of the comfort and peace the Lord has promised his followers. It can also deprive the exclusivist of the *knowledge* that (1) and (2) are true, even if they *are* true and he *believes* that they are. Since degree of warrant depends in part on degree of belief, it is possible, though not necessary, that knowledge of the facts of religious pluralism should reduce an exclusivist's degree of belief and hence of warrant for (1) and (2) in such a way as to deprive him of knowledge of (1) and (2). He might be such that if he *hadn't* known the facts of pluralism, then he would have known (1) and (2), but now that he *does* know those facts, he doesn't know (1) and (2). In this way he may come to know less by knowing more.

Things *could* go this way with the exclusivist. On the other hand, they *needn't* go this way. Consider once more the moral parallel. Perhaps you have always believed it deeply wrong for a counselor to use his position of trust to seduce a client. Perhaps you discover that others disagree; they think it more like a minor peccadillo, like running a red light when there's no traffic; and you realize that possibly these people have the same internal markers for their beliefs that you have for yours. You think the matter over more fully, imaginatively recreate and rehearse such situations, become more aware of just what is involved in such a situation (the breach of trust, the breaking of implied promises, the injustice and unfairness, the nasty irony of a situation in which someone comes to a counselor seeking help but receives only hurt) and come to believe even more firmly the belief that such an action is wrong—which belief, indeed, can in this way acquire more warrant for you. But something similar can happen in the case of religious beliefs. A fresh or heightened awareness of the facts of religious pluralism could bring about a reappraisal of one's religious life, a reawakening, a new or renewed and deepened grasp and apprehension of (1) and (2). From Calvin's perspective, it could serve as an occasion for a renewed and more powerful working of the belief-producing processes by which we come to apprehend (1) and (2). In that way knowledge of the facts of pluralism could initially serve as a defeater, but in the long run have precisely the opposite effect.

## NOTES

1. *Colloquium Heptaplomeres de rerum sublimium arcanis abditis,* written by 1593 but first published in 1857. English translation by Marion Kuntz (Princeton: Princeton University Press, 1975). The quotation is from the Kuntz translation, p. 256.

2. Thus Joseph Runzo: "Today, the impressive piety and evident rationality of the belief systems of other religious traditions inescapably confronts Christians with a crisis—and a potential revolution." "God, Commitment, and Other Faiths: Pluralism vs. Relativism," *Faith and Philosophy* **5** (1988), 343.

3. As explained in detail in Robert Wilken, "Religious Pluralism and Early Christian Thought," *Pro Ecclesia* **1** (1992), 89–103. Wilken focuses on the third century; he explores Origen's response to Celsus and concludes that there are striking parallels between Origen's historical situation and ours. What is different today, I suspect, is not that Christianity has to confront other religions but that we now call this situation "religious pluralism."

4. Thus Gary Gutting: "Applying these considerations to religious belief, we seem led to the conclusion that, because believers have many epistemic peers who do not share their belief in God . . . , they have no right to maintain their belief without a justification. If they do so, they are guilty of epistemic egoism." *Religious Belief and Religious Skepticism* (Notre Dame: University of Notre Dame Press, 1982), p. 90 (but see the following pages for an important qualification).

5. "Here my submission is that on this front the traditional doctrinal position of the Church has in fact militated against its traditional moral position, and has in fact encouraged Christians to approach other men immorally. Christ has taught us humility, but we have approached them with arrogance. . . . This charge of arrogance is a serious one." Wilfred Cantwell Smith, *Religious Diversity* (New York: Harper and Row, 1976), p. 13.

6. Runzo, "Ethically, Religious Exclusivism has the morally repugnant result of making those who have privileged knowledge, or who are intellectually astute, a religious elite, while penalizing those who happen to have no access to the putatively correct religious view, or who are incapable of advanced understanding." "God, Commitment, and Other Faiths," p. 348.

7. "But natural pride, despite its positive contribution to human life, becomes harmful when it is elevated to the level of dogma and is built into the belief system of a religious community. This happens when its sense of its own validity and worth is expressed in doctrines implying an exclusive or a decisively superior access to the truth or the power to save." John Hick, "Religious Pluralism and Absolute Claims," in Leroy Rouner, ed., *Religious Pluralism* (Notre Dame: University of Notre Dame Press, 1984), p. 197.

8. Thus John Cobb: "I agree with the liberal theists that even in Pannenberg's case, the quest for an absolute as a basis for understanding reflects the long tradition of Christian imperialism and triumphalism rather than the pluralistic spirit." "The Meaning of Pluralism for Christian Self-Understanding," in Rouner, *Religious Pluralism,* p. 171.

9. "God, Commitment, and Other Faiths," p. 357.

10. Smith, *Religious Diversity,* p. 14. A similar statement: "Nor can we reasonably claim that our own form of religious experience, together with that of the tradition of which we are a part, is veridical whilst others are not. We can of course claim this; and indeed virtually every religious tradition has done so, regarding alternative forms of religion either as false or as confused and inferior versions of itself. . . . Persons living within other traditions, then, are equally justified in trusting their own distinctive religious experience and in forming their beliefs on the basis of it. . . .let us avoid the implausibly arbitrary dogma that religious experience is all delusory with the single exception of the particular form enjoyed by the one who is speaking." John Hick, *An Interpretation of Religion* (New Haven: Yale University Press, 1989), p. 235.

11. "The only reason for treating one's tradition differently from others is the very human but not very cogent reason that it is one's own!" Hick, *An Interpretation of Religion,* p. 235.

12. To speak of a choice here suggests that I can simply choose which of these three attitudes to adopt; but is that at all realistic? Are my beliefs to that degree within my control? Here I shall set aside the question whether and to what degree my beliefs are subject to my control and within my power. Perhaps we have very little control over them; then the moral critic of exclusivism can't properly accuse the exclusivist of dereliction of moral duty, but he could still argue that the exclusivist's stance is unhappy, bad, a miserable state of affairs. Even if I can't help it that I am overbearing and conceited, my being that way is a bad state of affairs.

13. See my "Justification in the Twentieth Century," *Philosophy and Phenomenological Research* **50,** supplement (Fall 1990), 45 ff., and see Chapter 1 of my *Warrant: The Current Debate* (New York: Oxford University Press, 1993).

14. See the three editions of *Theory of Knowledge* referred to in Note 23.

15. Some people think there is, and also think that withholding belief, abstaining from belief, is always and automatically the safe course to take with respect to this duty, whenever any question arises as to what to believe and withhold. But that isn't so. One can go wrong by withholding as well as believing: there is no safe haven here, not even abstention. If there is a duty of the Chisholmian kind, and if I, out of epistemic pride and excessive scrupulosity, succeed in training myself not to accept ordinary perceptual judgments in ordinary perceptual circumstances, I am not performing works of epistemic supererogation; I am epistemically culpable.

16. In Aquinas's sense, so that the analogy may include causality, proportionality, resemblance, and the like.

17. But then (because of the Russell paradoxes) we can no longer take it that the deliverances of reason are closed under self-evident consequence. See my *Warrant and Proper Function* (New York: Oxford University Press, 1993), Chapter 6.

18. See my *Warrant and Proper Function,* Chapter 6. Still another analogical extension: a *person* can be said to be irrational if he won't listen to or pay attention to be deliverances of reason. He may be blinded by lust, or inflamed by passion, or deceived by pride: he might then act contrary to reason—*act* irrationally but also *believe* irrationally. Thus Locke: "Let never so much probability land on one side of a covetous man's reasoning, and money on the other, it is easy to foresee which will outweigh. Tell a man, passionately in love, that he is jilted; bring a score of witnesses of the falsehood of his mistress, 'tis ten to one but three kind words of hers shall invalidate all their testimonies . . . and though men cannot always openly gain-say, or resist the force of manifest probabilities, that make against them; yet yield they not to the argument." *An Essay Concerning Human Understanding,* ed. A. D. Woozley (New York: World Publishing Co., 1963), bk. IV, sec. xx, p. 439.

19. Among those who offer this objection to theistic belief are Brand Blanshard, *Reason and Belief* (London: Allen and Unwin, 1974), pp. 400ff.; Antony Flew, *The Presumption of Atheism* (London: Pemburton, 1976), pp. 22ff.; and Michael Scriven, *Primary Philosophy* (New York: McGraw-Hill, 1966), pp. 102 ff. See my "Reason and Belief in God," in Alvin Plantinga and Nicholas Wolterstorff, eds., *Faith and Rationality* (Notre Dame: University of Notre Dame Press, 1983), pp. 17ff.

20. Oliver Sacks, *The Man Who Mistook His Wife for a Hat* (New York: Harper and Row, 1987).

21. In this sense of the term, what is properly called an "irrational impulse" may be perfectly rational; an irrational impulse is really one that goes contrary to the deliverances of reason; but undergoing such impulses need not be in any way dysfunctional or a result of impairment of cognitive faculties. To go back to some of William James's examples, that I will survive my serious illness might be unlikely, given the statistics I know and my evidence generally; perhaps we are so constructed, however, that when our faculties function properly in extreme situations, we are more optimistic than the evidence warrants. This belief, then, is irrational in

the sense that it goes contrary to the deliverances of reason; it is rational in the sense that it doesn't involve dysfunction.

22. Hick, *An Interpretation of Religion*, p. 234; Runzo, "God, Commitment, and Other Faiths," p. 348; Smith, *Religious Diversity*, p. 16.

23. See his *Perceiving: A Philosophical Study* (Ithaca: Cornell University Press, 1957), the three editions of *Theory of Knowledge* (New Jersey: Prentice Hall, 1st ed., 1966; 2nd ed., 1977; 3rd ed., 1989), and *The Foundations of Knowing* (Minneapolis: University of Minnesota Press, 1982); and see my "Chisholmian Internalism," in David Austin, ed., *Philosophical Analysis: A Defense by Example* (Dordrecht: D. Reidel, 1988), and Chapter 2 of *Warrant: The Current Debate.*

24. Of course, there are many variations on this internalist theme. Consider briefly the postclassical Chisholm (see his "The Place of Epistemic Justification," in Roberta Klein, ed., *Philosophical Topics* **14,** no. 1 (1986), 85, and the intellectual autobiography in *Roderick M. Chisholm*, ed., Radu Bogdan [Dordrecht: D. Reidel, 1986], pp. 52 ff.), who bears a startling resemblance to Brentano. According to this view, justification is not *deontological* but *axiological.* To put it another way, warrant is not really a matter of justification, of fulfilling duty and obligation; it is instead a question whether a certain relation of fittingness holds between one's evidential base (very roughly, the totality of one's present experiences and other beliefs) and the belief in question. (This relationship's holding, of course, is a valuable state of affairs; hence the axiology.) Can the exclusivist have warrant from this perspective? Well, without more knowledge about what this relation is, it isn't easy to tell. But here at the least the postclassical Chisholmian pluralist would owe us an explanation why he thinks the exclusivist's beliefs could not stand in this relation to his evidence base.

25. *An Interpretation of Religion*, p. 2.

26. Actually, this conditional as it stands is probably not true; the point must be stated with more care. Given my parents and their proclivities, if I had been born in Madagascar, it would probably have been because my parents were (Christian) missionaries there.

27. See Richard Feldman, "Reliability and Justification," *The Monist* **68** (1986), 159–74, and Chapter 9 of my *Warrant and Proper Function.*

28. See Chapter 10 of my *Warrant: The Current Debate* and the first two chapters of my *Warrant and Proper Function* for exposition and defense of this way of thinking about warrant.

29. See William P. Alston, "Religious Diversity and Perceptual Knowledge of God," *Faith and Philosophy* **5** (1988), 433 ff. [reprinted as Chapter 11 in this volume].

CHAPTER 11

# Religious Diversity and Perceptual Knowledge of God

WILLIAM P. ALSTON

## I

The existence of a plurality of religious communities, each with its own belief system that is incompatible in various respects with each of the others, poses a serious and well advertised problem for the claims of each community. After all, it looks as if Moslems, Hindus, and Buddhists have grounds of the same general sort (revelation, religious experience, miracles, authority, etc.) as my fellow Christians and I have for the truth of our respective systems of doctrine. But then, unless I have sufficient reason for supposing that Christians are in a superior position for discerning the truth about these matters, why should I suppose that we are right and they are wrong? How can I be justified in continuing to affirm my Christian beliefs?

Note that this is hardly a crucial epistemological problem unless there are substantial grounds of belief within each community. If Christian beliefs are without any significant internal justification, then they lack positive epistemic status quite apart from competition from other religions, and so for the others.[1] I have no time in this essay to argue that this condition holds for the major religions of the world. I shall simply assume that it does, so as to throw the distinctive difficulties posed by religious pluralism into sharp relief.

One response to this problem is to argue that, despite appearances, there are no incompatibilities, or no fundamental incompatibilities, between the major world religions, thereby removing another fundamental condition of the problem. This line can take different forms. (1) The strongest would be the contention that the existent doctrinal systems, as generally understood, are not incompatible. To show this would be a brilliant feat indeed. (2) A more modest and feasible-seeming project would be to try to trim each system of various "excesses" so that what is left in each case is compatible with what is left in the others. (3) We might follow John Hick and others in introducing a

From William P. Alston, "Religious Diversity and Perceptual Knowledge of God," *Faith and Philosophy* 5 (October 1988): 433–48. Reprinted by permission of the author and *Faith and Philosophy*.

level distinction, contending that though the various belief systems conflict with each other that is because they constitute different "pictures," "images," or "representations" of the one ultimate reality, which is represented in each adequately enough for practical (salvific) purposes but the real nature of which is adequately captured in none of them. And there are other variants. However, for purposes of this paper I am going to take none of these enterprises to succeed in eliminating at least a stubborn residue of incompatibilities.

The most obvious move, in the face of genuine incompatibilities, is to try to show that the beliefs of one's own religion are true and those of the competition are false. If this maximally direct approach is to have any chance of success, it must proceed on the basis of considerations that are common to all parties, like sense perception, rational self-evidence, and common modes of reasoning. For if the Christian tries to show that her beliefs are true, and that Hindu beliefs are false, by appealing to God's self revelation in the Bible, we are, it would seem, no further forward. Now I do not want to assert that it is impossible to show by general metaphysical and empirical arguments that the system of Christian belief is superior to its rivals; nor do I want to assert the contrary. Again I shall simply set that enterprise aside and consider the epistemic situation on the assumption that it cannot succeed.

A less direct solution would be to argue, on the basis of common grounds, that the Christian is in a better epistemic position to get the truth about these matters than the adherents of other religions. I have no idea how this would go, and so I shall ignore this maneuver.

My discussion presupposes a realist theory of truth and its applicability to religious belief. I assume that religious beliefs are true or false according to whether what is believed is the case, whether or not we have any way of deciding this. Philosophers sometimes avoid the whole problem of religious pluralism just by eschewing a realist theory of truth, at least in application to religious belief. If the truth of religious belief simply means something like "passes the standard tests of that 'form of life,' 'language game,' or whatever," then the beliefs of all the major world religions could be equally true. I refrain from taking this easy way out.

The form our problem takes for my own work on the epistemology of religious belief is determined by the major thesis I have been concerned to defend.

> P. The experience (or, as I prefer to say, the "perception") of God provides prima facie epistemic justification for beliefs about what God is doing or how God is "situated" *vis-a-vis* one at the moment ("M-beliefs," "M" for "manifestation").

Examples of M-beliefs would be the belief that God is sustaining one in being, pouring out His love into one, communicating a certain message to one, or simply presenting Himself to one as supremely good or powerful. The experiences I take to constitute (putative) perceptions of God range over any cases in which the subject takes herself to be aware of God as presenting

Himself to her experience. This includes, but is not restricted to, "mystical" experiences of the classic type in which one seems, momentarily, to lose one's identity in merging with the divine. It also includes dim background experiences of the presence of God as well as more vivid and shorter lasting focal experiences. And it ranges over both experiences that are and those that are not mediated by sense perception of the physical and social environment. I take it that perception of God, thus broadly construed, is a widespread phenomenon among religious folk.

To explain how religious pluralism poses a problem for this thesis I will first have to lay out the general epistemological framework in which the thesis is set.

## II

We engage in a plurality of more or less distinct "doxastic practices," i.e., practices of belief formation, each of which involves distinctive sorts of input to "belief-forming mechanisms" and distinctive "input–output functions" that yield beliefs related in particular ways to the outputs.[2] Thus, to take the easiest case to describe, a deductive inference practice will feature a variety of mechanisms that take beliefs as inputs, each mechanism operating according to a function defined by some form of reasoning. (Unfortunately these are not restricted to valid inference forms.) The sense perceptual practice involves functions that are harder to describe, each of which goes from some characteristic pattern of sensory experience to a belief about the physical environment. Other familiar examples of doxastic practices involve the formation of beliefs on the basis of memory, introspection, and non-deductive reasoning of various sorts. Built into each practice is also a set of checks and tests for the beliefs so formed, in other terms, a series of possible "overriders" for the prima facie justification conferred on a belief by its emergence from that practice. For the sense perceptual practice (hereinafter "SP"), e.g., a particular perceptual belief may be overridden by sufficient independent reasons to think the belief false (I seemed to see an elephant, but there couldn't have been one there), or sufficient reasons to suppose that one's perceptual faculties were not working properly. A doxastic practice will typically operate on certain basic assumptions that cannot be justified within the practice but rather serve as presuppositions of any exercise thereof. Thus SP presupposes the independent (of experience) existence of physical objects and the by and large reliability of sense perception. In some cases a practice will also deal with a distinctive subject matter and will feature a distinctive conceptual scheme. This is true, e.g., of SP, but not of the inferential practices. Finally, a doxastic practice is typically acquired and engaged in well before one is explicitly aware of it. When one arrives at the age of reflection, one finds oneself with a mastery of many such practices and ineluctably involved in their exercise. And whatever role innate mechanisms play in the matter, such practices are socially established by socially monitored learning and are socially shared.[3]

I don't want to give the impression that different doxastic practices (hereinafter "DP") operate in isolation from each other. On the contrary, they depend on each other in various ways. Inferential practices obviously depend on others for their (ultimate) belief inputs. And the overrider system connected with, e.g., SP, makes use of a general picture of the physical world built up by applying memory and reasoning to the output of SP.

How are DP's to be assessed, epistemically? My answer is based on the point that our belief forming activity essentially aims at maximizing truth and minimizing falsehood. Therefore our basic term of positive epistemic evaluation, "justification," "rationality," or whatever, should be truth-linked, should be such that a positive rating carries with it at least a strong probability of truth. That is, I am justified in believing that p only if the belief is formed in such a way that it is thereby likely to be true. Hence, getting back to DP's, a practice will yield mostly justified beliefs only if it is reliable, only if it is such that the input–output mechanisms it involves are, by and large, reliable ones.[4] But then the most fundamental epistemological question to ask of a DP is as to whether it is reliable.

But how do we determine whether a DP is reliable? The most direct approach would be to compare its output beliefs with the facts that make them true or false, and determine the track record of the practice in a suitable spread of cases. Sometimes this is possible. It is possible, e.g., when we are dealing with what we might call "partial" or "restricted" practices, like determining temperature on the basis of mercury thermometers, or recognizing vintages of wine by taste. In these cases we have other modes of access to the facts in question, modes which we can use to check the accuracy of the practice under examination. But we fairly quickly arrive at more inclusive practices where this technique is no longer available. If we are assessing SP in general, e.g., we have no independent access to the facts in question (facts concerning the physical environment of the perceiver), i.e., no access that neither consists in nor is based on reliance on sense perception; and so we have no non-circular check on the accuracy of the deliverances of SP. We might try a more indirect approach, e.g., arguing "pragmatically" that the success in predicting and controlling nature we have achieved by basing our activities on sense perception indicates that SP is a reliable guide to the environment. But this exhibits circularity in a more subtle form. How do we tell that we have been successful in prediction? By making observations to determine whether what was predicted actually happened. We aren't informed of this by an angel. Thus it appears that when we try to assess the reliability of the likes of SP, we are unable to find any otherwise cogent argument for reliability that does not involve a reliance on the very practice under scrutiny. And the same holds, I make bold to say, for memory, introspection, and deductive and inductive reasoning. Let's call any socially established DP for which this is true "basic."

What, then, is the most rational attitude to take toward basic DP's? When we eschew circular arguments none of them can be shown to be reliable, and if such arguments are admitted a demonstration of reliability is, of course, quickly forthcoming in each case. If we use the outputs of a DP to check the accuracy of that DP, it can easily score 100%; we simply use each output twice, once as testee and once as tester. In this respect all DP's are on a par. Insofar as reliability is the crucial consideration, and pending the possibility of a demonstration of unreliability, it would seem that we are confined to either taking all of them to be acceptable (i.e., regarding them as reliable) or taking all of them to be unacceptable. It would be arbitrary to distinguish between them. Clearly, abstention from all such practices is not a live option; therefore the only rational alternative open to us is to accord prima facie acceptance to all basic socially established practices (regard them as prima facie reliable), pending a demonstration of unreliability, or the invocation of any other disqualifying consideration.

Just a word as to how a basic practice might be shown unreliable. First, there is the possibility of a massive and persistent inconsistency in its output (not just the sporadic inconsistency that pops up from time to time in the best behaved DP's). Second, there is inconsistency between its outputs and the outputs of more firmly established DP's. To be sure, even if a DP runs into trouble in one or more of these respects, it may well be modified so as to get back in line without losing its distinctive character. I take it that this has repeatedly happened with religious DP's.

We should also note that there is a kind of "self-support" by which a basic DP can strengthen its claim to rational acceptance. This is illustrated by the predictive success we attain on the basis of SP and associated practices (call the whole complex the "empirical DP"). This is not a non-circular support, for, as we have seen, we have to use the practice to ascertain that the success was forthcoming. Nevertheless it is far from trivial, since it is quite conceivable that the practice should not display it, and, in fact, many empirical DP's, e.g., the reading of tea leaves, do not exhibit anything analogous, even on their own showing. From now on I shall take it that the secular DP's I have been discussing are all basic, free from massive intra- or inter-inconsistency, and significantly self-supporting. Even after it has passed all these tests a practice is still only prima facie rationally acceptable, since there is always the possibility that trouble may develop in the future, particularly in the way of inconsistency with more firmly established practices. But a practice that satisfies all the conditions specified is in a very strong epistemic position indeed.

Now consider the practice of forming M-beliefs about God on the basis of experiences one takes to be direct experiential presentations of God: e.g., forming the belief that God is pouring out His love into one on the basis of what one takes to be an experience of God's doing just that. I want to suggest that this too is a basic DP, or rather, as we shall shortly see, more than one such DP. The phenomenology of religious experience indicates that we have distinctive sorts of experiential inputs here, especially where the experiences in question are non-sensory. And with this come distinctive input–output functions for going from a certain kind of experience to a correlated belief content. Finally, there are distinctive checks and tests to be used in the assessment of particular M-beliefs. It is at this point that we are forced to recognize that, unlike the SP situation, there is not one unique DP of forming M-beliefs about God, much less one unique DP of forming M-beliefs about Ultimate Reality. For the overrider system will vary from one religious tradition to another. It will be heavily based on the canonical scriptures of a tradition, together with whatever other sources there are for its general picture of the Ultimate and our relations thereto. For the major constraint on particular M-beliefs is that they do not conflict with that authoritative picture of the situation. Other tests too will vary from one tradition to another, e.g., whether the M-believer exhibits in his/her life the marks of genuine communion with the Ultimate; for these marks will vary somewhat from one tradition to another. The present point is that if we consider a particular religious community we will find an overrider system of the sort just indicated. For present purposes let's construe "religious community" fairly broadly so as to embrace many differences on points of detail. In that spirit we can identify what I shall call a "mainline Christian community" that relies on the picture of God and His relations to mankind derived from the Bible and from church tradition, allowing, of course, for changes in the understanding of these through time, and allowing for differences of emphasis and of detail. Let's use the acronym "CP" for the practice of forming M-beliefs within the Christian community, subject to the Christian overrider system.[5]

I am going to assume for purposes of this paper that CP is a basic practice, that it is impossible to establish its reliability in a non-circular way.[6] Since it is a socially established basic practice it will count, by the general epistemological principles I have enunciated, as prima facie acceptable, i.e., as prima facie reliable. I will also assume that we have, if necessary, purified the practice, and the system of Christian beliefs it embodies, so that it exhibits no massive and persistent inconsistencies, either internally or *vis-a-vis* other more firmly established practices. Finally, I will take it that it exhibits an appropriate kind of self-support. This will be quite different from the self-support that attaches to SP, just because the character of the practices are so different. Whereas SP is significantly self-supported by its success (as judged internally) in prediction and control, CP, to which those aims are foreign, is significantly self-supported by the fact that the promises held out to its devotees in the way of spiritual development can be seen (from within) to be fulfilled significantly often. As a result of all this CP makes a strong prima facie claim to reliability and hence to rational acceptance.[7]

> T. CP is prima facie reliable, and hence prima facie rationally acceptable.

I have in previous writings examined a number of objections to this thesis, e.g., that there are no objective intersubjective tests of particular M-beliefs, that the experience involved can be adequately explained in terms of natural factors, and that many people claim to have no such perceptions. I have argued that all these objections, and others as well, are based either on epistemic chauvinism (arbitrarily using the standards of one DP to judge another) or on arbitrarily holding different practices subject to different requirements (the double standard).[8]

However there is one difficulty I have not been able to deal with in these ways and that is the one posed by the diversity of religions. To bring religious diversity to bear on my thesis T, I will further stipulate that, in addition to CP, there are other experiential DP's in other religious traditions that are basic practices, not discredited by internal or external inconsistencies and enjoying the same degree of self-support.[9] Thus CP is confronted with DP's that yield outputs incompatible (on the whole) with its own, each of which has the same sort of claim to rational acceptance and none of which are discredited by any neutral standards. All this being the case, how can it be deemed rational for me to form M-beliefs in accordance with CP rather than in accordance with one of the rival religious DP's?

It might appear that the problem posed by religious pluralism for my thesis is much more restricted than the problem posed for total systems of religious belief. For M-beliefs constitute only one segment of the beliefs of a religion, and not the most prominent at that. However important they may be for the individual believer, their importance for the community as a whole lies in the empirical support they provide for the system, rather than in being themselves components of the basic faith of that community. It is no part of the common faith of the church that God sustained *me* in being yesterday. Nevertheless, in attempting to deal with the problem as it impinges on the empirical support of M-beliefs we will be led into the larger problem. First, M-beliefs make use of the basic conceptual and doctrinal scheme of the religion. In supposing that I have been directly aware of God communicating a certain message to me, I suppose that it is the God of Abraham, Isaac, and Jacob, creator of heaven and earth, Father of our Lord Jesus Christ, that is communicating that message to me. I do not learn from that experience that the source of the message is the creator of heaven and earth, the Father of our Lord Jesus Christ, etc., but it is part of what I take to be true in forming the M-belief.[10] And hence the complete M-belief cannot be prima facie justified for me, unless I am prima facie justified in that identification of the communicator. Second, as we have seen, the idea that a particular experience provides *prima facie* justification for a particular M-belief presupposes an overrider system that involves the general picture of God (the Ultimate) and our relations thereto that has been built up in the community over the centuries. But this means that in defending, or assessing, the general *practice* of basing M-beliefs on experience, we have to defend or assess the general system of belief in the community. Hence it is impossible to isolate the epistemology of M-beliefs from the epistemology of that wider system. And so anything that threatens the epistemic status of the latter will ipso facto threaten the epistemic status of the former.[11]

## III

Against this background let us try to be as explicit as possible as to the difficulty the fact of religious pluralism is alleged to pose for my thesis T. Just how is the fact of conflicting religious doxastic practices supposed to make it irrational for me to regard CP as a source of epistemic justification for M-beliefs? Given what I have been saying, religious pluralism would have such a bearing only if it constitutes a reason for thinking CP to be unreliable. And why should we suppose that it does? In considering possible answers to this question I shall move from the less to the more weighty reasons.

First, religious pluralism shows that practitioners of CP cannot appeal to a general consensus, even among those who take themselves to experience Ultimate Reality. All normal adults engage in pretty much the same doxastic practice of forming perceptual beliefs about the physical environment, but the ways of finding out about the Ultimate on the basis of experience differ sharply among the world religions. Therefore, with sense perception we will get general agreement both on particular perceptual beliefs and on the reliability of a particular doxastic practice, while no such consensus exists for CP.

This difference obviously holds, but it is not so clear what its bearing is on the case at hand. Why suppose that it has any tendency to show that CP is *unreliable?* As pointed out earlier, CP has a claim to reliability just by virtue of the fact that it is a "going concern." Even though that claim cannot be strengthened in one of the ways the claim of SP is strengthened, we cannot conclude that it is unreliable. We could draw that conclusion only if we had reason to think that if it were reliable it would be used world wide. But why should we suppose that every reliable doxastic practice will be universally shared? I see no reason to assume this; it is a mere prejudice, based on the overwhelming prominence that universally shared practices have in our lives.

A more serious line of argument is this. The best explanation of religious pluralism will leave the claims of CP, or any other religious DP, discredited. We can distinguish a more and a less strong form of this argument. The stronger form takes a hard naturalist line and contends that the best explanation of the facts of religious diversity is that there is no objective reality with which any of the contenders are in cognitive contact. For if there were, there would not be such persistent disagreements as to what it is like and how we are related to it. But this is only a rehash of the contention we have just dismissed, to the effect that any genuine cognitive contact with an objective reality would be shared across all cultural boundaries. There is no (sufficient) reason to suppose that religious diversity is best explained by an internal, non-veridical origin of all the experiences on which the beliefs are formed. The facts are at least as well explained by the hypothesis that there is a transcendent reality, or dimension of reality, with which some or all of these practices are in touch, though of course they cannot all have it exactly straight.[12]

A more modest argument would be that the diversity is best explained by supposing that none of the competing practices is reliable. For if one of the practices were reliable, that would show itself to us in such a way as to distinguish it from the rest. But no such distinguishing marks are evident. Therefore the best explanation of the diversity is that they all miss the mark to such a degree that none of them can be considered sufficiently reliable for rational acceptance.

But why should we suppose that any reliable doxastic practice will bear external marks of its reliability for all, participants and non-participants alike, to see? That is not the case for familiar, universal, non-controversial practices like SP. SP's marks of reliability are displayed, as we have seen, only from within the practice. Why should we suppose it to be otherwise with respect to religious, non-universal practices? Why suppose that if CP is a by and large reliable cognitive access to certain aspects of God, that reliability could be ascertained from other practices, when that is not the case with SP? And from *within* CP, just as from *within* SP, there are abundant indications of reliability. For example, God is experienced within CP as telling us that He will be present to us.

## IV

What's happening here? Is religious pluralism merely a paper tiger? Surely there is something to the idea that I have less reason to trust the reliability of CP than I would have if it were not for religious diversity? What about the idea presented at the outset, that since the participant of one religious DP has no non-question-begging reason to suppose herself in a superior epistemic position to her competitors, she is not justified in supposing that it is her DP that is the reliable one? Well, I think there is something to that idea, and I will now try to bring out just what there is to it and what there isn't.

Let's begin by spelling out the idea more fully. "We have premised that only one religious doxastic practice can be (sufficiently) reliable. But why should I suppose CP to be that one? I would need some reason for supposing that it puts me in a superior epistemic position for getting the truth about God. But I have no such reason. That is, I have no such reason that proceeds from ground common to all the contenders. Within CP I have such reason; CP "tells" me that God has revealed Himself to mankind in the Old and New Testament and in the Christian church. But the adherents of other religions have analogous reasons within their traditions for their epistemic superiority. And why should I suppose that my internal reasons are more likely to be correct than their internal reasons? The same difficulty again. Unless I have some external reason to suppose that my practice provides a more reliable cognitive access to the Ultimate than the others, I am being arbitrary in picking mine as the one that is sufficiently reliable for rational acceptance."

Note that there is no claim here to show that CP is *un*reliable, but only a claim to undermine the antecedent reasons for supposing it to be reliable. Religious diversity is a reason for *doubting* the reliability of any particular religious doxastic practice. Given religious pluralism, we lack sufficient reason for affirming the reliability of CP or any other particular religious DP.

In assessing the force of this argument it will be useful to focus on analogies that readily spring to mind, e.g., cases in which the witnesses to an automobile accident give divergent accounts of what happened. Unless a given witness, H, has sufficient reasons for regarding herself as in a better position to make accurate observations of the accident, the fact that she is confronted by several accounts that diverge from hers should reduce her confidence in her own. These disparities reduce, or nullify, her justification for believing that the accident was as she takes it to be.

However, there are two important differences between this kind of case and religious diversity. First, the former has to do with the epistemic status of particular beliefs, while the latter has to do with the status of entire DP's. We could find a closer analogue in this respect by switching to competitions between methods.[13] Consider ways of predicting the weather: various "scientific" meteorological approaches, going by the state of rheumatism in one's joints, and observing groundhogs. Again, if one employs one of these methods but has no non-question-begging reason for supposing that method to be more reliable than the others, then one has no sufficient rational basis for reposing confidence in its outputs.

But whether the examples concern particular beliefs or belief-forming procedures, there is still a crucial difference between these cases, where it is clear that uneliminated alternatives reduce or eliminate one's basis for one's own belief or practice, and the religious situation. That difference can be stated very simply. In the clear cases the competitors confront each other within the same DP, and hence it is clear what would constitute non-circular grounds for supposing one of the contestants to be superior to the others, even if we do not have such grounds. We know the sorts of factors that would disqualify an observer of the accident (inattention, emotional involvement, visual defects, a poor angle of observation), and we know what would decisively show that one account is the correct one (e.g., agreement with a number of new witnesses). In the weather prediction case it is, in principle, a simple matter to run a statistical test on the predictive success of the various methods and choose between them on that basis. It is just because of this that in the absence of sufficient reasons for supposing himself to be in a superior position, one the contestants, H, is not justified in continuing to be strongly confident of his alternative. It is because the absence of such reasons (for one's superiority to one's rivals) is the absence of something there is a live possibility of one's having, and that one knows how to go about getting, that this lack so clearly has strongly negative epistemic consequences. But precisely this condition is lacking in the religious diversity case. Since, as we are assuming, each of the major world religions involves (at least one) distinct DP, with its own way of going from experiential input to beliefs formulated in terms of that scheme, and its own system of overriders, the competitors lack the kind of common procedure for settling disputes that is available to the participants in a shared DP. Here, in contrast to the intra-DP cases, my adversary and I do not lack something that we know perfectly well how to go about getting. Hence the sting is taken out of the inability of each of us to show that he is in an epistemically superior position. And so this lack does not have the epistemically deleterious consequences found in the intra-DP cases. Or, at the very least, it is not clear that it has those consequences. To put the point most sharply, we have no idea what a non-circular proof of the reliability of CP would look like, *even if it is as reliable as you please.* Hence why should we take the absence of such a proof to nullify, or even sharply diminish, the justification I have for my Christian M-beliefs?

This conclusion, that the lack of a common ground alters drastically the epistemic bearings of an unresolved incompatibility, can be illustrated by secular examples. Consider the methodological opposition between psychoanalysts and behaviorists concerning the diagnosis and treatment of neurosis and, more generally, concerning human motivation. Psychoanalytic formulations are heavily based on clinical "insight" and "interpretation." Behaviorists typically reject these as data and restrict themselves to "harder" data, the observation of which can be easily replicated under controlled conditions. Since psychoanalysts do not reject the legitimacy of the behavioral data, but only hold that they are insufficient for dealing with the problems with which they are concerned, the issue is over the status of the analysts' "data." Let's say that there is no common ground on which the dispute can be resolved.[14] Here we are not so ready, or should not be so ready, to judge that it is irrational for the psychoanalyst to continue to form clinical beliefs in the way he does without having non-circular reasons for supposing that his method of forming clinical diagnoses is a reliable one. Since we are at a loss to specify what such non-circular reasons would look like even if the method is reliable, we should not regard the practitioner as irrational for lacking such reasons.

Let's now consider a counter-factual analogue. Suppose that there were a diversity of sense perceptual DP's as diverse as religious experiential DP's are in fact. Suppose that in certain cultures there were a well established "Cartesian" practice of construing what is visually perceived as an indefinitely extended medium that is more or less concentrated at various points, rather than, as in our "Aristotelian" practice, as made up of more or less discrete objects of various kinds scattered about in space. Let's also suppose that in other cultures a "Whiteheadian" SP is equally socially established; here the visual field is construed as made up of momentary events growing out of each other in a continuous process.[15] Let's further suppose that each of these practices serves its practitioners equally well in their dealings with the environment. We may even suppose that each group has developed physical science, in its own terms, to about as high a pitch as the others. But suppose further that we are as firmly wedded to our "Aristotelian" mode of conceptualizing what is visually perceived, as we are in fact. The Cartesian and Whiteheadian *auslander* seem utterly outlandish to us, and we find it difficult to take seriously the idea that they may be telling it like it is. However we can find no neutral grounds on which to argue effectively for the greater accuracy of our way of doing it. In such a situation would it be clear that it is irrational for us to continue to form perceptual beliefs in our "Aristotelian" way, given that the practice is proving itself by its fruits? It seems to me that quite the opposite is clear. In the absence of any external reason for supposing that one of the competing practices is more accurate than my own, the only rational course for me to take is to sit tight with the practice of which I am a master and which serves me so well in guiding my activity in the world. But our actual situation with regard to CP is precisely parallel to the one we have been imagining. Hence, by parity of reasoning, the rational thing for a practitioner of CP to do is to continue to form Christian M-beliefs, and, more generally, to continue to accept, and operate in accordance with, the system of Christian belief.

I have been suggesting that if there actually were a diversity of sense perceptual practices, we would be faced with an epistemological problem with respect to SP exactly parallel to that we actually face with respect to CP. But why shouldn't we say that the mere *possibility* of an SP diversity implies that the problem already arises. If it is so much as possible that human beings should construe what is presented in visual perception in a radically different way, and so much as possible that the practice so constituted should be as internally viable as our actual SP, then doesn't that *possibility* raise the question of why we should suppose that it is rational to form beliefs in the SP way, given that we have no reason to suppose it to be more reliable than these other possibilities? And if in that case it is rational to engage in SP, despite the lack of any non-circular reason for regarding our Aristotelian SP as more reliable than its possible alternatives, that conclusion should carry over to the CP problem.

And yet it is difficult to work ourselves up into worrying about these possibilities, and even difficult to convince ourselves that it is our intellectual duty to do so. Insofar as this has a respectable basis, it is that it is not really clear that the alleged possibilities are indeed possible. At least they may well not be real possibilities for us, given our actual constitution and the lawful structure of the world. It may be that we are innately programmed to perceive the environment in Aristotelian terms, and that this program does not allow for social reprogramming into a "Cartesian" or a "Whiteheadian" mode. Nevertheless, I want to reiterate that *if* these alternatives really are possible, then they give rise to difficulties for the rationality of engaging in SP that are quite parallel to those arising from the actual diversity of religions for the rationality of engaging in CP. And so, in that case, if it is rational to engage in SP despite these difficulties, the same conclusion follows for CP.

Although I have been speaking in the first person for the most part, it goes without saying, I hope, that the conclusions I have been drawing concerning my epistemic situation as a practitioner of CP hold, *pari passu,* for practitioners of the other internally validated religious DP's. In each case the person who is in the kind of position I have been describing will be able to justifiably engage in his/her own religious DP despite not being able to show that it is epistemically superior to the competition. It may seem strange that such incompatible positions could be justified for different people, but this is just a special case of the general point that incompatible propositions can each be justified for different people if what they have to go on is suitably different.

## V

I have been arguing that despite appearances, religious pluralism does not show any irrationality in the use of CP, and, by parity of argument, in the use of any other such religious experiential DP. But does that imply that it in no way constitutes a problem for the Christian, Moslem, or Buddhist? By no means. In conclusion I will enumerate some of the problems that remain.

I will begin with the non-epistemic ones. First, there is, from within any particular religion, a theological problem. In a theistic religion this will take the form: why does God allow such a diversity of incompatible systems of belief about Himself? This is allied to the more general question: why doesn't He make at least the main outlines of the truth about these matters clear to everyone? And both are simply particular versions of the familiar problem of evil. As with other versions, there have been many attempts to deal with them. Then there are social–psychological problems as to what factors lead to the particular forms taken by religious belief, organization and practice in the various world religions. And so on.

Turning to epistemic difficulties, I have been arguing only that the facts of religious pluralism do not establish that it is *irrational* for one to engage in CP and other religious experiential practices. But I have not denied that religious pluralism should diminish the confidence one has in the reliability of CP. On the contrary, I think we can see that there is a negative influence here just by asking ourselves whether we would not be entitled to repose more confidence in CP if all religious persons formed M-beliefs in the CP way, than we are in the present situation. If all those who take themselves to be experientially aware of God's presence in their lives were to tell stories that agree with each other in broad outline, wouldn't we be more certain that we are in cognitive contact with God in CP than we are in fact? I think this cannot be denied. An epistemic as well as a theological load would be lifted from our shoulders. Thus, I would acknowledge that it is right and proper for one to be worried and perplexed by religious pluralism, epistemically as well as theologically, though not to the extent of denying the rationality of CP.

This conclusion is, admittedly, very imprecise. One's justification for engaging in CP is diminished by religious pluralism, but not to the extent of its being irrational for one to engage in that practice. But just what is the order of magnitude of this diminution from "ideal justification?" How far is the resulting degree of justification from each of the extremes of full justification and complete lack of justification? I don't see any basis for answering such questions. I don't see any basis for quantifying degrees of justification, in any event. I will have to content myself with saying that the degree of justification that remains is such as to make it not irrational for one to engage in the belief-forming practice and to hold the beliefs so formed. The facts of religious diversity do not suffice to override the positive considerations on the other side (the presumptive reliability of any socially established DP, plus the internal self-support involved) to such an extent as to show that the practice lacks a degree of reliability appropriate to rational acceptance. We are warranted in supposing CP to be a reasonably reliable mode of belief formation, one that at least gives us approximations to the truth about God and our relations thereto that suffice for our condition.

I do not take the practical implication of this conclusion to be that the Christian, or the member of another religious community, is free to shut herself up within the boundaries of her own community and ignore the rest of the world. On the contrary. The knowledgeable and reflective Christian should be concerned about the situation, both theologically and epistemically. Actuated by the latter concern, she should do whatever seems feasible to search for common ground on which to adjudicate the crucial differences between the world religions, seeking a way to show in a non-circular way which of the contenders is correct. What success will attend these efforts I do not presume to predict. Perhaps it is only in God's good time that a more thorough insight into the truth behind these divergent perspectives will be revealed to us.

## NOTES

1. Of course there will be serious theological, apologetic, and evangelical problems posed by the persistence of incompatible faiths.

2. The use of the term "practice" is not intended to carry any implication that this activity is under voluntary control. To avoid such a suggestion, terms like "process," "disposition," or "habit" could be used as alternatives.

3. It will not have escaped the reader's notice that this account owes much both to Reid and to Wittgenstein, though in spirit is closer to the former. As will become clear in the sequel, I do not accept Wittgenstein's verificationist, non-realist assumptions that we cannot so much as sensibly attempt to evaluate a practice, or the beliefs generated therein, from the outside, or that different practices involve different concepts of truth and reality.

4. I omit consideration of the complication that a belief might be determined by an unreliable input–output function that is involved in a mostly reliable doxastic practice.

5. At this point the reader may well wonder just what epistemic status I take this "general picture" to have. Is it based on the pooled experience (or the pooled M-beliefs) of the community throughout its history? Is it based on divine revelation, and if so are we thinking of this revelation as communicated otherwise than through the formation of M-beliefs from particularly crucial individual encounters with God? Do innate tendencies play a role? And what about natural theology? These are all crucial questions for the epistemology of religious belief, but I will forego consideration of them at this time.

6. This is controversial. Traditional appeals to miracles, history, and natural theology have been used to do just that. But I shall take it that none suffices to give strong enough support to a claim to reliability.

7. CP is no more independent of other DP's than is SP and other secular practices. For one thing, reasoning of various sorts, as well as sense perception and memory, are used in building up the general system of doctrine that provides the overrider system and the scheme in terms of which God is identified and characterized.

8. See my "Religious Experience and Religious Belief," *Noûs* **16** (1982), pp. 3–12; "Christian Experience and Christian Belief," in *Faith and Rationality,* ed. A. Plantinga & N. Wolterstorff (University of Notre Dame Press, 1983), pp. 103–34; "Perceiving God," *The Journal of Philosophy* **83** (1986), pp. 655–66.

9. To be sure, as I am depicting the situation, the outputs of each religious DP are in fundamental contradiction to the outputs of other religious DP's. Nevertheless, since I will also be taking it that none of these DP's is more "firmly established" than the others, these incompatibilities do not serve to discredit any of them.

10. See Fred Dretske's distinction between the "incremental" knowledge provided by a particular case of visual perception and the "proto-knowledge" that is brought to that perception, in Chapter III of his *Seeing and Knowing* (London: Routledge & Kegan Paul, 1969).

11. To be sure, we can consider a more rudimentary perceptual belief-forming practice in which the beliefs formed on the basis of experience are much less specific than those that are formulated in terms of the conceptual and doctrinal scheme of a particular religion. Such a practice could be defended without getting into

the defense of the basic belief system of any religion. And, indeed, if the beliefs involved are unspecific enough, they may be confronted by no opposition from other religions. This is the tack taken by Gary Gutting in his *Religious Belief and Religious Skepticism* (University of Notre Dame Press, 1982). In Chapter V he argues that religious experience can justify a "core" belief in the existence of a very good and very powerful being, but that it cannot justify the more distinctive beliefs of any particular religion. Since I take it that belief formation on the basis of experience in religion always takes place in terms of the conceptual and doctrinal system of some particular religion, I do not feel that what Gutting defends is actually realized in human affairs, and therefore I shall not consider it further.

12. Whether one has it much more nearly straight than all the others, or whether some or all have it straight to varying degrees, or, indeed to the same degree, is a question we would need other resources to answer.

13. William Hasker puts forward an example of this sort in his "On Justifying the Christian Practice," *The New Scholasticism*, L, no. 2, Spring 1986.

14. One might think that there is a predictive test in terms of the success of the therapies based on the respective methodologies. But, alas, parallel methodological controversy will break out over the assessment of therapeutic success. I am also assuming that psychoanalytic theories do not have implications that have been disconfirmed by ordinary empirical investigation; or if there have been such, the theories have been modified to take account of them without losing their distinctive thrust.

15. Many questions would have to be settled if we were to pursue these fantasies. For example, does the environment *look* different to the people in these different cultures, or is it only that they use a different conceptual scheme to form perceptual beliefs about what they are seeing? I think that the former alternative will be more suitable for present purposes.

CHAPTER 12

# Religious Experience and Religious Diversity:

## *A Reply to Alston*

J. L. SCHELLENBERG

William Alston's *Perceiving God: The Epistemology of Religious Experience* (Ithaca, NY: Cornell University Press, 1991)[1] is a most significant contribution to the philosophy of religion. The product of 50 years' reflection on its topic (xi), this work provides a very thorough explication and defence of what Alston calls the "mystical perceptual practice" (MP)—the practice of forming beliefs about the Ultimate on the basis of putative "direct experiential awareness" thereof (pp. 103, 258). Alston argues, in particular, for the (epistemic) rationality of engaging in the Christian form of MP (CMP). On his view, those who participate in CMP are (in the absence of specific overriding considerations from within CMP) justified in forming beliefs as they do because their practice is "socially established," has a "functioning overrider system" and a "significant degree of self-support"; and because of the "lack of sufficient reasons to take the practice as unreliable" (p. 224).[2]

Now Alston recognizes that his view faces certain difficulties. The most serious of these he considers to be the problem posed by a "plurality of incompatible religious perceptual doxastic practices" (p. 255). Indeed, so formidable is the problem of religious diversity held to be that a whole chapter of his book (Chapter 7) is devoted to dealing with it. There is much of interest and of value in this chapter, especially in the sections leading up to Alston's detailed response to the problem in Section v, but unfortunately, the response itself is less than convincing. Furthermore, a slightly revised version of the objection Alston addresses seems (on its assumptions, accepted by Alston) completely successful. In what follows I shall develop and defend these claims, and point out the implications of my conclusions for the epistemology of religious experience.

From J. L. Schellenberg, "Religious Experience and Religious Diversity: A Reply to Alston," *Religious Studies* 30, 2 (June 1994): 151–59. 

# I

The problem posed for religious experience by religious diversity is formulable in a diversity of ways. Alston considers several possible formulations, discussing and rejecting each in turn until he arrives at the following, which he considers to be by far the most powerful:

> Since each form of MP is, to a considerable extent, incompatible with all the others, not more than one such form can be (sufficiently) reliable as a way of forming beliefs about the Ultimate. For if one is reliable, then most of the beliefs that issue from it are true; and hence, because of the incompatibility, a large proportion of the beliefs issuing from each of the others will be false; and so none of those others is a reliable practice. Now why should I suppose that CMP is the one that is reliable (if any are)? No doubt, *within* CMP there are weighty reasons for supposing it to be much more reliable than its rivals; in the practice of CMP we find God telling people things that imply this. It is claimed from within the Christian tradition that God has assured us that His Holy Spirit will guide the church in its decisions, will keep it from error, will provide a "testimony" to the accuracy of the words of Christ, and so on. But, of course, each of the competing traditions can also produce conclusive internal reasons in support of its claims. Hence, if it is to be rational for me to take CMP to be reliable, I will have to have sufficient *independent* reasons for supposing that CMP is reliable, or more reliable or more likely to be reliable, than its alternatives. But no such reasons are forthcoming. Hence, it cannot be rational to engage in CMP; and by the same reasoning it cannot be rational to engage in any other particular form of MP (pp. 268–69).

Alston accepts, for the sake of discussion, the assumptions of incompatibility and epistemic parity between religious reliability claims essential to the success of this objection, claiming that even if these assumptions are true, the objection fails.[3] His defence of this view depends crucially on certain secular analogies—for example, a case in which the witnesses to an automobile accident give contradictory accounts of what happened:

> Consider . . . the familiar sort of case in which different people give conflicting sense perceptual reports of an automobile accident, and in which there is no neutral ground on which it can be determined which account is most likely to be correct or which witness was in the best position to determine what happened. A particular one of these witnesses, X, lacks sufficient reason, aside from the question-begging reason drawn from her own account or her own self-confidence, to regard herself as in a better position to make accurate observations of the accident. Therefore the fact that she is confronted by several accounts that diverge from hers should drastically reduce her confidence in her own. Here it seems clear that the existence of these uneliminated conflicting alternatives nullifies whatever justification she otherwise would have had for believing that the accident was as she takes it to be (pp. 270–71).

The same conclusion, says Alston, must be drawn in cases of competition between *methods,* which provide a closer analogy to the conflict between belief-forming practices with which he is concerned:

> Consider ways of predicting the weather: various "scientific" meteorological approaches, going by the state of rheumatism in one's joints, and observing groundhogs. Again, if one employs one of these methods but has no non-question-begging reason for supposing that method to be more reliable than the others, then one has no sufficient rational basis for reposing confidence in its outputs (p. 271).

Now, these secular analogies, as Alston concedes, seem at first to *support* the critic's claim. They appear to show that justification for belief must be *removed* by an unresolved incompatibility. Alston's next step, however, is to point out what he takes to be a very important and relevant feature of the analogous cases. This is that in these cases the competitors confront each other within the *same* belief-forming practice, and so it is clear what would constitute independent, non-question-begging grounds for favouring one claim over the others, even if we do not have such grounds. For example:

> We know the sorts of factors that would disqualify an observer of the accident (inattention, emotional involvement, visual defects, a poor angle of observation), and we know what would decisively show that one account is the correct one (e.g., agreement with a number of new witnesses) (p. 271).

Alston then argues that it is because of *this* feature that we are inclined to think that, in the absence of sufficient independent reasons, any one of the competitors, e.g., any one of the witnesses to the automobile accident, would be irrational if she continued to be strongly confident of her alternative account:

> It is just because of this that in the absence of sufficient reasons for supposing himself to be in a superior position, one of the contestants, X, is not justified in reposing complete confidence in his alternative. It is because the absence of such reasons is the absence of something there is a live possibility of one's having, and that one knows how to go about getting, that this lack so clearly has negative epistemic consequences (p. 271).

The final step of Alston's argument is his claim that this crucial condition is *absent* in the religious case. The world's religious believers confront each other from within *different* experiential belief-forming practices, and hence do not have access to common procedures for settling disputes:

> Here, in contrast to the intra-practice cases, my religious adversary and I do not lack something that we know perfectly well how to get. Hence the sting is taken out of the inability of each of us to show that he is in an epistemically superior position. The lack does not have the deleterious consequences found in the intra-practice cases (pp. 271–72).

So that's Alston's argument. First he presents secular analogies which seem to throw the problem into clear relief. Then he points out what it is about those cases that, he thinks, makes us want to say that belief is not justified in them. Thirdly, he points out that this condition is absent in the religious case, whence it follows (on his view) that even though there are conflicting religious experiential belief-forming practices, and even if no independent, non-question-begging reasons for supposing one to be more reliable than the others are available, religious believers may still be justified in continuing to believe in the reliability of their own practice.[4]

## II

I have found much to admire in Alston's work, but the argument just described is, I suggest, inadequate. I will approach my defence of this claim indirectly, by first considering what Alston must do to make his argument a *valid* argument. The condition isolated by him as justification-removing in cases of unresolved incompatibility is important in this context, so let us begin by bringing it more clearly into focus:

> (C) The absence of independent reasons—reasons providing for a non-question-begging resolution of the dispute—is the absence of something there is a live possibility of one's having, and that one knows how to go about getting.

The important point here is that to defend successfully his argument's validity, Alston must hold the obtaining of C to be not just sufficient but also *necessary* for a removal of justification in cases of unresolved incompatibility. Alston must claim that it is *only if* C obtains that belief is, in such cases, unjustified. For unless C's obtaining is held to be necessary for the removal of justification, he cannot validly infer (as he does infer) that its absence in the religious case signals that *there* justification for belief is retained.

This point can be made more precise. Let *r* represent the religious situation of incompatibility. Alston can be construed as putting forward an argument, the second premise of which is

> (2) C does not obtain in *r*,

and whose conclusion is

> (3) It is not the case that justification for belief is removed in *r*.

So what is his first premise? Surely not

> (1′) If C obtains in *r*, then justification for belief is removed in *r*.

For (1′), (2), and (3) comprise an argument that rather plainly commits the fallacy of denying the antecedent. To turn Alston's argument into a valid argument, we must suppose instead that its first premise is

(1) If justification for belief is removed in *r*, then C obtains in *r*.

Let us assume, then, that this is how Alston understands his argument.

The cost of validity in this case is, however, a false premise. For contrary to what (1) states, the obtaining of C is *not* necessary for the removal of justification for belief in *r*. It may be sufficient, if we think of the situation in question as one in which the believer has an epistemic *duty* to seek non-question-begging reasons for believing and fails to fulfil this duty; but it is not necessary. Why then (it may be asked) would *Alston* suppose it to be necessary? As it seems to me, Alston is implicitly reasoning as follows: "If C does *not* obtain, the religious believer cannot be blamed for not having reasons of the relevant sort in her possession: since in that case they are in principle unavailable, the claim that she *must* have such reasons is unreasonable. After all, "ought," implies "can." Hence, if C does not obtain, the believer does not need reasons of the sort in question—which is to say that the obtaining of C is necessary for the removal of justification in this case." But what this argument fails to recognize is that there is more than one sense in which we can say of the believer that she *must* have independent reasons. In particular, even if the "must" of *obligation* is inappropriate where C is absent, a *logical* necessity may still obtain. And this is in fact the case: another, more fundamental, justification-removing condition is indeed present in *all* cases of unresolved incompatibility and so in all cases Alston discusses, secular *and* religious—a condition which removes justification whether C obtains or not. Alston's terminology obscures this fact, but when it is brought out into the open and clarified, we can on its basis infer both that Alston's argument fails (its first premise must be rejected), and that his conclusion—that justification for belief is not removed in *r*—is false.

To see this, we need only develop a little further the automobile accident analogy—a case which is, in the relevant respect, representative of all cases of unresolved incompatibility. Alston refers to "a particular one" of the witnesses to the accident as "X." Assume that there are two more; call these Y and Z. Assume, moreover, that each of X, Y, and Z continues to believe that her account is correct even after noting the challenge posed for her claim by incompatible accounts and the lack of a non-question-begging response. Just what has gone wrong here? How have X, Y, and Z fallen afoul of the standards of epistemic respectability in believing as they do? Is it only—as Alston would suggest—that they have not found independent reasons for accepting or rejecting their opponents' claims when it was in their power to do so? It seems to me that something rather important has been missed if this is all we say.

Let us call X's claim that her account of the accident is correct C1; and let us call the corresponding claims of Y and Z C2 and C3, respectively. It seems clear that X's knowledge of the situation must include the knowledge that her claim entails not-C2 and not-C3. And the same goes for Y and Z and the denials of *their* counterparts' claims. For to know that certain claims are mutually incompatible is to know that at most one can be true, that the truth of any one entails the falsity of each of the others. Now it is a necessary truth that if I am justified in believing some proposition, I have a justification for believing any proposition which I know to be its entailment.[5] And since if *p* is a sufficient condition for *q*, *q* is a *necessary* condition for *p*, we can easily derive that, necessarily, I am justified in believing some proposition *only* if I have a justification for believing any of its known entailments. It follows that X is justified in believing C1 only if she has a justification for believing not-C2 and not-C3; for these she knows to be entailments of C1. And similarly for Y and Z and the denials of their counterparts' claims. Here a problem arises, however: What justification could X, Y, and Z possibly have for denying each other's claims? The only reasons each has at her disposal are, as we have noted, inadequate in this context—question-begging reasons, drawn (in Alston's words) "from her own account or her own self-confidence." Indeed, the absence of justification for such a move seems *built into* the story as told by Alston and elaborated by us. Hence we must allow that none of the witnesses has justification for supposing the others' claims false. But then it follows (by modus tollens) that none is justified in *holding her own claim to be true.* Put more formally, and applied now to the question at hand, the argument is as follows:

(1) Necessarily, for any person S and proposition *p*, S is justified in believing *p* only if, for any proposition *q* known by S to be entailed by *p*, S has justification for believing *q*.
(2) Participants in the various religious experiential belief-forming practices, insofar as they are aware of the problem of religious diversity, know the denials of many other reliability claims to be entailed by their own.
(3) For each such participant, continued belief in the reliability of her own practice is justified only if she has justification for a denial of the others' claims (from (1) and (2)).
(4) Each lacks justification of the latter sort.
(5) Hence each lacks justification of the former sort (from (3) and (4)).

So even if believers are (as Alston is assuming) in a situation where independent grounds for belief are in principle unavailable, and therefore cannot be *faulted* for lacking them—cannot be said even to *have* a duty to seek such grounds—justification is still removed by an unresolved incompatibility for the reason specified by the critic's (revised) argument. If I am to be justified in believing my claim, then I *logically* must have good reason to believe all its known entailments; and this condition cannot be satisfied in the case of an unresolved incompatibility of the sort represented by the problem of religious diversity. Since this is so, we can, as suggested above, draw two conclusions: (i) that Alston's main premise—(1)—must be rejected (C need not obtain in *r* in order for justification for believing to be removed in *r*); and (ii) that Alston's conclusion (that justification for believing is not removed in *r*) is false.

## III

I anticipate several objections to my reply to Alston. It may be objected, first of all, that my argument requires us to accept a principle which is ideally suited to the purposes of the sceptic. Specifically, the principle I have affirmed, according to which anyone justified in believing that *p* has justification for believing any known entailment of *p,* can be used by the sceptic to argue that none of us is justified in believing the deliverances of the senses, since none of us has justification for their known entailment "I am not a brain in a vat." And surely there is strong reason to resist any principle that in this way renders us vulnerable to sceptical attack.

But it may be replied to this objection (in the spirit of G. E. Moore) that the best *response* to the sceptic requires that the very same principle be utilized: using modus ponens instead of modus tollens, this response argues that since we *are* justified in accepting certain perceptual claims, we also have a justification for believing their known entailments—even the entailment "I am not a brain in a vat"! As the objector should realize, this sort of reasoning is quite popular in epistemology nowadays.[6]

But the objector will no doubt wish to know how, given my endorsement of this response to the sceptic, I can fail to concede that the three witnesses in our example—X, Y, and Z—may use the *same* approach. Surely, by parity of reasoning, I must allow that (for example) X can argue on the basis of the confidence *she* feels plus the principle in question that *C1's* entailments—not-C2 and not-C3—are true. But if this is allowed, my argument obviously fails.

I would suggest, however, that there is an important disanalogy between the two cases, in light of which we are not required to accord to X, Y, and Z the privilege we have extended to the anti-sceptic. *Competition* is obviously a factor in the case of an unresolved incompatibility. The important question in such a case is "*Whose* confidence (if anyone's) is well-placed?" Here an answer in terms of one of the contestants' own confidence would—as Alston sees—clearly be question-begging, and so illegitimate. But the same cannot be said in the case of the sceptic. Perhaps if the sceptic's argument claimed that there is reason to be confident that we *are* brains in a vat, and reported competing observations to support this—perhaps then we could not respond to it simply by appealing to our own observations and our own confidence without begging the question. But of course, whatever else it may entail, the sceptic's argument does *not* represent competing reason to believe that we are brains in a vat. It simply suggests that we *lack* reason to *deny* that we are.[7] Hence we may without inconsistency or (apparently) any other impropriety respond to the sceptic in the manner outlined while denying that X, Y, and Z are justified in using the same approach.

It may, finally, be said that Alston himself has a reply to our argument, represented by the factual and counter-factual examples he gives later in Section v of Chapter 7 to "illustrate" his position (p. 272). Critics may argue that our readiness to accept the situations he describes as ones in which belief is justified despite an unresolved incompatibility, *because of the lack of a common ground,* provides (sufficient) support for Alston's position even in the face of arguments like those presented in this paper.

So what are these situations? First cited is the "methodological opposition between psychoanalysts and behaviorists concerning . . . human motivation" (p. 272). Here Alston argues that, assuming "there is no common ground on which the dispute can be resolved," we should allow that practitioners of these opposed methods are rational in continuing to form beliefs as they do. As he puts it: "Since we are at a loss to specify what . . . noncircular reasons would look like even if the method is reliable, we should not regard the practitioner as irrational for lacking such reasons" (p. 273). Next we have a counter-factual analogue referring to diverse sense perceptual doxastic practices. This is detailed as follows:

> Suppose that in certain cultures there were a well established "Cartesian" practice of seeing what is visually perceived as an indefinitely extended medium that is more or less concentrated at various points, rather than, as in our "Aristotelian" practice, as made up of more or less discrete objects scattered about in space. In other cultures we find a "Whiteheadian" [practice] to be equally socially established; here the visual field is seen as made up of momentary events growing out of each other in a continuous process. . . . In the absence of any external reasons for supposing that one of the competing practices is more accurate than my own, the only rational course for me is to sit tight with the practice of which I am a master and which serves me so well in guiding my activity in the world (pp. 273–74).

What should we say about the force of these examples? Do they serve to rescue Alston's case? I think not. It seems false that any inclination we may have to accept Alston's analogies could or should survive the recognition that the position they are used to support is incompatible with so basic a principle of epistemic logic as that enunciated and defended above. In any case, Alston's analogies are not very persuasive. In each there is a tendency to muddy the distinction between the *actual* absence of noncircular reasons and the practitioners' *recognition* of their absence. The examples are not relevant unless both conditions are assumed, and when both *are* assumed, Alston's conclusion seems less than intuitively obvious.

But there are other difficulties too. The force of the counter-factual analogy is apparently held to derive from the fact that it would be *imprudent* or *practically impossible* to cease to form beliefs in the specified way upon recognition of the lack of a common ground. But in that case it would seem to be irrelevant: we have been concerned only with questions of *epistemic* rationality; hence pragmatic considerations are not to the point. The psychology analogy faces its own problems. This example is apparently supposed to derive its force from the fact that an obligation to seek neutral reasons cannot exist in the circumstances in question, and so succumbs to our point that the critic need not base her argument on a failure to fulfil such an obligation. Alston's argument here also neglects the distinction between belief and acceptance: even where it is irrational to *believe* it may yet be possible to rationally *accept* the proposition(s) in question—to act on the *assumption* that it is true (while not believing), in order to see what may result from doing so. (One of the results might of course be the discovery of evidence sufficient for belief.) This attitude is indeed common among scientists, and recognition of it is surely sufficient to show that the choice here is not, as Alston suggests, between conceding the rationality of belief in this situation and denying that the relevant method of forming clinical diagnoses ought to be pursued at all.

For these reasons—in particular the first—I suggest that Alston's case cannot be saved by analogies of the sort he has presented.

## IV

We may conclude, therefore, in view of the failure of the objections we have considered, that Alston's response to the problem of religious diversity does not succeed, and furthermore, that on its assumptions, the critic's revised argument is completely successful. But if so, then contrary to Alston's claim, a solution to this problem is possible only if one or other or both of these assumptions can reasonably be denied. Religious believers sensitive to the issue of religious diversity must find some plausible way of arguing that the "facts" of pluralism assumed by the critic and (for the sake of argument) by Alston are not facts after all—that there are no incompatibilities of the sort in question (at least not on fundamental matters) and/or that there *are* strong independent reasons for viewing one of the relevant alternatives—their own—as epistemically preferable to the others. It is because this task will not be easily carried out that our conclusion is, it seems to me, a significant one.[8]

## NOTES

1. Further references to this book will be made parenthetically in the body of the paper.

2. A practice is *socially established,* for Alston, if it is "established by socially monitored learning and socially shared" (p. 163). It has a *functioning overrider system* if there is a "background system of beliefs against which a particular perceptually supported belief [generated by the practice] can be checked for possible overriders" (p. 79). It enjoys significant degree of *self-support* if the results achieved by engaging in it and using its "fruits" are best explained by supposing it to be reliable (p. 174). And it is *reliable* if it "will or would yield mostly true beliefs" (p. 104).

3. Alston is, as he puts it (p. 270), carrying on this discussion on a "worst-case scenario," endeavoring to show that even if that scenario accurately represents the truth (which, he suggests, may not be the case), the problem of religious diversity this objection poses can be resolved.

4. It should be noted that Alston concedes in Section vi of the chapter (for reasons that are not entirely clear) that religious diversity *does to some extent* reduce the epistemic status of beliefs in a given religion, but he claims that the reduction is not such as to render it irrational to engage in MP (p. 275).

5. Note that I am not suggesting that justification is closed under known entailment—that my being justified in believing some proposition $p$ is sufficient for my *being* justified in believing those of $p$'s entailments known to me. I am affirming, instead, the more modest claim that by being justified in believing $p$, I *have* a justification for believing its known entailments—where having a justification for believing a proposition $q$ implies knowing (or justifiably believing) propositions that constitute (sufficient) support for $q$, but does not imply that any other condition necessary for being justified in believing $q$ is satisfied. The stronger claim is perhaps questionable (could I not, for example, be justified in believing $p$, know that $p$ entails $q$, and yet fail to believe $q$ on the *basis* of $p$ & $(p \rightarrow q)$?), but surely the weaker one is not; and the weaker one is all we need for our purposes.

6. For a recent and interesting development of such a move, see John L. Pollock, *Contemporary Theories of Knowledge* (London: Hutchinson, 1986), pp. 4–6.

7. And in this *it* seems to beg the question.

8. I am grateful to Terence Penelhum, William Alston, and Philip Quinn for their comments on the penultimate draft of this paper.

CHAPTER 13

# Religious Experience and Religious Pluralism

William J. Wainwright

Alston's account of religious experience lies at the center of his defense of Christian theism. Alston believes we can't establish the reliability of sense-perception, induction, rational intuition, or any basic doxastic practice without relying on what we learn from engaging in the practice. Why, then, trust them? (1) The practices are socially established. (2) They are self-supporting; their outputs support their claim to reliability. (3) They are internally consistent. (4) Their outputs are also consistent with the outputs of other well-established doxastic practices. Similar considerations show that we are justified in engaging in Christian mystical practices.

In my opinion, Alston's defense succeeds in defusing the standard objections to the veridicality of Christian mystical experience. One objection, however, can't be set aside so easily. "An apparent experiential presentation of God as ø will provide only *prima facie* justification of the belief that God is ø. . . . But the concept of prima facie justification has application only where there is a system of knowledge or justified belief about the relevant subject matter, against which a particular prima facie justified belief can be checked." Our "religious perceptual doxastic practices" must therefore be construed as including within them "at least the main lines of the body of beliefs of the religion[s] within which" they "flourish." But these belief systems "are, as wholes, seriously incompatible with each . . . other."[1] The mystical practices that incorporate them are thus also incompatible. It follows that at most one is reliable. "Now why should I suppose that CMP [Christian mystical practice] is the one that is reliable (if any are)?" Although each tradition can produce internal reasons for thinking its practice is reliable, there seem to be no *external* reasons for doing so. "Hence, it cannot be rational to engage in CMP;

From William J. Wainwright, "Religious Language, Religious Experience and Religious Pluralism," in *The Rationality of Belief and the Plurality of Faith,* edited by Thomas D. Senor. 

An earlier version of this essay was presented to the 1991 Central Division meeting of the American Philosophical Association. I wish to thank William Rowe, who commented on an early draft, and my respondent, William Alston. My essay has benefited from their criticisms.

and by the same reasoning it cannot be rational to engage in any other particular form of MP [mystical practice]" (p. 269).

Alston addresses this issue in "Religious Diversity and Perceptual Knowledge of God"[2] and, more fully, in Chapter 7 of *Perceiving God*. His discussion is interesting and helpful. I doubt whether it is sufficient.

He begins by inviting us to consider situations in which "different people give conflicting sense perceptual reports [about an accident, for example] . . . and in which there is no neutral ground" for resolving the conflict, or to consider various "ways of predicting the weather" where there is "no non-question begging reason for supposing that [one] method is more reliable than the others." In cases like these one has "no sufficient rational basis" for confidence in one's report or in one's method. But there is "a crucial difference" between these cases and the religious situation. In the former, "it is clear what would constitute non-circular grounds for supposing one of the contestants to be superior to the others even if we do not have such grounds." (The accident might have been videotaped. More accurate statistical data could show that one method is more successful than the other.) "It is because the absence of such reasons . . . is the absence of something there is a live possibility of one's having, and that one knows how to go about getting, that this lack so clearly has negative epistemic consequences. But precisely this condition is lacking in the religious diversity case." "We have no idea of what non-circular proof of the reliability of CMP would look like, *even if it is as reliable as you please.* Hence why should we take the absence of such a proof to nullify, or even sharply diminish, the justification I have for my Christian M-beliefs?"[3] (pp. 270–72).

Or consider "the methodological opposition between psychoanalysts and behaviorists." The dispute hinges on whether "clinical 'insight' and 'interpretation'" counts as evidence. "There is no common ground on which the dispute can be resolved." It is not, however, "irrational for the psychoanalyst to continue to form clinical beliefs in the way he does." Similar considerations apply, mutatis mutandis, to our continued use of a mystical practice (pp. 272–73).

Or imagine "a diversity of sense perceptual doxastic practices"—an Aristotelian one in which we see what is visually perceived "as made up of more or less discrete objects scattered about in space," "a Cartesian practice of seeing" it "as an indefinitely extended medium that is more or less concentrated at various points," and a Whiteheadian practice of seeing "the visual field . . . as made up of momentary events growing out of each other in a continuous process. . . . Let's further suppose that each of these practices serves its practitioners equally well in their dealings with the environment." Finally, suppose "that we are as firmly wedded to our 'Aristotelian' form of SP [sense-perceptual practice] as we are in fact." "In such a situation" it is not "irrational" for us to continue to form perceptual beliefs in the way we do. "By parity of reasoning, the rational thing for a practitioner of CP to do is to continue to form Christian M-beliefs" in the way she does (pp. 273–74).

Note finally that the very possibility of alternative sense-perceptual practices "gives rise to the same problem." For their mere "possibility raises[s] the question of why we should suppose that it is rational" to form sense-perceptual beliefs as we do, "given that we have no reason to suppose" that our practice is "more reliable than these other possibilities." Yet, of course, it *is* "rational to engage in [our] SP, despite the lack of any non-circular reason for regarding our Aristotelian SP as more reliable than its *possible* alternatives." A similar conclusion follows for CMP (p. 274).

In my opinion, Alston's defense is only partly successful. Suppose I am not already engaged in a mystical practice. Has Alston provided me with reasons for accepting the outputs of CMP? He believes he has. I am justified in believing *p* provided that "X is justified in believing that *p* . . . X tells me that *p*," and "I am justified in supposing that X is justified in believing *p*." Since Alston believes he has shown not only that "CMP endows its products with prima facie justification" but also that "mystical perceivers can be justified, all things considered, in their perceptual beliefs," he concludes that I (who do not engage in the practice) can have good reasons for accepting these perceivers' testimony and hence for believing their claims (pp. 280–81; cf. p. 283).

I am not sure this will do. For I have similar reasons for believing that Buddhist mystical practice (BMP) or Hindu mystical practice (HMP) "endows its products with prima facie justification," and so on. Since I do, I have similar reasons for accepting the testimony of those who engage in these practices. But these practices and their products are, by hypothesis, incompatible with CMP. Hence, whatever reasons I have for assenting to the products of BMP are reasons *against* assenting to the products of CMP (and vice versa). And this seems to be a good reason for withholding assent altogether. The existence of incompatible mystical practices seems to provide the religiously uncommitted with a rather decisive reason for suspending judgment.

Alston's discussion, however, is primarily addressed to those who are already engaged in CMP (or some other mystical practice). Has Alston shown that it is reasonable for Christians (or Buddhists) to retain their commitments? I am not sure he has.

Consider his examples. In the case of conflicting perceptual reports or rival meterological methods, we can specify in concrete detail precisely what sorts of evidence would settle the issue—tape from a suitably situated video camera, the testimony of better-placed witnesses, statistical information about the comparative success of rival forecasting methods, and so on. We cannot do this in the religious case. Yet why should this matter?

It might matter if the religious dispute *couldn't* be resolved, for, in that case, we could argue as follows. Our conflicting perceptual reports and rival meteorological methods lack positive epistemic features that they *might have had*. Our competing mystical practices do not. (For *no* evidence could resolve the issue.) Now nothing can properly be faulted for failing to exhibit a good-making feature that things of that kind can't have. Hence, the existence of unresolved disputes matters in the first case but not in the second.

But this can't be Alston's argument. In the first place, we *do* know how the religious dispute *could* be resolved. As Alston recognizes, it could be resolved by historical and metaphysical arguments based on neutral premises that show that the overrider systems and doxastic outputs of some mystical practices are closer to the truth than those of others.[4] In the second place, Alston thinks that the plurality of mystical practices should diminish (though not destroy) our confidence in our practice's reliability and hence in its epistemic rationality. It shouldn't (or so I have just argued) if the dispute *couldn't* be resolved.

The difference, at most, comes to this. We know exactly what sort of evidence would settle the issue in the nonreligious cases and can describe it in some detail. In the religious case, we have a general idea of the kind of evidence we are looking for (neutral metaphysical or empirical arguments) but can't specify it with any precision. And even this isn't clear. For can't we describe (a series of) miracles that would be rationally conclusive? (Cf. the story of Elijah and the priests of Baal.) Although it may be *unreasonable* to expect this sort of evidence to be forthcoming in the foreseeable future, expectations of this kind can also be unreasonable when perceptual reports or meteorological methods conflict.[5]

The difference, then, seems to be a difference in degree, not in kind. I fail to see how it justifies treating these cases differently.

There are other reasons for according more weight to the diversity objection than Alston does.

Many traditions contain doctrines that (if developed in certain directions) imply that other mystical practices are (at least) partly reliable. Examples are that God is love, the universality of the eternal Buddha nature, and so on. Alston thinks the problems these doctrines create are primarily theological and not epistemic (see pp. 257 and 266 n. 13). I am not sure this is true. For any reason for believing that an incompatible doxastic practice is reliable is a prima facie reason for thinking one's own is not. (This problem does not arise with respect to sense-perception. Our Aristotelian perceptual practice provides no reasons for thinking that a Cartesian perceptual practice is reliable [and vice versa].) It is always possible, of course, for Christians or Buddhists to accommodate the claim that other mystical practices are partly reliable by accepting products of those practices that are consistent with Christian or Buddhist doctrine and discounting the rest. They can also accommodate it by reinterpreting the products of other practices so as to *make* them consistent with the products of their own. The more worth one ascribes to competing practices, however, and the more one respects their integrity by refusing to edit them selectively or reinterpret them radically, the less confident one can be about the reliability of one's own. The degree of tension will be determined by *how* reliable one thinks alternative mystical practices are. If God really is loving, however, or the Buddha nature *is* universally accessible, they must be reliable enough to provide adequate opportunities for salvation.

One reason why it is rational for me to continue to engage in CMP (if I do) is that it seems to work; the practice is self-supporting (cf. pp. 275–76). Hick has argued that other mystical practices also work. Not only does each provide a payoff, truthfully assuring its adherents that engaging in it will yield certain fruits; but the payoffs are essentially the same, namely, "the transformation of human existence from self-centredness to Reality-centredness"—a transformation expressed in lives exemplifying "the ethical ideal, common to all the great traditions of agape/karuna (love/compassion)."[6] If Hick is right, our situation is similar to that of someone confronted with alternative sense-perceptual practices where "each . . . serves its practitioners equally well in their dealings with the environment" (*Perceiving God,* p. 273). It would be unreasonable for a person in this situation to abandon her Aristotelian perceptual practice, for she has no reason to think the alternatives are better.

But I think she *does* have a reason for doubting that what Aristotelian practitioners have conceptually "added" to what is visually presented has more purchase on (is more firmly grounded in) reality than the conceptual contributions of those engaged in Cartesian or Whiteheadian practices. Wouldn't the most reasonable attitude for her to take toward her perceptual reports,[7] then, be "acceptance" rather than belief? (I have in mind something like Van Fraassen's account of the right attitude toward empirically equivalent scientific theories.)[8] Mutatis mutandis, shouldn't Christians or Buddhists (only) *accept* rather than believe reports that have been structured by specifically Christian or Buddhist concepts—perceptual reports like "God spoke to me," for example, or "I entered into Nibbāna"?

Alston has argued that in spite of the inability of the psychoanalyst to show that psychoanalysis is superior to behaviorism, it is rational for him to continue to form his clinical beliefs in the way he does. The Christian's (or Buddhist's) situation is similar. CMP (or BMP) is not only "a socially established doxastic practice that has not been shown to be unreliable"; it is also significantly self-supporting (pp. 275–76). It is thus as rational for the Christian (or Buddhist) to adhere to her views as it once was for an advocate of Aristotelian, Galilean, or Cartesian physics and chemistry to adhere to his. But *why* was it rational for (e.g.) the Cartesian to stick to his guns, given that there was, at the time, no neutral way of resolving the conflict between him and his opponents? For the same reason it is rational for the psychoanalyst to stick to his. Because it is unreasonable to abandon a research project that is still promising.[9] But what follows? Clearly, that it is reasonable to *engage* in the project or to continue to act *as if* one's favorite theory were true. It *isn't* clear that it is reasonable to *believe* it.

There is, however, a significant difference between *theories* like Aristotelian, Cartesian, and Galilean science, or psychoanalysis and behaviorism, and *doxastic practices.* According to Alston, engaging in a doxastic practice involves thinking it reliable and, hence, accepting its outputs as (for the most part) *true,* that is, *believing* them.[10] If so, one can't engage in a doxastic practice by merely acting *as if* it were reliable. Engaging in CMP, for example, involves thinking it reliable and thus believing (most of) its outputs. The distinction I have tried to draw between accepting and believing, or acting as if and believing, collapses.

I think this is right. Nevertheless, I believe one can, from time to time, step back from one's doxastic practices and ask whether there are independent reasons for or against their epistemic rationality. A person who does this might (without making any obvious errors) come to the conclusion that although it is pragmatically rational to engage in the practice, it isn't epistemically reasonable to do so. If the pragmatic reasons are strong enough, he might further conclude that he should suppress any doubts he may have and continue to engage in the practice, or that he should try, as it were, to live on two planes of consciousness at once—engaging in the practice on one level and hence trusting in its reliability while, on another, doubting it. Something like this appears to have been the goal of some ancient skeptics with respect to believing in general. Alston's defense of the pragmatic rationality of continuing to engage in CMP thus seems compatible with certain forms of epistemic skepticism. Whether the latter is *reasonable* is another matter. But the considerations that implied that "acceptance" might be the most rational attitude suggest that it may be.

How strongly does diversity count against CMP's reliability? I have argued that the answer partly depends on whether we are already engaged in a mystical practice or not.

Those of us who aren't are confronted with an analogue of one of Hume's arguments against miracles. Since miracles support incompatible religious systems, cases for miracles destroy one another. There are two ways of undercutting Hume's argument. One can show that the alleged conflicts between religious systems aren't real or one can show that the cases for miracles aren't equally strong. Similarly here. Now Alston thinks that overrider systems and hence the practices that incorporate them really do conflict. Hence, the first avenue of escape isn't open to him. He must therefore show that the practices aren't equally well founded. It is difficult to see how he could do this without introducing empirical and metaphysical arguments that establish the superiority of (e.g.) the Christian world-view.

Yet what about people who *are* engaged in CMP or some other mystical practice? It is epistemically rational to engage in a doxastic practice if there are good reasons for regarding it as reliable.[11] It is epistemically irrational to engage in it if there are good reasons for thinking it unreliable. In the absence of good reasons either for or against a doxastic practice's reliability, it is epistemically nonrational to participate in it.[12] Alston believes that the fact that CMP is socially established and significantly self-supporting, and that it hasn't been shown to be unreliable, is a good reason for regarding it as prima facie reliable. This seems right. But whether it is a good reason for regarding it as rational *überhaupt* depends on the strength of whatever overriders there may happen to be. In the case of CMP, the most significant overrider is the diversity of mystical practices.

Are there good reasons for regarding CMP as *un*reliable? There are; the prima facie reliability of incompatible mystical practices is a good reason for thinking that CMP is prima facie unreliable. Whether it is a good reason for regarding it as unreliable *überhaupt* depends once again on how much weight should be placed on diversity.

Alston has offered reasons for thinking that the diversity of mystical practices doesn't override the evidence for CMP's reliability. I have argued that these reasons aren't as compelling as he thinks and that the overrider is therefore stronger than he allows. Is it or is it not, then, epistemically rational to engage in CMP? This question is difficult to answer, because, as Alston says, we lack "the conceptual resources to quantify degrees of rationality" (p. 275). I am skeptical, however, of the possibility of a completely successful defense of the epistemic rationality of a mystical practice on what Alston calls a "worst case scenario" (p. 270). If the metaphysical and empirical arguments for a Christian (or Buddhist) world-view really are no better than those for its rivals, then I doubt whether his remarks are sufficient to show that it is rational to regard CMP or BMP as reliable. If it isn't, then it isn't epistemically rational to engage in it. Whether it is epistemically *ir*rational to do so depends on whether the diversity of mystical practices overrides the reasons for regarding CMP as reliable or simply offsets them. If (as I suspect) it simply offsets them, it isn't irrational.

So where do we stand? Suppose there really were well-established non-Aristotelian perceptual practices. In the absence of arguments showing that an Aristotelian framework is preferable to its rivals, I doubt that it would be epistemically rational for me to continue to engage in my practice, although it *would* be pragmatically rational for me to regard it as reliable and might not be epistemically *ir*rational for me to do so. Similarly here; on the "worst case scenario," the most that follows is that it is pragmatically rational, and not epistemically irrational, to engage in CMP. Whether one can establish more than this depends on the prospects for Christian metaphysics.

My conclusion, then, is this. Whether one is committed to a mystical practice or not, metaphysical and empirical argumentation of a familiar sort (arguments for God's or Nibbāna's existence, Christian or Buddhist "evidences," etc.) is probably needed to show that commitment to an MP is fully rational. Alston's defense of CMP is impressive and, on the whole, convincing. To be fully successful, however, I believe it must form part of a persuasive cumulative case argument for the Christian world-view.[13]

## NOTES

1. William P. Alston, *Perceiving God: The Epistemology of Religious Experience* (Ithaca: Cornell University Press, 1991), p. 262. Subsequent page references appear in parentheses in the text.

2. *Faith and Philosophy* **5** (October 1988), 433–48 [reprinted as Chapter 11 of this volume].

3. An M-belief (manifestation belief) is a belief about God or the Real acquired on the basis of one's religious experience.

4. The situation would be different if we knew that proofs of this kind were impossible, but Alston hasn't attempted to establish this.

5. For example, we sometimes have compelling reasons for believing that a dispute between witnesses will never be resolved. (We know that there were no other witnesses, that the event wasn't videotaped, etc.)

6. *An Interpretation of Religion*, pp. 14 and 36.

7. With the exception, if any, of reports about perceptions that aren't structured in specifically Aristotelian or Cartesian or Whiteheadian ways. (Would "'Red' is instantiated over there" be an example?)

8. Acceptance, however, involves more than using a theory for "important purposes" like prediction. One also uses it "as a source of explanations, as a means of formulating questions and pursuing answers," and so on. (Richard Miller, *Fact and Method* [Princeton: Princeton University Press, 1987], pp. 158–59.)

9. I think that *this* is why the psychoanalyst's continued commitment is reasonable and not (as Alston seems to suggest) because we have no idea how to resolve his dispute with the behaviorists.

10. See *Perceiving God,* Chapter 4, Section ix.

11. I am using "rationality" in an "objective" rather than "subjective" sense. A belief is objectively rational if a fully informed and properly functioning agent would hold it. An action or policy is objectively rational if an agent of this kind would endorse it. But we often aren't fully informed and aren't ideal epistemic agents. Hence, beliefs, actions, and policies that are objectively rational aren't always rational *for us.*

12. One might suggest that it is epistemically irrational to engage in a doxastic practice if there is *no* reason to believe that it is reliable even if there is also no reason to believe that it is *un*reliable. I think, however, that an analogue of the Principle of Credulity is true of doxastic practices. Apparent perceptions and established doxastic practices are both innocent until proven guilty. The fact that a doxastic practice is engaged in is thus *a* reason for trusting it. (Although one that can, of course, be overridden.)

13. The same is true of other mystical practices. Most of what Alston says in defense of CMP could be adopted to justify (e.g.) BMP. Commitment to BMP is fully rational only if one has good reason for thinking that the Buddhist world-view is superior to its rivals.

CHAPTER 14

# Towards Thinner Theologies:

## *Hick and Alston on Religious Diversity*

PHILIP L. QUINN

Western Christianity has never been ignorant of religious diversity. Early Christianity had to make its way in the religiously pluralistic environment of late antiquity. During the medieval period, Islam put cultural and military pressure on European Christendom. And religious diversity has often been seen by Christians as an intellectual challenge to which a response must be made. Origen wrote *contra Celsum* to defend Christianity against pagan critique. Thomas Aquinas wrote *contra gentiles* to make the case for the rationality of Christian belief. So Western Christianity has never been without a philosophical problem of religious diversity of some sort.

But there seems to me to be something special about the form the problem of diversity assumes for Christians today. Frequently in the past the problem has been taken to be vindicating Christian exclusivism about doctrinal truth or access to salvation by writing polemics against the beliefs and practices of other religions. However many Christians have lost confidence in exclusivism, and even among the remaining exclusivists there are few with a taste for polemical warfare with other religions. Though armchair theorizing is no substitute for empirical research, I think it would not be excessively speculative to number among the causes of this change in attitude better acquaintance with religions other than Christianity and increased acknowledgement of evils associated with Christian exclusivism. Those Christians who live in pluralistic democracies have numerous opportunities to develop first-hand familiarity with religions other than their own. Modern scholarship has produced good translations of powerful texts from religious traditions other than Christianity, and cultural anthropologists have provided fascinating thick descriptions of the practices of such traditions. Educated Christians find it increasingly easy to discover much to admire in religions other than their own and hard to hang on to negative stereotypes of such reli-

From Philip L. Quinn, "Towards Thinner Theologies: Hick and Alston on Religious Diversity," *International Journal for Philosophy of Religion* **38**, 1–3 (December 1995): 145–64. 

gions. When religions are considered as social movements, they must, of course, be assigned a share of the responsibility for various social evils. But Christianity is no exception. Many Christians are now prepared to acknowledge that attitudes and practices informed by Christian exclusivism have contributed to evils derived from colonialism and antisemitism. The upshot is an attitude toward religions other than Christianity that is more respectful, less inclined to denigrate them and less concerned to engage them in intellectual combat. Needless to say, there have been similar developments in other religious traditions. As a result exciting new possibilities for conversations among the world religions have opened up, and the philosophical discussion of religious diversity now takes place in a transformed intellectual climate.

Two of the best recent treatments of religious diversity by analytic philosophers of religion occur within this new climate. In his Gifford Lectures, published as *An Interpretation of Religion,* John Hick shows his respect for all the world religions by proposing a pluralistic hypothesis according to which there is parity among their truth claims. In his *Perceiving God,* William P. Alston shows his respect by proposing an account of mystical doxastic practices according to which the mystical practices of other religions are not precluded from achieving epistemic parity with the Christian practice. I think there is much to be learned, as well as something to criticize, in each of these discussions. In this paper I try to spell out one of the lessons to be drawn from them. I argue that movement in the direction of a refined version of Hick's position, which amounts to movement towards thinner theologies, is a rational course of action within the framework of Alston's doxastic practice approach to religious epistemology.

The paper is divided into two parts. The first is devoted to Hick, and the second focuses on Alston.

## 1. HICK'S RELIGIOUS PLURALISM

According to Hick, what the great religious traditions have in common is that each offers a path to salvation, which involves a transformation of human existence from self-centeredness to reality-centeredness. As far as we can tell, all of these traditions are of roughly equal effectiveness in producing this transformation. This suggests to Hick that a single ultimate reality is being differently conceived, experienced and responded to from within different religious traditions. He develops this suggestion with the assistance of terminology and ideas borrowed from Kant. Like Kant, he distinguishes between the phenomenal and the noumenal. Using this distinction, he proposes that "the noumenal Real is experienced and thought by different human mentalities, forming and formed by different religious traditions, as the range of gods and absolutes which the phenomenology of religion reports."[1] These gods and absolutes, these divine *personae* and metaphysical *impersonae,* are phenomenal, and so they "are not illusory but are empirically, that is experientially, real as authentic manifestations of the Real" (p. 242). On a naturalistic interpretation of religion, according to which there is no noumenal Real, the various divine *personae* and metaphysical *impersonae* are illusory because they reduce to purely human projections. As Hick sees it, his is a religious interpretation of religion precisely because it postulates the noumenal Real.

Hick is not a slavish disciple of Kant; he himself draws attention to some of the ways in which their views differ. Thus, for example, Kant was driven to postulate God in response to moral demands, but Hick postulates the noumenal Real to explain the apparently equal salvific efficacy of the great religious traditions. Yet there is a difficulty in interpreting Hick's use of the distinction between the noumenal and the phenomenal that neatly parallels a difficulty Kant scholars find in interpreting his use of that distinction.

According to what is sometimes called the "double aspect" interpretation of Kant, his distinction between the phenomenal and the noumenal is not a distinction between two kinds of objects, appearances and things in themselves.[2] An analogy proposed by George Mavrodes can be used to illustrate the point.[3] Suppose a prince wants to get an undistorted idea of what the lives of his people are like and so decides to travel among them in disguise. In one village he appears and is experienced as an itinerant monk; in another he appears and is experienced as a journeyman stone-mason. One and the same prince visits both villages, but he appears and is experienced in different ways in the two villages.

When this disguise model is applied to Hick's appropriation of the Kantian distinction, Hick's pluralistic hypothesis is to be understood as postulating a single noumenal Real and diverse ways in which *it* appears and is experienced in different religious traditions. Some of the things Hick says when he introduces his pluralistic hypothesis call for this interpretation. Thus he tells us that Kant distinguished "between a *Ding an sich* and *that thing as it appears* to human consciousness" and that, for Kant, "the noumenal world exists independently of our perception of it and the phenomenal world is *that same world as it appears* to our human consciousness" (p. 241, my emphasis). And, speaking for himself, he claims that, though the noumenal Real is not directly known as such, "when human beings relate themselves to it in the mode of I–Thou encounter they *experience it as* personal" but "when human beings relate themselves to the Real in the mode of non-personal awareness they *experience it* as non-personal" (p. 245, my emphasis). On this interpretation, the noumenal Real itself is experienced, but it is experienced as personal in some religious traditions and is experienced as non-personal in others.

According to what is sometimes called the "two object" interpretation of Kant, his distinction between the phenomenal and the noumenal is a distinction between two kinds of objects.[4] Mavrodes provides us with another helpful analogy.[5] Imagine that two artists, who work in different non-representational styles, sit side by side, looking back and forth from a common landscape to their easels, and paint. When their paintings are finished, we find that they do not resemble one another and neither resembles the common landscape. Nonetheless both artists are confident that, had the landscape been significantly different, their paintings would have been noticeably different. The landscape furnished real input to the paintings, and they depend on it in some way. But of course they also depend on artistic decisions made by the painters. They are human constructs. And the two paintings are diverse from one another and from the landscape.

When this construct model is applied to Hick's appropriation of the Kantian distinction, Hick's pluralistic hypothesis is to be understood as postulating not only a single noumenal Real but also many phenomenal Reals that are joint products of the interaction of the noumenal Real and various human religious traditions. Some of the things Hick says when he proposes the pluralistic hypothesis call for this interpretation. Acknowledging that the noumenal provides informational input to human experience, he cautions us that "all that we are entitled to say about the noumenal source of this information is that it is the reality whose influence *produces,* in collaboration with the human mind, the phenomenal world of our experience" (p. 243, my emphasis). On this interpretation, the noumenal Real itself cannot be experienced, but it contributes to producing phenomenal objects, the divine *personae* and metaphysical *impersonae* of the religious traditions, that are experienced.[6]

Having distinguished the single noumenal Real, on the one hand, from either the many ways in which it is experienced in various religious traditions or the many phenomenal Reals it contributes to producing in collaboration with various religious traditions, on the other, Hick proceeds to make claims about the conclusions that can be drawn from his distinction. He says:

> It follows from this distinction between the Real as it is in itself and as it is thought and experienced through our religious concepts that we cannot apply to the Real *an sich* the characteristics encountered in its *personae* and *impersonae.* Thus it cannot be said to be one or many, person or thing, substance or process, good or evil, purposive or non-purposive. None of the concrete descriptions that apply within the realm of human experience can apply literally to the unexperiencable ground of that realm (p. 246).

In this passage Hick's use of both the disguise model and the construct model leads him into inconsistency. In its first sentence he says that the noumenal Real is experienced, albeit through our concepts. This claim holds within the disguise model. And in its third sentence he implies that the noumenal Real is not experienced, because it belongs to a world that is the unexperiencable ground of the realm of human experience. This claim holds within the construct model. Hence it seems that Hick will be forced to choose between the two models in order to achieve consistency at this point. But no matter how he chooses, these conclusions do not in fact follow from his distinction unless he makes at least one additional assumption.

Consider first the disguise model. A prince can appear as and be experienced as a prince, clad in royal robes and seated on a throne. In order to exclude this possibility from the model, we must assume that every guise in which something can appear is a disguise. Less picturesquely but more accurately, Hick must assume that the noumenal Real cannot appear as or be experienced as it is in itself. Otherwise put, he must make the strong negative assumption that none of the ways in which the noumenal Real appears can be ways it is in itself. Exclusivists from all religious traditions will, of course, reject this assumption. They will insist that at least some of the ways in which the noumenal Real appears in their tradition are, or at least are closely analogous to, ways it is in itself. In short, Hick must not only distinguish between the phenomenal and the noumenal; he must also make a strong negative assumption about how they are related in order to get to the conclusion that we cannot apply to the Real *an sich* the characteristics encountered in its *personae* and *impersonae.*

Consider next the construct model. Artists who work in a representational style can paint landscapes. In order to exclude this possibility from the model, we must assume that there can be no representational landscape paintings. More accurately, Hick must assume that the noumenal Real cannot possess any positive attribute that is also possessed by the phenomenal Real of any of the great religious traditions. Otherwise put, he must make the strong negative assumption that no positive attribute of any of the phenomenal Reals of the great religious traditions can be an attribute of the noumenal Real. Exclusivists from all the traditions will also reject this assumption. They will insist that at least some of the positive attributes of the phenomenal Real of their own tradition, or at least closely analogous attributes, are also attributes of the noumenal Real. In sum, Hick must not only distinguish between the phenomenal and the noumenal; he must also make a strong negative assumption about how the various phenomenal Reals are related to the one noumenal Real in order to get to the conclusion that none of the concrete descriptions that apply within the realm of human experience can apply literally to the unexperiencable ground of that realm.

Hick does not argue directly for such strong negative assumptions. He certainly does not prove that those who reject them are mistaken. But if we grant such assumptions, it is easy to see how they can be used to establish parity among the truth claims of the great religious traditions.

In the disguise model, apparently conflicting claims about ultimate reality will be construed as truths about how the noumenal Real appears to various groups but falsehoods about how it is in itself. There is nothing contradictory in supposing that the noumenal Real appears as and is experienced as personal by Christians, and appears as and is experienced as impersonal by advaitic Hindus, but is in itself neither personal nor impersonal.[7] So all the great religious traditions will be on a par in two senses: they are all equally correct if their claims are taken to be about the ways in which the noumenal Real appears to them, and they are all equally mistaken if their claims are taken to be about the ways in which it is in itself. Similarly, in the construct model, apparently conflicting claims about ultimate reality will be construed as truths about the positive attributes of the diverse phenomenal Reals of the various religious traditions but falsehoods about the positive attributes of the noumenal Real. Neither is there anything contradictory in supposing that the phenomenal Real of Christianity is personal, the distinct phenomenal Real of advaitic Hinduism is impersonal, but the noumenal Real, which is yet a third thing, is neither personal nor impersonal. So, once again, all the great religious traditions will be on a par in two ways: they are all equally correct if their claims are taken to be about the positive attributes of their diverse phenomenal Reals, and they are all equally mistaken if their claims are taken to be about the positive attributes of the noumenal Real.

Honesty demands the admission that Hick's pluralistic hypothesis purchases such parity at a very high price. It must be viewed as an alternative and rival to the main lines of self-understanding within the great religious traditions. As one perceptive commentator notes, it proposes "a revisionist conception of religions and religious diversity."[8] A great many of the members of the great religious traditions would reject the claim that their religious beliefs are true only of the ways in which the ultimate religious reality appears to them, or only of phenomenal objects it contributes to producing, and not true of that reality as it is in itself. For example, an ordinary Christian theist who grasped the distinction between the phenomenal and the noumenal would be likely to insist that the noumenal Real itself, and not just its way of appearing in Christian experience or a phenomenal object partly derived from it, is personal or, at least, that the noumenal Real itself is closely analogous to one or more human persons. Hick does what he can to accommodate such views, but the logic of his position does not permit him to do much. He recognizes that literal and analogical language about objects of religious worship or meditation always intends to be about the noumenal Real itself, but he holds that such language actually functions mythologically with respect to the noumenal Real. As he sees it, "we speak mythologically about the noumenal Real by speaking literally or analogously about its phenomenal manifestations" (p. 351). But, according to the definition he proposes, "a statement or set of statements about X is mythologically true if it is not literally true but nevertheless tends to evoke an appropriate dispositional attitude to X" (p. 348). All that Hick can concede to the ordinary Christian theist is that it is mythologically but not literally true that the noumenal Real is personal. However, such Christians typically believe or have beliefs which imply that it is literally true that the noumenal Real is personal. Similarly, all that he can concede to the ordinary advaitic Hindu is that it is mythologically but not literally true that the noumenal Real is impersonal. But such Hindus typically believe or have beliefs which imply that it is literally true that the noumenal Real is impersonal. So Hick's pluralistic hypothesis attributes large errors to a great many members of these two traditions. I doubt that such people would be consoled by the thought that it also attributes equally large errors to a great many members of all the other great religious traditions.

But perhaps there is massive error in the great religious traditions. The fact that Hick's pluralistic hypothesis is revisionary is, by itself, no proof of its falsehood. So it at least merits further consideration. Such consideration quickly reveals a problem with the formulation of the hypothesis.

According to the pluralistic hypothesis, the noumenal Real, the Real *an sich,* "cannot be said to be one or many, person or thing, conscious or unconscious, purposive or nonpurposive, substance or process, good or evil, loving or hating" (p. 350). To say such things of the noumenal Real is to say things that are not literally true of it. Yet Hick realizes that he is committed to some claims that have to be taken as literal truths about the noumenal Real if the pluralistic hypothesis is to make sense. Thus he supposes we can, presumably with literal truth, "say of the postulated Real *an sich* that it is the noumenal ground of the encountered gods and experienced absolutes witnessed to by the religious traditions" (p. 246). And the question is how the claims that are literally true of the noumenal Real are to be demarcated from those that are not. Hick tries to demarcate in terms of a distinction between concepts and statements that are purely formal and those that are not. He is aware that some such distinction is needed if his view is to escape self-refutation. Thus, for example, if the noumenal Real does not fall under any concepts that are not purely formal, then it must fall under the purely formal concept of being such that it is beyond the scope of other than purely formal concepts. Unfortunately, however, Hick does not provide a definition of purely formal concepts or statements, and so we are left to gather as best we can the distinction he has in mind from the examples he presents. Hence, we must conjecture about how he demarcates the claims he takes to be literally true of the noumenal Real from those he considers not literally true of it, and in framing such conjectures we have only his examples to go on. But the examples create difficulties.

At one point Hick asks why pluralism postulates a single noumenal Real. He concedes that there is "no reason, *a priori,* why the closest approximation that there is to a truly ultimate reality may not consist in either an orderly federation or a feuding multitude or an unrelated plurality" (p. 248). Indeed, Hick's explanandum, the roughly equal salvific efficacy of the great religious traditions, could be accounted for by postulating that each tradition is in contact with a distinct religious reality, each of which is roughly as it is experienced and conceived in its tradition and all of which are roughly equal in salvific power. Hick appeals to the theoretical virtue of simplicity to justify postulating a unique noumenal Real; he regards the issue as finding "the simplest hypothesis to account for the plurality of forms of religious experience and thought" (p. 248). But the appeal to theoretical simplicity in this context is problematic in several ways. One might deny, as some philosophers of science do, that theoretical simplicity is indicative of truth, viewing it instead as a merely pragmatic virtue. More importantly, Hick's claim that the Real *an sich* cannot be said to be one or many seems to be inconsistent with his insistence that we can, for reasons of simplicity, say that it is not a plurality, whether orderly, feuding or unrelated. In addition, the claim that the Real *an sich* is a single thing and not a plurality, a one and not a many, appears to be not a purely formal statement. And, finally, if theoretical considerations can justify a substantive claim about the noumenal realm in this instance, what if anything is to prevent them from doing so in other cases?

Recall, too, that Hick claims that the Real *an sich* provides informational input into the human mind and that we are entitled to say about the noumenal source of this information that its influence produces, in collaboration with the human mind, the phenomenal world of human experience. Presumably the pluralistic hypothesis, when understood in terms of the construct model, requires that these be claims to literal truth. But they entail claims about the causal powers of the noumenal Real, its powers to transmit information to the human mind and to contribute to the production of experience in it, and such claims must also be claims to literal truth. But they are substantive claims, albeit fairly abstract ones, and hence the statements making them appear to be not purely formal. It may be that the statement that the postulated Real *an sich* is the ground of the divine *personae* and metaphysical *impersonae* of the religious traditions is purely formal in some sense. But even if that is so, the statement that it performs this grounding function by transmitting information to the human mind and collaborating with it in the production of religious experience makes a substantive causal claim.

There is also something to worry about in one of Hick's most prominent examples of a purely formal statement we can make. He says that

> The most famous instance in western religious discourse of such a formal statement is Anselm's definition of God as that than which no greater can be conceived. This formula refers to the ultimate divine reality without attributing to it any concrete characteristics (p. 246).

But maximal conceivable greatness may well entail other divine attributes. Anselm himself argued that it does, and several contemporary philosophers of religion follow in his footsteps. For example, Alvin Plantinga, in his well known ontological argument for God's existence, appeals to the property of having maximal greatness. According to Plantinga, the property of having maximal greatness entails the property of having maximal excellence in every possible world and the property of having maximal excellence entails the properties of omniscience, omnipotence and moral perfection.[9] Moreover, the property of being morally perfect entails the property of being personal. Hence, the property of having maximal greatness entails the property of being personal. Similar lines of argument are contained in work by George Schlesinger and Thomas Morris.[10] Even if it is epistemically possible that such authors are mistaken about the entailment relations in question, it is far from clear that they have in fact fallen into error on this point. And if they have not, Hick's position is in trouble. According to Hick, the statement attributing maximal greatness to the noumenal Real is purely formal, and so it is an instance of those statements we can make about the postulated Real *an sich*, presumably with a claim to literal truth. But it entails and thus logically commits us to a statement, presumably with the same claim to literal truth, attributing personhood to the noumenal Real, which commitment is not consistent with Hick's claim that the noumenal Real cannot be said to be person or thing and, hence, that personhood cannot literally be one of its attributes. What is more, things would not be any better for Hick's position if being maximally great did not entail being personal but instead entailed being impersonal.

So Hick's attempt to formulate the pluralistic hypothesis in a way that defines clearly what is literally true of the postulated noumenal Real runs into trouble. As I see, the best way to respond to the difficulties I have pointed out is to refine the hypothesis rather than to abandon it. Since it is his hypothesis, Hick will to some extent be authoritative about how to resolve problems in formulating it with clarity and precision. But I would like to propose a strategy for making refinements that I take to be in the spirit of Hick's thought, as I understand it.

At bottom, Hick finds religious diversity problematic because the great religious traditions attribute contrary properties to the religious ultimate.[11] Advaitic Hindus say it is impersonal; Sunni Muslims say it is personal. The members of a pair of properties are contraries if, as a matter of logic, nothing can have but something can lack both members of the pair. Hick's basic move is to deny that the religious ultimate really has either member of any such contrary pair. So the first steps in constructing a pluralistic hypothesis are these. Fix the religious traditions that are to fall within the scope of the hypothesis and determine what properties they attribute to the religious ultimate. Next check these properties for pairwise contrariety. Then postulate a common religious ultimate that has no property which entails either member of any contrary pair. Once you have gotten this far, there are a couple of explanatory options. Following the disguise model, you can explain apparent contrariety in terms of diverse ways in which the common ultimate appears in different traditions. Or, following the construct model, you can explain apparent contrariety by postulating different objects for different traditions to bear the members of contrary pairs. And you may then flesh out the hypothesis by attributing further properties, formal or substantive, to the common religious ultimate, as theoretical considerations dictate, provided you refrain from attributing to it any property that entails either member of any of the contrary pairs previously enumerated. I suggest that this recipe will allow you to construct coherent pluralistic hypotheses if such constructions are possible.

Of course this strategy will not yield interpretations of religion that would be acceptable to most current members of the great religious traditions. But those traditions have undergone development in the past, and no doubt they will continue to change in the future. Hence it is worth asking whether the belief systems of the great religious traditions ought to be altered to bring them into conformity with the truth of the matter as it is understood by some refined pluralistic hypothesis. Would it be rational for members of such a tradition to endeavor to change its belief system in the direction of such conformity? I address this question by means of a discussion of William P. Alston's treatment of the problem of religious diversity.

## 2. ALSTON ON RELIGIOUS DIVERSITY

It is only in the penultimate chapter of his book, *Perceiving God,* that Alston addresses what he takes to be "the most difficult problem for my position."[12] It is a problem posed by religious diversity. What is it? How does Alston propose to solve it within the framework of his religious epistemology?

The notion of a doxastic practice is central to Alston's general epistemology. He thinks of a doxastic practice as a way of forming beliefs and evaluating them epistemically in terms of a background system of beliefs that furnish potential defeaters or overriders. He argues that it is practically rational to engage in socially established doxastic practices that are not demonstrably unreliable or otherwise disqualified for rational acceptance. In the religious sphere, Alston thinks of mystical perception as religious experience in which a presentation or appearance to the subject of something the subject identifies as the Ultimate occurs. When the notion of a doxastic practice is applied to mystical perception, Alston urges us to acknowledge that there are different socially established mystical practices in diverse religious traditions because there are substantial differences in their overrider systems of background beliefs. One such practice is Christian mystical practice (CMP). Alston argues at length that it is not demonstrably unreliable. It does not display massive and persistent internal inconsistency in its outputs; nor does it display persistent and unresolvable conflict with more basic secular doxastic practices. However, both the outputs of CMP and its overrider system appear to be massively inconsistent with their counterparts in the mystical practices of other religious traditions. Does this disqualify CMP and its equally well established rivals in other traditions from being rationally engaged in? Considerations that count in favor of a positive answer to this question give rise to Alston's problem of religious diversity. What are these considerations?

It is a presupposition of the claim that religious diversity renders the rationality of engaging in any mystical perceptual practice problematic that the belief systems of the great religious traditions are massively incompatible. On the face of it, they seem to be, but attempts have been made to construe them as mutually compatible, appearances to the contrary notwithstanding. Alston considers two such attempts. One might, he notes, "trim each system of its 'exclusivist' claims, so that it presents only one possible way to salvation, only one part of the story as to what the Ultimate is like and how we are and should be related to it" (p. 263). Though he expresses skepticism about whether the strategy of abandoning exclusivist claims would succeed in resolving all doxastic conflict among the great religious traditions, he declines to follow this path for another reason. His project is the epistemic evaluation of doxastic practices that are socially established and widely engaged in, and there are no mystical perceptual practices of a nonexclusivist sort that are actually engaged in by any significant community. Though it might be nice if there were such practices, evaluating merely hypothetical practices of this kind is not part of Alston's enterprise.

Another attempt to resolve doxastic conflict among the great religious traditions involves reinterpretation of what is going on in actually existing religious doxastic practices. Alston takes Hick's religious pluralism to be the most prominent representative of this position on the current scene because he construes Hick as holding that the apparently incompatible beliefs associated with various mystical perceptual practices are not really incompatible, since they are not about the one noumenal Real but are instead about the many phenomenal Reals of diverse religious traditions. Thus construed, Hick's position encounters a difficulty mentioned previously. As Alston puts it, Hick's proposed interpretation of religion is not faithful to the self-understandings embedded in existing religious doxastic practices because "most practitioners of one or another religion are pre-Kantian in their realist understanding of their beliefs" (p. 265). In other words, on Hick's view, most such practitioners misunderstand what is going on in their own religious doxastic practices, for they take their beliefs to embody true accounts of the noumenal Real and its relations to them. For the sake of fidelity to their self-understandings, Alston proposes to take the great religious traditions to be making noumenal truth claims that are logically incompatible with one another and to assess the implications of this assumption for his view that it is nonetheless practically rational to continue engaging in CMP.

But how, exactly, does the incompatibility of various forms of mystical perceptual practice threaten the rationality of engaging in any of them? After canvassing several defective ways of posing the problem, Alston settles on the following formulation. On account of the incompatibility, at most one form of mystical practice can be a sufficiently reliable way of forming beliefs about the Ultimate to be rationally engaged in. But why should one suppose that CMP in particular is the one that is reliable if any is? To be sure, CMP can come up with internal reasons for supposing that it is more reliable than its rivals. However, each of its rivals can do the same. Hence, according to the objection, "if it is to be rational for me to take CMP to be reliable, I will have to have sufficient *independent* reasons for supposing that CMP is reliable, or more reliable or more likely to be reliable, than its alternatives" (p. 269). But no such independent reasons are forthcoming. Thus it is not rational to engage in CMP. And, by parity of reasoning, it is also not rational to engage in any other particular form of mystical perceptual practice.

A slightly different way of expressing what is essentially the same point goes as follows. All the competing mystical practices are equally well socially established; none of them has greater prima facie credibility than its rivals on grounds of deeper social entrenchment. So each of the competing practices is confronted with a plurality of uneliminated alternatives. According to the objection, the following conclusions are to be drawn in these circumstances: "Thus, in the absence of some sufficient independent reason, no one is justified in supposing her own practice to be superior in epistemic status to those with which it is in competition. And hence, in this situation no one is being rational in proceeding to employ that practice to form beliefs and to regard beliefs so formed as ipso facto justified" (p. 270).

As Alston notes, this line of argument takes it for granted that there are no independent reasons for an epistemic preference of one form of mystical practice over its rivals, and this assumption can be challenged. But successfully mounting such a challenge on behalf of CMP would involve telling a very long story about evidences for Christianity, and Alston chooses not to undertake this project except in a sketchy form in his final chapter. Instead he proceeds at this point in accord with a worst-case scenario in which it is just assumed that there are no independent reasons for preferring CMP to its rivals. He seeks to show that, even on this assumption, the justificatory efficacy of CMP is by no means dissipated, though it is significantly weakened. Of course, if the assumption is false and there are such independent reasons for the reliability of CMP but none for the reliability of its rivals, things are all the better for CMP and all the worse for its rivals.

But just how bad are things for CMP in Alston's worst-case scenario? How much is its justificatory efficacy actually weakened in those circumstances? In discussing the genuine epistemic consequences of religious diversity, Alston invites us to look at the matter this way. Suppose our sole respectable basis for a positive epistemic evaluation of CMP were the fact that it is a socially established doxastic practice that has not been shown to be unreliable. On that assumption, Alston admits, religious diversity would reduce its epistemic status to an alarming degree. Given the equal social establishment of several mutually incompatible mystical practices, he thinks that "it is at least arguable that the most reasonable view, even for a hitherto committed participant of one of the practices, would be that the social establishment in each case reflects a culturally generated way of reinforcing socially desirable attitudes and practices, reinforcing these by inculcating a sense of the presence of Supreme Reality and a way of thinking about it" (p. 276). And that in turn, he allows, would imply that the justificatory efficacy of all of these practices had been altogether dissipated.

It is worth noting that Alston does not explicitly endorse the claim that he says is at least arguable. But he does not dispute it. Instead he observes that so far the whole story has not yet been told. We must also take into account the significant self-support CMP derives from the way in which promises it represents God as making are fulfilled in the spiritual lives of its practitioners, fulfilled in growth in sanctity, joy, love, and other fruits of the spirit. As Alston sees it, "in the face of this self-support it is no longer the case that the most reasonable hypothesis is that none of the competing practices provide an effective cognitive access to the Ultimate" (p. 276). Hence, "one may quite reasonably continue to hold that CMP does serve as a genuine cognitive access to Ultimate Reality, and as a trustworthy guide to that Reality's relations to ourselves" (p. 276). And, again by parity of reasoning, a similar conclusion may be drawn for any of the alternative mystical practices that enjoy comparable self-support.

I concur with Alston in thinking that self-support counts, epistemically speaking, in favor of the rationality of engaging in a doxastic practice. So I agree that things are not as bad for CMP in his worst-case scenario as they would be in the absence of self-support. Just how bad are they? In the absence of self-support, the justificatory efficacy of CMP arguably would be altogether dissipated. So, in the presence of self-support, the justificatory efficacy of CMP is, at the very least, not altogether dissipated. Of course, this conclusion is consistent with Alston's claim that, given the self-support CMP enjoys, it is no longer the case that the most reasonable hypothesis is that none of the competing mystical practices provides an effective cognitive access to the Ultimate. But it is also consistent with the claim that, despite the self-support CMP enjoys, it remains the case that the most reasonable hypothesis is that none of these practices provides such access. For all that has been shown thus far, then, it may be that, though CMP has some justificatory efficacy because of the self-support it enjoys, it does not have enough to make it reasonable to hold that it serves to yield genuine access to the Ultimate.

Hence, as I see it, the difficulty religious diversity generates for Alston's position may be summarized in this way. The fact that CMP is a socially established doxastic practice that has not been shown to be unreliable counts in favor of the rationality of engaging in it. It derives therefrom a certain amount of justificatory efficacy. In the context of the worst-case scenario, there being equally well established rival practices that also have not been shown to be unreliable weakens its justificatory efficacy, but its significant self-support strengthens its justificatory efficacy. Either it enjoys enough self-support to make engaging in it rational despite the weakening effect of there being uneliminated rivals, or the self-support it enjoys falls short of what is required to make engaging in it rational in the face of that effect. What reasons are there for preferring one of these alternatives to the other?

Alston offers reasons of two sorts for preferring the first alternative. I next examine the arguments in which he sets them forth.

His first argument plays off of a disanalogy between conflict within a single doxastic practice and conflict among diverse doxastic practices. Consider alternative methods of predicting the weather such as scientific meteorology, going by the aches in one's joints and observing groundhogs. Since these competitors confront one another within sensory perceptual practice, it is clear what would constitute noncircular grounds for supposing one of them to be superior to the others, even if we do not have such grounds. Observed predictive success provides neutral grounds for choosing among methods of weather forecasting, and the lack of such grounds has negative epistemic consequences for the competing methods. Indeed, according to Alston, "it is because the absence of such reasons is the absence of something there is a live possibility of one's having, and that one knows how to go about getting, that this lack so clearly has negative epistemic consequences" (p. 271). But in the case of conflict among mystical perceptual practices the competitors lack the kind of common procedure for settling disputes that is available to the participants in a shared practice, and so participants in rival mystical practices do not lack something they know how to get. Hence, as Alston sees it, we may conclude: "The lack does not have the deleterious consequences found in the intra-practice cases. Or, at the very least, it is not clear that it has those consequences" (p. 272).

Alston's conclusion must not be interpreted as the claim that religious diversity has no bad epistemic consequences. He explicitly acknowledges that "it can hardly be denied that the fact of religious diversity reduces the rationality of engaging in CMP (for one who is aware of the diversity) below what it would be if this problem did not exist" (p. 275). Rather his claim is that this bad consequence is not, or at least is not clearly, the same as the deleterious consequences found in the intrapractice cases, and surely he is right about at least this much. In the intrapractice cases, something we know how to get by way of justification for beliefs or methods is lacking. It is because of the presence of this feature in the cases that there are those deleterious consequences. How bad are they? At worst, according to Alston, they amount to nullification of one's justification or elimination of one's basis for a belief or practice. This feature is absent in the case of conflict of mystical practices. In this interpractice case, what is lacking, for example, a proof of the reliability of CMP, is not something we know how to get. Of course, it does not follow from the absence of the feature in question that nullification or elimination does not occur in our interpractice case. What follows is only that nullification or elimination does not occur because of the presence of that feature. If it occurs in the case of conflict of mystical practices, it occurs for some other reason. But it is not clear that there is any such reason, and so it is not clear that nullification or elimination occurs. What might such a reason be? Since I have none to propose, I am prepared to grant for the sake of argument that nullification or elimination does not occur in our interpractice case.

But this is not the end of the story. The bad consequences of religious diversity amount to a reduction that falls short of nullification of one's justification for engaging in CMP; they involve a weakening of its justificatory efficacy. What is the extent of this reduction or weakening? It is probably impossible to answer this question with quantitative precision, but two possibilities remain open. One is that it is small enough that engaging in CMP remains rational, and the other is that it is large enough that engaging in CMP is not rational. The absence of the crucial feature of the intrapractice cases is, in effect, the absence of a reason for thinking that the latter possibility is realized. By itself, however, this absence does not furnish a reason for thinking that the former possibility is realized. In other words, the disanalogy between the intrapractice cases and our interpractice case undercuts a reason that might be offered for thinking that it is not rational to engage in CMP but does not provide a reason for thinking that it is rational to engage in CMP. Thus Alston's first argument does not show that it is rational to engage in CMP. As he is well aware, it serves only to block one path to the conclusion that it is not rational to engage in CMP.

But I think Alston's second argument is meant to yield the conclusion that engaging in CMP is rational. It proceeds by way of an analogy between the actual diversity of mystical perceptual practices and a merely hypothetical diversity of sensory perceptual practices. We are to imagine there being a plurality of sense perceptual doxastic practices as diverse as forms of mystical practice are in fact. As Alston fleshes out the story, "suppose that in certain cultures there were a well established 'Cartesian' practice of seeing what is visually perceived as an indefinitely extended medium that is more or less concentrated at various points, rather than, as in our 'Aristotelian' practice, as made up of more or less discrete objects scattered about in space" (p. 273). We are to imagine in other cultures an established Whiteheadian practice in which the visual field is seen as made up of momentary events growing out of each other in a continuous process. Further suppose that all these practices are equal in terms of the fruits they produce; each serves its practitioners well in their dealings with the environment and has associated with it a developed physical science. Imagine also that in this situation we are as firmly wedded to our Aristotelian practice as we are in fact yet can find no neutral grounds on which to argue effectively that it yields more accurate beliefs than the alternatives. It seems clear to Alston that "in the absence of an external reason for supposing that one of the competing practices is more accurate than my own, *the only rational course* for me is to sit tight with the practice of which I am a master and which serves me so well in guiding my activity in the world" (p. 274, my emphasis). But this imagined situation is precisely parallel to our actual situation with respect to CMP. Hence, by parity of reasoning, the only rational thing for a practitioner of CMP to do is to stick with it and, more generally, to continue to accept and operate in accordance with the system of Christian belief.

Beyond saying that it seems clear to him, Alston gives no reasons for supposing that, in the imagined situation, the only rational course is to sit tight with the sensory practice of which one is a master. But there is a line of argument that can be deployed to support this supposition. Declining to engage in any sensory perceptual practice is presumably not a live option for me. Hence it seems that my options are restricted to sitting tight with my Aristotelian practice and switching to one of its established rivals. However switching would carry with it very large costs in terms of resocialization. I would have to spend a lot of time and energy getting trained to see things in new ways. And even if I could be successfully trained, what assured benefits would accrue to me as a result? By hypothesis, I would not be better off in terms of fruits; I would not be better at coping with my environment or have access to a more advanced physical science. Of course, it could be that I would be swapping inaccurate beliefs for accurate beliefs and thereby getting closer to my epistemic goal. But again, by hypothesis, I have no neutral ground on which to base an argument that this would be the outcome. And switching would be risky because it could equally well be that I would be swapping accurate beliefs for inaccurate beliefs. I also have no neutral ground on which to base an argument that this would not be the outcome. Hence cost–benefit considerations, which surely count for a lot in deliberations about practical rationality, weigh very strongly in favor of sitting tight with my Aristotelian practice.

In my view, this argument is flawed because, appearances to the contrary notwithstanding, I do not have to obey the injunction to sit tight or switch. There is another live option that ought to be considered. I also have the choice of revising my Aristotelian practice from within and working toward a situation in which my revised practice becomes socially established. A precedent for making revisions in one's sensory perceptual practice is to be found in the way people respond to learning that such things as phenomenal colors are not mind-independent. Revisions of my sensory practice might proceed in a Kantian direction. Suppose it occurs to me that a plausible explanation of the success of the diverse sensory practices in the imagined situation is the hypothesis that each of the established practices is reliable with respect to the appearances things present to its practitioners but none is reliable with respect to how things are in themselves. Motivated by this consideration, I decide to modify the functions of my sensory practice so that they map sensory inputs onto doxastic outputs about the appearances things present to me but not about how things really are independent of me. I also do what I can to see to it that my revised sensory practice gradually becomes socially established.

Transforming my Aristotelian practice into a Kantian practice would in some ways be like switching to a Cartesian or Whiteheadian practice. I see no reason to suppose I would be worse off in terms of fruits as a result. I would not lose the ability to deal well with my environment; nor would I lose access to a developed physical science, though some reinterpretation of its metaphysical import would probably be required. In addition, I would lack neutral grounds on which to base an argument that my revisions are going to get me closer to my epistemic goal by improving the reliability of my sensory practice. But there are salient differences too. Instead of having to be trained to acquire substantially different inputs to my sensory practice, I would only have to make the slight modifications in its functions needed to produce slight alterations in its doxastic outputs. Because I think this change would not require costly resocialization, I do not think cost–benefit considerations count strongly against revising my Aristotelian practice in a Kantian direction.

It is doubtful that the costs and benefits of sitting tight with Aristotelian practice and those of transforming it into a Kantian practice can be quantified precisely enough to allow us to say with much confidence which of the two is the more rational course. So I do not wish to conclude that it is irrational to sit tight with Aristotelian practice. But I submit that we can conclude that it is not the only rational thing to do. In our imagined situation, then, it would be rational to stick with our Aristotelian practice but it would also be rational to transform it into a Kantian practice. Each of these courses of action would be rationally permitted; neither of them would be rationally required.

And, of course, our imagined situation is, in the relevant respects, parallel to the actual situation in regard to competing mystical practices.[13] Hence, by parity of reasoning, though it is rational for practitioners of CMP to continue to engage in it, it is not *the only* rational thing for them to do, there being more than one thing it is rational to do in the face of competing mystical practices. Another thing it is rational for them to do is to revise CMP from within in ways that would improve its reliability if some refined pluralistic hypothesis were true. Each of these courses of action is rationally permissible in the light of religious diversity. Neither of them is irrational, but neither is rationally required. And absent any relevant dissimilarities, the same goes for those engaged in other socially established mystical practices with significant self-support.

Alston's views do not rule out the possibility of the great religious traditions evolving in such a way that they converge on consensus about a self-understanding in the neighborhood of a refined pluralistic hypothesis. He explicitly notes that "the system of Christian belief has undergone a great deal of change in its history, and we cannot be sure that it will not continue to do so; the same holds for other major religions" (p. 278). And he allows that future developments in the great religious traditions might be in the direction of greater consensus. But he does not explicitly acknowledge the rationality of trying to bring such consensus about by revising the belief systems and doxastic practices of the presently existing world religions, including Christianity, so that they are no longer pre-Kantian in their understandings of their beliefs. Thus his advice to the knowledgeable and reflective Christian is that "she should do whatever seems feasible to search for common ground on which to adjudicate the crucial differences between the world religions, seeking a way to show in a non-circular way which of the contenders is correct" (p. 278). I do not think it would be irrational to follow this advice. However I also think it should not be taken for granted that any of the contenders in its present form is correct. Hence I think it would be rational for a knowledgeable and reflective Christian to revise CMP from within in ways that are designed to bring it into line with a Kantian understanding of Christian belief of the sort expressed by some refined pluralistic hypothesis and to try to get CMP thus revised socially established.

If I am right about this, Alston's second argument gives him what he needs to solve the problem of religious diversity he has posed. It builds a good analogical case for the conclusion that it is rational for practitioners of CMP to continue engaging in it despite the fact of religious diversity. And, as Alston notes, this conclusion holds, *pari passu,* for practitioners of other established and internally validated forms of mystical perceptual practice. But the argument does not establish the stronger claim that is its stated conclusion, for it is not a good analogical argument to the effect that this is the only thing it is rational for practitioners of CMP to do. Thus it does not impugn the rationality of those Christians whose response to religious diversity is to seek a more inclusivist or pluralist understanding of their own faith and who are, accordingly, interested in altering CMP in order to bring the beliefs that are its outputs into line with such an understanding. In particular, it does not impugn the rationality of those Christians who are prepared to move in the direction of thicker phenomenologies and thinner theologies, even if they are not yet ready to go all the way to the Hickian view that it is nothing but phenomenology almost all the way down. And I would say this too holds, *pari passu,* for practitioners of other established and internally validated forms of mystical perceptual practice.[14]

# NOTES

1. John Hick, *An Interpretation of Religion* (New Haven and London: Yale University Press, 1989), p. 242. Hereafter references to this book will be made parenthetically in the body of my text. Hick also discusses religious diversity in "Religious Pluralism and Salvation," *Faith and Philosophy* **5** (1988), pp. 365–77 [see pp. 54–66 in Chapter 3 of this volume] and in *Disputed Questions in Theology and the Philosophy of Religion* (New Haven: Yale University Press, 1993), Part IV.

2. Karl Ameriks, "Recent Work on Kant's Theoretical Philosophy," *American Philosophical Quarterly* **19** (1982), pp. 1–24. This interpretation might also aptly be described as the one world view.

3. George I. Mavrodes, "Polytheism," in *The Rationality of Belief and the Plurality of Faith,* Thomas D. Senor, ed. (Ithaca: Cornell University Press, 1995), pp. 261–86 [reprinted as Chapter 8 of this volume].

4. Ameriks, *op. cit.* This interpretation might also aptly be described as the two worlds view.

5. Mavrodes, *op. cit.*

6. This explains why Hick is included in the treatment of polytheism by Mavrodes. Within the construct model, the divine *personae* are distinct objects, and so Hick is a polytheist at the phenomenal level and not a theist at all at the noumenal level.

7. At least this is so if we construe being personal and being impersonal as *contrary* properties. A charitable reading demands that we construe as contraries, not contradictories, all the pairs of attributes both of whose members Hick denies are possessed by the noumenal Real. This works well enough for such pairs as substance and process or good and evil, but I do not see that it so much as makes sense for such pairs as one and many or purposive and non-purposive. But let that pass.

8. Sumner B. Twiss, "The Philosophy of Religious Pluralism: A Critical Appraisal of Hick and His Critics," *The Journal of Religion* **70** (1990), p. 543 [see p. 75 in Chapter 4 of this volume].

9. Alvin Plantinga, *The Nature of Necessity* (Oxford: Clarendon Press, 1974), p. 214.

10. George N. Schlesinger, *New Perspectives on Old-Time Religion* (Oxford: Clarendon Press, 1988), Chapter 1; Thomas V. Morris, *Anselmian Explorations* (Notre Dame: University of Notre Dame Press, 1987), pp. 433–48.

11. See Note 7 above.

12. William P. Alston, *Perceiving God: The Epistemology of Religious Experience* (Ithaca and London: Cornell University Press, 1991), p. 255. Hereafter references to this book will be made parenthetically in the body of my text. Alston also discusses religious diversity in "Religious Diversity and Perceptual Knowledge of God," *Faith and Philosophy* **5** (1988), pp. 433–48 [reprinted as Chapter 11 of this volume].

13. A disanalogy is worth mentioning. Since mystical practice is not universal, ceasing to engage in any mystical practice is a live option in at least some cases. Limitations of space preclude a thorough discussion of the costs and benefits of this course of action, and so I shall confine myself to remarking that it should not be assumed that in all cases exercising this option would result in the uncompensated loss of benefits of spiritual fruits. Religious life is often very hard. If we attend only to what can be observed in this life, it is easy to imagine cases in which opting out of mystical practices would be tantamount to shedding a burden rather than foregoing a benefit.

14. An earlier version of the second part of this paper was presented at an Author Meets Critic Session on Alston's *Perceiving God* at the 1993 APA Pacific Division Meeting. I am grateful to Bill Alston for a response to my criticism that helped me in making revisions.